D0754541

The Jeffersons at Shadwell

RECENT TITLES

Furs and Frontiers in the Far North: The Contest among Native and Foreign Nations for the Bering Strait Fur Trade, by John R. Bockstoce

War of a Thousand Deserts: Indian Raids and the U.S.–Mexican War, by Brian DeLay

Defying the Odds: The Tule River Tribe's Struggle for Sovereignty in Three Centuries, by Gelya Frank and Carole Goldberg

The Bourgeois Frontier: French Towns, French Traders, and American Expansion, by Jay Gitlin

"Liberty to the Downtrodden": Thomas L. Kane, Romantic Reformer, by Matthew J. Grow

The Comanche Empire, by Pekka Hämäläinen

Oceans of Wine: Madeira and the Emergence of American Trade and Taste, by David Hancock

Hell on the Range: A Story of Honor, Conscience, and the American West, by Daniel J. Herman

Frontiers: A Short History of the American West, by Robert V. Hine and John Mack Faragher

Bordertown: The Odyssey of an American Place, by Benjamin Heber Johnson and Jeffrey Gusky

William Clark's World: Describing America in an Age of Unknowns, by Peter Kastor

Emerald City: An Environmental History of Seattle, by Matthew Klingle

Making Indian Law: The Hualapai Land Case and the Birth of Ethnohistory, by Christian W. McMillen

The American Far West in the Twentieth Century, by Earl Pomeroy

Borderlines in Borderlands: James Madison and the Spanish-American Frontier, 1776–1821, by J. C. A. Stagg

Fugitive Landscapes: The Forgotten History of the U.S.–Mexico Borderlands, by Samuel Truett

Bárbaros: Spaniards and Their Savages in the Age of Enlightenment, by David J. Weber

The Spanish Frontier in North America: The Brief Edition, by David J. Weber

The Jeffersons at Shadwell

Susan Kern

Yale

UNIVERSITY PRESS

New Haven and London

Published with assistance from the Annie Burr Lewis Fund and
from the foundation established in memory of James Wesley Cooper
of the Class of 1865, Yale College.

Yale University Press books may be purchased
in quantity for educational, business, or promotional use.
For information, please e-mail sales.press@yale.edu (U.S. office)
or sales@yaleup.co.uk (U.K. office).

Designed by Nancy Ovedovitz and set in Adobe Caslon type by
Westchester Book Group, Danbury, Connecticut.
Printed in the United States of America.

Library of Congress Cataloging-in-Publication Data
Kern, Susan (Susan A.)
The Jeffersons at Shadwell / Susan Kern.
p.   cm.—(The Lamar series in western history)
Originally presented as the author's thesis (doctoral-College of
William and Mary).
Includes bibliographical references and index.
ISBN 978-0-300-15390-3 (clothbound : alk. paper)   1. Jefferson,
Thomas, 1743–1826—Childhood and youth.   2. Jefferson, Thomas,
1743–1826—Birthplace.   3. Jefferson, Peter, 1708–1757.   4. Jefferson,
Jane, 1720–1776.   5. Plantation life—Virginia—Albemarle
County—History—18th century.   6. Excavations (Archaeology)—
Virginia—Albemarle County.   7. Shadwell (Va. :
Plantation)   8. Albemarle County (Va.)—Antiquities.   I. Title.
E332.25.K37 2010
973.4′6092—dc22   2010017494

A catalogue record for this book is available from the British Library.

This paper meets the requirements of ANSI/NISO Z39.48-1992
(Permanence of Paper).
10 9 8 7 6 5 4 3 2 1

Contents

Acknowledgments

Among the privileges of research that crosses disciplinary boundaries are the opportunities to work with people who have a wide range of expertise and affiliations.

Archaeology is never a lone endeavor. Bill Kelso founded this search into the first years of Thomas Jefferson at Shadwell before leaving to find the first years of Virginia at Jamestown. I thank him for entrusting me with his legacies. Barbara Heath was instrumental in establishing the research design for our first years of work at Shadwell. Ben Ford's research along the river on the mill sites contributed to the whole. The identification and catalogue organization of the artifacts was instrumental to making sense of them. Cynthia Whitley, Drake Patten, and Jonathan Farris performed this often-behind-the-scene role. Drake's further research and interpretation has been especially relevant to telling the stories of people who lived at Shadwell. Allison Tillack supplied any kind of support that was needed, at almost any time. The Shadwell archaeology reports include the names of legions of field school students and excavators who moved dirt and documented Shadwell and moved artifacts in the Monticello Archaeology Lab.

In the post-Shadwell era, the Monticello Archaeology Department still supports my research and writing. I thank director Fraser Neiman for keeping the door open. I thank archaeologists Derek Wheeler, Leslie McFaden, Karen Smith, and Sara Bon-Harper for help with photographs, files, and drawings and thinking about what it all means.

Also at the Thomas Jefferson Foundation, Monticello colleagues past and present, Cinder Stanton and Ann Lucas have readily answered questions and helped consider evidence. Their ongoing inquiries into various topics related to everyone who lived and worked at Monticello have been models to which I aspire. Bill Beiswanger, Elizabeth Chew, Peter Hatch, Anna Koester, Zanne MacDonald, Wayne Mogielnicki, Kris Onuf, Kathy Revell, and Doug Wilson have shared opinions, evidence, sources, and access to information. Leah Stearns's exuberant expertise with visual materials enhanced the photographs in this book.

The various and ever-changing members of the Williamsburg Material Culture Reading Group, especially Barbara Carson, Betty Leviner, Colleen Isaac, and Ann Martin, have produced many substantive discussions of sources, interpretation, meaning, and ways of thinking about material culture during semiregular meetings.

The Colonial Williamsburg Foundation is home to some of the world's specialists in Chesapeake and early American studies. Many people have offered time for casual questions and in-depth responses about objects, inventories, and ways of looking at the past. I thank Lorena Walsh for sharing thoughts on amenities indexing, probate inventories, and monetary values. Linda Baumgarten offered observations on clothing in the Jefferson inventories and took time to show me examples in CW's collections. John Hyman and John Davis took time to consider the silver spoon from the Shadwell house cellar. Kevin Kelly and Lou Powers answered queries about education, Indians, and other aspects of early American life. Wayne Randolph's extensive knowledge of early agricultural tools informed much of my discussion of plantation labor. Robin Kipps shared her expertise about medical and apothecary topics. Bill Barker shared his special knowledge of Jefferson.

The members of Colonial Williamsburg's Architectural Research Department have offered fieldwork, opinions, examples, drawings, photographs, and a husband. This group's contribution to ways of thinking about and knowledge of the Chesapeake is beyond compare. Carl Lounsbury, Ed Chappell, Willie Graham, Mark Wenger, and Michael Bourne all offered their expertise at various times. Carl has read and reread, carried books, and contributed many good ideas to my project.

Other scholars who contributed thoughts about the site or materials include Garrett Fesler, Anna Koester, Turk McCleskey, Doug Sanford, Camille Wells, Jim Deetz, Seth Mallios, Martin Gallivan, Jeff Hantman, Buck Woodard, Steve Clements, and Rick Berquist. (I apologize for anyone I've forgotten.) I thank friends who listened and read and offered comments: Ann Lucas, Lisa Crutchfield, Claire Dempsey, Stuart Kern, and Rosemarie Kelley. Bennie Brown helped me research aspects of Peter Jefferson's book list, and Brett Charbeneau helped me understand the physical aspects of books. Tracy Lounsbury translated Latin, and Margaret Robertson shared GIS skills. Betty Leviner and John Hyman shared books, ideas about early American furnishings, and good food. Barbara Carson and Cary Carson gave encouragement and good cheer, and conversations about material culture and rendering them in ways that make sense. Rhys Isaac is a colleague and friend whose engagement with the challenges of researching history and interpreting Virginia's plantation culture make it more fun than it ought to be.

Helpful curators, librarians, and archivists make researching easier and enjoyable. At Swem Library, in particular, I thank Margaret Cook for being especially helpful to researchers. At the Rockefeller Library I thank Marianne Martin, visual resources editorial librarian. Thanks, too, to the special collections librarians, especially Heather Riser at the University of Virginia. At the Huntington Library, Olga Tsapina willingly engaged with particular problems of the accounts of Peter Jefferson's estate there. Peter Drummey has made the Massachusetts Historical Society a rewarding destination for scholars.

The fine maps in this book are original drawings by the talented historian and cartographer Rick Britton.

A Beehive-Mills Lane Architecture Fellowship at Museum of Early Southern Decorative Arts, Winston-Salem, N.C., offered an opportunity to sort out early Piedmont building information. A fellowship at the Robert H. Smith International Center for Jefferson Studies in Charlottesville, Va., enabled more work on Jefferson documents. Minor research grants and summer research grants from the College of William and Mary funded microfilm of county records and library travel. Travel money from William and Mary's history department made possible my research at the Huntington Library.

A version of chapter 1 appeared as "The Material World of the Jeffersons at Shadwell," in the *William and Mary Quarterly* (April 2005). The whole work is better for the close attention that the editors and readers at the *Quarterly* gave to my writing and ideas. Part of chapter 6 appeared as "Where did the Indians Sleep? An Archaeological and Ethnohistorical Study of Mid-Eighteenth-Century Piedmont Virginia," in *Historical Archaeology, Identity Formation, and the Interpretation of Ethnicity,* ed. Maria Franklin and Garrett Fesler (1999). I thank Maria and Garret for their reading and comments.

An earlier version of this book was my dissertation at the College of William and Mary. I thank my readers, advisers, and now colleagues James Whittenburg, James Axtell, Barbara Carson, and Dale Hoak for their enthusiasm, criticism, and ongoing interest in my work. I thank colleagues in the history department who have read and offered opinions: Jody Allen, Julie Richter, Brett Rushforth, Ron Schechter, and John Selby. I am honored to have worked among the many talented historians at William and Mary who are the best of critical readers and unyielding editors.

Williamsburg is also home to the Omohundro Institute of Early American History and Culture, whose colloquia are the best game in town for people who study early American history. Quite a few portions of this book are better for surviving the sharpened minds and fresh pens of the many and varied participants there. Special thanks to Ron Hoffman for inviting my papers and to Fredrika Teute and Mendy Gladden for challenging me to think about what makes a good book. Earlier versions of chapters 1, 3, and 6 benefited from the willing engagement of participants in these colloquia.

In true colonial Virginia fashion, I have a great and long-lasting debt to Virginia Scharff for her interest in my work and pointing me toward Yale University Press as its home. Thanks to Chris Rogers and Laura Davulis at Yale University Press for shepherding, prodding, and waiting. I thank the anonymous readers for their candid observations. I am both humbled and honored by Laura Jones Dooley's copyediting expertise, which improves my work in both subtle and great ways.

Among my deepest debts is to Ann Lucas for all our conversations about research, writing, Jefferson, Monticello, and just about everything else. She and Roger Birle made many research trips possible by offering a place to stay and all the good cheer that goes with it. A special thanks to Eleanor, Thomas, and Susanna Birle for sharing their home on my visits to Charlottesville.

I thank my parents, Anne and Stuart Kern, for pitching in with their grandchildren, especially when I needed time away to research or write. Reavis and Anne Lounsbury have contributed to this project in many ways, even when that meant reading a book sitting for way too long on the floor of a library or computer lab. And thanks to Carl, for understanding what it takes.

The Family of
Peter Jefferson and Jane Randolph Jefferson

Children of Peter Jefferson (1707/8–1757) and Jane Randolph Jefferson (1720–1776)

Jane (1740–1765) (unmarried)
Mary (1741–1804) m. January 24, 1760
    John Bolling (1737–1800)
    Children: Martha, John, Edward, Archibald, Mary, Robert, Jane, Thomas, Ann
Thomas (1743–1826) m. January 1, 1772
    Martha Wayles Skelton (1748–1782)
    Children: Martha, Jane, son, Mary, daughter, Lucy Elizabeth
Elizabeth (1744–1774) (unmarried)
Martha (1746–1811) m. July 20, 1765
    Dabney Carr (1743–1773)
    Children: Jane Barbara, Lucy, Mary, Peter, Samuel, Dabney
Peter Field (1748, died in infancy)
Son (1750, died at birth)
Lucy (1752–1784) m. September 12, 1769
    Charles Lilburne Lewis (1747–1831)
    Children: Randolph, Jane, Isham, Charles, Anna Marks, Elizabeth, Martha
    Ann Cary, Lucy, Mary, Lilburne
Anna Scott (1755–1828) m. October, 1787
    Hastings Marks (d. 1811)
Randolph (1755–1815)
    1. Anne Jefferson Lewis (d. 1808) m. July 30, 1780
    Children: Isham, Thomas, Field, Robert, James, Anna Scott
    2. Mitchie B. Pryor, m. 1809
    Children: John

The Enslaved African Americans of Shadwell

At least seventy-six enslaved African Americans lived at Shadwell during its use by Peter, Jane, or Thomas Jefferson. Many of these names have different spellings in different documents. Where a name appears more than once there is clear evidence that multiple people had that name.

Adam
Agey
Bellinda
Bella
Bellow
Bellow
Betty
Betty
Billey
Cachina
Cate
Cesar
Charlotte
Cloe
Crummel
Cyrus
Dinah
Eady
Ephey
Eve
Fan
Fany
Fany
Farding
Flora
Gill

Goliah
Hannah
Harry
Hercullus
Jack
Jack
Jammey
Jenny
Jesse
Juno
Jupiter
Jupiter
Leah
Lucey
Lucinda
Lydia
Minerva
Moll
Myrtilla
Nan
Nanney
Nell
Nimrod
Orrange
Patt
Peter

Phebe
Phill
Phillis
Pompey
Quash
Rachel
Rachel
Sall
Sall
Sally
Samson
Sandy
Sancho
Sanco
Sarah
Sawney
Simon
Squir
Squire
Suckey
Syphax
Tobey
Toby
Val

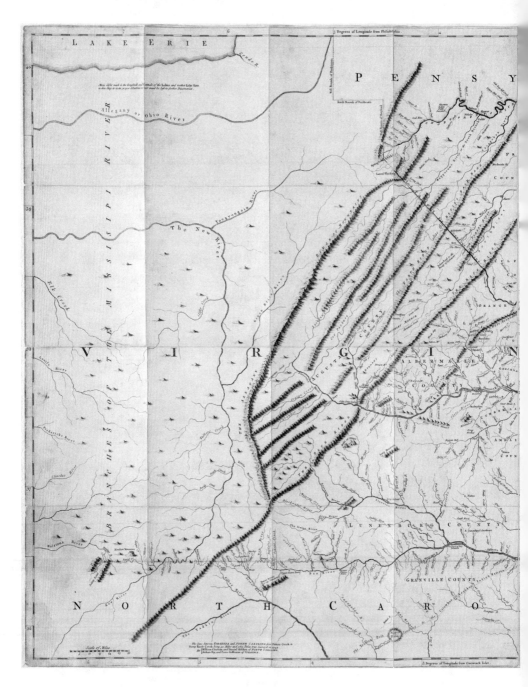

The Fry-Jefferson Map of Virginia: "A map of the most inhabited part of Virginia containing the whole province of Maryland with part of Pensilvania, New Jersey and North Carolina. Drawn by Joshua Fry & Peter Jefferson in 1751." Shadwell is in the center of the map, located at the break in the mountain

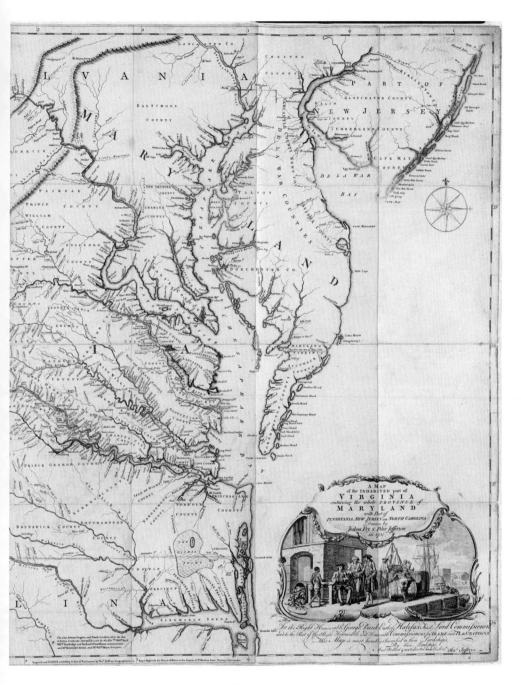

range that lies to the left of the "N" in "VIRGINIA." Williamsburg is to the lower right. Courtesy Special Collections, University of Virginia Library.

Introduction

On his retirement from the presidency, Thomas Jefferson proclaimed "inexpressible pleasure" at "returning to the scenes of my birth and early life, to the society of those with whom I was raised, and who have been ever dear to me." In this address to his fellow "citizens and neighbors," he called on the place, people, and manners that defined his native Albemarle County.[1] Jefferson invoked place often: a favorite oak tree, his view of the Maison Carrée, his own dear Monticello, which we today hold up as Jefferson personified. Even though Jefferson himself acknowledged over and over the importance of place in defining people, one of the places important in Jefferson's life has long been missing from our picture of him. Shadwell, the scene of Jefferson's birth and early life, has long been lost beneath the plowed earth at the foot of the hill that he so famously named Monticello. This book returns to Shadwell to bring forth tangible stories about the place, people, and manners of Thomas Jefferson's earliest home.

Thomas Jefferson was born at Shadwell, in what is now Albemarle County, Virginia, in 1743, on April 2 in the calendar of that year (April 13 in the new-style calendar adopted in 1752). From the 1730s through the 1770s Shadwell was home to Jane and Peter Jefferson, their eight children, more than sixty slaves owned by them, and numerous hired workers. It is impossible to write a history of one of the people who lived there without considering everyone who lived and worked there: the artifacts and documents from the site bear many stories.

As part of the preparations for celebrating the 250th anniversary of Thomas Jefferson's birth in 1993, the Monticello Archaeology Department entered into documentary and field investigations at Shadwell.[2] That fieldwork continued through 1995 and provided material to answer initial questions about the character of Peter and Jane Jefferson's family home. Research concentrated on the location of the Jeffersons' house, a slave quarter site, and the plantation landscape, details of which fell into place during those field seasons. Yet much of the basic physical description of the site could not be explained from the artifacts and features located through archaeological investigation. In fact, the range and complexity of the artifact assemblage and the seeming formality of the landscape plan prompted a rereading and new interpretation of familiar documentary sources.

Archaeological and documentary research at Shadwell reveals a picture of a well-appointed gentry house at the center of a highly structured plantation landscape in a period when the Piedmont was undergoing frontier settlement. The Jeffersons clearly accommodated, in their house, landscape, material goods, and behaviors, the most up-to-date social expectations of Virginia's elite tidewater culture. The material circumstances of Shadwell raise questions about the character of this frontier and how people could maintain a style of living that reflected their high social status. Shadwell seems to extend the boundaries of tidewater culture to include a world that was at least five days' journey from the colonial capital of Williamsburg.

The common themes throughout these chapters have to do with the material and cultural influences of the Jeffersons. Their wealth enabled them to enjoy the fashionable material goods they desired and permitted them to influence the character and development of their community in profound ways. In providing their family with a home and consumer goods that served the familiar functions of elite society, the Jeffersons fostered the growth of a local community of craftspeople whose skills they needed. The Jeffersons' slaves worked agricultural jobs, but they were also cooks, servants, and children's nurses and had a variety of skills to support the Jeffersons' material needs and heightened social position. The number of African Americans at Shadwell also meant that slaves had opportunities to form effective families and communities. The Jeffersons' various agricultural investments required the building of an infrastructure that small planters nearby also used. Social connections and economic power translated into political authority, which meant that the Jeffersons and their peers who held public office affected not only how their county grew but also how Virginia developed. These local leaders made policy and practiced laws that ensured that their way of doing things in tidewater would work in newly formed Albemarle County and across the Blue Ridge Mountains.

The archaeological discoveries at Shadwell give new meaning to many of the historic documents about the Jeffersons because the material culture recovered there has prompted fresh reading of much that had seemed familiar. The results of the research ultimately offer new views of the Jefferson family, a rich description of the lives of the slaves who worked for them, and new perspectives on Thomas Jefferson himself.[3]

Two historiographical problems haunt interpretations of Shadwell. The first is the tension between the scholarly and popular perceptions of Thomas Jefferson's origins. The second is the nature of findings from earlier excavations of Shadwell.

In 1909 University of Virginia professor William Thornton proclaimed that Jefferson bore the "plebeian red [blood] of Peter" and the "aristocratic blue of Jane," an analogy meant to challenge partisan political groups to find common ground in distinctly American combinations of high and low culture. But Thornton's analogy heightened the idea of an oppositional relationship between the political and social origins of Thomas Jefferson's parents. In *The Jefferson Image in the American Mind* (1960), Merrill D. Peterson traced the popular embrace of this view even after the complete scholarly repudiation of it by Marie Kimball in 1943. Marie Kimball certified Peter Jefferson's gentry status in *Jefferson: The Road to Glory, 1743 to 1776*, and Dumas Malone reiterated her findings five years later in the first volume of his celebrated six-volume biography of Jefferson. Most scholars since cite Malone on the parentage of Thomas Jefferson, but they are left, as Malone was, with architectural historian Fiske Kimball's earlier tentative thesis about Shadwell on the *material circumstances* of earlier Jeffersons.[4]

Interpretations of the social and material worlds of the Jeffersons have been difficult to reconcile. Fiske Kimball excavated portions of Shadwell in 1943, and his assessment still reverberates through Jefferson historiography. Kimball uncovered the cellar to the Jeffersons' house, but he could not understand the archaeological evidence because it did not fit what he wanted to find: a formal "five-part Palladian plan." Kimball wanted to find a "mansion" to dispute the idea then current among some scholars that Thomas Jefferson rose from yeoman origins. Early in the twentieth century, politically liberal scholars and politicians described Jefferson as being born of an overseer class, a characterization made to ennoble the Everyman as a descendent of common American beginnings, but Colonial Revival conservatism responded with a desire to certify the pedigrees of great American patriots. Kimball excavated the mid-eighteenth-century brick cellar and called it an outbuilding. He thought the later eighteenth-century stone cellar might be part of the early Jefferson house because he made the incorrect assumption that stone was necessarily earlier construction than brick. He also uncovered the two kitchen-related cellar pits nearby. Based on the extent of the buildings, he declared that there was little evidence that Jefferson was "a son of the frontier." But Kimball could not bolster his argument with further material evidence, and later interpretations echo his tentativeness. Malone summed up Kimball's findings: "No mansion ever stood on this homesite but his father erected a substantial group of plantation buildings before he died." Citations of Fiske Kimball via Malone have been augmented only by those who cite Jack McLaughlin's book *Jefferson and Monticello: The Biography of a Builder* (1988), in which McLaughlin sets up a formalistic contrast between Shadwell and Monticello and extends the oppositional paradigm from the social world to the material.[5]

Among historians, Jane Jefferson's Randolph parentage left little doubt as to her prestige; it is Peter Jefferson's ancestry and fortunes that have driven the discussions. Jan Lewis cites Malone and the gentry status of Thomas's grandfather but still chooses to highlight Peter's "own exertions" as his identifying characteristic. Noble E. Cunningham, Jr., calls Shadwell "a modest frame house" and describes Peter as "a rising young planter" yet says that Thomas was born to the gentry. Willard Sterne Randall uses a safer tactic of noting that in his autobiography Thomas himself said his father was a surveyor and did not mention his father's elected offices. In other words, Thomas downplayed his father's achievements. Randall cites McLaughlin that Shadwell was a "typical Virginia farmhouse," as does Andrew Burstein, who chooses to embrace Peter as a "self-reliant frontiersman." Joseph J. Ellis uses "moderately successful" to describe Peter, and Gordon S. Wood calls Peter Jefferson "wealthy but uneducated and ungenteel." Norman K. Risjord calls Peter "a man of some substance" but avoids describing Shadwell at all.[6]

This study of Shadwell demands reinterpretation of historians' characterizations of Peter Jefferson, Jane Randolph Jefferson, and Thomas Jefferson's boyhood experience. The material provisions of the plantation suggest that Peter and Jane Jefferson fashioned a world wholly familiar to Virginia's elite. Though Peter Jefferson is often described as a self-made frontiersman, the imprint of a talented surveyor on Shadwell's landscape speaks of a man who knew what social and political returns came from a carefully planned estate. The provisions for social ritual within the Jefferson dwelling house and the attention to the children's well-rounded education show Jane Jefferson's concern with refined manners. The role of these parents in shaping their children is implicit in the material goods that filled their home and in the constant presence of enslaved African Americans to ensure that each and every Jefferson understood the entitlements of being born white and wealthy in colonial Virginia. This study of Shadwell requires us to think of the Jeffersons as a family, a social unit whose function was to perpetuate genetic lines and to preserve socioeconomic investments within their cultural system. Evidence from Shadwell shows just how successful the Jeffersons were at promoting the family's interests.

This study begins with the walls of the house—actually with the archaeological remains of those walls—and spirals outward from there to explore the connections that the Jeffersons had from Shadwell across Virginia and beyond (fig. Intro.1). The buildings and objects at Shadwell suggest that the Jeffersons invested in running a plantation but also concerned themselves with furnishing their house for entertaining and as a way of displaying their status. The house was a physical object that both defined and was defined by the social needs of those who lived and worked in it. Its users operated within the building and beyond its walls with the relentless details of everyday life and the workings of a household that included Jefferson family members, their slaves, and occasional hired help. Peter Jefferson owned more than sixty slaves who performed tasks as part of the Jefferson household, of their own households, and of the agricultural enterprise of the plantation. The plantation population made contact well beyond the property's physical bounds as commerce included local hired help, craftsmen, merchants, and visitors. And the family, business, and professional dealings of Peter and Jane and other members of the plantation

Figure Intro.1. Brick cellar of Jefferson house at Shadwell. The brick cellar was under the eastern end of the Jefferson dwelling house that burned February 1, 1770. Photo taken during 1991 excavations, facing northwest. Courtesy Monticello/Thomas Jefferson Foundation, Inc.

community ensured that the Jeffersons were not cut off from the larger social landscape of Virginia or the material wealth of the British colonial world.

This project is by nature descriptive, but it is not merely so. To describe this plantation and its inhabitants required the collection and cataloging of artifacts and evidence. The detailed analysis of objects and documents, statistics and individuals, and historical context are what make the description possible. Yet this is not a study of material culture; it is a history of people written from the things they used and the things they did. The material remains, just like the account books, are a means for investigating the history on this site. The objects set the stage upon which the people acted. Until recently scholars have been uneasy with using material culture as a source for history, since for so long old objects had been merely curiosities or the domain of the specialized formalist language of people who study decorative arts. A generation of historians, material culture specialists, museum professionals, architectural historians, archaeologists, and others has changed that and proven that dynamic and meaningful histories come from what had previously been considered "interdisciplinary" at best. The physical setting helps us move through the plantation; each chapter describes a different subset of the whole population, as the focus expands from house to household to slave houses to plantation and to Piedmont Virginia and beyond.

A word is in order here about certain conventions I have chosen to use in rendering this image of Shadwell. Names are an issue for both the white and the black families in this book, but for different reasons. Readers who are used to the word "Jefferson" may be challenged by the presence of so many Jeffersons. In most cases I call each Jefferson by her or his first name, which is also cumbersome since there are three Martha Jeffersons, two Jane Jeffersons, and other family members with the same name at some point in their lives. The names of the people whom we know only from documents that list them as slaves are complicated by our knowing only their given names, often rendered in nonstandard spelling. In most cases, I use the spellings from the 1757 inventory, even when other spellings occur in later documents. I have tried to be clear in the notes about multiple versions of names.

In the first chapter I describe the Jefferson family's house at Shadwell, springing from its fullest flowering as recorded in the 1757 inventory of Peter Jefferson's estate. The comprehensive house renovations in the early 1750s present an opportunity to see how the house and its furnishings represented the aspirations and met the needs of the family during those years. In particular, I examine how the house served public functions, family life, and labor and craft production. The house was the enclave for a wealthy family but a place of work for slaves given tasks as various as tending babies or grown gentry, setting up a tea service, or making candles. This was where Jane Jefferson ensured that children learned to dance and where Peter Jefferson hung maps, kept accounts, and inscribed important boundaries on paper. The house contained many objects that encouraged learning; whether from books or teacups or a finely finished room, the house and its furnishings were didactic. The house was also the center of a substantial plantation, and the relationship of the parts of the plantation in the landscape shows how the Jeffersons carefully ordered their world.

Chapter 1 involves critical methodology dealing with objects and buildings. The give and take between the material remains and the documentary evidence drives this study. There is tension between the two types of sources; neither is complete, and each is made both more and less so with consideration of the other. The joining of the material and the documentary sources creates new ways to discuss the Jeffersons' lives. Artifacts are three-dimensional and require consideration of how people used them as well as the space they took up. They require that the actions of the people who used them be described in deliberate and concrete ways: actions take up space as well as time. The artifacts enable the historian to animate the site and enliven the now-past landscape, but the documents ground the discussion to a particular time and place. Documents such as inventories function as snapshots to capture single moments in people's lives. The objects provide the colors and textures that distinguish the character of the everyday.

In the second chapter I look at running the household, the purview of Jane Jefferson. Her oversight extended beyond the walls of the house into the separate kitchen building and home slave quarters and even into the homes of local women who produced goods for Shadwell. The house set the stage for both household and social activities, and running the household relied on the work of Jane Jefferson and her organization of other family members and slaves. Jane's projects can be divided into two broad categories: work that sustained the household, from everyday cooking to seasonal crafts; and work that preserved and perpetuated the family's important social standing vis-à-vis the proper training of both her children and the slaves who served them. This home belonged to a family of wealthy colonial Virginia planters. That meant that the household included the members of that family, the slaves who tended them and worked in and around their house, and other people whose expertise or labor was hired to aid in the Jeffersons' fortunes and comforts.

Chapter 2 focuses on the lives of Jane Jefferson and other women at Shadwell because the history of the household was in large part a history of the women who were its primary keepers. The children also occupied a substantial portion of this landscape. Their daily care and the investments made in their upbringing were among the basic functions of the household. The history of the household, and of these women, is a history of the everyday and the immediate. It relies on our thinking about the most basic functions of various objects and what work those objects facilitated. This means thinking about the time and actions it takes to dress and feed and educate children, to tend animals, to make clothing, to give orders to slaves, or, if a slave, to do all these things for your own children *and* someone else's. And no one—in the eighteenth century or now—wrote down how many buttons they sewed onto clothing each day or how many spoons they set on the table or picked up off the floor or picked up off the floor again.

The Jeffersons' riches and power rode on the backs of African or African-American slaves. The slaves and their material and social lives are the focus of chapters 3 and 4, which depend on archaeological as well as documentary evidence. The sixty or so slaves who lived at Shadwell inhabited a materially rich world, very different from what most Virginians experienced. Shadwell offers an opportunity to explore how the work of slaves was affected by their owners' access to consumer goods and investments in elite material culture; yet for all the manufactured goods at Shadwell, the people there augmented their provisions through local resources. The slaves' lives were tied not only to the large-scale production of tobacco and grain but also to the tending of the plantation kitchen and to the combing and dressing of young gentry-in-training. The Shadwell slave lists lend themselves to analysis through aggregate statistics, and archaeology offers insights into objects of the slaves' material culture and reveals domestic landscapes and social opportunities. Their lives, from birth to death, from sunup to sundown, were inextricably intertwined with those of the Jefferson family, and those relationships drive much of what we know about these people.

The home-quarter slaves are the subjects of chapter 3. Although slavery at Shadwell was very much like slavery elsewhere, there were differences within the plantation, particularly between the experiences of home-quarter slaves and field laborers, though in the end, an enslaved person's life responded to her or his owner's demands. The Jeffersons practiced some management strategies that historians have come to label as somewhat "better" for the slaves' personal well-being, such as recognizing slave families in the organization of housing and work. But the most brutal aspects of slavery—of not being able to control the destinies of one's own body and family—were enacted within the Jeffersons' holdings. Slaves were moved within and between plantations, their jobs were changed, they were sold, and one was murdered. Only a few of the people who were slaves at Shadwell in 1757 died there; most followed Jefferson family members to other places, along trajectories set in place when both the black and white children were infants. The lives of the Shadwell slaves changed as their owners' legal status changed. Instead of a life lived on one patch of land doing the same work for years, most of these slaves experienced at least one major change to home or job, and some experienced many changes during their lives. The evidence of these changes appears in the archaeological and documentary records and suggests that a life that was never quite settled was a common story of slavery. Archaeology at Shadwell, coupled with the Jefferson documents, offers an unusual opportunity to explore both the mundane and the exceptional events in the lives of a single group of enslaved people on the home quarter of a plantation.

In chapter 4 I explore the Jeffersons' slaves as a group and how they reflected the experience of slavery in early Albemarle County and Virginia. Shadwell housed one of the largest populations of African Americans in colonial Albemarle County. The lives of these slaves were unusual because of the size of the group. Yet in other ways Shadwell represented a common experience, especially for the field hands. Staple-crop production at Shadwell, the keeping of a large labor force, and the maintenance of the plantation ensured regular commerce with people outside the plantation population. Business and social visits that brought people and material goods to Shadwell expanded the experience of those who lived on the plantation.

The plantation and agricultural investments at Shadwell I define in chapter 5. Peter Jefferson organized his enslaved and hired labor force to make the most of the resources of the vast Shadwell enterprise. Jefferson established local relationships that supported the household and plantation businesses as well as those that fulfilled familial responsibilities. This chapter relies heavily on account books kept for the plantation and on family records to explore the status and influence of Peter Jefferson, as well as how his personal, professional, business, and family relationships describe a man charged with extensive power and responsibility. The material and social worlds of Shadwell support an argument that the spread of culture occurred through socioeconomic means rather than by geographical diffusion; Peter Jefferson's many business and personal alliances provide an interesting map of how his associations connected his family across a range of social and geographic settings. Just what was Peter Jefferson's business? How far geographically did his associations reach, and how pervasive was his influence in Albemarle County and abroad? In this chapter I define the web of the Jeffersons' local relationships and begin to chart their geographic horizons, which expand further in chapters 6 and 7.

The associations that Peter Jefferson had through elected offices or government appointments that connected him to people across Virginia and beyond are explored in chapter 6. Sources for this chapter include public records and the documents generated by land speculation and mapmaking, yet certain artifacts from Shadwell illustrate how Jefferson's public roles were symbolically and literally brought home. Artifacts of surveying, office holding, and hosting Native Americans let us tell these stories from the grounds of Shadwell, bringing them into the lives of everyone who lived there. There is significant overlap between the names of family members, friends, and colleagues who appear in chapter 5 as part of Jefferson's personal business and those who appear in chapter 6 as professional associates or fellow officeholders. Much of the business that benefited the colony, for which Jefferson acted as agent, also benefited Jefferson the person. Peter Jefferson's story is one of commonwealth, empire, and a worldview that extended far beyond Albemarle County, Virginia.

In chapter 7, I follow the occupants of Shadwell, both the Jeffersons and their slaves, into their post-Shadwell lives. Jane and Peter Jefferson left intangible legacies that connected their children and grandchildren to generations past. The futures of sons, daughters, and family slaves were determined in part by the industrious attentions of Peter and Jane Jefferson. The genealogical notations made by Jane and Peter Jefferson and their heirs, as well as the mechanics of wills and funerals, provide evidence of many ways of remembering family. In addition to preserving the family's wealth and status, Jane and Peter Jefferson instilled in their children a strong sense of family that enabled them to support and care for one another and their descendants. The possibility for an affectionate history of this generation of Jeffersons has been hinted at in documents but has remained unexplored by historians (who often find greater entertainment in exposing the possibility of pathologies among their subjects). This chapter relies heavily on letters written between the Jefferson children that show how their adult relationships reveal gestures of love and concern among them. In this chapter I also examine the kin networks among slaves who once lived at Shadwell and moved away or who stayed at Shadwell, Monticello, or Snowdon and facilitated exchanges among members of the Jefferson family. The histories of the slave families and their owners' families continued together.

Chapter 7 is one of the most "text-based" parts of this project, yet documents, too, are artifacts and offer up evidence beyond the words they bear.

As the context in which men like Thomas Jefferson lived becomes as important to historians as the man himself, the value of various documents changes. A surprising number of letters written by the family of Thomas Jefferson survive. These have not been handled in any comprehensive way, and their association with Thomas Jefferson has been both an asset and a liability in how historians have presented them. Many of the Jefferson family letters also contain glimpses into the lives of the slaves who came and went with the various siblings.

As I explain in chapter 8, the final chapter, the archaeological assemblage from Shadwell, coupled with the surviving documents, offers a unique opportunity to examine the lives of many people who passed over this place more than two centuries ago. Throughout this study new details about the Jeffersons' lives bring up opportunities to reassess family stories and myths surrounding the early years and family of Thomas Jefferson. Some family stories are reinforced by the material record: the description of the Shadwell house, for instance. Other stories are revealed to have their origins in the minds of nineteenth- or twentieth-century historians. This story of Shadwell brings us again to essential questions about Thomas Jefferson.

How does this picture of the early years of Thomas Jefferson challenge our view of him? The image of Jefferson as the self-made scholar, epicure, and republican who bursts forth onto the American landscape is at once more complex and simpler. His parents' participation in a Virginia-wide social world and larger Atlantic economy explains Jefferson's worldliness as well as his attention to refinement, taste, and manners. Jefferson knew intimately the hierarchical social and physical structure of large plantation landscapes, which he applied with rigor at both Monticello and Poplar Forest. Enslaved Africans and African Americans of all ages surrounded Jefferson from birth to death; he spent his lifetime negotiating relationships with people he owned. He knew that to appear successful in Virginia meant fostering relationships with slaves and laborers and with itinerant, poor, and improvident neighbors, as well as with kin and powerful officeholders. Young Thomas becomes one of many privileged young gentry in this, his family's culture, instead of the exception to a circumstance from which he alone escaped. Like the landscape at Shadwell, he bears the imprint of Jane, Peter, and other family members, of the talented enslaved blacks who made their lives possible, and of the view that Shadwell was peculiarly positioned to take advantage of unknown potential for new enterprise on this edge of the British Empire.

Just as Peter Jefferson helped chart the bounds of British colonial expansion in North America, the Jeffersons' Shadwell marked the limits of the colonial gentry's domain. Peter and Jane prepared their children and their enslaved workers to continue in that world, but it was not to be. The challenges of administering the law to people spread along the edge of the American continent fell from the British government to a new government designed by men like the younger Jefferson and authorized by a war for independence. The fire that altered the character of gentry life at Shadwell coincided with political, social, and economic upheaval that changed it anyway. Despite the heroic evidence here of strong families and social networks that served both black and white residents of Shadwell, the entire structure rested uneasily on the violence that everyone knew because they were complicit in this slave society. How Shadwell's most famous son grappled with that legacy is perhaps the most enduring conversation begun at Shadwell.

1 The House: The Material World
of the Jeffersons at Shadwell

Scholars who study Thomas Jefferson have had a difficult time defining his origins in the context of late colonial Virginia culture. On no topic is Jefferson scholarship more mired in previous generations of interpretation than that of Shadwell, his birthplace, in what is now Albemarle County. The popular mythology of Thomas Jefferson contends that Peter Jefferson was a backwoodsman, a native of the frontier, and that Jane Randolph Jefferson brought her gentry standards to the household, though her influence was not strong. The Jeffersons were a successful planter family, but, the story goes, the young Thomas left his Shadwell and Tuckahoe homes, his boyhood schoolmasters, and went to the metropolis, where he acquired his manners and tastes for finer things, first in Williamsburg, then in Philadelphia, Paris, and London.

In contrast to the popular perception, many scholars acknowledge that Peter Jefferson, Gent., had nearly the status his wife had; he was, after all, a county surveyor, a county justice, a burgess, and an acquaintance of many important people in mid-eighteenth-century Virginia. Yet historians still embrace a story that Thomas Jefferson necessarily moved between dramatically different worlds when he left Shadwell for the best tables in Williamsburg and to the refined home that he ultimately created at Monticello. The material world of Shadwell shows, however, that young Thomas and his siblings did not have to seek refinement elsewhere: they grew up with it and carried it with them. Shadwell was full of the proper tools for entertaining and for teaching children manners: the objects there and the behaviors they imply reveal who the Jeffersons were and what they expected from their world. Their expectations, moreover, were not dictated by their location, for Albemarle County indeed was still a frontier in many ways. Instead, the Jeffersons acquired both the consumer goods and the manners that allowed them to participate in the colonial gentry world wherever they could find—or make—it. In remote regions where there were no store displays with the latest goods, those concerned with status had to actively pursue their acquisition of objects and behaviors; they could not come by them casually. The material world of the Jeffersons at Shadwell illustrates the pervasive reach of the gentry and how their world of goods extended their political and social dominance across Virginia.[1]

The recent work of archaeologists and architectural and social historians has enabled a better understanding of just how most of the gentry, and the larger body of folk who were not gentry, lived. Gentry houses were alike, not because of appearance, but because of function: how people arranged activities within their living spaces and what those activities were. In the mid-eighteenth century, many prosperous people lived in relatively small houses made of wood with wooden chimneys, even as they added specialized spaces and new furnishings for entertaining and created private rooms for family in their homes. This readjusting of historians' expectations proved that many of our extant models for colonial architecture were in fact outliers. The most visible grand houses of Virginia, such as Rosewell and Westover, were extraordinary creations of a very few wealthy families. Scholars have put houses and their families in context by looking at buildings and furnishings as records not simply of design details but as artifacts that can show how people thought of themselves and how they related to other members of their households and communities.[2] Ironically, recent research at Shadwell, backed by a generation of social history and archaeology of the common man, began looking for the yeoman model—a frontier cabin, perhaps—and found, instead, Peter Jefferson's mansion.

The Jeffersons occupied the high end of the social scale in a culture that produced leaders through its members' regular participation in the militia, the church vestry, and county and colonial government. Of course, the heights to which Thomas Jefferson rose were exceptional, yet he neither struggled against excessive economic or material hardship nor occupied an exclusive existence. Rather, he grew up in a culture of plantation owners whose responsibilities included public service and the professional tasks of hiring and coordinating such workers as overseers, slaves, road crews, and militia, as well as the social tasks of educating family members to these roles that perpetuated the civic culture.

The geography of this settlement is important. Tidewater refers to both the location and the dominant culture of the Virginia Chesapeake region. This culture was characterized by a gentry class who lived on large tobacco plantations worked by slaves. It extended along Chesapeake Bay and its tributaries, including the James River, inland to the fall line. Piedmont refers to the terrain between the fall line and Blue Ridge Mountains, west of which lies the great Shenandoah Valley of Virginia. Historians consider both the Piedmont and the Shenandoah Valley as frontiers of English settlement late in the first half of the eighteenth century. The central Virginia Piedmont and the valley settlements differed in their dominant agricultural practices and their ethnic makeup. The Piedmont continued the tobacco culture of the eastern regions and the domain of second sons or lesser gentry of the great tidewater families. The valley accommodated a few of these same gentry offspring, but also became home to a variety of German, Scots, Irish, and Welsh settlers, many of whom entered Virginia through the northern end of the Shenandoah and never set foot in tidewater. This period of Virginia settlement marked the Piedmont and the valley as distinctly different cultural regions. Historians have noted that Piedmont society was more like that in the tidewater region than not, but the Piedmont is often omitted from studies of Chesapeake society and culture. In terms of institutional structures, patterns of slaveholding and agriculture, and slave life, the Piedmont ultimately extended the character of tidewater culture in the second half of the eighteenth century rather than replicating an earlier stage of tidewater development.[3] Evidence from Shadwell suggests that at least some who settled the Piedmont early thought of themselves as very much a part of the older Virginia culture: distance did not preclude the persistence of culture for very wealthy Virginians.

Contemporaries thought of the Piedmont as remote. Jefferson's friend James Maury lived about eight miles from Shadwell. Maury's uncle Peter Fontaine lived about a hundred miles east at Westover in Charles City County and described Maury's parish as "amongst the mountains." Maury referred to his situation as "we mountaineers." Fontaine's son Peter lived in southside Piedmont, which, as Fontaine wrote to his brother in England, was "threescore miles, in the woods back from the river. I can send a letter to you in as short a time as to him. No post travels that way, and I have not heard from him at all this two months." Distance did not keep Fontaine's wife from visiting her grandchildren there. Her complaining husband was the same Peter Fontaine who had traveled with William Byrd to survey Virginia's southern boundary in 1728 and appears (often in ill humor) in Byrd's account of that adventure. The Reverend Devereux Jarratt called 1750s Albemarle "nearly a frontier county." Thomas Jefferson did not use the word "frontier" but described what historians now call a frontier of settlement. In Jefferson's granddaughter's retelling, Shadwell was in the midst of a "thinly peopled and densely wooded" country. Jefferson's nineteenth-century biographers used "wilderness" and "primeval forest" to describe early Albemarle, features that Ellen Coolidge credited with causing her grandfather to become "well versed in all the ways of the woods and fields . . . a fearless rider, a bold hunter and skillful in the use of his gun." But the post-Turnerian Jefferson historians took these lessons in wilderness skills and transformed them into lessons of frontier culture. They linked Jefferson to the idea that the frontier nurtured the growth of democratic ideals because a still-forming community ensured that its members learned life lessons from the necessary interaction of people of different social ranks there. In the twentieth century, Jefferson became known as a "child of the frontier."[4]

In his autobiography, Thomas Jefferson stated that his father was "the third or fourth settler about the year 1737" in what became Albemarle County. Peter Jefferson, partner to Joshua Fry in making the famed 1751 *Map of the Inhabited Part of Virginia,* perhaps first saw this land on the Rivanna River during an early surveying venture (see fig. Intro.1). Jefferson acquired land in this region in 1734 and obtained the homesite of two hundred acres from his friend William Randolph for the price of "Henry Weatherburn's biggest bowl of Arrack punch" in 1736 at a tavern in Williamsburg. Peter may have moved to Shadwell as early as 1737, from Fine Creek, also in Goochland County. Jane joined him after their marriage in 1739 (fig. 1.1). They named their home Shadwell after the London parish where Jane was born, and daughter Jane, the first of their

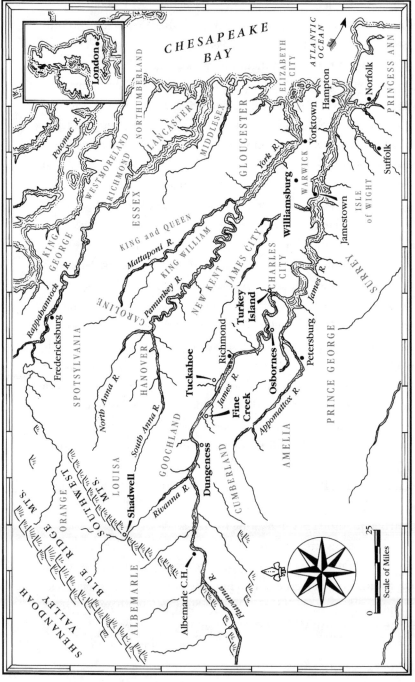

Figure 1.1. Both Jane Randolph and Peter Jefferson lived at various homes along the James River, moving west almost at the same pace as the newly forming counties. Jane's family moved from London to Williamsburg, Turkey Island, and Dungeness before she married Peter and moved to Shadwell. Peter was born at Osbornes and moved to Fine Creek, then Shadwell. The Jeffersons moved to Tuckahoe for seven years, then back to Shadwell. (Map spellings as rendered on the Fry-Jefferson Map.)

ten children, was born at the Virginia Shadwell in June 1740. Before his death in 1757, Peter Jefferson amassed more than fifteen hundred acres along the Rivanna River adjacent to this tract (including the mountain that his son later named Monticello) and other land in the Piedmont and beyond to total more than seventy-two hundred acres.[5]

Peter's own peers noted the honorific "Gent." behind his name in court documents as early as 1736—before he married a Randolph—and Peter's parents and grandparents held office and had important associations.[6] Though Thomas Jefferson called his father's education "quite neglected," Peter Jefferson shows attributes of many other gentry whose education came from a tutor instead of a school. Peter was an accomplished surveyor and a respected public official, a keeper of accounts who had fine handwriting and a decent library, the husband of the literate Jane Randolph, and a father concerned with the education of both daughters and sons.[7] The sophisticated house and landscape at Shadwell matched the company Peter Jefferson kept in his professional work and social life.

Peter's wealth ensured his wife, Jane Randolph Jefferson, the material provisions needed to raise their sons and daughters to the same standards of propriety that the parents knew. Born in London, Jane grew up in the household of the well-established Virginia and London merchant and agent for the colony Isham Randolph and his English wife, Jane Rogers. Their Virginia home, Dungeness, included extensive gardens enclosed with brick walls, specialized plantation buildings, including a coach house, mill house, well house, and henhouse, horses and a chariot for riding, and family portraits. A contemporary offered a glimpse of the social and material standards expected by these Randolphs. An impending visit to Dungeness by John Bartram in 1738 prompted Bartram's sponsor, Peter Collinson, to advise his colleague:

> I know no person will make thee more Welcome than Isham Randolph. He lives 30 or 40 miles above the falls of James River in Goochland above the other settlements. Now I take his house to be a very suitable place to make a settlement att for to take several Days' Excursions all Round, and to return to his House at Night. One thing I must Desire of thee and do Insist that thee oblige Mee therein that thou make up that Druggett Clothes, to go to Virginia In and not appear to Disgrace thyself or Mee for tho I would not Esteem thee the less to come to Mee in what Dress thou Will, yet these Virginians are a very gentle, Well Dress'd people, & look phaps More at a Man's Outside than his Inside, for these and other Reasons pray go very Clean, neat & handsomely Dressed to Virginia.

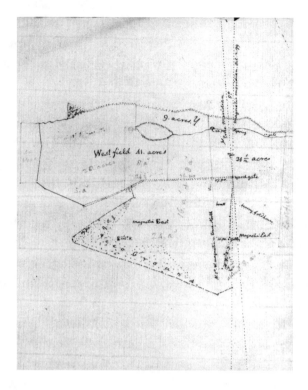

Figure 1.2. Shadwell lands as surveyed by Thomas Jefferson in 1799. The legend
"magnetic East" at lower center is the southern limit of the ten-acre domestic center of
the plantation. The diagonal line just above that reads "bearing of old house." Jefferson
used the east chimney of the house as a reference point for surveying from nearby hills.
The 1799 surveys of the property reveal remnants of earlier plantation use, including the
cemetery (marked "cedars," lower center), the Three-Notch'd Road along the northern
boundary, and the farm road to Monticello (dotted line from "yard gate" that leads west
to the Rivanna River). The Rivanna River runs just outside the southern and western
boundary of the plat. HM 9379-4, HM 9379-5. By permission of The Huntington
Library, San Marino, California.

Bartram reported being treated with "all ye expression of kindness & Civil-
ity."[8] Accounts kept for Shadwell after Peter Jefferson's death indicate Jane
Jefferson's attention to and investment in teaching her children as well as in
surrounding them with fine consumer goods.

Though the Jefferson family moved east to Tuckahoe from about 1746 to
1753, Shadwell remained an active plantation, worked by Jefferson slaves and

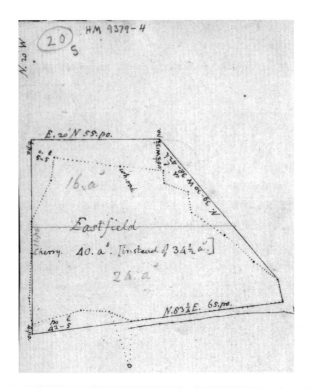

Figure 1.2. *(continued)*

hired managers, and visited by family members.[9] In the early 1750s, when the family was to return, Peter Jefferson repaired and improved the dwelling house and outbuildings at Shadwell. The Jeffersons' pending move from Tuckahoe back to Shadwell was an opportune time to think about furnishing this plantation as a cohesive statement of the growing family's physical needs and social status. Agricultural investments at Shadwell included cleared land, dwellings, stores, and barns, vegetable and flower gardens, tobacco and grain cultivation, a grist mill, brewing, and livestock, including horses, cattle, pigs, and sheep, for transportation, draft, food, hide, and fiber. Peter Jefferson died at age forty-nine in 1757 in good gentry standing. He held major public office, serving on the vestry at Saint James, Northam, as county justice, lieutenant colonel of the militia, and county lieutenant. He represented Albemarle County to the Virginia House of Burgesses. He left his wife, six daughters, and two sons a fashionable house, sixty slaves, two improved plantations, speculative landholdings, rental properties, and, unlike many of his peers, no debt.[10] He bequeathed the plantations and most of the slaves to his sons. His daughters received money for their education, dowries, and personal servants. Jane retained life rights to Shadwell, her slaves, and other property, which she disposed of in her own will in 1776.

This ideal gentry world at Shadwell ended on February 1, 1770, when the house burned to the ground. The houses and plantation landscape described here are reconstructed from the archaeological recovery of building remains and material goods, the wills, account books, and documents left by the Jefferson family, and the inferences allowed by these methods of research.[11] The physical landscape of Shadwell reveals the social landscape of the plantation explicitly (fig. 1.2). In the early 1990s archaeologists for the Thomas Jefferson Foundation excavated house sites and work areas for both white and black residents and exposed part of the layout of the plantation. Specialized spaces indicate a clear hierarchy of slave and owner, domestic and industrial, and public and private across the center of the plantation and within the dwelling houses of Shadwell's white and black residents, reflecting the familiar patterns of plantation architecture adopted by Virginia's slaveholding elite. Peter Jefferson's accomplishments as a surveyor emerge in the landscape plan, but the enslaved occupants used the same landscape in ways that seem counter to the planter's grander scheme. The plantation landscape offers the first clue to the formality of the Jeffersons' world at Shadwell.

The Shadwell Landscape

The Jeffersons' dwelling house at Shadwell occupied the literal and figurative center of this plantation world. It sat on a ridge, facing south to the Rivanna River and north to the mountains, at the middle of a ten-acre square (fig. 1.3). This ten-acre area was the domestic seat of the plantation. Within this curti-

---

Figure 1.3. Peter Jefferson laid out Shadwell on a ridge between the Rivanna River to the south and the Three-Notch'd Road to the north. The Jefferson house sat at the center of a ten-acre square that defined the home quarter. At least two buildings to the east served kitchen activities and housed a small group of slaves. A slave quarter site farther east contained at least four houses for slaves. Fence lines and gates controlled access and marked space within this domestic complex.

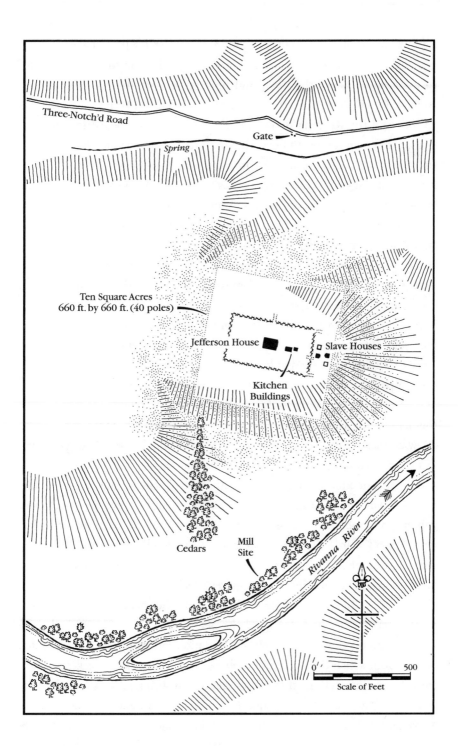

Three-Notch'd Road

Gate

Spring

Ten Square Acres
660 ft. by 660 ft. (40 poles)

Jefferson House

Slave Houses

Kitchen
Buildings

Cedars

Mill
Site

Rivanna River

0   500
Scale of Feet

lage, or improved area, were the outbuildings, quarters, shops, barns, stables, gardens, and orchards. Beyond this central area lay the tobacco fields and pastures, mills along the river, and unimproved woodlands. The "Three-Notch'd Road" that connected the Shenandoah Valley of Virginia to tidewater followed the Rivanna River past Shadwell. Archaeological research has located the main house, a kitchen building that also served as slave housing, and one group of slave quarters, forming a line east-west along the ridge. Fences and gates defined the approaches to the main house and separated the house and kitchen from the quarters. A fence line running north-south toward the east end of the ten-acre square provided a visual and physical barrier between the Jefferson family and quarters for some of the Shadwell slaves. Archaeological evidence indicates that the major components of the landscape were planned and put in place before work on and enlargement of the main dwelling house around 1750.[12]

The ten-acre center of this plantation reflects the mind of its maker, Peter Jefferson. Ten acres equals 660 feet, or forty poles, on a side. The gates and fences within the square divide the ten acres mathematically and geometrically. A pedestrian-scale gate north of the house places a fence line one-third of the way from the house to the curtilage edge. The split-rail fence between the house and quarter area had larger gates on its north and south ends to allow carriage or wagon access to the main dwelling house. These gates, 220 feet apart, divided by one-third the total ten-acre square. The axes of the fences and the line of buildings describe a highly ordered schema laid on the land by Peter's surveying tools (fig. 1.4). The Jeffersons organized vegetable and flower gardens in numbered beds that they then ordered in rows designated by letters. A sundial in a prominent position in this landscape suggests that the ordering of time was as important as the ordering of space in this world: both passions would be inherited by the surveyor's elder son.[13]

The Shadwell landscape, like the house and other material goods, had explicit social functions. It arranged the people who lived and worked there according to the familiar divisions of plantation society—that is, it separated master from servant, planter from laborer, and white from black, and controlled their interactions through hierarchically arranged spaces and routes of access. Slaves left the main quarter site via a small gate in a split-rail, or Virginia, fence, and passed by the kitchen building and up a slight rise to arrive at the south porch of the main house, where they might receive work

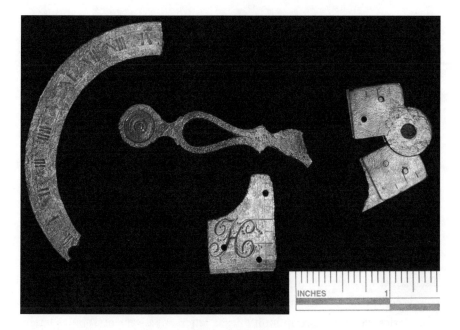

Figure 1.4. Eighteenth-century surveying and drafting instruments found at Shadwell (clockwise from upper left): brass ring for an "inclining" or "equatorial" sundial that was mounted in a box and carried by a surveyor or traveler to tell the time at any latitude; brass hinge for wooden scale, marked at 1/8 inch; brass plate or hinge for wooden drafting scale, marked with "H," 1/8 inch; brass hinge or arm for rectangular protractor. Courtesy Monticello/Thomas Jefferson Foundation, Inc.

assignments or enter the house to finish domestic tasks. The slaves who lived and worked in the plantation kitchen building occupied a physical and social space in between the Jeffersons in their house and the site farther east that served as a center of African-American life. Slaves who worked and slept in the Jeffersons' house formed a social niche that regularly separated them from both the black and the white members of their larger community. The landscape also mediated between those on the plantation and those entering the bounds from outside. From the passing road, visitors climbed the hill, entered through a gate, and crossed a yard before reaching the door that may or may not have allowed them into the passage of the house. From the passage a slave or family member judged whether the visitor would then enter into one of the Jeffersons' better rooms.[14] The landscape clearly communicated the customary order of plantation society to those within this particular community and to those outside it.

The landscape that separated white and black people and their activities also contained the spaces in which they interacted. Thomas Jefferson's earliest memory reveals physical intimacy with family slaves when one carried him on horseback in their move to Tuckahoe. For the planter child and the family slaves, common experiences were inescapable. The shared material culture of the plantation community extended beyond pots and bowls to language and music, events surrounding birth and death, and even patterns of work and leisure that may at first glance separate the activities of planters and slaves. Family stories remembered by Thomas Jefferson's granddaughters recounted that a slave summoned their grandfather on the night the Shadwell house burned: they had not rescued Thomas's books, but a slave saved his fiddle. The planter may later claim to not remember the Africans' songs, yet the fiddle stands conspicuously as a meaningful and perhaps valuable object across the boundaries within this community. Isaac Jefferson, a slave of Thomas Jefferson's at Monticello, recalled Thomas's younger brother, Randolph Jefferson, as "a mighty simple man [who] used to come out among black people, play the fiddle and dance half the night." This planter did not deny the community or the pleasure he knew in his extended household. Isaac Jefferson's authority on the familiar names of Thomas Jefferson's sisters, referring to Mary as "Polly," Martha as "Patsy," and Anna Scott as "Nancy," reveals further the intimacies among these residents of the same household.[15]

The Jeffersons' House

The strong spatial order that allowed separation of the different social functions and cultural groups on the landscape also informs the physical evidence for the main dwelling house. The archaeological record for the Jeffersons' house at Shadwell is somewhat diffuse. The Shadwell ridge was plowed throughout the nineteenth century, and earlier excavations wiped out any physical remains of the western end of the house and most of the stratigraphic artifact record for the house proper. Only a few intact archaeological deposits can be associated with the Jefferson occupation of the main house, though period artifacts exist across the site in the plowed earth and in other valid contexts. Yet the scant archaeological record, augmented by the copious furnishings listed in Peter Jefferson's account book, will, and probate inventory, offer a fairly complete picture of the house and how it functioned during the 1750s. The Shadwell house of the previous decade was smaller, yet the landscape plan indicates that it occupied the formal center of the plantation, and the furnishings Peter inherited from his father suggest that social activities as represented by such amenities as table linens, seating furniture such as chairs and couches, and silver eating utensils had long been a priority for the Jeffersons.[16]

A great English-bond brick cellar outlines the eastern portion of the house (figs. 1.5, 1.6; see also figs. I.1, 1.3 center). The cellar measures eighteen and a half by thirty-two and a half feet outside and was probably raised well above grade, as the cellar entrance suggests its use for large-scale storage. Scaffolding holes outside the cellar mark the location of the east outside chimney (referred to in survey notes) and locate the fireplaces that heated both the parlor and chamber above the cellar and the upstairs chamber above those rooms. Three postholes designate a porch on the south side of the house, added during the 1750s renovations. The total length of the house cannot be determined from what remains archaeologically, nor is there any remaining evidence of the chimney to the west that demanded a surveyor to denote the other as "east" when referring to the house chimneys.[17] The porch aligns with the gate to the north of the house and defines a center passage axis that extended through the house into the landscape.

Peter Jefferson's estate inventory supports the earliest recorded family history of Shadwell, describing a house "a story and a half in height [with] four spacious ground [floor] rooms and hall[way], with garret chambers above." The inventory lists an unheated room first, which served as Peter Jefferson's office and contained his desk and bookcase, books, maps, and mathematical instruments. The inventory then follows the pattern observed by architectural historians in listing a formal entertaining room—known as a dining room or hall—furnished with the best goods; a parlor that served as best bedchamber, entertaining, and secondary food-preparation area; and a lesser chamber that accommodated beds and odd storage. Like some other houses of the period, such as George Mason's Gunston Hall in Fairfax County or George Wythe's house in Williamsburg, the two public rooms—the dining room and office— were paired on one side of the passage, with the two private chambers opposite them. The upstairs had two heated bed chambers, both of which held

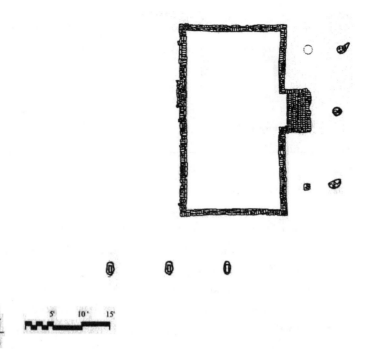

Figure 1.5. Jefferson house at Shadwell: archaeological remains at cellar level. The conjectural plan of Shadwell is based on archaeological evidence, documents pertaining to Shadwell, and studies that examine the various functions, arrangement, and proportions of rooms in eighteenth-century domestic architecture. Shadwell's largest artifact, the brick cellar, represents the oldest (eastern) part of the house, and the chimney evidence here indicates it was below two adjoining rooms that were listed as heated in the 1757 inventory: the more private rooms of parlor and chamber. These rooms were on the east side closest to the separate kitchen building, whose role was directly related to the function of the parlor as secondary dining and also food preparation space. The cellar gives the dimensions for the house depth at thirty-two and a half feet. Drawing by author.

bed furniture and case furniture.[18] The special-purpose rooms and fine furnishings at Shadwell displayed more than simply Peter and Jane Jefferson's refined tastes, however; the material goods reveal that the Jeffersons invested in the spaces and equipment to entertain properly and also to teach their children the social rituals required to occupy an elevated status in Virginia.

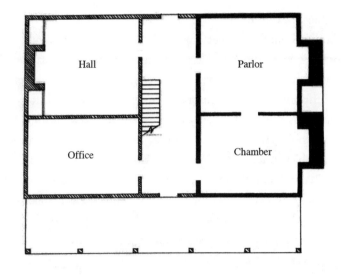

Hall

Parlor

Office

Chamber

5'   10'   15'

N

Figure 1.6. Jefferson house at Shadwell: conjectural ground-floor plan. The ten-foot intervals for the three existing porch postholes on the south side of the building are the best tool for approximating the length of the house in conjunction with the proportions of the rooms above the cellar. The Three Notch'd Road and gate to the north of the house describe a formal route of access, and most likely the hall and parlor were on the north front. With a ten-foot-wide passage, the porch extends west twenty feet more, for a total length of fifty feet. Dell Upton's idea of "social molecule" illustrates the customary communication between rooms. The proportions of the hall are based on Upton's observation that the hall was generally square. The hall chimney is interpreted as internal in order to allow space for the cupboards or closets implied by the lack of case furniture in this room that was filled with dining equipage. Walls are drawn six inches on the exterior and four inches on the interior, approximating the average sizes for frame houses. Drawing by author.

The Shadwell house shows that the Jeffersons participated in gentry culture and expected to continue to do so, even if they lived on a "frontier."

The formal entertaining room, the dining room, held an array of furnishings that set the Jeffersons apart from most people who lived in Virginia in the eighteenth century. Peter Jefferson ordered a substantial quantity of furniture for this room from joiner Francis West in 1750, concurrent with the expansion of the house. The movable goods listed in the inventory describe a range of social activities at Shadwell, and archaeological finds augment the spare legal descriptions in the inventory with details of material, form, and color. The Jeffersons could seat twenty people for dinner (twenty-one if one counts the closestool chair that hid a chamber pot there) at two large and two smaller oval tables. If ten chairs held Peter, Jane, and their children, at least ten guests could join them, though younger children were probably fed out of the dining room. The Jeffersons set the tables with knives, forks, spoons, and napkins, in an era when many people still ate with only a spoon or their hands. They had silver soupspoons, tablespoons, and teaspoons, and ladled punch with silver. They served two courses on silver-plated or white salt-glazed stoneware plates, and a soup course in silver-plated soup plates. Both the silver-plated and the white salt-glazed plates were new to the consumer market in the 1740s. Chafing dishes show that the food served at Shadwell demanded tools for finer detail than the large kitchen fireplace, spits, and pots and pans offered. A lacquered plate oven by the fire warmed the dishes that waited for the table, and a cruet stand and silver "salts" held spices to adjust seasonings in the food.[19]

The Jeffersons served tea, coffee, and punch in their hall using equipment that elevated these luxuries to the status of ritual. They had a tea service of silver, a "China teapot," and a "Black teapot" to put on their three tea tables. Fragments of teapots in blue-and-white Chinese porcelain and of a "Jackfield"-type ware, a lustrous black-glazed earthenware, denote two of these pots. There was a white salt-glazed stoneware teapot and small rectangular tea chest, and at least one item of black basalt, a fashionable English-made earthenware frequently made in Neoclassical forms. Eight guests could sip from matching china cups and saucers. White stone tea ware and "Glass" (perhaps glazed china) teacups rounded out the service that could include at least fourteen, and probably a few more, participants. Tea bowls and saucers were blue-and-white Chinese porcelain or white salt-glazed stoneware. Some of the porcelain was augmented with overglaze decoration in gilt and other colors or Batavian porcelain with its rich brown exterior finish. The inventory lists two milk pots, in china and silver, and a china sugar dish. The Jeffersons also had a tea strainer, a tong, a tea chest, a silver-plated basket, and two tea kettles for hot water to aid in this affair. The inventory lists eight teaspoons and two "old tea spoons," as well as

"6 old silver spoons" of unspecified type. A single silver teaspoon recovered in the remains of the dwelling house at Shadwell was made around the middle of the eighteenth century (fig. 1.7). Tea-related items in the parlor suggest that family members also took tea in this more private room. In addition to tea, Jane Jefferson administered coffee from a silver coffeepot to a set of coffee cups. The "silver coffee pot teapot & milk pot" at £17 10s. was the costliest entry in the inventory, except for slaves. A silver ladle and two wooden ones completed the service for punch, which may have been served from the large china bowls, one of which was painted with a polychrome overglaze decoration. Wine glasses had elegant air-twist stems. Peter's funeral expenses included 2s. 6d. for sugar, used for punch and other beverages for guests that day.[20] Punch, or at least social drink, had a role in Jefferson's initial coming and final parting from Shadwell.

At midcentury, the variety of spoons, table knives, forks, porcelain tea wares, and tables put this room among the more fashionable in all of Virginia. Peter Jefferson specified oval tables in his order to furniture maker Francis West in 1750: tables without corners ensured ease of conversation. West also made at least a dozen of the eighteen black walnut chairs and the two armchairs that encircled these tables, ensuring that at least fourteen diners sat in matching chairs. The pair of armchairs allowed Peter and Jane to preside together at their table, a fairly new style of performance as host and hostess.

Figure 1.7. Silver teaspoon recovered from Jefferson house at Shadwell (5 5/16 inches long, rat tail, midrib handle; marked but maker unknown). Edward Owen photograph, Courtesy Monticello/Thomas Jefferson Foundation, Inc.

The lack of case furniture in this room suggests that built-in cupboards held the finery, perhaps within paneled walls. A "Large Looking Glass Cherry tree frame & Candlesticks" lit the room with candlelight reflected from a framed mirror.[21] In addition to social gatherings, Peter Jefferson may have entertained in his public role as county justice or held occasional official functions in this well-appointed room that surely impressed both family members and strangers alike with its finery.

Parlor

The parlor served as secondary entertaining as well as private space and workspace for Jane, Peter, other family members, and whatever slaves attended them. This room was furnished for sleeping—it was the best bedroom—and minor entertaining, for small-scale food and drink preparation and finishing, and for the safekeeping or control of precious commodities. The parlor was the closest room to the kitchen building and may have had a side door through which to usher food and attendants en route to the dining room, though having slaves pass through the main door and the passage to the dining room was perfectly within the bounds of acceptable accommodation at midcentury. Entertaining in the parlor required two oval black walnut tables and two square tea tables. There were two chairs of unspecified material that were almost but not quite as good as the black walnut chairs in the hall. Four chairs upholstered in harrateen, a wool fabric, were the most valuable chairs in the house (not counting the closestool). One large and one small teakettle and a tea chest occupied this room to aid both tea-making and tea-taking there. Whereas the tea chest and twenty-two tin canisters held tea and seasonings to be doled out under the watchful eye of the plantation mistress, the dining wares stored in the parlor were not the status objects kept and displayed in the hall. The parlor contained silver-plate plates, a serving basket, and soup plates; old pewter, glasses, and knives and forks of less expensive material; and various dishes, basins, and porringers. A pair of scales and weights and a mortar and pestle aided whoever used the bell-metal and copper skillets there. Although slave women did most of the larger-scale cooking in the separate kitchen building a little more than a hundred feet east of the main house, Jane and others coordinated the movement of food from storage to kitchen and from kitchen to table, perhaps with adjustments at the parlor hearth. In the parlor or in the passage, Jane oversaw and coordinated the activities of the slaves who worked in or around the house.[22]

To serve as a bedroom, the parlor held two sets of beds with bed furniture, a chest of drawers, two dressing glasses, four upholstered chairs, and one warming and one bedpan by the fireplace. Peter and Jane's bedroom suite included a harrateen bed and furniture, valued at £12, the most expensive piece of furniture at Shadwell. The bed matched the four harrateen upholstered chairs. The second bed and furniture was valued at £6 10s., a substantial sum but only half of what the best bed cost. The chest of drawers probably held clothing, and the two dressing glasses served Jane and Peter in their daily grooming. For their comfort, they had a warming pan and a bedpan, a reference that could mean either an object for heating or for sanitation. Five brass candlesticks augmented light from the fireplace for work, dining, or reading.[23]

Office

Peter Jefferson's office served his professional needs and also as the family library. Historians often analyze the library holdings of a person in order to discuss the possible impact of the books' intellectual content, but there are other ways to talk about books. Besides educational content, books had status as objects that cost money and displayed taste, and they were physical objects that occupied space and required furniture to hold and display them. Peter Jefferson's Shadwell library is most often discussed as the seed of Thomas Jefferson's first—and lost—library. Peter's 49 volumes, worth £16 17s. 9d., grew to a collection worth over £200 under his son's attention. By Thomas's report, "almost every book" of his burned in the Shadwell fire. But what kind of books did he and his siblings grow up with? In short, Peter owned books on a range of topics that reflected the tendencies of other educated men in colonial Virginia. Just over half were books of history and literature (28 of 49 volumes, or 57 percent), followed by books relating to his duties as a magistrate (11 of 49, or 22 percent), augmented by books on religion, practical skills, and natural philosophy. The topics suggest that the library listed in Peter's inventory served the whole family. The Jeffersons were the only women in colonial Albemarle whose books were recognized as their own: Jane owned "a parcel of books," in addition to her Bible, and Jane Jr. owned six books (see appendix, table 1).[24]

The books represent a negligible portion of the estate in terms of money spent. The value of the books, £16 17s. 9d., equaled less than 1 percent of the estate and just under 8 percent of the value of household items. The appraised value of the books was less than the three-piece silver tea service, valued at £17 10s. But the choice of topics tells us what the Jeffersons found important or interesting, and one title stands out as a large investment. While the greatest number of volumes (39 percent) was in the periodical collections that included the *Spectator, Guardian, Tattler,* and *Addison's Works,* the greatest monetary investment was in history at 43 percent. The combined categories of history and literature made up 57 percent of the books and 68 percent of the investment. The legal category occupied 18 percent of the investment in books, while three religious books used 10 percent (see appendix, table 2).

Peter Jefferson's legal books included summaries of court cases (Salmon) and lists of laws (Laws of Virginia). Two titles instructed how to carry out various public offices: Nelson's *Office of a Justice* and Webb's *Virginia Justice.* In addition to advising justices, these books offered advice, respectively, "for constables, commissioners of sewers, coroners" and "sheriffs . . . church-wardens, surveiors of highways . . . and officers of militia." *Scrivener's Guide* advised "all gentlemen, but chiefly . . . those who practice the law" on the correct form for writing wills, articles of agreement, indentures, and other legal documents. Except for *State Trials,* all of the legal books were octavos or smaller, which made them easy to hold, carry, and use.[25]

The two titles with practical application also were octavos. Brewer William Ellis published *The London and Country Brewer* in 1744. He explained the art of brewing malt liquors "as practised both in town and country," after touring "several counties" in England for more than four years. He also explained preserving in the cask and bottling beer. This book was likely used by Jane in overseeing the making and bottling of beer for the cellar at Shadwell. The family also owned Stephen Switzer's *Practical Husbandman and Planter,* which, like Switzer's other work, included observations on horticultural and ornamental aspects of administering a country seat. Switzer's book invoked classical as well as eighteenth-century scientific ideas about horticulture and was aimed at the estate nurseryman or elite hobbyist. His illustrations were horticultural in nature, such as diagrams of tree grafting.[26]

The history books included works that were popular in Virginia: Rapin's *History of England* and Chamberlayne's *Magnæ Britanniæ* or *Present State of*

Great-Britain. Other Virginians also owned the titles on natural history and discovery, such as Ogilby's *Description of America* and *Anson's Voyage Round the World. The Secret History of the White-Staff* . . . or "Queen Anne's Ministers" written by Daniel Defoe, was less common among Virginia libraries.[27]

One entry, "Trents Astronomy," remains tantalizing. Astronomy appears in the titles of eighteenth-century books on stars, almanacs that include sun and moon charts, and guides to navigation. Astronomy also enters into the philosophical and religious realms, in books on the nature of man and God and the universe, and it is a word used in practical mathematics. This volume may thus have served the Jeffersons' professional, scientific, natural history, or religious interests. It cost 5s., making it worth more than *Anson's Voyage,* an octavo volume at 4s. had plates and maps, and more than a single volume of the quarto-sized periodicals at 4s. 6d. each. Thus it may have been a substantial size or have had illustrations, but it was not as impressive a book as Ogilby or Rapin.[28]

Another way of analyzing a book collection is as a group of objects that had shape, color, and size as well as unique storage and display needs. When we think about the Shadwell books as artifacts, we enter an interesting room. Peter's books resided in his office, where he kept his mathematical instruments and a collection of maps. This was a room that spoke of charting and exploration, both in the real woods and mountains of Virginia and on paper around the world. The books were part of the intellectual apparatus for that exploration, and indeed, the maps and other illustrations contained in the books added the books to the decorative as well as intellectual landscapes. Peter owned ten maps that were not part of books, including "Maps of the 4 Quarters of the World," "A map of the city London . . . Do of Virginia," and "Four old maps." The maps not only announced Peter's profession and the Jeffersons' worldliness but asserted the place of Shadwell within the larger British realm and the place of the British realm in the world. Like the maps, some of the books dominated in their presence. They were not content to line a small shelf in the background, waiting to be called on behind a glass-front door.

Of the forty-nine volumes, three were smaller than octavo and might have been called pocket books, small enough to fit in a pocket, be carried on horseback, or taken in a carriage. Nine were octavos, about six by nine inches, the size Thomas Jefferson preferred because books of this size were easily held in the hand for reading. This is the size of most of the legal and practical books at Shadwell. Over half the family books, however—twenty-one—were quartos, about nine by twelve inches. Quartos were serious, impressive books, generally used at a table or bookstand, and often the size chosen for family Bibles by those who could afford to pay for things to impress other people. Then there were folios, measuring sixteen to eighteen inches high, and perhaps twelve inches wide. A folio could seem magical to a small child and required a space of its own, not an ordinary library shelf. A book in folio was an investment in art and object, not a mere manual for helping the reader attend to some other business. In 1769 Thomas Jefferson contracted with a Williamsburg cabinetmaker to make a large reading desk capable of holding and possibly displaying folios. The desk required a person to stand or use a tall stool to read there. It was to be surmounted by a "[Chinese?] railing at the back and ends of top," and so had a decorative as well as functional nature.[29] Folios were an investment in more ways than one, as this specialized desk shows.

Twelve volumes comprised the three titles in folio at Shadwell and were impressive books indeed. Salmon's *State-Trials* impressed with its gravitas. It compiled "proceedings for high-treason, and other crimes and misdemeanours," from the late fourteenth century under Richard II to the early eighteenth-century reign of George I. Its six volumes were a history of English rule as well as a collection of court cases.

Like many early books, Ogilby's work had a long title meant to invoke a sense of wonder in a would-be reader:

> *America: Being the Latest, and Most Accurate Description of the New World: Containing the Original of the Inhabitants and the Remarkable Voyages Thither, the Conquest of the Vast Empires of Mexico and Peru and Other Large Provinces and Territories: With the Several European Plantations in Those Parts: Also Their Cities, Fortresses, Towns, Temples, Mountains, and Rivers: Their Habits, Customs, Manners, and Religions, Their Plants, Beasts, Birds, and Serpents: With an Appendix Containing, Besides Several Other Considerable Additions, a Brief Survey of What Hath Been Discover'd of the Unknown South-Land and the Arctick Region: Collected from Most Authentick Authors, Augmented with Later Observations, and Adorn'd with Maps and Sculptures.*

This book offered an encyclopedia of the Americas and shared the Old World fascination with the New, leading the reader through the exploration and discovery (for Europeans) of America's natural and cultural history. Ogilby's work included thirty-two plates, as well as six portraits and nineteen maps (some larger than the book and folded to fit within). Ogilby's maps were decorated with both exotic and familiar heroic imagery: naked natives present their continents' wonders to the cartographic order of the (always dressed) Europeans. On many maps, the scale for measuring the world is presented by winged putti, naked messengers from above who bring the legitimacy of the Christian heaven and the classical world to the empirical (and imperial) enterprise. Ogilby was a single volume but, at 674 pages, a very substantial one. Though not a folio, *Anson's Voyage* also contained images of exploration, including "charts of the southern part of South America, of part of the Pacific Ocean, and of the track of the *Centurion* round the world."[30]

Ogilby's work was no doubt as impressive and favorite a book as Rapin's *History of England,* a five-volume folio set that included seventy-seven copper-plate engravings of maps, genealogical tables, and "heads and monuments of kings." The imagery in Rapin also invoked the classical past, of "Britannia Romana," and the ancient past, of "Britannia Saxonica." Maps connected the pasts of England and Wales, Scotland, Ireland, France, and western Europe. Genealogies of kings legitimized royal authority from the combined inheritance of Essex, Sussex, Mercia, and other English counties. And putti presented royal portraits in Baroque frames, championed by allegorical images of victory or justice. Rapin's *History of England* was the most expensive title in the library. In fact, this work cost more than many pieces of furniture in the house. At £6, the five-volume Rapin cost the same as "A set of surveyor or other mat. Instruments," the same as one of the upper chamber beds (others cost £2 10s., and one with curtains cost £9), more than "10 black walnut chairs" at £5 in the hall, and more than a cart and wheels at £4. Rapin was a luxury good.[31]

A record of Peter Jefferson and his colleagues exchanging books reveals another title that was not listed in the inventory. In 1746 Robert Rose "wrote Col. Jefferson . . . & sent home, Brown's Vulgar Errors to him." Other Virginians owned works by Sir Thomas Browne. This particular book, called *Pseudodoxia Epidemica; Enquiries into Very Many Commonly Received Tenets and Commonly Presumed Truths,* contained what might be called late superstition and early science. Chapters covered such topics as unicorns' horns, griffins, and the phoenix, and proposed "That Storks will only live in Republics and free states" and "That the Chicken is made out of the yolk of the egg." Inquiries into social science and the biblical world included "That the forbidden fruit was an Apple," "That Jews sin," and "Of the blackness of

Negroes." In the book, Browne traced man's deception in—or inability to understand—all things, from Adam's original deception by the serpent in the Garden of Eden. Browne cataloged mankind's errors in ancient Egypt and in the classical world in a continuum across the ages that sought to explain why there was errant judgment of natural philosophy in the seventeenth century. The format of the book, of a single statement—given as the title of the chapter—followed by a multipage response, was used by many philosophers who tried to make sense of the world for others, including Thomas Jefferson in his *Notes on Virginia*. The 1650 edition of this book was in folio, but others were quarto.[32]

The largest group of books in the library was the nineteen volumes of belles lettres contained in the periodicals the *Tattler, Guardian, Spectator,* and *Addison's Works.* This group of related publications was influential in its presentation of literature and poetry, plays, satire, opinion, and, in the *Guardian,* politics of the Whig persuasion. It is impossible to know from the descriptions what volumes the Jeffersons owned and thus what stories, plays, poems, essays, or images they encountered in them. The family remembered that Peter Jefferson liked "reading historians, essayists, and even poets." Also that "Addison, Swift, and Pope were prime favorites with him—but Shakespeare was his great favorite! His well-worn and fine old edition of the work is still extant." The periodicals at Shadwell were part of the popular culture of eighteenth-century Virginia, and their influence extended beyond the set volumes to essays republished in the *Virginia Gazette* and reflected in letters written by Virginians to the *Gazette.* As with popular history books, the material contained within these titles was a medium for communication among literate people of taste. Popular works served their readers in many ways and offered another form of cultural currency for the Jeffersons.[33]

The Other Rooms

The array of furnishings listed in the rest of the inventory offered every white and free member of the household a striking level of accommodation and comfort. There were eight beds for ten family members, though three children were under age five at the date of the inventory. In addition to Peter Jefferson's cherrywood desk and bookcase in his office, a walnut desk and bookcase in the hall and a desk in the smaller downstairs bedchamber encouraged family members in scholarly pursuits or to keep plantation accounts. Other clues to the social life at Shadwell appear in accounts kept for Jane Jefferson after Peter's death. She paid for dancing lessons and attendance at a dance for the children, and at least three of her children, and probably all, had musical training. The Jeffersons owned all of the amenities that signal to historians positive changes in standards of living over the mid-seventeenth through the late eighteenth century.[34]

The physical and social standards at Shadwell clearly suggest that the Jeffersons thought of themselves as participants in elite society. In fact, their social world included both tidewater and Piedmont families. The tobacco economy extended into this part of Virginia, and with it, tobacco culture. The Jeffersons built at the head of navigation on the North Branch of the James, later called the Rivanna River, and thus shipped tobacco to market via the same waterway as other great planters. For people of wealth such as the Jeffersons, the connection to the markets was direct, not secondhand. At Shadwell, stockpiles of cloth and such building materials as glass, lead, and nails suggest that the Jeffersons, like many planters whose seats were on the periphery, operated a store for neighbors, influencing the material expectations of the county further through this mercantile role. The location of Shadwell did not prohibit the Jeffersons from contact with major markets. In fact, they placed orders directly with ship captains for leather gloves, riding traces, letter seals, coffee, salt, and nails from Bristol, England (see appendix, table 3).[35] From Shadwell, in the Piedmont, they were as connected with the supplies of the British Atlantic realm as any merchant in Williamsburg. Mobility between the Piedmont and the tidewater must have been a simple and usual thing for some, despite the distance.

When we understand the connections of Shadwell to crop markets, labor, crafts, and material goods, the geographical limitations suggested by the word frontier melt away. In fact, there is almost nothing about the material world of this plantation only thirteen years after the county's founding to support the argument that establishing a fashionable home was somehow limited by locating it on Virginia's midcentury frontier. Yet the frontier was not a myth. The access to goods and information that the Jeffersons had was unavailable to poorer Virginians; most people in these new Virginia counties had only remote contact to any metropolitan center of politics and fashion. Unsettled lands and non-English immigrants, such as French Huguenots, Scottish, Irish, and Germans, ensured that the region remained a zone of cultural interaction. Shadwell also hosted Cherokees traveling between Tennessee and the colonial capital in Williamsburg, adding the role of ambassador to the plantation community. Indian visits doubled the population of the plantation for a day or two and affected its cultural and material world, as well as reminding its members that unfamiliar realms lay nearby. From Shadwell, nestled on the east side of the Blue Ridge, Peter Jefferson authorized surveying parties as far west as the Mississippi. Closer to home, men like Jefferson who were wealthy planters, large-scale land speculators, surveyors, and public officials played formative and lasting roles not only in their new county governments but also in the way immigrants imprinted on their new land and how the local society grew from that. The fences and curtilage defined the Jeffersons' realm as separate from the untamed beyond and signaled improvement in this recently settled region.[36] Peter and Jane Jefferson used the recognizable idioms of the gentry in a conscious material display that advertised their standing and enforced social ritual within the plantation and beyond it.

No colonial Virginia town was the standard for a plantation such as Shadwell. The material world of wealthy Virginians in this period cannot be classified in terms of urban versus rural, expecting that high culture filters through a small tidewater capital out to a vernacular hinterland. Many large plantations were towns unto themselves, with craft-manufacturing and imported goods flowing directly into their storerooms. Francis West, the craftsman who made the Jeffersons' fashionable tables and chairs for Shadwell, worked at Tuckahoe, and also for Colonel Nicholas Cabell at Liberty Hall in Nelson County, Virginia. He did not, however, work among Williamsburg craftsmen. He plied his trade for an elite culture that defined itself through its country seats.[37] Virginia's gentry were the makers and keepers of culture; they did not wait for it to be passed to them second- or thirdhand.

Though a young Thomas Jefferson, home from the College of William and Mary, complained about the remoteness of Shadwell, he was more likely lamenting the lack of companionship other than his sisters and brother. Peter and Jane Jefferson built a home that prepared in every material way for the social expectations of their planter class. The site on a ridge signaled to the passerby that this was an important home. The landscape showed the visitor how to approach the house and told the servants where they could relax. The house told guests how to enter, the rooms showed them where to sit, and the teacups told them how to act. In this frontier there was plenty of room to grow, but there was no room for mistaking whose world would grow there.

2 *The Household: Making Women's Work Apparent*

On August 17, 1757, Jane Jefferson became a widow. She was thirty-seven years old and the mother of eight children, ranging in age from seventeen to almost-two-year-old twins. Two more children, boys who died in infancy, would have been nine and seven that year. She may have begun preparations for widowhood in advance of her husband's death. In mid-July, about a month before his death, Peter wrote his will, and Dr. Thomas Walker visited the ailing patriarch fourteen times that summer. When Peter died, Jane's immediate job was to make funeral arrangements for her husband and to participate in the legal processes of probate that would settle her husband's estate and ensure that his wishes for the care of his family were carried out. Her long-term charge was what it had been since she married and bore her first child: to raise her children to their roles as young Virginia gentry. Her day-to-day tasks were little changed. Children needed still to be fed and dressed and house slaves to be guided through their work. Jane spent almost nineteen more years at Shadwell following Peter's death. During this time she would see two young men off to school, four children marry, two daughters die unmarried, and the house where she and her remaining children lived burn to the ground.

We know Jane through few documents, but—beyond bearing children—two roles can be assigned to Jane Jefferson as the mistress of the Shadwell household. One of her roles was the organization of the daily household activities that ensured that each person was fed and clothed. To those ends, she had oversight of everyone, her children or her slaves, who prepared food, clothing, and other basic household items. In 1757 the family enjoyed the labor of sixty slaves (sixteen adult males, sixteen adult females, ten boys, and eighteen girls) and various hired help, whose positions Jane oversaw if they worked in the house or on tasks related to household consumption. Jane's other major role was the preservation and perpetuation of her family's important social standing through proper training of her children and the slaves who served them. Her acceptance of this role is evident in the few documents she left. Her training for this role came from her own upbringing as the eldest daughter in a gentry family.[1]

The history of women at Shadwell comes from both traditional and nontraditional sources. More detail about their lives exists for those Jefferson women who, like Jane, outlived their husbands or who died unmarried, for the fortunes of these women were not hidden in their husband's legal documents. Archaeological finds illustrate the history of those whose lives we know something of from documents; for those whose history is not written in detail, each artifact, even the tiniest shard, contributes a larger piece to the whole. What do artifacts tell us about Peter Jefferson that is more important than what we know from documents? Not much: they mostly illuminate people around him. Of Jane, however, her history murkier in documents, and the Jefferson children—especially the girls—each artifact, whether known through a document or through archaeology, carries more meaning. The slaves, whose names are in a list, have a history from artifacts that is more articulate than what is written: their history is greatly enriched by archaeological finds.[2]

Using objects and spaces to write history requires the proper identification of artifacts and the roles people played within their families and the plantation economy. Artifacts reveal only a few of the experiences of the women who were slaves at Shadwell; the rest, we must conclude, were much like those on other large plantations in the eighteenth century. The history of these women remains painted with a broad brush, a few details added. Finding Jane Jefferson in her husband's inventory requires making assumptions about her activities, based on what were the domestic labors of gentry women. But the same objects in her own inventory suggest that her activities reflected choices about how she used her time and expertise. Some of her labor was her own, and she expended it on objects and lessons of refinement for her family, not in the public acts recorded in the name of men. Peter Jefferson's inventory and account books give a sense of the plantation whole and its connections across Virginia and the Atlantic world; sons Thomas and Randolph went off to the College of William and Mary and wrote part of their histories in public places. Jane and her daughters shared books, fine clothes, and other genteel pastimes, filling the domestic spaces with their histories as wives, mothers, sisters, and daughters, as teachers and taskmasters, investing everyday objects with their legacies as the bearers of stories about the women who used them.

Family

To say that a history of Peter Jefferson could be written without knowing much about his family is not to say that family did not matter to him. He named Shadwell for the London parish where his wife was born. He was most deliberate in his will to provide for his wife and children. He thought enough of his wife to give her life rights to his estate and "houshold stuff" (as he referred to his furniture) and the provision to dispose of said "stuff" and her portion of the slaves. To each daughter by name he provided an education and £200 for her "fortune," and he named each slave trained as a personal servant who was to go to each of his children. Each of his two sons received a trained slave, land, and one half of the remaining slaves after the distribution of the named slaves. The elder Jefferson made one specific bequest, of his books, mathematical instruments, and cherry desk and bookcase to his son Thomas. Peter's bequests performed a number of functions that affected the landscape of the household following his death. He arranged the future relationships of certain slave children with his own children. The careers of these young, and even tiny—some were two years old—servants and masters were set when Peter wrote his will. It also meant that certain areas of the house inhabited by these bequests remained the patriarch's. By leaving his desk and bookcase, books, and mathematical instruments—essentially the defining contents of his office—to his eldest son, he conferred both the space and the roles that had presided there to his heir. Jane, with Peter's executors, carried

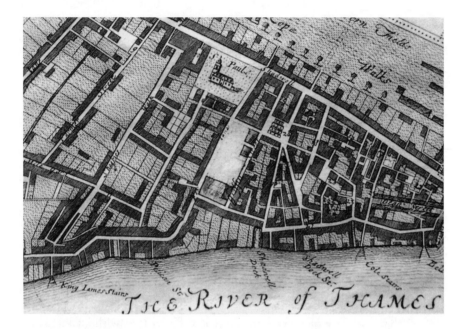

Figure 2.1. In 1720, when Jane Randolph was born, the East London suburb of Shadwell was a growing shipping district. Her father, Isham Randolph, was a merchant on Shakespeare's Walk (here labeled Shagbies Walk). Saint Paul's Parish Shadwell, 1755, Stow's Survey. Collection of author.

out her husband's charges and continued his legacy in the spirit in which he had intended: this was her legacy, too.[3]

Jane Randolph married Peter Jefferson on October 3, 1739. She had known many homes in her life. She was born in Shadwell Parish, London, on February 9, 1720, to Isham Randolph, a Virginian, and his English bride, Jane Rogers. She was their second child of ten; an older brother named Isham was born but lived only ten days in June 1718. Her father had an address in Shakespeare's Walk and was listed as "merchant" there (figs. 2.1, 2.2). When Jane was four, her family lived in nearby Whitechapel Parish, where her younger brother Isham was born. The next year they moved across the Atlantic to Williamsburg, Virginia, where Mary was born in October 1725 (see fig. 1.1). Sister Elizabeth was born in the years between Mary and William. In July 1729 Jane's younger brother William was born at Turkey Island in Henrico County, the home of Jane's (now dead) grandparents and her father's older brother

Figure 2.2. Jane was baptized at the parish church of Saint Paul's Shadwell, shown here in 1756. Collection of author.

William. Jane's sister Dorothea, born in 1730 when Jane was ten, was the first of their family born at Dungeness in Goochland County (formed from Henrico in 1728), their family's own home. Younger siblings Thomas (born and died 1732), Anne (1734), Thomas (1736), and Susanna (1738) were all born at Dungeness. The next year Jane married Peter Jefferson and moved with him to Shadwell. By the time Jane was twenty, she had lived in six different locations. In a few more years she would add one more address to this list, when her own family moved to her cousin's house, Tuckahoe, then back to an enlarged Shadwell in 1753. When the Shadwell house burned, Jane lived at Shadwell six more years in a smaller dwelling. At the end of her fifty-six years she had moved at least eight times.[4]

Jane was not the only Randolph to move to the part of Goochland that became Albemarle County, however. She was part of a kin network that ranged within a few miles of Shadwell. The nearest was her younger sister Mary, who married Charles Lewis in 1744 and moved to his plantation called Buck Island, about five miles from Shadwell. Some of Jane's children shared schooling with the Lewises, and two marriages came from the Jefferson and Lewis connection. Another of Jane's sisters, Anne, may have been the Anne who married Daniel Scott, on whose farm Albemarle Courthouse was established, about twenty miles south of Shadwell. With the exception of her youngest sister, Susanna, who moved to Cumberland County, Jane's other siblings remained in Goochland County. Their connections within Goochland were already strong, from the Randolph cousins on their father's side at Tuckahoe to their mother's brother Robert Rogers on Lickinghole Creek. They strengthened these connections through multiple associations and marriages in each generation. Jane's cousins sold Peter land in what would become Albemarle County. Peter surveyed in Goochland with John Woodson, a prominent Goochland County officeholder who would marry Jane's sister Dorothea. Jane's grandchildren would someday visit Dungeness with descendants of Jane's brother Thomas. These kin networks were an engine in the social and political workings of Virginia.

Family mattered to Jane Jefferson. She not only married and bore children but recorded their history and provided a legacy for her heirs of these facts. Two years following the Shadwell fire in 1770, Jane acquired a new family Bible and in it recorded important information about her family. She listed births and birthplaces (Shadwell and Tuckahoe) and, for two of her children and her husband, their deaths. This family Bible reveals a number of things about Jane Jefferson. First, there are the facts—births, deaths—of her own family, which Jane reconstructed. The Bible also confirms the early family histories that remark that Jane was literate, able to write about people and places and events; indeed, her penmanship is elegant and well wrought. Her inscriptions offer insight into both the creation of her family and what she thought they should remember.[5] Jane's son Thomas, the most prominent of the Jeffersons before or since, left voluminous writings that give historians cause to celebrate his interests in books, gardening, food, and music, among many other pastimes and passions. There are few documents from his siblings, but enough writings survive to reveal that his sisters and brother shared many of these same interests. These interests were undoubtedly formed at Shadwell from the domestic landscape established by Peter and Jane Jefferson there.

Thomas Jefferson wrote to his own daughter when she was thirteen outlining what she should know of the "domestic arts." He advised, "go on . . . in your reading, in attention to your music, in learning to manage the kitchen, the dairy, the garden, and other appendages of the household." He also advised her to "[suffer] nothing to ruffle your temper or . . . good humor."[6] These were the traits she should have to enter adulthood. The ideal planter's wife should be a capable learner, teacher, and hostess. She should read and perform musically, master the diverse parts of the household devoted to foodways, and she should do it with good humor. Jane Jefferson was this sort of planter's wife.

Childbearing and Health

Jane lived to be fifty-six, past the life expectancy for women of forty-some years, and past the half-century mark that her husband almost reached. In some ways, these Jeffersons reflect the demographic averages for midcentury Piedmont: in other ways they do not. Although Jane was an immigrant, not native born, she married at nineteen, within the typical range of late teens to early twenties in which white Virginia women married. Peter married at the older age of thirty-one, past the average of five years older than his wife. Jane's age follows the pattern some demographers have found of women marrying younger when land was readily available. However, Peter's age fits better into a pattern of limited land availability, when men waited until they could acquire land before starting a family.[7] Jane's marriage age allowed her ample time to bear children.

Jane's reproductive history can be reconstructed from the record she left in her family Bible. Jane had ten pregnancies in sixteen years. Between October 3, 1739, and October 1, 1755, assuming her pregnancies were full-term, she was pregnant almost fifty percent of the time (90 out of 192 months, 46.8 percent). Women in the Chesapeake who married in their late teens or early twenties gave birth, on average, every thirty months. Jane's average was just over nineteen months (19.2). The actual birthrates of her children offer a number of observations about Jane and life at Shadwell. In women with high fecundity, which Jane appears to have had based on the number of healthy children she bore, pregnancy follows relatively quickly following the onset of ovulation. Jane became pregnant less than ten and a half months following five of her births and, in three of these, less than nine and a half months (see appendix, table 4). Her three pregnancies with longer intervals from the last birth to conception ranged from just under to just over two years.[8]

A number of factors may account for these birth patterns. Studies of natural fertility populations find an average duration of postpartum amenorrhea (during which ovulation is suppressed) at 20.1 months.[9] The birthrates of her first five children, and of the son who died at birth, suggest that Jane did not nurse her babies; likely a slave performed the important duty of nourishing and nurturing the young Jefferson children. The longer periods between last birth and conception may reflect periods of stress or illness in Jane's life or a time when Peter was traveling. There may be unrecorded miscarriages in her history as well. Women who did not nurse their babies did not receive the benefits that nursing offers the mother's body. For instance, they were at higher risk for conditions such as a prolapsed uterus, which normally contracts with nursing. Had Jane nursed her children herself, she likely would have had fewer pregnancies during the seventeen-plus childbearing years she and Peter were married. Giving birth to twins may have been in the family genes because Jane's daughter Martha also bore twins.[10]

That a slave wet nurse was part of the family circle and that Jane did not nurse her babies herself is in keeping with ideas about childbearing and nursing in the eighteenth century. Philip Fithian noted a dinner with his patrons, the Carters, and Dr. Walter Jones, where the topic of conversation was nursing children. Fithian was surprised to find that "it is common here for people of Fortune to have their young Children suckled by the Negroes!" Mrs. Carter said that several of her thirteen children had been nursed by "wenches," and Dr. Jones said that his child was now with a nurse. For this mixed company to discuss this topic at supper suggests that neither nursing nor nursing by a slave was taboo in polite conversation. Although some people in the early modern world feared that the baby might absorb any character flaws of the nurse, this must have been reconciled by the same mechanism that rationalized so many other parts of the slave system. Many elite women in both England and America used wet nurses in the first days following birth, inadvertently decreasing the likelihood that they could develop a good milk supply for their infants. Contemporaries noted the inability of elite women to nurse and even blamed this "curse" on their stays, which were not worn by working women, who seemed to have little trouble nursing their babies. Elite women knew a tradition of passing their babies to others to nurse, and some women feared for their own health from the demands of nursing. There is no evidence that using a wet nurse diminished maternal affection and concern in any way.[11]

The slave woman (or women) who nursed the Jefferson babies bore more than the demands of feeding another. One of these nurses was Sall, who had a child of her own to nurse at the same time as each Jefferson child. Perhaps Peter Jefferson's bequests of slaves to his children reflected a relationship formed at the breast of the woman who nursed them. The nurse likely was an expert in child care from her own experience. She now tolerated Jane's scrutiny at the care of her mistress's children and likely from time to time had to deny maternal care to her own children in order to see to the Jeffersons to whom she was assigned. If she had sore nipples, fatigue, or breast infections, she bore them as well. Planters gave extra care—at Shadwell generally a measure of sugar and brandy—to slaves in childbirth, but there is no evidence that women who were nurses to the planter's children received any extra provisions. Their proximity in the master's house, however, may have given them access to different fare than that at the quarter. Isaac Jefferson recalled that his mother, Ursula, suckled Thomas Jefferson's daughter Martha and described himself as "one year's child with Patsy Jefferson." Although historian James Bear discounts Isaac's claim about his mother nursing both babies because Martha was born in 1772 and Isaac in 1775, Isaac tells us something of the arrangement of slave women, their babies, and the babies of their owners. Being born in the same year was a way of identifying the children as a group—an age cohort—tied to the same nurse. That he was aware of this relationship with Patsy was something he had to have been told, not something he could have remembered; thus Isaac made this personal and individual connection to his owner's child via a story told in the slave quarters.[12] Slave nurses were part of the mechanism for forming and remembering bonds that began at infancy.

There are few references to Jane's health, good or bad, but her ability to bear children, move numerous times, and keep her own house and affairs following the death of her husband and the burning of her house suggests that she was strong in body and in mind. Jane's family remembered her with these words: amiable, lively; of cheerful, sweet, and hopeful temper; mild, peaceful, and gentle. While none of these words describe health necessarily, none bespeak an ailing or frail person. Jane retained Dr. George Gilmer numerous times during the years 1770–74, but for whom and for what is not clear. He sold the Jeffersons medicines in the form of pills, tinctures, drops, lotions, and plasters. He sometimes treated slaves on visits and sometimes members of the Jefferson family, and Jane may have had periods of illness. She wrote her will sometime between January 1, 1772, when Thomas married, and September 29, 1773, when she deeded slaves to Thomas. She also acquired and began to record her family history in her Bible in September 1772. Illness was often what motivated people to write wills and otherwise settle their estates, and her will coincides with Dr. Gilmer's period of visits. She may have lived in good health the last two years of her life because his visits to Shadwell ended in 1774. Jane's probate inventory contains no items of a specifically medicinal or nursing application. The only suggestion of medicine in the entire archaeological assemblage for the Jefferson house was a fragment of a pale aqua-colored, blown glass vial, of the sort used for medicine in the eighteenth century.[13]

A single comment about illness comes after Jane's death. Three months following his mother's death, Thomas reported to his friend William Randolph (Jane's nephew) that Jane died on March 31, 1776, "after an illness of not more than one hour. We suppose it to have been apoplectic." Her dying was not a lingering illness but likely something quick, such as a stroke. The family histories speak of Jane as "educated," able to write "readily and well," and of "clear and strong understanding." Jane was also described as "a notable housekeeper."[14] Her intellectual pursuits we shall see more below.

Child Rearing

Jane's household changed as her children and their slaves grew, married, and moved away or back again. Visiting among these households seems to have been a regular and customary practice. When he died, Peter left a household of nine—Jane and eight children—although Thomas was away at school much of that time and Randolph some of it. During the 1760s three daughters married and one died. Mary was the first to marry, with John Bolling in January 1760. Mary and John Bolling and the slave Nan lived at Fairfields in Goochland County, although they may have lived at Shadwell for a time after their marriage. Jane later gave her daughter Mary the slave Fanny in 1766, "In & of consideration of the Natural love & affection which I have and so bear unto my Daughter Mary Bolling also for Divers Other good Causes & considerations me Hereunto moving."[15]

Eldest daughter Jane next crossed a legal threshold, to majority, though not to marriage. On June 27, 1761, she turned twenty-one, and her father's estate was charged "By pd. Mrs. Jane Jefferson Junr. Cash £200 & a Negroe Girl bequeathed her Valued at 55" that same day. Peter had bequeathed a slave girl, either Cloe or Pat, to Jane; Jane chose Pat. Although the ownership of Pat changed on paper, it probably altered little the day-to-day workings of the household. Jane Jr. remained at home and so did Pat, each probably performing the same roles they had before Jane's majority, except that by 1768 Pat also had two children, Betty and Sancho. Pat may have had a husband at Shadwell, the father of these children, but his name is not known to us. Jane never moved away from Shadwell and never married. She died of an unnamed illness on October 1, 1765, at the age of twenty-six. Her estate was probated by the court and the settlement disbursed among her siblings. The appraisers valued her three slaves, Pat, Betty, and Sancho, at £50, £15, and £13, respectively.[16]

Jane Jr.'s furnishings do not describe a complete room, so it is likely that she continued to share a room with a sister or two throughout her life. Her furnishings included a bed and two bed quilts, a table, and items for storage: a large trunk, a large "half worne portmantean trunk," three smaller old trunks, and a small box. She did not own her own fireplace equipment, nor did she own cooking tools, past those for making tea, which suggests she remained part of the family circle for meals and household activities. She had entered into the womanly realm of keeping and drinking tea, and she owned "a Large Copper Kittle & Hook" and a tea chest. Her only other food-related property was a large earthen jar. The "ring for keys" in her possessions was a marker of a plantation mistress whose job it was to control access to regulated foods and supplies among various household staff. "Carrying the keys" was part of a girl's household training and one that Thomas Jefferson's grand-daughters disliked. They complained of boredom "locking and unlocking the doors" during their month to practice this aspect of housekeeping.[17] Jane Jr. may have continued this role as an adult.

Like the other Jefferson women, Jane Jr. spent time reading, riding, and spinning and working fibers. She owned six books, "an old saddle without a pad," and a single riding chair, on which the estate paid extra taxes. She had a spinning wheel, cards for cleaning wool, a small workbasket for her tools, and a pair of flatirons. Jane owned a substantial inventory of clothing, more details of which are below. From her brother we know that she took an interest in plants, music, and the outdoors. The only indication of a medical condition is her ownership of "one smelling bottle seal," but this may also have been for fashion.[18] In short, Jane Jr.'s estate reflects the household roles, fashionable pursuits, and intellectual pastimes of elite Virginia women.

Thomas boarded at least part of the year with his teachers, as many young gentlemen did. During the 1750s he lived first with the Reverend William Douglas from 1752 to 1757, then with the Reverend James Maury until 1760. He entered the College of William and Mary in March 1760, and two years later he left the school to read law with George Wythe in Williamsburg. In Williamsburg young Thomas stepped into the embrace of his father's associates and his mother's kin. His arrival prompted a warm welcome from such cousins as Archibald Cary and John and Peyton Randolph. Thomas returned to Shadwell and continued to live there even after he reached majority in 1764. His personal slave Sawney, inherited from his father, probably moved with him to Williamsburg and back. Thomas's major impact on the house must have been the addition of his ever-growing book collection—both legal subjects and general reading—to the office where his inherited desk and bookcase and books resided. Thomas also kept plantation accounts after 1765, when executor John Harvie's account keeping ended. Thomas later acted legally responsible for Shadwell and his father's estate as well as for the estates of his minor siblings.[19]

At the age of ten Randolph left home to board with his Lewis cousins at Buck Island, where Benjamin Sneed was their teacher. Randolph lived with the Lewises, possibly to absorb the role of a plantation owner from his uncle in addition to the academic training that Sneed offered. Randolph spent at least two years with the Lewises. In 1771, when he was sixteen, he left Albemarle County for the grammar school at William and Mary and returned in 1772. He ultimately married his cousin Anna Jefferson Lewis, whom he had known since childhood. His slave Peter and half of his father's field slaves moved with him to the land he inherited on the Fluvanna River.[20]

Martha married Dabney Carr in 1765. The slave Rachel became part of Carr's household at Spring Forest in Goochland County. Carr was Thomas's close friend and now his brother-in-law. The Carrs lived about forty miles away, but they were at Shadwell in May 1773 when Dabney died there. Thomas served as an executor of Dabney's estate and arranged for the Reverend Charles Clay to read at his funeral. Martha continued to live at Spring Forest and to visit Shadwell and the homes of her siblings. She lived for a time at

Monticello, where Thomas looked after her sons' and daughters' educations. Although she later moved back to Spring Forest, she died at Monticello in 1811.[21]

Elizabeth reached majority in 1765 and remained at home. Her father had bequeathed her the slave girl Cate, although she may have taken a maid with equivalent training. She and the slave called Little Sall died trying to cross the Rivanna River during the winter of 1774. Elizabeth's mental capabilities have been questioned and may be the source for speculation about the health and ability of other family members. A family friend wrote: "I have always understood that she was very feeble minded if not an idiot—& that she and her maid were drowned together while attempting to cross the Rivanna in a skiff." Thomas entered in his account book the payment to the Reverend Charles Clay "for performing the funeral service this day on burying my sister Elizabeth."[22]

At age sixteen Lucy married her cousin Charles Lilburne Lewis in 1769 and took her inheritance, which included slaves Cachina and her daughter Phebe. They lived at Monteagle, part of Lewis's father's Buck Island estate, about five miles from Shadwell. Lucy's husband was the brother of the woman who would eventually marry Lucy's brother Randolph.[23]

Thus in February 1770, at the time of the Shadwell fire, the regular occupants of Shadwell were Jane, and two adult and two minor children: Thomas, then twenty-six, Elizabeth, twenty-five, and Randolph and Anna Scott, who were fourteen. Other families came on visits and spent time at Shadwell. The requirements for a new house at Shadwell were quite different from the house the family had known there. Jane and two daughters and two sons needed places to sleep and perform their respective daily duties. Jane needed to be able to run her household and plantation, Thomas his law practice and plantation, and Elizabeth, Randolph, and Anna Scott their roles as students and as daughters and son. Thomas filled the office at Shadwell—his accounts of his library and papers relating to his legal practice reveal that his loss from the fire was great. He had already begun clearing and leveling Monticello Mountain and had begun construction on what would be his house there when the fire occurred.[24]

Jane's probate inventory reveals some of what was important to her and the family following the fire, if we accept that what she replaced and did not replace is meaningful. If Jane's inventory describes the whole house, it was indeed smaller than the house the family had known for the previous two decades. Thomas's daughter Martha repeated the story she heard from her parents about their nighttime journey to Monticello as newlyweds, only to find the fires out in the small brick pavilion that was Thomas's house there. They decided to stay and make the best of it: "The house that had been fitted up for [Thomas's] mother's use after the burning of the Shadwell house was too small for the accommodation of the two families, and was still four miles farther."[25]

Household Economy

Managing a plantation household was greater than coordinating the activities of a single family—not that the latter is any small feat. The plantation household had a broad and changing membership, and Jane Jefferson was in a position to oversee it closely. The years spent at Tuckahoe between 1746 and 1753 meant mothering nieces and nephews as well as her own children. Some decisions about running the plantation were clearly her own, and others must have been: Peter Jefferson traveled extensively, sometimes for weeks or even months while on duty as a surveyor and public officer in this still-young region of the colony. The account books for the years 1757–65, kept by estate executor John Harvie, reveal a few of the more personal family expenditures, although most of the entries involve running the plantation. The few documents to which Jane was party during her widowhood were of a legal or financial nature, in which she deeded slaves to a daughter, lent laborers to a son, and sold agricultural products. These reflect the broader economic relationships in which she engaged; the probate inventory taken after her death reflects more personal aspects of her world.

The inventory of Jane Jefferson's estate, made after her death six years following the Shadwell fire, offers a glimpse into what was important to Jane by showing what she reestablished after the loss of her house and its contents. First were the necessities: the beds and blankets, things for preparing, storing, and eating food, and tables, chairs, and livestock, although the range of these items and their values indicate that they were, for the most part, fine versions of what was available. Then there were the things for craft production, such as fiber work and the candle molds. Jane's more personal interests can be seen in the "parcel of books" and a "Large Bible," in which she recorded her family genealogy following the fire. Jane owned good clothing and a looking glass.[26]

The three probate inventories from Shadwell, of Peter, Jane Jr., and Jane, also suggest that the Jeffersons considered different types of property as belonging to different family members—and that the estate appraisers were advised of this. The differences may reflect ideas about what appropriately represented the wealth of these wealthy people or ideas about men's and women's estates. Jane's inventory contained things not listed in Peter's. The appraisal of Peter's estate included textiles for kitchen and dining but not bedroom use. Jane's held £10 15s. worth of bedroom textiles, including three counterpanes, three blankets, "oznabrig sheets," and "ruggs and matts." Yet the inventories of other wealthy men, such as Joshua Fry, included bedroom textiles. Peter's estate listed nothing for spinning or weaving, activities in which the Jefferson women engaged, as evidenced by Jane and Jane Jr.'s inventories and account book entries; yet other men's inventories included tools for textile processing and production.[27]

Anther difference had to do with clothing. Peter's inventory is completely silent about clothing, except for some ornaments of military office. Jane Jr.'s inventory provides a substantial list of clothing, "which the administrator was advised not to offer for appraisement but of which he thought himself Pledged to Subjoin an Inventory." In other words, her clothing was itemized but not assigned a monetary value. Jane Sr.'s inventory appraisers did not include her clothing, either by item or by value, with the other contents of her estate. Roughly one-third (46 of 143) of Albemarle inventories included clothing as an item that had value to the estate, most of these for men.[28]

Certain categories of household objects rarely showed up in inventories. Objects specifically related to childhood such as toys or cradles that may have been in the house when Peter died were absent in the Shadwell inventories and rare in other county inventories. There were no musical instruments included in the Jefferson inventories, though smaller instruments such as fiddles appeared from time to time in other Albemarle inventories. Musical skills were part of the training a young lady or gentleman was expected to have— and the Jefferson children did. In fact, a granddaughter described Thomas's violin accomplishments as "gentlemanly proficiency." Their father's ability to purchase luxury goods may be why their violins, violoncellos, and spinets are absent from the documentary record. When parents gave their children pianofortes or other large gifts, they became the property of the child, even while that child lived at home. Accordingly, children's musical instruments do not appear in parent's probate inventories, even if the objects were in the house. The dining room at Shadwell contained folding tables that could be repositioned along the walls when not in use. The dining room was most likely the dancing classroom, music room, and no doubt the room for dancing when the Jeffersons entertained.[29]

Jane was a wealthy individual and a very wealthy woman. The contents of her probate inventory total only £73 1s., placing her in the second lowest quartile of Albemarle decedents. However, if her estate total is corrected with the value of the eleven slaves she deeded to Thomas in 1773, her estate rises to £623 1s., making her the nineteenth wealthiest person in the county during the colonial period. Her clothing was not included in her estate value. Jane Jr. was the next wealthiest woman at £114 15s. 6d., including her slaves but not her clothing. Jane Jr. was wealthier than 55 percent of all decedents in colonial Albemarle. The only female rivaling the two Jane Jeffersons may have been Mary Fry, wife of Joshua Fry; her estate was inventoried but not valued. The colonial Albemarle court ordered probate of the estates of only three other women, and all were in the lowest quartile of estate value: Elizabeth Massons, £28 14s. 3d.; Susanna Ballow, £27 9s., and Sarah Fitzpatrick, 10s.—the value of her woman's saddle—the lowest valued estate recorded. None of the inventories of women included clothing in the value of the estate. None of the three women in the lowest quartile owned slaves. The Jeffersons were the only women in colonial Albemarle County who had books listed among their property.[30]

Jane Jefferson, Slave Owner

The plantation system required its members to know the boundaries between master and servant, household worker and laborer. The overseer of the household—Jane Jefferson—had to help both family members and slaves learn their roles. The slaves that Peter Jefferson bequeathed to his children in 1757 became part of each child's daily experience. With two exceptions, each Jefferson child was paired with a slave who was the same sex and just younger than him or herself. By 1762, when the children ranged from age seven to twenty-two, and their servants from seven to nineteen, Jane charged the estate for "clothing for the children's slaves," a separate charge from the clothes for the rest of the plantation labor force.[31] These slave children were well on their way to learning their specialized roles and the differential treatment they would receive as personal attendants or house slaves. Although the plantation culture surely aided in the domestic training of this combined group of fourteen children, one can only imagine the demands on Jane and enslaved adult household workers in guiding all these children toward adulthood: slave children as servants and gentry children toward their roles of domination. Peter's attention to family did not stop with his own. The Shadwell quarter system housed slave families together, which suggests that slaves maintained some control over the raising of their children and some assurance of a spouse at home. For the members of a planter family, this meant learning to understand and cultivate their slaves' personal lives within the plantation. Although planters saw this as an investment that could benefit the entire community, it also ensured that planters had still more ways to coerce their bondspeople.

In 1760 Jane chose her "sixth," the portion of slaves allotted to her in the legal settlement of Peter Jefferson's estate. Eleven slaves became hers, and she was "lent" three others to "allow the Children were not divided."[32] Part of Jane's strategy—as had been Peter's—for running this household and this labor force was to maintain the slaves' own family ties. At least seven of the eleven slaves Jane chose belonged to three families (see appendix, table 5), including that of Sall, her children's nurse. Probably the parents of the children's slaves also knew about being household slaves and they helped train their children for these roles. Jane had learned the paternalism necessary to be a planter, or, perhaps she knew that this seemingly compassionate method of dealing with her charges would benefit her and her family in the end.

Clothing

Maintaining clothes for themselves, children, and slaves was one of the many regular tasks of women, although investment in dressier clothing for family also incorporated the taste and connections of the planter. Jane and her daughters were spared the job of making clothes for the slaves; account book entries recorded payments to local women for this, as well as for knitting stockings for the Jefferson children. Jane and her daughters and sons made choices about their wardrobes. The Jeffersons hired tailors John Bell and George Twynman and invested in professionally made garments for the family. The Jeffersons imported cloth from England, India, and Ireland, and some was Virginia made. Jane purchased tabby stays for children, shoes for the girls and young Randolph, and gloves from England. Jane Jr. left a collection of clothing that included a dozen fashionable gowns, of various silk, chintz, "callico," and Virginia cloth, hats, stays, "satten" shoes, and gold and silver rings, buckles, and buttons. She had a pattern—fabric printed with dress parts—for another gown of Virginia cloth. Most of the clothing suggests participation in genteel visiting and dining, with one more formal and a few everyday pieces. Jane Jr.'s clothes reflect the premarriage acquisitions of a young lady whose eligible status required an expensive wardrobe. Jane the mother specified in her will that "all [her] wearing apparel" was to go to her unmarried daughter Elizabeth. Jane Sr.'s wearing apparel was not specified but was probably equivalent to what her daughter owned.[33]

Other objects for personal adornment appear in the archaeological collections, including two clothing buckles, one of brass and the other silvered. Wigs were probably part of the elder Jeffersons' dress, although they are not mentioned in the probate inventories. The younger generation wore wigs: Thomas did, and in 1770 he made a note to "Get a pr. Curls for A.S. Jefferson ordered to measure" from Williamsburg's peruke maker. The eight dressing tables at Shadwell confirm that attention to clothing went beyond merely covering the body. Peter and Jane's records do not reveal which of them made the decisions about fashionable investments in clothes, but clothing must have been part of the discussions when the family visited other gentry. Peter made purchases when he was "abroad" in Williamsburg or meeting with friends recently returned from another metropolis, just as Thomas's account books reveal his role in acquiring fashionable goods for his siblings and for his wife and daughters. The tailors Bell and Twynman picked up and reported on the latest styles when they came to Shadwell.[34]

Young planters and their wives in-training needed to learn how to attend to their own appearance and how to read the subtle clues packaged in the fabric, cut, and adornment of clothing worn by others, as Peter Collinson advised his friend John Bartram on his impending introduction to Virginia. The quality and fashion of dress of others could offer important information that both daughters and sons needed to help them make judgments about potential spouses. This lesson was not lost on the rising Jeffersons. Thomas revealed these lessons many times in raising nephews and nieces, daughters, and grandchildren. In a letter to another uncle (and executor) of his nieces, he recognized that the young ladies were required "to be clothed more expensively than at any earlier period." In his travels he often purchased clothing for his sisters, daughters, and granddaughters and instructed recipients on the wearing of these gifts. For instance, in a pair of letters written from Philadelphia to his daughter Martha, he described a "kind of veil lately introduced here," then included the veil and rather complicated instructions for wearing it down over a hat or wearing it up.[35] His admonitions to his daughters about their appearance were part of his role as a parent, especially since their mother had died, but his instructions extended beyond neatness and hygiene to fashion. Attention to clothing and appearance was part of the training for young gentry—males as well as females—and for their personal servants, who learned these same skills because they were involved in the public presentation of the family.

Crafts and Hobbies

There is no evidence of spinning or other textile production in Peter Jefferson's inventory, but later documents show that the white women at Shadwell participated in this activity. Jane had a cotton wheel, a hackle, brushes, a bag and cotton, and a parcel of spun cotton in her inventory when she died in 1776. In September 1775 Thomas Jefferson paid William Sumpter 12s. (of 16s. due) for a spinning wheel. Later that month he sent Jane "20. lb wool in dirt & 4 lb of picked cotton." The unwashed wool that Thomas sent his mother ties her craft also to the sheep listed in her and Peter's inventories. When she died, Jane owned "22 Sheep with 8 Lambs" valued at £12 2s. In 1757 the family owned only eleven sheep valued at £3 6s. Jane had a flax wheel for which her son paid merchant William Sumpter after her death. In 1762, Miss Pattey Jefferson, who was almost sixteen, purchased a "wheel, &c" to pursue her own spinning.[36] Jane Jr. also had a spinning wheel and a pair of cards. There is no evidence to suggest that money was tight following Peter Jefferson's death or that the women took on fiber production because of necessity. Spinning was a polite activity for ladies and augmented the family wardrobe, no doubt, but perhaps when it was not perceived as an integral part of the household economy it was not included in a man's list of property.

The wheel purchase for a young lady suggests her coming of age in a craft that was the women's domain. Young gentry women learned these pastimes both as play and as part of their "formal" education. Philip Fithian was amused by the girls at Nomini Hall "imitating what they saw in the great house; sometimes tying a String to a Chair & then run[ing] buzzing back to imitate the Girls spinning." The young girls also took sticks and pretended to knit "small round stockings, Garters &c," or pretended to wash clothes or scrub the floor. The Jefferson daughters learned to knit as well and may have enjoyed this as both a craft and a duty to do well. Much later in their lives, Martha and Lucy involved themselves in knitting stockings for their brother, who was then president of the United States. Thomas's daughter Martha Randolph, in an apologetic letter to her father, sent stockings to him but feared they would not be to his satisfaction. Martha Carr had tried to send her brother's stockings out to be made, but Lucy took the stockings home for her and her daughters to make. Except for a few straight pins, all archaeological evidence of sewing at Shadwell occurred in the areas where slaves lived on the kitchen and slave quarter sites. There is no archaeological or documentary evidence of weaving at Shadwell.[37]

A book on brewing and four candle molds represent traditionally female-centered craft production in Peter's inventory. The Jeffersons kept the book in the office with other books, but it was likely Jane's job to brew, bottle, and store beer—or to oversee the daughters and slaves who did it under her direction. Jane's inventory included a corkscrew and a variety of "Carry boys," bottles, and jugs for brewing or storage. Thomas took stock of the Shadwell cellar in September 1769. It contained at least 250 bottles of alcohol, including rum (85 bottles), Madeira (15 bottles), cider (54 bottles), Lisbon wine (4 bottles [+52 more?]), small beer, and empty bottles, some of which had just been purchased from a Hanovertown merchant. In the next month he received sixty gallons of rum from a tavern keeper in Staunton. Jane may have spent that month brewing beer and bottling spirits. In early September the cellar contents included empty bottles: 12 "in possn of Mrs. Jefferson" and 28 in Thomas's, and, he added, "Note this day take out [14] bottles of J. Smith's for small beer." On October 2, Thomas counted 434 bottles of alcohol, including 66 bottles of small beer and new stocks of rum and Lisbon wine, in addition to the Madeira and cider there. Processing other beverages is not mentioned specifically, but it remained women's work, and the women who lived at Shadwell had experience with it. In 1808 Anna Scott, or Aunt Marks, as she became, visited her niece Martha and Martha's daughter at Monticello and helped them and Thomas's butler Burwell bottle wine. They decanted 203 bottles and drew off the contents of a large cask to two smaller ones for safe storage.[38]

Candle molds were the only craft item to occur in both Jane's and her husband's inventory. Jane kept the candle molds in the parlor with kettles, scales, and food preparation items. The four candle molds in 1757 were worth 5s., but the four in 1777 were valued at 6s. Jane's may have been larger or simply worth more money at the later date.[39]

Cookery and Foodways

Jane maintained specialized cooking equipment, tools that had the potential to elevate cooking from mere food production to the level of craft in its preparation and display. In fact, redefining this category, from the *labor* of food to the *craft* of presentation changes the way we can talk about women's roles. Her most basic task was to provide sustenance, but elevating that to a craft lets the historian speak of it in terms of choices she made rather than drudgery she tolerated. The Jeffersons may have owned tools for basic eating, yet what stands out are the amenities they owned for dining. Jane kept rarer tools for finishing food, including chafing dishes, irons, toasters, and ovens, in the parlor, separate from the tools in the main plantation kitchen. The parlor was her center of operations for some of the details of finer cooking and food presentation. Like most gentry wives, Jane was the keeper of seasonings and expensive foodstuffs such as tea, coffee, sugar, pepper, and other spices. She owned the sugar box and bag, the tea basket, the pepper box, and the spice mortar. These accoutrements and skills worked in conjunction with the recent addition of specialized spaces for dining in the Jeffersons' house; the Jeffersons invested heavily in furnishings, utensils, food, and skilled slaves that displayed their status as people of cosmopolitan taste.[40]

Elaborate cooking demanded a variety of ingredients unknown to or beyond the time constraints of most Virginia farmers. The Jeffersons kept livestock to provide beef, pork, mutton, dairy products, and turkey and other poultry, and they could hunt deer and other game as well as fish. They imported oysters from tidal regions. It is possible that the passion for gardening shared by multiple Jefferson children came from Jane, if not both parents. Thomas Jefferson's earliest garden book entries reveal that the diet at Shadwell included asparagus, different varieties of peas, celery, Spanish onions, lettuce, radishes, broccoli and cauliflower, cucumbers, English and black walnuts, and cayenne pepper—in short, enough variety for the vegetable-focused diet that Thomas continued at Monticello. Fruits included both hearty and desert fruits: cherries, gooseberries, plums, and strawberries. Thomas, Randolph, and sisters Martha, Jane, and likely others all shared an interest in plants, seeds, and horticultural pursuits.[41]

In Jane's nine years at her parents' plantation, Dungeness, she knew the gardens there, and the family enjoyed horticulture as an intellectual pursuit in addition to the food it produced. Brick walls and "a double ditch of 300 feet square" enclosed Isham Randolph's gardens. Isham hosted botanist John Bartram on his travels through Virginia and corresponded with Bartram and his patron Peter Collinson in their efforts to collect and document plant and animal life. On Bartram's 1738 travels in Virginia, Isham traveled with him as a guide and lent Bartram "his man" to continue when he could not. Isham may have introduced Bartram to Peter Jefferson on this trip. In a 1739 letter to Bartram, Isham apologized: "I wish I could entertain you with an acct. of Some new discovery Since your progress here; but for the want of a penetrating genius in the curious beauties of Nature, I must make it good in assuring you that I am with great sincerity of heart." Isham and Jane's entire family joined some of these conversations. Isham signed this letter with the note that "my wife & family join in their best respects to you & Mrs. Bartram." Even after Isham's death, Collinson corresponded with Jane Randolph to acquire seeds from her.[42]

Jane Jefferson was a mother, the guardian and guide of privileged, well-connected, white Virginians. She made choices about their education—provided for in her husband's will—and their training for gentry society. Both sons and daughters could read and write, and Jane paid for dancing lessons, music lessons, good clothes, and the accessories, including a well-trained servant, that each child needed in order to participate in their world. The boys took their schooling out of the house, but the daughters learned at home. Thus the house also had to accommodate a visiting tutor. Benjamin Sneed instructed Martha in 1757 and 1758 when she was about ten to twelve. He taught Lucy from 1762 to 1764 when she was ten to twelve. Sneed also taught Jefferson children in 1761, but they were unnamed in the account. Peter's estate paid £6 a year for Randolph to board with his cousins. Sneed received £1 10s. a year for teaching Randolph, £1 for each year teaching Martha, and 13s. 4d. for eight months teaching Lucy. In both 1759 and 1760, James Maury received £20 for the schooling and board of Thomas Jefferson.[43] Values for intangible investments, such as education, become more meaningful when compared to physical property. A year's education with a schoolmaster such as Sneed was worth about the same as twenty-two pigs or a pair of harrateen window curtains. Randolph's board could have replaced a bed and furniture, a moderately priced horse, "seven cows and steers," a set of surveyor and mathematical instruments, or two copper kettles. The annual expense for Thomas's education and board with Maury, on the other hand, was equivalent to the value of the elderly field hand Phillis or the young slave girl Eve, who was destined to be a lady's maid.[44] Of the items listed in Peter Jefferson's inventory, only slaves cost more than Thomas's annual education expense.

What part of the house belonged to Jane? She does not seem to have had a room of her own. Peter's office contained items that reflected his numerous professional roles, including surveyor, justice, and planter, and held books for general reading that likely served the entire household. There was no space that was so specifically female; instead, the activities of Jane Jefferson, as defined above, inhabited parts of a number of rooms. The dining room furnishings reflected an investment in the type of status display required both for Peter Jefferson's public role within the county and colony and for the family's participation in gentry society. The acquisition and display of status objects— the expensive and fashionable equipment for social dining and drinking—was in Jane's purview, and this room reflected her taste and attention to detail. Most likely, it was she who entertained with the fine tea service, but both Jane and Peter presided at their finely appointed table when they had guests.

The parlor is the room to which we could most easily assign Jane as the center of her daily work. This room was furnished for sleeping—it was the best bedroom (Peter's and Jane's)—and for minor entertaining, but also for small-scale food and drink preparation and finishing, as well as candle making. Cooking on a larger scale was done by slave women in the separate kitchen building a little more than a hundred feet east of the main house. Most likely Jane coordinated the movement of food from storage to kitchen and from kitchen to table. In the parlor or in the passage, Jane oversaw and coordinated the work and activities of the slaves who worked in or around the house. The desk in the dining room may have served for Jane's own writing and account keeping.

Peter's will included the clause that "all my Family live & be maintained & my Children Educated out of the Profits of my Estate" and that Jane should have her Division "ascertained and laid out for her." When Peter died, he bequeathed to Jane "dureing her Natural Life or Widdowhood the use and profits of the House & plantation whereon I now live." In addition to the sixth part of the slaves, a third of the cattle, hogs, and sheep, and "two Good serviceable Work Horses," he willed that she should have and enjoy "all my Houshold Stuff," with the exception of the desk and bookcase that were to be Thomas's. In 1760 Jane claimed her allotment of the slaves and also "By Household Furniture deliverd Mrs. Jefferson as pr. Inventory £202.2.6." By keeping separate the estates of Peter and Jane, they ensured that Jane could enjoy her fortune and that the children's inheritances would be preserved. Additionally, Jane would dispose of her estate, both goods and slaves, as she saw fit. Like her mother before her, Jane wrote her will to make bequests to her unmarried children. Jane's will is undated, but she wrote it between the time Thomas married in January 1772 and Elizabeth died in February 1774. Thus, Anna Scott and Randolph received slaves, and Elizabeth received "all my wearing apparel with one good bed an[d] furniture." Jane appointed Thomas her executor with the charge to divide everything else equally among all.[45]

Jane's probate inventory of 1776 differs from her husband's of twenty years earlier in a number of ways. First, it is not spatial; the appraisers did not proceed from room to room in their listing, and thus the historian cannot reconstruct from it the house Jane and her family occupied at Shadwell following the destruction of the first house. Second, it includes items not listed in her husband's inventory and leaves out other items. The house where Jane lived following the Shadwell fire was small. Jane's family was no longer growing— she had no need for a big house.

It is not known where Jane and her remaining family moved immediately after the fire, but archaeological evidence suggests that a new house at Shadwell was built just west of and almost on the remains of the earlier one. A veneer of finer goods from the late third quarter of the eighteenth century presents itself in the statistical artifact distributions for the site. Just west of the brick cellar remains of the Jeffersons' house is a smaller stone-lined cellar that also

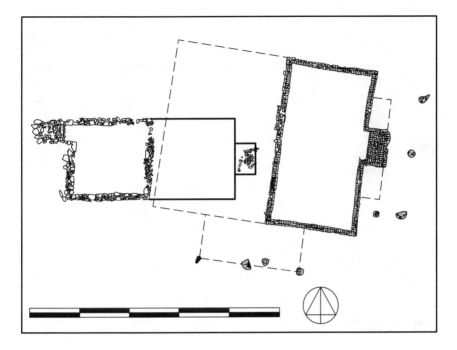

Figure 2.3. Archaeological plan of Shadwell cellars. The large brick cellar (to right) and porch posts (below) belonged to the Jefferson house that burned in 1770. The smaller stone cellar to the west (left) post dates the brick cellar—bricks from the first house were reused to build the stairway in the stone cellar. The surface distribution of status goods from the later eighteenth century points to the stone cellar as part of the house built for Jane Jefferson following the fire (see fig. 2.4).

has been excavated with each excavation of the main house (fig. 2.3). The builders of this smaller, stone-lined cellar used bricks recovered from the brick cellar to build the stairs to the cellar floor. The reused bricks had been the only evidence that the stone cellar was built later than 1770, but there are no artifacts from within the cellar to date it further. However, distribution studies of artifacts across the whole site create a distinct pattern of later-eighteenth-century occupation in the vicinity of the stone cellar (fig. 2.4). The distribution studies pinpoint the use of the earlier house site—in its central location—as the site of Jane's continued occupation. The creamware and some finer porcelain suggest elite occupation during the 1770s, Jane's final years. Following Jane's death, younger children moved to the homes of older siblings.

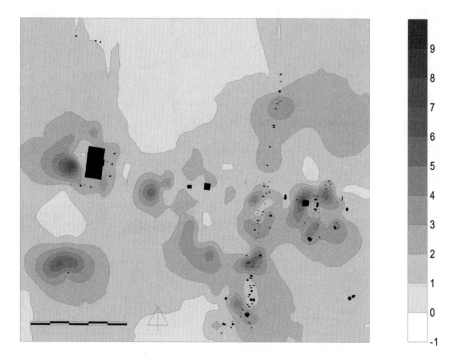

Figure 2.4. Surface distribution of artifacts suggesting location of post-1770s house, with peak of activity just west and north of earlier house. The map shows porcelain (both Chinese and European), which continued to be fashionable during Jane Jefferson's era at Shadwell. Various types of porcelain were available during the entire Shadwell period, yet the statistical distribution of porcelain was the first suggestion that elite domestic activity continued on this area of the site following the fire.

Shadwell became a quarter farm in Thomas's plantation system, and his over-seers or tenants occupied the house, leaving a veneer of lesser-status pearl-ware that marks their later occupation. Thus the general orientation of the plantation remained consistent throughout the eighteenth century, from its use as the seat of an estate to its use as a quarter farm in a larger plantation system.[46]

Jane's inventory suggests a number of activities, but not the rooms in which they occurred. The duplicate sets of fireplace equipment, "2 pr. Hand Irons" and "2 pr. Tongs Shovel & poker," may come the closest to objects that de-scribe specific architectural features, in this case, two heated rooms. But the contents of the inventory describe areas of activity: for sleeping, dining or other "polite" pursuits, and food preparation and other work. Jane had three bedsteads with bedding (mattresses), and a chaise bed, as well as sheets and blankets for them all. Three chamber pots may have resided beneath the three beds. Two feather beds were valued at £6, while a "Virginia Tick [Bed] Bolster and Pillow" was worth £4 10d. In Peter's inventory beds ranged from £2.10 to £12, with £6 being about average for the eight beds in the house. In addition, "3 bedsteads & 2 Cords 13/6" may have been bed parts in storage or may indicate space for servants. Jane had twelve chairs and two tables that were probably for better use. These included three cherry chairs, two walnut chairs, an elbow walnut chair, and five flat-bottomed chairs. It appears the luxury of the closestool was not replaced following the fire and that chamber pots sufficed.[47]

Jane's kitchen equipment offered a similar range of cooking possibilities to those she had before the house fire. She had heavy hearth cookware, including a Dutch oven, grid irons, pots, and pot hooks, as well as a spit and rack and camb for roasting and a frying pan. She also had a "peperbox," a spice mortar, and, as before, a stand of cruets for adjusting seasonings. As in the house she shared with Peter, Jane maintained serving wares for various beverages. She had a tea basket and tea, a "tea kittle & Trivett," another kettle, and a tea board. She owned coffee, a coffeepot, and sugar and a sugar box.[48] Teapots and cups were not specified but were likely included in the "parcel China" or "parcel of Old Silver." She had a corkscrew, a pair of horn tumblers, and the requisite bottles and jugs, but the glassware was undifferentiated. Jane's tableware included knives and forks, and spoons may be included in the "Old Silver," listed above. Her twenty-one plates valued at 44s. cost about as much as the silver-plated plates in Peter's inventory, where three dozen plates had a value of 70s., or twelve soup plates were 24s. The two dozen "Earthen plates and bowl" valued at 10s. may have been creamware, the latest fashionable ware on the English market, which became available about the time of the Shadwell house fire. For Jane to replace her dining assemblage with the latest wares was in keeping with the attention the Jeffersons paid to other details of their lifestyle. Yet the plantation was a place of work, and a workspace in or near Jane's house was just that. It contained two old tables and "Pails Tubs & Box." Among general tools, Jane owned an ax. Her livestock included seven turkeys, twenty-two sheep, eight lambs, one cow and a calf, a bull, and a heifer. The inventory did not include her horses.[49]

Jane conveyed her slaves to Thomas in 1773, so they were not part of the estate to be settled and thus not listed. At various times Jane leased slaves to Thomas, and ultimately she deeded them to him. Jane's house at Shadwell, the house "fitted up" for her following the fire, served the same purposes as the earlier Shadwell house. It provided a place to work, to sleep and eat, and to dine and entertain with some finer wares, but overall likely on a more modest scale than the bigger house. Like the family house, the retirement house was a place to enjoy such polite pastimes as reading and spinning, as well as time with her family.

The Jane Jefferson Image in the American Mind

Jane is little known from documents, yet historians have sought her and made much of her in their quest to explain her son Thomas, and especially his relationships with women. Jane suffered greatly during the twentieth century at the hands of the Momists, psychohistorians, psychosexual historians, and worshipers of the patriarchy—who often simply left her out of the histories altogether. In the twentieth century, Jane Jefferson was less than celebrated. Somehow in the charge to elevate the mothers of the Founding Fathers, Jane, instead, fell. Jane Jefferson stands as the often-maligned mother to whom her son Thomas just could not relate. Historians have evaluated his move to Monticello as a rejection of her world at Shadwell, his birthplace and her home until her death in 1776, even though he chose to live with her for seven years beyond his majority. Yet the family remembrances of Jane—and the nineteenth-century biographers of Thomas Jefferson who relied on those remembrances—present Jane in glowing terms, suggesting that in her own time she was revered.

Merrill Peterson's 1960 masterwork, *The Jefferson Image in the American Mind,* offers the best insight into the twists and turns of interpreting Thomas Jefferson and his ancestry. Around the turn of the twentieth century, commentators held up the idea that Thomas Jefferson was a profoundly American mixture of "the blood of the democrat and the blood of the aristocrat." Though this turn of phrase was meant to propose a constructive way to approach American politics, later writers took Thornton's useful imagery and imagined in it an oppositional relationship between Peter and Jane. As Peterson points out: "The tendency around 1900 was to emphasize the 'backwoodsman' side of [Jefferson's] heritage; then, with the recognition of Monticello a quarter century later, the emphasis shifted to the 'aristocrat.'" Marie Kimball's *Jefferson: The Road to Glory* (1943), offered the first scholarly revision that Thomas Jefferson came from prominent, propertied ancestors on both sides of his family line, but this became recognized in only some of the *academic* literature on Jefferson. The mythological power of the frontier Jefferson continues to permeate *popular* literature, including children's books, plays, and movies. The lusty backwoodsman has been a more acceptable revolutionary hero than his opposite, a prim and grand lady. Historians who have favored one side of this have done so at the expense of the other; those who cast the masculine frontier father in triumph in Thomas Jefferson's character or political successes have generally diminished the maternal, feminine strengths of his mother in order to do so.[50]

Those historians who see conflict between Thomas and Jane Jefferson base their arguments on a number of circumstances. One is that the extant references to Jane in Thomas's writing are perceived to lack affection, although there is evidence that Thomas burned his correspondence with her, just as he later burned letters between himself and his wife; he was careful with intimate correspondence. The remaining accounts between mother and son are just that, accounts, keeping separate the charges and debts for each plantation to facilitate bookkeeping, and in a way, a clever tool to prevent the younger generation from bearing the charges that could be assumed by the parents' estate. In his book *The Head and Heart of Thomas Jefferson* (1954), John Dos Passos used the word "frigid" to describe Thomas and Jane's relationship, a term that by the 1950s had become associated with sexual dysfunction, especially in women. Dos Passos suggested that Thomas's "scanty references" to his mother "may well betoken real dislike."[51] Dos Passos planted a seed that other writers and historians cultivated.

A second circumstance that has led historians to interpret Jane and Thomas's relationship as cold is the misogynist strain in many of the early entries in Thomas's literary commonplace book. This has been interpreted as the "inescapable suggestion" that Jane Jefferson was "the implied antagonist of these unique tirades." According to Kenneth Lockridge, Thomas's frustration was strongest in his teen years, when his mother was in control of the household and he was denied access to patriarchal resources, what should have been "his first exercises of masculinity." Jack McLaughlin credits Jefferson's decision to build his own house on Monticello Mountain as a "conscious desire to escape from the rule of his mother and the crush of too much family in too little space." Although there is evidence for the "too little space," there is scant evidence that the rule of his mother drove Thomas's action, unless we consider the normal young adult response to growing up and wanting to establish oneself.[52]

Even an advocate of material culture must admit that it may be difficult or even impossible to use artifacts to decipher the complex relationships between a mother and son two and a half centuries ago. Yet the material culture of Shadwell nonetheless shows that, following her husband's death, Jane Jefferson carefully attended to the physical and social world her children would inhabit. Shadwell represented gentry Virginia, a place where manners and social ritual mattered, and Jane Jefferson was the agent who procured these social tools for her children. Certainly parents can hand children material wealth and social opportunity without also handing them love and affection, but family histories and the legacy of family ties suggest this was not the case at Shadwell.

Nineteenth-century stories about Jane Jefferson are glowing, as the style of biography tended to be in that period. Henry S. Randall culled stories from Thomas Jefferson's granddaughters to write about Jane: "She was an agreeable, intelligent woman, as well educated as the other Virginia ladies of the day, of her own elevated rank in society—but that by no means implying any very profound acquirements—and like most of the daughters of the Ancient Dominion, of every rank, in the olden time, she was a notable housekeeper. She possessed a most amiable and affectionate disposition, a lively, cheerful temper, and a great fund of humor. She was fond of writing, particularly letters, and wrote readily and well." Ellen Coolidge, granddaughter of Thomas Jefferson, supplied some of the earliest family history in letters she wrote to Randall answering his queries for his biography. Coolidge wrote that Jane Rogers Randolph, the wife of Isham, mother of Jane Randolph Jefferson, was "a stern and strict lady of the old school, and feared and little loved by her children." She went on to report that Mrs. Jefferson (as she called Jane Jefferson) was "mild and peaceful by nature, a person of sweet temper and gentle manners." Sarah Randolph, herself a descendant, related that her great-grandfather's "mother, from whom he inherited his cheerful and hopeful temper and disposition, was a woman of a clear and strong understanding, and, in every respect, worthy of the love of such a man as Peter Jefferson."[53]

With a single exception, each of Peter and Jane Jefferson's children who had children named a daughter "Jane" (see appendix, table 6). Mary and John Bolling's third daughter was Jane, following Martha, Mary, and sons. Thomas and Martha Jefferson's second daughter was Jane Randolph; their first daughter was named for her own mother, Martha. Martha and Dabney Carr's first daughter was Jane Barbara. Lucy and Charles Lewis's first daughter was Jane Jefferson. Randolph and his wife, Anna Jefferson Lewis, had only one daughter, but she was named for Randolph's twin sister, Anna Scott (who never had children). Lucy also named a daughter for her sister Anna Marks, Anna Scott's married name. Of the four children who bore sons, only Martha used the name Peter. Other names of siblings, grandparents, and family reverberate through the next generation in homage to the important people and connections already in the family. These names include Martha (three uses), Mary (three), Lucy (three), Thomas (two), Isham and Isham Randolph, Field, Randolph, Elizabeth, and Lilburne. There is no denial of family in the making of these families.

Thomas Jefferson buried his mother at Monticello, in the graveyard begun three years before when his childhood friend Dabney Carr died. He paid family friend the Reverend Charles Clay to read at her funeral and had her burial marker inscribed: "Jane Randolph, wife of Peter Jefferson. Born in London 1720—Died at Monticello 1776." This inscription is the only suggestion that she died other than at Shadwell. Whether she in fact moved up the mountain in her final days or whether her son now thought of Shadwell as part of his Monticello estate is unclear. What is clear is that in his mind they were part of the same household. Thomas's only entry in his memorandum book that day read: "[1776 Mar.] 31. My mother died about 8. oclock this morning in the 57th year of her age." Other matters of business did not take his attentions that day. A year later, in April 1777, Thomas paid Clay for "preaching my mother's funeral sermon 40/."[54] Thomas assumed responsibility for his mother's estate as well as for his youngest sister and brother, half a year from their majority.

Thomas acted as legal guardian as well as caretaker, companion, and adviser to his siblings and their children following their mother's death and throughout the rest of their lives. His sister Anna Marks lived (and died) at Monticello and was a great favorite of her brother's daughters and grandchildren. Sister Martha Carr was buried in the Monticello graveyard, and her children spent much time at Monticello. Thomas's daughters and granddaughters visited Lucy Lewis and kept their grandfather supplied with news of the Lewis family. Thomas and Randolph exchanged letters and agricultural products, and the younger sought the older brother's advice on numerous occasions. Letters among family reveal that the grandchildren of Thomas and his siblings knew and held affection for one another. Strong family ties and close commerce were regular and expected parts of the Jeffersons' social landscape. We will revisit this theme in a later chapter. For now it shows that family ties were established early and deeply, between parents, siblings, and generations. If Jane's charge in life was in creating a caring and involved family, she created a lasting legacy.

3 The Home Quarter: Material Culture and Status

In the summer of 1757, Sall watched someone she had known all her life die. Her feelings must have been mixed. Peter Jefferson, the man who died, owned her, her children, and likely her husband. The man wrote a will in which he legally transferred ownership of her black children to his white children. Her children would move to other plantations as their new owners reached majority. Ironically, within the plantation system that she knew, she and her children were being honored for their reliable work in learning and carrying on the cultural practices of their owners. As personal attendants and status symbols for wealthy planter children, Sall and her children lived in better material comfort than many Virginians, regardless of their skin color or condition of servitude, which meant that they had status, albeit at the top of an underclass of enslaved people.

Sall also had a physically intimate relationship with her owner's family: his children had probably suckled at her breasts as babes. She had practically lived in his house, nursing his children, often at his wife's side. Her own children grew because of her skill with small children, despite having to spend long hours away from their mother. Sall taught her children how to be near and yet remain distant from this family they would know so well. Her son Jupiter would spend most of the next forty-three years at the side of the planter's son born in the same year—1743—as this slave. Like his mother, Jupiter had an often-intimate relationship with his owner, spending some of his years as the planter's valet. When Jupiter died, the planter mourned the death of his lifelong companion, and his comments reflected both his caring and frustration with and his disapproval and respect for this person who had always been part of his world.[1]

Slave Life and the Consumer Revolution

The people who lived on the home quarter at Shadwell knew the material culture of two very different worlds—that of planters and an opposing one of slaves. As they served the household needs of the Jeffersons, their world changed during the middle of the eighteenth century because of the choices made by their owners to invest in the increasing waves of fashionable goods that we call the consumer revolution. Enslaved African Americans experienced the consumer revolution in ways both similar to and abruptly different from their white owners. New access to goods altered the material culture of colonial America as people with money invested in houses, landscapes, furniture, and dining wares that showed increased specialization in purpose and form, often with an expected return measured in social capital. On the most basic level, the consumer revolution meant that more people had more things. Archaeology on plantation sites shows that slaves of wealthy whites often had access to more and better goods as well. The home quarter slaves at Shadwell owned and used things beyond their documented ration, yet despite the availability of consumer goods, they also chose to make some of the things they owned.

The increased quantity and newly varied material goods meant changed patterns of both work and living for slaves whose owners concerned themselves with fashion. The work of slaves was affected by the general availability of consumer goods and by the material investments of their owners. Scholars have noted the increased specialization in the roles of slaves as the eighteenth century progressed. Most often, they have proposed that the shift in staple agriculture from tobacco to grain produced changes in the seasonal work calendar that forced planters to find ways to engage their slaves when they were not in the field; the planting and harvest cycles of wheat meant that field slaves had many weeks of time during the year to make casks or nails or weave cloth. The needs of the fashion-conscious household, however, were great enough to demand specialization that went beyond finding jobs for redundant field workers. The shift in staple agriculture and the revolution in consumer goods occurred in close temporal proximity and reflected the personal preferences and newly defined needs of elite planters.

The household slaves at Shadwell were themselves a product of the consumer revolution. They belonged to a planter who was wealthy enough, with sufficient land and tobacco returns, to spend money on slaves who did not labor to generate salable agricultural or craft products. The families who lived on the home quarter worked to produce social capital. They performed work that augmented amenities—the superfluous material investments made by their owners—and they became part of the machinery of the fashionable house.

Living Arrangements

The home quarter was the domestic center of the plantation, the area that included the Jeffersons' house, kitchen, slave houses, and other service outbuildings, arranged within concentric boundaries in a ten-acre square. This was the part of the plantation that the Jeffersons constructed to impress their guests. Many of the slaves who worked there were part of the formal face of the plantation and of plantation life in the Old Dominion. Some of their roles were public, and although the public moments may have been infrequent and brief, they were very important in determining whether a slave continued to work around the planter's family or whether he or she worked "out." At Shadwell the slaves who lived at the plantation center had varying degrees of contact with the material goods that wealthy white Virginians thought were important. In some ways the material richness of their everyday lives gave these people an unusual experience for slaves. Yet in many ways, they were never far from experiencing the worst that slavery had to offer. The material record at Shadwell presents contradictions and adds much complexity to the story of how slaves lived in the eighteenth century.

Slaves on the home quarter lived near the Jeffersons' house in at least two areas: the plantation kitchen, located a little more than a hundred feet east of

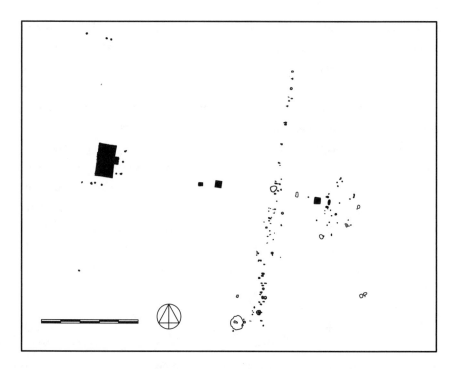

Figure 3.1. Archaeological site plan of Shadwell showing imprint of eighteenth-century activity. Slaves worked in almost every part of this domestic center of the plantation. Enslaved workers may have lived in the Jeffersons' house (to left) some of the time. Their regular homes were in the kitchen building (cellar at center left) and at least four buildings on the home quarter site (right-Building I was over the large square cellar). The fence line between the kitchen buildings and quarter site created the almost north-south line of postholes. Site plan by Derek Wheeler, Courtesy Monticello/ Thomas Jefferson Foundation, Inc.

the house, and a quarter site of slave houses another hundred feet east of the kitchen (fig. 3.1). Some slaves may have slept in the Jeffersons' house along with whomever they attended there. One of the most explicit statements planters made about the social structure on plantations lay in how they located and controlled the movements of enslaved people within their planta-tion landscapes. The relationship of the buildings in size, finish, and proximity conveyed immediately the underlying social status of the people who used and inhabited the buildings. At Shadwell all of the outbuildings continued the axial arrangement of the plantation laid out by Peter Jefferson. The physical structure of the plantation helped train both enslaved and free workers, as well as visitors and family members, about the established hierarchies of colonial Virginia society.

The two separate areas where slaves lived on the home plantation exhibit certain cultural practices in common among all the slaves there, as well as patterns of use that make each living area distinct. A kitchen area with two buildings—a kitchen and a smokehouse or dairy building—served the work of the cook and her family. The activities of their daily personal lives concentrated within and around the kitchen building that was their home. Excavation of slave houses on the east end of the ten-acre plantation center uncovered the remnants of two of four houses on this site. The home quarter site, separated by a fence away from the kitchen and the main plantation house, was a community with its own local center. The yard between the buildings there was the site of a range of activities, including cooking, eating, and craft work, such social activities as smoking pipes and playing games, and spiritual or medicinal rituals. Yet archaeology shows that all of the people who lived on the home quarter, whether they lived in the kitchen buildings or in the slave houses, shared many activities and, despite their separate living areas, were at times part of the same community.

People

The thirty-one people who lived on the home quarter in 1757 comprised the largest grouping of slaves within the Jefferson plantation holdings and one of the largest single groups of slaves in colonial Piedmont Virginia (see appendix, table 7). The six men, six women, seven boys, and twelve girls had training as house servants, as personal attendants, and in other skills. Many of the children in this group grew up learning to wait on the Jefferson children and wore the better clothes that such a job demanded. This group included all of the slaves Peter Jefferson bequeathed by name to his children and all but one of the slaves claimed by Jane Jefferson as her sixth portion of her husband's estate. They had the greatest monetary worth of any slaves on the plantation, revealing that local appraisers acknowledged the value of their domestic skills. These people also seem prominent to the historian because the Jeffersons mentioned them by name in various roles. For instance, Sawney received notice as Peter's, then Thomas's, attendant, a role in which young Jupiter followed. Samson and the older Jupiter worked on the mill. Mothers were a reference point for their children, who were called "Nan Sall's daughter" or "Peter Myrtilla's son," for instance. It is likely that they were prominent within the larger African-American community as well.[2]

Families appear in the list according to the mother's name. In 1757 five of the six women in this group claimed at least one child at home: the remaining children were theirs also but old enough to not be listed with their mothers. Some of the women must have had husbands at home, but at least one did not. Bellinda married Squire, who lived on a Jefferson field quarter. Only Nan, the adult daughter of Sall, cannot be linked directly to children of her own, but she may have just reached adulthood. All six adult women were of childbearing age. The paternal relationships are less clear. Four of the men may have been husbands and fathers to the women and children of the home quarter, but at least two had wives across the plantation. Phill married Moll, who lived at a field quarter, and many years later Hercules married a slave called Island Betty, whom Thomas Jefferson inherited in 1774.[3] In many cases slave families lived together within the Shadwell quarter system. For the women, this meant some chance to raise their children and have some assurance of a husband at home. For at least one older woman, the field hand Phyllis, this meant living with her son's family, which may have provided comfort to her and also made her a plantation babysitter when she was beyond field work. Other women shared houses with multiple families or unrelated adults. Everyone had close neighbors.

Plantation Kitchen: Hearth and Home

The Jeffersons' cooks were home quarter slaves. They lived in the frame plantation kitchen buildings where they worked and probably moved with regularity between their own workspace there, the Jeffersons' house, and the slave houses to the east. There is no indication which of the slaves was trained in cookery and so no telling which family or families lived in this building. The main kitchen held "1 bed and covering" that may have accommodated a single person or a whole family who slept among "4 potts & 3 pr pot hooks" and "2 old Tables" (fig. 3.2). The cook had two old chairs for comfort during work and leisure hours, although the surrounding dishes, andirons, tubs, pails, copper kettles, and pot racks were constant reminders of work. Other

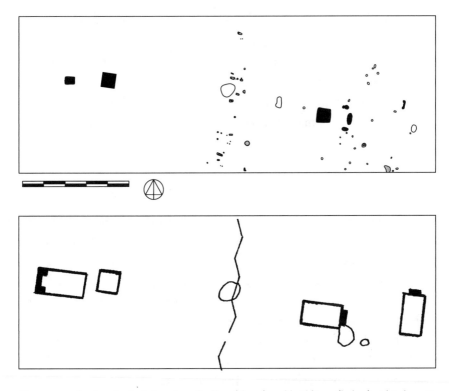

Figure 3.2. Archaeological site plan of cellars (above) and buildings (below) at kitchen site
and home quarter site at Shadwell. Site plan by Derek Wheeler, Courtesy Monticello/
Thomas Jefferson Foundation, Inc. (above), building reconstructions
drawing by Carl Lounsbury (below).

people slept in the two beds in a separate storeroom or wood shed, amid
meal bags, a cask, two barrels, tight casks, old lumber, and a cleaver. The main
kitchen had a broad open hearth with "1 Pr Large Kitchen HandIrons," and
pothooks, pot racks, and spits. This room was designed for food preparation
for the planters' family and guests, but it also provided space for food preparation and domestic activities for the cook's family. The cook's chamber pots
attest to her personal needs being met in the building where she worked.
A small clay-walled cellar (about two feet by three feet) beneath the floor
likely served the cook's professional and personal needs, storing root crops
and family items. The building had windows to offer some light and relief

from heat and smoke.[4] The cooking, child rearing, and beds may have been shared by other related or unrelated adults; either arrangement was within the bounds of the system. If children were small, they spent the day underfoot while their mother worked, or they went to another slave house nearby to someone whose job it was to watch young children for the community. These boys and girls may well have shared the company of kinfolk while their mother worked.

Kitchen Work

The cook performed a variety of skilled and unskilled labor for the Jeffersons; her long list of equipment is the catalog of her abilities (see appendix, table 8). She maintained tools that describe a variety of cooking styles, including pans for savory and sweet baking, spits for roasting, pans for braising and grilling, pots for stewing, dishes and pans for baking, pans for frying, a gridiron for broiling, and irons for toasting. She prepared food that simmered or roasted without much attention, and she used tools that required constant monitoring. She had iron implements for use at the fireplace, but also smaller bone-handled utensils for dressing or serving food, or for her own dining (fig. 3.3). She also preserved food and processed food for storage, as well as managed stocks of food using milk pans, jugs, jars, bottles, and casks. The open hearth, with its three pairs of pothooks, pot racks, and spits, allowed cooking over flame, near flame, or right in coals. She or an assistant—maybe a child—turned the spit if there was no clock reel to do that job. A separate oven for baking would have been part of the brick structure of the chimney and would not show up in the inventory but was likely part of the kitchen. The cook, or perhaps a younger slave under her direction, brought wood and kept the fires the right size for various jobs, carried water to heat in great copper kettles, washed dishes in the tubs and pails, swept, and carried produce in and trash out. She used the tablecloth and brushes to aid in hygiene and food preparation. The cook may well have visited the vegetable garden to supply the kitchen, or others may have brought to her what the Jeffersons directed. She had a cleaver for dispatching fowl and chopping large cuts of meat and probably game. She handled fishhooks from catch and processed dairy products. She probably helped salt, smoke, and preserve meats, perhaps under the direction of Jane Jefferson, and helped store wine and brew beer. A second

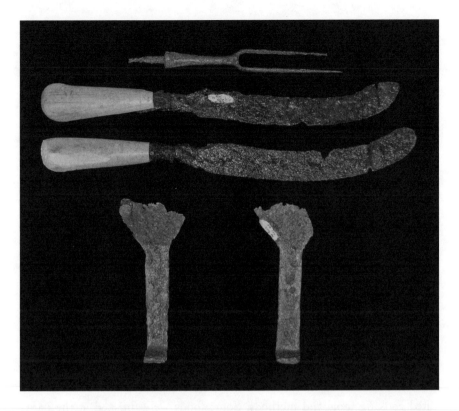

Figure 3.3. People on the home quarter had an array of utensils for preparing and eating food, including iron- and bone-handled forks (above) and knives (center), and a variety of iron and ceramic pots (iron pot legs shown below, note brass rivet on left leg). Courtesy Monticello/Thomas Jefferson Foundation, Inc.

building next door had a brick-lined cellar and may have served as a smoke-house or dairy.[5]

The material culture of the Jeffersons indicates that their cooks needed to be versed in distinctly Anglo-Virginian manners of food preparation; it is likely that the domestic slaves and kitchen workers were people who had been in Virginia since birth. Although the 1757 inventory lists the better wares with the contents of the Jefferson house, the kitchen area contained the archaeological remains of numerous items of tableware, glass stemware, and eating utensils, evidence of the everyday circulation of dishes from kitchen to table to scullery. The slave cook and others who worked in the kitchen had first-hand experience with a full range of the ceramic wares available in the British

Atlantic consumer world. They handled English-made white salt-glazed stone-ware, which was fashionable at midcentury; delftware from England and Holland; stoneware and earthenware from various European manufactures such as the Rhineland and England; and Chinese porcelain that passed through European ports before making its way across the Atlantic. The kitchen staff also had to learn when to serve on ceramic or pewter, when to prepare for a table set with silver, and the difference between a coffeepot, a teapot, a chocolate pot, and a cream pot. The slave cook and related staff probably knew more about how to use and to care for silver, pewter, and porcelain wares than most Virginians of any color who still ate from wooden plates and bowls using only spoons.[6]

The women who lived and worked in the plantation kitchen probably ate the best grade of food of any slaves because, in addition to their ration, they no doubt tasted and ate extra from what they prepared for the Jefferson household. But they may have eaten only when they were finished meeting the demands of those dining in the big house, whether they served a small family meal or a great dinner. The wares associated with the Jeffersons' dining room indicate that the Jeffersons practiced an elite style of dining that could involve multiple courses and fine seasonings prepared with sophisticated cooking tools and methods. Some foods were finished at the parlor hearth on the way to the dining room, and some were seasoned at the table. The cooks who worked there knew a style of food preparation very different from the one-pot meals that were probably the staple at the field quarter sites. The cooks had to calculate preparation times (though there was no clock in the inventory) and how to protect and move the dishes from the kitchen buildings to the main house. They may have had to tend dishes in the house parlor for servers to take to the dining room across the passage, closely watched by Jane Jefferson, her older daughters, or a male slave who acted as butler. Their work involved great performances between bouts of the mundane. They needed to process beef, lamb, pork, poultry, fish, and game, and maybe catch some of it. The plantation garden included vegetables to be cooked, such as peas, asparagus, broccoli, and cauliflower; others to be eaten raw, such as lettuce, radishes, cucumbers, and berries; and others that were preserved, such as peas, cucumbers, berries and other fruits, and nuts. They hauled water, chopped wood, washed pots and dishes, and protected their own small children from knives, flame, and other harm. They may also have had to cook separate food for other slaves who worked in the house or when all hands were in the fields.[7]

The cook occupied a position that put her at an advantage over others in the slave community, but she was also required to work closely with the Jeffersons. The needs of Jeffersons no doubt limited her ability to socialize with other slaves, but her access to regulated foodstuffs gave her special privilege. She needed to work with the mistress of the house—either Jane or one of the daughters as mistress-in-training—who carried the keys to locked storerooms for spices or better cuts of meat. She worked according to the Jeffersons' and their guests' meal schedules, with occasional time off. She probably spent some of her time in the Jeffersons' house, finishing or transferring food to vessels over the parlor fire, unless she directed other slaves to do so. The cook had currency in the scraps and leftovers from foods that were seasoned and cooked with implements different from those that most slaves had. She may have had the opportunity to use these extras as social or economic leverage in her exchanges with other slaves who might otherwise resent her position. She could invoke a celebration or trade with sugar, cinnamon, a beef roast, or a pork chop that offered a dramatic break from a diet of cornmeal and salted meat, or she might have the ability to alert others to unlocked storerooms so they could choose for themselves occasionally.[8] She needed to be trusted by the Jeffersons and included in the broader slave community—her skills and her access gave her the tools to do both if she was clever.

Home Quarter: House and Yard

A number of the home quarter slaves lived in a group of four small houses located on the eastern edge of the ten-acre center of the plantation (see fig. 3.2). Despite Peter Jefferson's formal arrangement of the plantation elements, the slaves' daily use of the space reflected a few of their own needs and desires. These homes contained the full range of life—enslaved people cooked, ate, slept, raised families, and kept company there. Archaeological evidence supports the Jeffersons' attention to slave families and indicates that these buildings housed families, as opposed to single-sex gang living arrangements that have been the model for discussing slavery in this region during this period.[9]

One slave house—called Building I here—left prominent archaeological remains: a large (six-and-a-half-foot-square) clay-walled cellar pit; a pit marking a hearth area just east of the cellar; and two large postholes flanking the hearth pit, which held post supports for the chimney. This building was likely frame, at least ten feet deep by twelve feet long—the minimum size of a room that would extend from the hearth area past the cellar. The building had glazed windows, and artifact distributions show that the building opened to the south. The cellar reached about three and a half to four feet below modern grade and was large enough to serve a variety of storage needs. The cellar dated to at least 1737, based on the mean ceramic date of the cellar fill, and artifacts from the chimney structure confirm its date before the middle of the eighteenth century. The single large cellar in the building suggests the building housed a family. There is no evidence of later major repairs or alterations to the building—at least not to any substructure.[10]

A second building—Building II—is marked only by a small sill of brick rubble between two postholes that indicate a doorway. The only artifacts from the sill were wrought nails, wine bottle glass, and an animal tooth. Like all the other buildings at Shadwell, there is no footprint to indicate its dimensions. Like Building I, it had glazed windows, and distribution studies show that the front of Building II was on its western side, toward the yard area between the two buildings. Based on the Jeffersons' attention to the location and orientation of the components of their plantation, Building II was most likely of the same frame construction and finish as Building I.[11]

The yard around and between these two buildings was a space for raising food, for cooking food, and a common living space. Artifacts here testify to an array of domestic activities across the area. Though the Jeffersons dictated the buildings and their placement in the landscape, archaeology indicates ways that enslaved people used their allotted space that fell outside the carefully constructed plantation plan. Just off the southeast corner of Building I, six small postholes form an almost circular enclosure that kept small livestock such as poultry or protected garden plants. Just beyond the enclosure, further southeast, was a pit for cooking or smoking fish and meats. This yard, with space for raising and cooking food, was also a center of local community within this small plantation compound, a community that had some degree of autonomy behind a fence that separated it from its white overseers.[12]

A split-rail fence enclosed the quarter buildings and their yard and separated them from the center of the plantation, where the Jeffersons' house and
the kitchen building stood. The physical landscape of the plantation offers
some clues as to the freedoms and limitations of slaves' movements around
that space. A fence can be both a permeable barrier—something that provides access—and a shield—a defense from noise and activity or people that
might be intrusive. This fence was not a palisade or security wall for humans:
it did not imprison enslaved adults. Rather, it may have offered slaves a bit of
security and aided their efforts to raise poultry and garden crops and keep
roving animals at bay. It may have offered those who resided within a degree
of privacy away from the plantation center, providing the opportunity to be
out from under the watchful eyes of others. On the other hand, it may have
been a constant reminder to those whom it enclosed that people in the big
house wanted to keep them separate and not have the rustic elements of the
plantation quarter intrude on the refined elegance of the Jeffersons' house.
The fence was recognized as a barrier that separated people and activities on
both sides.[13]

The fence line persisted—archaeological evidence showed four periods of
fence repair. Its purpose also persisted, even during the quarter farm period
(1776–90s), when there was no longer a plantation house at Shadwell as the
center of things. Just north of the quarter buildings was a trash pit that strad-
dled the fence line. That trash lay on both sides suggests that people on both
sides of this boundary recognized it and dumped along it. Its location also
indicates that the quarter and the kitchen residents thought of the area north
of their houses as the back—or at least as less important than the south face.
Just outside the doors of the slave houses was a gate in the fence through which
a path led to the kitchen and to the porch of the house where the slaves' owners and taskmasters lived. The people who lived on the quarter were connected to the center of the plantation by this path. They followed it to report
for work, and it carried them home again. They used it to visit their friends in
the kitchen, who may have peered along the path for glimpses of what was
going on among their families in the quarter. Despite the hundred-foot distance, the slaves who lived on the home quarter, both in the kitchen and at
the quarter site, shared some things in common across their separate domestic landscapes. Probably much of their world was the product of shared labor

and shared culture. The fence in their midst did not limit exchange between the slaves in the kitchen and those on the quarter; rather, the fence offered a degree of privacy or autonomy that allowed the people who lived there to sustain a community.[14]

Foodways

Artifacts from the home quarter describe a variety of domestic activities, and much of the activity focused on food. No lists tell us what the Jeffersons gave their people as their regular ration. In general, planters gave slaves a weekly portion of cornmeal and salted meat, and occasionally salted fish. But artifacts from Shadwell offer information about cooking methods, if not what was cooked, and suggest food-related activities that provide some further insight into diet and the activities of slaves in their homes. The Jeffersons furnished each house on the home quarter with fireplace equipment—a set of pothooks—for preparing meals. The work routines and living arrangements of the home quarter residents were different from those of the field hands; on the home quarter, each household had equipment to cook for itself, suggesting that this was not always a communal world but one where individual households or families usually cooked and ate separately, with one exception.[15]

The inhabitants of the quarter site cooked in various types of cast-iron cooking pots. Some pots had legs to allow the cook to place pots right over the coals, or people could use pot hooks and hearth equipment to make stews in pots hung over the fire. Scraps of iron pans indicate baking or other cooking methods. Slaves may have earned or purchased this cookware themselves. Colono pots from the site also suggest stewing directly in a fire, although these pots may also have served other purposes. Artifacts show that slaves ate foods much more various than what is suggested generally in documents about slave rations. The pit near Building I shows that people smoked fish or meats outdoors. They had a small pen for keeping poultry, and they also had spades for keeping gardens.[16]

Slaves in Building I moved some of their food preparation from their hearth to the cooking or smoking pit outside their house (fig. 3.4). Although this mirrored the actions of wealthier Virginians in removing cooking heat and smells from houses, it also showed choices made by enslaved people about

Figure 3.4. Cooking pit in yard of slave quarter area. The circular rock with flat sides (seen to left of pit) sat on a bed of corncobs and other charred material. The fill in the pit included fish scale, fragments of bone, brick, and English Staffordshire slipware vessels. Courtesy Monticello/Thomas Jefferson Foundation, Inc.

their use of living space and their foods. Smoking required brining the food to be smoked, a place to concentrate heat and smoke, and a few days' time. People here dug a circular hole about two and a half feet wide and almost as deep. To smoke meat or fish, they layered the bottom of the hole with wood charcoal and corncobs, over which they put an almost-circular flat rock. They put the food on the rock, perhaps on a rack of sticks or on a grate, and put some kind of cover over the hole. Over the one to four days of smoking they tended the coals to keep a slow, steady burning. If they cooked in the pit, they layered coals in the bottom, placed the food in a pot on the rock, and piled coals around and over it. During use the raking of coals into and out of the pit pushed bits of building material—brick, glass, and nail—and shards of Staffordshire slipware pans into the hole, evidence of its active use during the Jefferson era at Shadwell. Although the pit appears to be associated with Building I, it may also reflect an invitation to the neighbors to be social or may represent special communally prepared foods or events.[17]

The residents of Shadwell's home quarter had a range of European ceramics that most slaves did not possess. Most of the ware types that occurred in association with the Jefferson dwelling house also appeared in the quarter area, with heavier concentrations of utilitarian wares on the quarter site. Ceramic vessels from across the quarter site indicate that people prepared, preserved, and stored food there, using larger vessels of both glazed and unglazed earthenware and salt-glazed stoneware. People had earthenware pans, mostly Staffordshire slipware, red-bodied ware with lead glaze, and Buckley ware, for processing milk or other food. The high frequency of storage containers such as stoneware bottles and glass wine bottles shows us that the people who lived there had alternatives well beyond a standard weekly ration; they put up stores of food or used foods that had been preserved. Although they might not have enjoyed quite the same access to foods as the plantation cook, they still had opportunities far beyond the expected slave fare (fig. 3.5).[18]

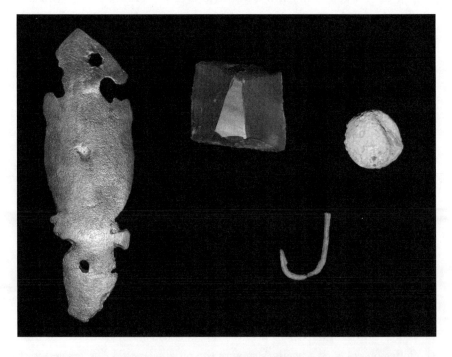

Figure 3.5. Slaves on the home quarter site had means to hunt and fish. Shown clockwise from left: brass escutcheon plate from a gun, English flint, lead shot, iron fishhook. Courtesy Monticello/Thomas Jefferson Foundation, Inc.

Questions of Fashion and Use

Ceramic tableware from the home quarter site reflect the forms and wares available to the Jeffersons in the eighteenth century—almost all the ceramic types used at Shadwell passed through the home quarter, from the most utilitarian to the finest goods. Since the Jeffersons acquired almost the full range of ceramic wares available in Virginia during the middle of the eighteenth century, the home quarter site reflects the breadth of the ceramic market in the colony. But there is no way to know which of the goods may have been secondhand and which might have been purchased or earned by slaves directly. Slaves on the home quarter at Shadwell used plates and bowls, tea wares and table forks. Access to and ownership of goods separated house slaves from field slaves, and house slaves for rich folks from all poorer folks— white, black, enslaved, or free. Slaves belonging to wealthy people experienced a different range of material goods than most people in the eighteenth century, but the interpretation of consumer goods as hand-me-downs is a "problem" of plantation archaeology. Fashion is limited by time, and at some point in their lives, fashionable goods become merely useful objects.[19]

Second- or thirdhand goods do not necessarily indicate the behaviors implied by these objects during their initial phase of consumption, and the possible interpretations are many. Wares without intrinsic value—that is, not made of silver or pewter or a material that could be sold or recast—still had value because of their usefulness and because of their fashion. For instance, we assume that the Jeffersons invested very consciously in a new and high-style teapot because the teapot's fashionable status held a return for the Jeffersons. The teapot was worth its expense because it played a role in reinforcing the social prestige of Peter and Jane. In a world where social prestige was currency, owners who displayed high-status goods perceived a financial return from them. When the teapot's design was not at the height of fashion, it was no longer a positive statement about its owner's taste and current ability to acquire goods. Yet it may still have been important to that owner as an object with sentimental value or as a vessel to serve tea or to hold another liquid.

When the initial owner discarded an item—to replace it with a more fashionable pot or because it was worn or chipped—the receiver may not have cared at all that the teapot was once fashionable and held in high regard. It may have become merely a useful vessel. However, because of the limited firsthand access of slaves to markets or because a slave might want to display certain privilege within the plantation community, the hand-me-down may still have been a status good, but within an altered scale. A chipped teapot may be more teapot than most laborers ever owned, or the teapot may illustrate within the slave community the personal relationship that a particular servant had with the master or mistress. The teapot may still bear a return as a status object, but it cannot—and should not—be measured on the same social scale as when it was first acquired.[20]

Slaves obtained and used secondhand goods in various ways. At Shadwell, people gave familiar objects new meaning by reworking them. Slaves made a number of gaming pieces or markers out of fragments of ceramic and shell, suggesting that certain objects held currency in the quarter even when broken. When the Jefferson house burned, the contents were presumably scattered. Then the site was cleaned up following the fire. Jane's postfire house included au courant purchases instead of replacing exactly what was lost to the fire. So with the 1770 fire and cleanup, there was a window of opportunity for higher status goods to move across the site. Some of the goods on the slave quarter may have been new, some hand-me-downs, some salvage, some refuse.[21]

Healing-Medicinal Activity

Someone in the slave community used and prepared medicine—perhaps she or he was a healer. Evidence of medicinal preparations on both the kitchen site and the home quarter area and along the fence line in between suggest that slaves managed medicines themselves and helped others in the community. Someone in the household of the Shadwell cook—very possibly the cook herself—lent a hand in healing, preparing, or working with others to manufacture remedies in the kitchen. The variety of artifacts with medicinal applications from both the kitchen site and the quarter site indicates a tradition of healing in the broadest possible sense in mid-eighteenth-century Virginia and represents a number of cultural practices. The kitchen housed a caudal cup of white salt-glazed stoneware for serving soft foods to an ailing person, an Anglo idea in an English vessel, but an idea not out of place in many parts of the world. Across the slave-inhabited area of the plantation were numerous

Figure 3.6. Shadwell slaves had a variety of English delftware ointment pots and may have had access to medicines prepared by apothecaries. The Shadwell ointment pots range from two to four inches in diameter and include the same variety of forms shown in this collection from the Dr. George Gilmer site in Williamsburg, Virginia. Courtesy The Colonial Williamsburg Foundation.

delft salve pots and different sizes of drug jars of stoneware and earthenware (fig. 3.6). The Jeffersons likely purchased these European-made jars filled with ointment compounded by a doctor or apothecary and gave the preparations to their slaves. Alternatively, the Jeffersons may have used prepared ointments and passed the empty pots on to their slaves for reuse, but in this case fragments of jars should also have appeared in the materials related to the Jefferson house, and they did not. The making of salves of local plant matter and animal fat was traditional in European, African, and Native American cultures. Knowledge and opinion of what ingredients soothed what conditions differentiated the practices. Glass vials and bottles fall into the same patterns of use as the drug jars; the vessel form implies the keeping of healing substances, but what that substance was could differ from user to user, even within the same cultural group.[22]

The ointment pots, drug jars, and vials illustrate the presence of "professional" medicine at Shadwell. Occasionally the Jeffersons or an overseer called someone recognized as a doctor to treat members of the plantation community. Doctor Thomas Walker treated Peter Jefferson, Arthur Hopkins visited as a physician, and Dr. William Wills treated the twenty-four-year-old Samson. Midwives Jane Hammock and Mrs. Lewis helped slave women deliver their babies. Dr. George Gilmer visited the plantation to treat slaves and may also have treated Jane Jefferson or other family members: in 1772 he looked after a boy with a leg injury. Peter Jefferson kept fleams (for bloodletting) and sundry medicine vials in the same strong house where he kept his militia weapons; he may have used them on the plantation, or they may have been reserved for military and surveying expeditions.[23] There is only a single vial in connection with the Jefferson house, but if the habit was to pass empty vessels to slaves, then pots may not have stayed in the house for long.

Knowledge about medicine and healing could be learned from books, from working with or watching doctors, or from practicing remedies at home—what people called professional and folk practice did not differ greatly. Slaves at Monticello practiced traditional medicine that Thomas Jefferson referred to as "poison," but healing was an inexact art and not so far removed from ideas about faith and spirituality. The women in the slave community no doubt passed their knowledge about nursing babies and tending small children from woman to woman. Nursing babies and helping women in childbirth was one of the skills women in early America almost had to practice. The women who could offer concrete solutions to problems such as diaper rash and postpartum pain also could make prayers and invoke faith as part of healing.[24]

Healing-Spiritual Activity

Other artifacts that relate to medicinal practices at Shadwell reflect the spiritual side of healing. Colonoware vessels had medicinal-spiritual applications that speak entirely of slave culture. Slaves or Native Americans made the pots—named colonoware by archaeologists—by taking local clays and tempering materials, shaping vessels by hand, and firing them directly in an open fire or hearth. The product was a coarse-fired earthenware that revealed the cultural traditions of its maker and the distinction of local materials. The

Figure 3.7. Colonoware from Shadwell quarter site: five distinctly different clay and temper combinations. All but one reflect the red clay of the catoctin limestone ridge on which Shadwell sits. The lighter, buff-colored pieces in the upper right are from a larger vessel (approx. eight inches diameter at the rim; shard shown is approx. four and a quarter inches wide), of nonlocal material, perhaps from the sandier soils of Virginia's tidewater. Courtesy Monticello/Thomas Jefferson Foundation, Inc.

pots made by slaves were a direct product of African craft or creole methods developed by Africans during their American slavery. Their function may have been to prepare African-style foods, practice traditional medicine, or represent to their owners a spiritual connection. Archaeologists recovered sixteen fragments of colonoware vessels on the kitchen and slave quarter area at Shadwell (fig. 3.7). They fall into five distinctly different vessels or types of material. Most of the pieces reflect the deep red color of Piedmont clays. The sandy buff color of one larger bowl indicates its production in the tidewater region from materials there. This may have been a treasured personal object, brought long ago from a family home on another plantation. Unless it was "just" a bowl, it was unlikely to have played a role in food preparation for the

Jeffersons. If this bowl served as cookware, then the cook and her family at least occasionally preferred their own food, prepared their own way, even though the technologically more advanced cooking utensils of another culture surrounded them. This redundancy makes the presence of the colonoware even more important. Although a colonoware bowl may have held a substance, it also served as a vessel for a spirit. Archaeologists have uncovered evidence elsewhere that slaves made colono pots to carry messages between spirits and people on earth. The treatment of a pot in both its making and its disposal provided the ritual relationship between people and spirits for healing both body and soul. The colonoware may have been among the most important things the slaves owned. Other objects performed similarly talismanic purposes, such as the quartz crystal that people found locally but that made its way into cultural deposits in the slave quarter.[25]

Many slaves retained spiritual practices such as healing while also finding usefulness in Christianity. The presence of one did not preclude the other. There is no evidence, except for some of their names, that the Shadwell slaves practiced a Christian religion like the Jeffersons, although it is likely that the Virginia-born among them did. The degree of accommodation that many of these slaves showed to Anglo-Virginian ways suggests that they might also have embraced activities relating the Jeffersons' Anglican church. Many of these slaves knew the clergy who visited Shadwell and must have known the slaves who worked for those clergymen. In addition, the Jeffersons had friends and family who were Dissenters from the Church of England. Dissenting religions were particularly popular with people who had less power than their gentry neighbors. Shadwell slaves had a good chance to hear the call of evangelical Christianity, with its promises of peace and justice in the afterlife and its potential to heal in the present.[26]

Tobacco was also considered medicinal in the eighteenth century. Tobacco pipes, like colono bowls, were vessels to carry important substances and slaves made both types of vessels on-site, though they used mostly commercially made pipes. Smoking tobacco in pipes reflected both African and Native American spiritual healing practices as well as fit with European ideas about balancing the humors. The home quarter site had the highest concentration of tobacco pipes across the whole ridge, and although their use may have been medicinal at times, I have considered them mainly with leisure activities.

Clothing and Dress

Slaves at Shadwell wore linen in the summer and woolen in the winter. Some of their clothing came ready-made from manufactories in Europe, while other garments came from women who sewed imported or country cloth to order in Albemarle County. A few of the slaves sewed their own clothes or had them tailored. The documents kept for Peter Jefferson's estate by John Harvie give the best detail of the ration of clothing and blankets, and archaeology offers a few glimpses into sewing and personal ornamentation not available in the documents. The clothing rations reflect the standard by which wealthier planters kept their "people" or "negroes," as they were called in the clothing lists. Many planters gave their people far less than the Jeffersons did.[27]

Except for a few references that differentiated house slaves, the Jeffersons distributed similar garments across the plantation as part of the annual ration (see appendix, table 9). Specialized clothing may have been passed out only occasionally. Male slaves received two shirts and two suits of linen for summer, one woolen suit for winter, and a pair of cloth stockings each year. Their summer breeches were the coarse linen called crocus. Women received two linen shifts for summer, a woolen suit for winter, and a pair of cloth stockings. Children received small shirts or frocks in both winter and summer weights. There is no mention of pants or stockings for children or stays for women, and the spare use of color description suggests a palette of unbleached brown and natural. Except for the stockings, neighboring women sewed almost all the above clothing. Purchased ready-made goods included knit wool Monmouth caps that went to men who worked outside in the cold, wool blankets, and plaid (woven wool cloth) stockings. One shipment of blankets was noted as being "bought in the Country," but most fabric came from England, collected there from all over the world and reexported, according to British trade laws. Imported fabric included brown Irish linen, cotton (a name for napped, woven wool), plains (another woven woolen), osnaburg (coarse linen or hemp from Germany), and crocus (linen). Additional imported supplies included thread and shoe thread.[28]

Local women, many of whom were wives of overseers or other white hired workers, made most of the rationed clothing. Some years the work was divided among five or more women who each made multiple items of clothing, possibly to supply the quarter each woman's husband oversaw. Other years one or two people performed the work, sometimes one was paid for cutting the cloth, another for making. In 1761, Eleanor (also Nel or Nelly) Shepherd cut as well as produced "46 Shirts & Shifts out of Dam[ask], 15 Small D[itt]o, 10 Do, 8 Cotton Frocks, 6 Frocks + 1 little Jacket & Breeches, 13 mens & 12 Suits of Wos. Wollen Cloths." The items distributed were a standard issue of a single size and the color, cut, and fabric advertised the wearer's status as a laboring slave.[29]

Slaves at Shadwell sometimes wore shoes made at home, and other shoes were purchased. In 1754, Peter Jefferson paid Alexander McCaul £4 6s. for twenty pairs of "Negroes Shoes." But Peter also owned shoemaking tools and fourteen lasts, had tanned leather and hide, and purchased shoe thread. Both Sawney and Sandy were trained as shoemakers, and shoe thread purchases indicate shoe making on the plantation in years both before and after the 1754 purchase of shoes. In 1747 Jefferson supplied overseer Martin Dawson with both shoes and shoe leather, but he supplied other overseers with just shoes. It is unclear whether Peter purchased shoes for his hired workers and passed on the cost or whether Sawney made shoes to sell as part of the plantation enterprise. Shoe thread purchases continued in the years after Peter's death. It was during this time that Sawney had the opportunity to practice his craft outside the plantation by working nearby with Joseph Bolling, a shoemaker. Bolling hired Sawney for six months in 1759, perhaps to help make shoes, perhaps to train young apprentices. Sawney's work was valuable: the estate received 27s. 6d. a month, for a nice sum of £8 5s.[30] Excavations on the home quarter produced needles and a large pair of shears that may reflect the leather working of Sawney or Sandy.

Sawney and Sandy and other men and women who practiced trades may have had work clothes that differed slightly from those the field hands wore. Leather aprons and leather breeches or fabric trousers signified skilled craftsmen, whether slave or free. Someone wore the leather caps that the estate purchased in 1759. The cook might have worn a waistcoat or aprons that signaled her position within the society. The house slaves differed more.[31]

The clothing lists mention only two slaves by name: Sawney and Cloe, but all the house servants received special clothing. Sawney's role as personal attendant to the past and rising masters of Shadwell was no doubt why he dressed differently. There is not evidence for or against him wearing livery, but it is likely he did. He received fabric instead of made clothes. Sawney may have sewn a suit or coat himself or had a cohort or a hired tailor work with him (fig. 3.8). His ration in terms of fabric was not out of the ordinary: in 1763, in addition to hose, he received four and half yards of cotton (woolen) and six yards of osnaburg.[32] But the individualized cut and style of clothes tailored for him indicated his status on the plantation. Unfortunately, though ceramic fragments survive to tell us the color of teapots and bowls, there are no cloth scraps to give color to the dress of this man Sawney.

Others who worked in the house also received different goods. In 1762 a special order for "Clothing for the Childrens Slaves" shows how those slave children were well on their way to differential treatment and performed specialized roles in the plantation community at early ages. One order included "to Mrs. Jefferson Cloths for Chloe," who must have worked separately from others on the ration lists—perhaps Cloe was Jane's maid. In 1761, Eleanor Shepherd sewed "6 Frocks" for girls in the house. Although the frocks may have been the same fabric as those sewn for the field hands, their companion suit of "1 little Jacket & Breeches" for a boy indicates that the house slaves dressed much more formally. The same year, Jane's slaves would get "2 Cotton Suits & 3 Wos. Shifts." Another year Jane covered her people using thirteen yards of cotton and twenty and a half yards of osnaburg, in addition to two men's suits and one woman's woolen suit. The slaves of the minor Jefferson children also benefited from the higher status accorded to house slaves. Their 1762 order "To Clothing for the Childrens Slaves" included "11 1/2 Yds Ozna at 1/1, 7 1/2 Yds Cotton at 2/6 1.11.2 1/2; and 1/4 # thread .1." This purchase clothed Elizabeth's girl Cate, Martha's Rachel, Lucy's Cachina and Lydia, Anna Scott's Eve, Randolph's Peter, and possibly Sawney. These slave children grew up learning to wait on the Jefferson children. Part of their training was learning to wear the better clothes that such a job demanded.[33]

On the home quarter site and the kitchen area, archaeological evidence of sewing as well as decorating with buttons, beads, and other ornaments reveals that slaves mended, reused, and decorated their clothing, perhaps even garments made for them by local women. They had a pair of small needlework

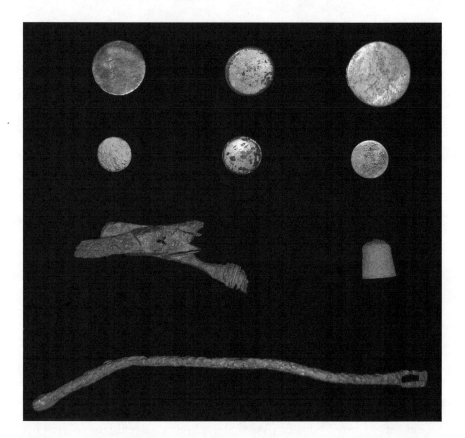

Figure 3.8. Clothing care and sewing, left to right: dozens of gilt, silvered, and brass buttons of matched sets and graded sizes indicate something of the degree of formality of clothing at Shadwell. People engaged in sewing had needlework scissors and thimbles. The large iron needle is six and a half inches long and may have been used for running ribbon or cord through cloth or sewing pack cloth for trade goods. Courtesy Monticello/Thomas Jefferson Foundation, Inc.

scissors and straight pins. Someone may have used the large iron needle found nearby to run ribbon or cord through cloth. Buckles of brass and other metal alloys fixed clothes and shoes of slaves, and gilt, brass, and plain metal alloy buttons and hooks and eyes secured or decorated clothing. The range of sizes of buttons of matching finish may indicate livery or at least more formal clothes. The detached fittings for making and fastening clothing may also indicate necessary clothing maintenance, including laundry activities, on this site.[34]

Plantation Work

All of the able-bodied slaves at Shadwell likely joined in agricultural work when demand was high, such as transplanting tobacco seedlings in the spring or bringing in wheat in the fall. Slaves on the home quarter worked tobacco with hilling hoes, broad hoes, and grubbing hoes; they prepared soil with a Dutch plow hoe and harrow hoes; and they gardened with spades. Someone also tended orchard fruit and livestock. But many of the home quarter slaves had occupations other than serving as agricultural laborers. Samson and Jupiter used their broadaxes to dress lumber that had been cut from logs. They hired out to carpenter John Biswell, who used their strength and expertise when he worked on the Shadwell mill in 1753. Jupiter and Samson each received £1 3s. for twenty days' work. Sawney hired out to a local shoemaker, and he and Sandy used the shoemaker's tools and lasts kept in a barn and the large shears found on the home quarter site to make the tanned leather into work shoes. Phill was a wagoner, and Sandy had skills as a jockey. Sandy and others kept the harnesses and riding chairs and carriages in good order. Thirteen of the twenty-two horses at Shadwell had names. These may have been the descendants of Thomas Jefferson II's racehorse, the horses that pulled the family carriages, and the trusted steed used by the militia colonel. A slave groom knew these horses better than the Jeffersons did and attended them accordingly. Peter Jefferson's inventory includes tools for making and marking casks and hogsheads, along with carpentry tools and materials for building, including window glass and lead, paint, putty, lime for plaster or mortar, and nails. Slaves at Shadwell witnessed or practiced the specialized trades that used these materials.[35]

Slaves did not have free access to the materials they used in their crafts and labor. Supplies of new goods were kept in storerooms, locked away. The Jeffersons regulated access to tanned leather, building materials such as hinges and nails, house paint, and cloth. The Jeffersons also kept supplies of new farm implements such as hoes out of general circulation. This may have been to preserve stock to sell to neighbors in addition to carefully managing the workers' relationships to the tools issued to them. The number of tools listed with each quarter corresponds fairly closely to the number of working individuals on each site. If a worker—a slave or an overseer—lost or tried to sell tools, the shortage would be readily apparent to whoever doled out replacements. When Sandy ran away in 1769, he had an opportunity to take his shoe making tools with him: his skills had value, but he needed the tools, too.[36]

Hired workers who came to Shadwell brought opportunities for slaves to develop skills, learn to use new tools, and hear news from abroad. Carpenters, coopers, blacksmiths, tailors, and shoemakers all entered the plantation, and evidence of all these skills except blacksmithing showed up among the slaves at Shadwell. Other skilled craft work came from local women who sewed, knitted, and wove for the slaves and the Jeffersons, but it is unclear if any of these women came to work on the plantation or simply sent batches of items they produced in their homes. Nevertheless, a slave interested in these techniques could study the garments brought to her. Other visitors included rollers and watermen who carried tobacco and other crops to warehouses and who probably had many colorful stories of life traveling along the James and other rivers. Phill's job as a wagoner meant carting goods between plantations and warehouses, making the acquaintance of many people along the way. Midwives and doctors visited the slaves and the Jeffersons. The teachers who visited the Jefferson children for reading and writing and for dancing and music no doubt made an impression on any slaves within earshot, and when the Jeffersons hosted traveling bands of Indians, the entire plantation community could not help but notice.[37]

Slaves from elsewhere also visited the plantation. "Capt. Charles Lewis's negro carpenter" had skills that allowed him to travel and perform work at Shadwell. Because the Lewises were family and visited with the Jeffersons often, the Shadwell slaves—especially those on the home quarter—probably knew all the attendants of the Lewis family. Some Lewis slaves and some Shadwell slaves may have become family after Lucy and Randolph Jefferson married Lewis children. The Jeffersons had many well-heeled visitors who likely traveled with a slave or two. Robert Rose, Joshua Fry, John Harvie, Thomas Walker, and most gentry friends of the Jeffersons probably had slaves who knew someone at Shadwell and vice versa. The slaves of William Randolph of Tuckahoe may have formed very close relationships with the Jefferson slaves who joined the family there for seven years. Slaves no doubt packed and drove wagons for the Tuckahoe move, and some returned to Shadwell to work alongside those who never left. A slave may have driven the carriage the Jefferson women rode in to Tuckahoe, and at least one slave rode along on horseback, carrying young Thomas on his or her lap. When Peter Jefferson traveled home during the family's years away, there were reunions for slaves, and when the whole family returned in 1753, slave families were mended. The slave Jack remained in the Tuckahoe vicinity, sold to a Mr. Charles Clarke there. It may be that Jack had family in that area and sympathetic owners arranged his stay. Regardless, he became yet another associate that the Shadwell slaves had somewhere else in Virginia. As the Jefferson children grew and claimed slaves as their own, the web of family and acquaintances for this group of slaves once again expanded to include more plantations where kin and colleagues could be found.[38]

Slaves in the Jefferson Household

The slaves who were part of the Jefferson household—the cook, the personal attendants, the wet nurse, and the children's nurses—all lived on the home quarter. They had to: their jobs were there. Sawney knew how to dress a man's wig, brush a coat, and hang a sword belt. He could pack his master's cases for attending the House of Burgesses or for hacking through the mountain woods following a surveying chain. He also knew how to dress himself for the jobs he performed. Sawney's counterpart, Jane's maid, had similar skills, and eight other slaves grew up learning to wait on the Jefferson children and wore the better clothes that such jobs demanded. Sall nursed the Jefferson children and had particular skills in caring for babies. Other women and girls fed small children, cleaned up their messes, and kept them from bothering their parents during important events.

Proximity to the Jeffersons and their guests meant opportunities for making money. Slaves with skills could ply their trades and keep some of their earnings. In addition, waiting on guests meant tips. Servants who attended to guests' horses, carriages, travel cases, and clothes commonly received monetary compensation from visitors. Thomas Jefferson called these "vales" or "vails," the English word for gratuities given to servants.[39] In a brief exchange with a visitor, a slave could make alliances and perhaps hear tidbits of news from the guest's plantation, where the slave might have family or friends. The slaves' use of these alliances was another skill that could give house slaves an advantage other slaves did not have. However, these momentary alliances made over offers of and payments for service also demonstrated to everyone that the structure of plantation society was firmly in place. These relationships confirmed the power of the patriarch and the subjugation of those people in bonds.

Leisure

Slaves on the home quarter devised a number of ways to spend their leisure time, the minutes a day or hours a week that their work was not solely for the benefit of the Jeffersons. The most prominent leisure activity to appear archaeologically was smoking tobacco. The home quarter area held the highest concentration of tobacco pipes, suggesting that slaves smoked during their hours at their homes, in addition to whatever smoking they did while they worked. Most of the pipes were the familiar long, white ball clay ceramic pipes of European manufacture. Slaves may have purchased these with their own funds or received these as payment for certain tasks. Slaves also made pipes. A "blank," a pipe-shaped piece of soft local stone that was in production, broke, and was discarded, shows that making pipes was a hobby of someone here (fig. 3.9).[40]

The distribution of tobacco pipe fragments on the site also informs something about family life and how men and women used space differently and

Figure 3.9. A slave on the quarter site tried to form a tobacco pipe from locally available sedimentary rock called Candler phyllite. He discarded it near his workplace after he carved out the bowl, drilled the stem, and the stone split. Approximately four inches long. Courtesy Monticello/Thomas Jefferson Foundation, Inc.

had varied leisure pursuits. Pipe stems have distinct discard patterns, as they were fragile and likely to break where people smoked them or put them down. The pipes appear in heavy concentrations in the yard of the quarter site, and dramatically less in the kitchen area (fig 3.10). Although some women smoked tobacco, it was primarily a male activity. The kitchen area was predominantly female during the working hours, and male slaves apparently did not or could not spend time there. Although this illustrates the use of kitchen space by nonsmoking women, the use of the quarter buildings and yard by men who smoked may tell us that the cook did not live with her husband or that her husband lived or socialized mainly in the quarter area when not at work. The fence obscured the view from the Jeffersons' house to the quarter area, and that may have made the yard there a desirable place to be. Clearly the area around and just south of the slave quarter houses was among the most desirable places to smoke and enjoy social activity.[41]

Other recreational or socially important objects include a slate pencil, a clay marble, and gaming pieces or markers made from ceramic, shell, and stone (figs. 3.11, 3.12). These small pieces of reworked and polished shell and ceramic served as markers for such games as mankala; however, such games often were not merely leisure but served important social functions by testing and establishing leaders among groups. One small piece of slate bears inscribed lines that may be writing practice or decoration. Many of the objects considered above as part of work or required clothing care may have served dual purpose for slaves' own choices about personal adornment. The buttons occurred in quantity on both the kitchen site and the quarter site. The variety of craft tools, needles, pins, scissors, and shears suggest the slaves did handiwork in their living quarters. Craft work for themselves could have included quilt making, jewelry making, or otherwise altering the materials they were given to make something of their own. The beads and gems here bespeak adornment of clothing or bodies (fig. 3.13).[42]

The main quarter and the kitchen area had in common many buttons, fragments of colonoware, and a few artifacts of American Indian origin. This last category of antiques speaks of collecting for the sake of remembering or curiosity, as people on the home quarter brought home Native American artifacts that they found or traded and kept. People who lived at Shadwell had contact with Indians who lived west of the mountains (in present-day Tennessee) and

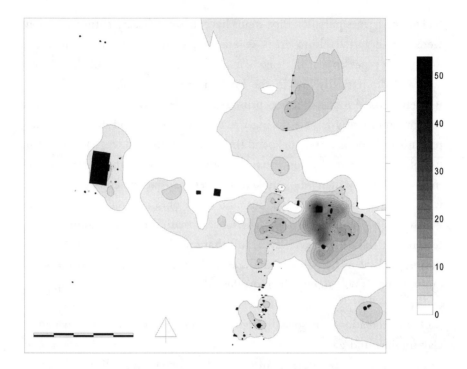

Figure 3.10. Surface distribution of European and locally made tobacco pipe fragments over all excavated areas of the home quarter.

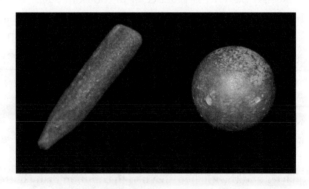

Figure 3.11. Slate pencil and marble from home quarter site. The pencil is about an inch long. Courtesy Monticello/ Thomas Jefferson Foundation, Inc.

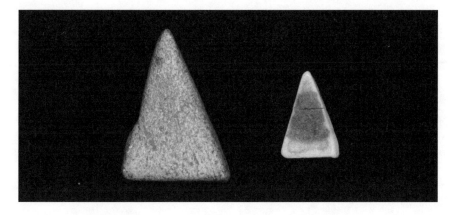

Figure 3.12. People living on the home quarter fashioned markers or gaming pieces by
working available materials into these deliberate forms. Left: shaped
and polished fragment of stone, approximately one inch high; right: shaped and
polished fragment of porcelain, approximately three fourths of an inch high.
Courtesy Monticello/Thomas Jefferson Foundation, Inc.

Figure 3.13. Ornamental accessories from the home quarter site include gems that were
not pierced but had to be used in a setting. Top, left to right: two paste glass gems, black
with reddish brown, gray, and white stripes (3/8 inch diameter); pressed clear glass or
paste gem (3/8 inch diameter); and polished stone, white with shades of brown and red
(9/16 inch long). Other ornament was in the form of beads pierced for stringing.
Bottom, left to right: blue glass bead (1/4 inch diameter), double pierced faceted clear
yellow bead (9/16 inch long); gray stone (slate?) double pierced bead (7/16 inch square).
Courtesy Monticello/Thomas Jefferson Foundation, Inc.

perhaps Albemarle County Monacans. But the artifacts the slaves owned were not everyday currency among Indians in the eighteenth century. They were quartz projectile points, collected during a period when Indians carried European firearms. They were small stone tools, kept during an era when metals served to do those jobs. And they were brass and iron tinkling cones, badges of ethnicity that sometimes served to open doors and other times forced their closure. Like the material world of the slaves at Shadwell, this small group of artifacts illustrates local and nonlocal materials, ethnic traditions, and cross-cultural contact.[43]

Beyond Shadwell

In a single cultural context the interpretation of objects—what they were and how they functioned—is usually straightforward. What motivated people from different times and places to choose certain objects and how they used them can have a range of possibilities. Sometimes the best a historian can do is pose multiple questions about how an object *may* have served. Although this discussion of a fairly "rich" material environment might evoke thoughts of comfort and occasional leisure activity, the people who inhabited these sites were still held in slavery. They had high material wealth relative to many Virginians of any color, but this picture of their world is not meant to indicate complacency on their part—nor on mine—in considering their unfree state. If anything, the material evidence creates a more complex palette for painting a picture of their lives within bondage, suggestions of small freedoms in certain choices, and no choices in many other things. Those who prospered within the rich environment of an enlightened patriarch such as Peter or Thomas Jefferson had little to complain about in terms of physical comforts; they needed strategies for survival motivated by intangible ideals.

The slaves on the home quarter were aware of their condition despite their material "wealth." Sandy chose to run away in the fall of 1769 and took his shoe making tools with him. The runaway notice recognized that he "will probably endeavour to get employment that way." The ad also noted that Sandy could do "coarse carpenters work" and could ride a horse, acknowledgment that skills, like skin color, clothing, and speech patterns, were identifying features. Slaves with skills were well aware of the market for their craft abilities. The advertisement posted for Sandy's return reveals some of the benefits

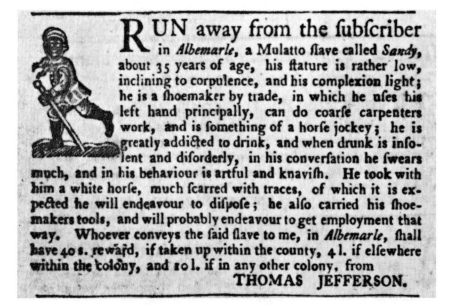

RUN away from the subscriber in *Albemarle*, a Mulatto slave called *Sandy*, about 35 years of age, his stature is rather low, inclining to corpulence, and his complexion light; he is a shoemaker by trade, in which he uses his left hand principally, can do coarse carpenters work, and is something of a horse jockey; he is greatly addicted to drink, and when drunk is insolent and disorderly, in his conversation he swears much, and in his behaviour is artful and knavish. He took with him a white horse, much scarred with traces, of which it is expected he will endeavour to dispose; he also carried his shoemakers tools, and will probably endeavour to get employment that way. Whoever conveys the said slave to me, in *Albemarle*, shall have 40 s. reward, if taken up within the county, 4 l. if elsewhere within the colony, and 10 l. if in any other colony, from
THOMAS JEFFERSON.

Figure 3.14. Runaway advertisement for Sandy. *VG*, Purdie and Dixon, Sept. 14, 1769. Courtesy The Colonial Williamsburg Foundation.

he had at home (fig. 3.14). He was well fed, "inclining to corpulence." He had training in shoe making that he hoped would give him work, but he also had other skills of carpentry and horsemanship. He communicated in ways that white owners called "artful and knavish," which may be their way of acknowledging that he was clever. His owners had let him practice his skill enough on his own to realize that he was left-handed. His propensity for swearing suggests both his connection to alternative cultures of other tradesmen and his unwillingness to abide by the codes of polite behavior that he surely learned at Shadwell. His unpleasantness when drunk revealed his underlying unhappiness. In his thirty-five years Sandy had learned enough about the world to know that his shoe making tools, a horse, and his light complexion might enable his safe passage to freedom. Sandy's flight did not last. He returned to Shadwell, and Thomas Jefferson sold him to Charles Lewis at nearby Buck Island in 1773. The £100 value assigned to his person and his skills lined the pockets of Thomas Jefferson instead of his own.[44]

The slaves who lived on the home quarter had families of their own, husbands and wives, brothers and sisters, sons, daughters, and parents there. But the purpose that brought them there was to be of service to the Jefferson family, which took them often from their own families. Little Sall was born at Shadwell about 1752. Her mother was Sall, the mother of so many of the privileged slaves at Shadwell, and this fact virtually ensured that Little Sall would also hold a position of status—at least to her owners and within the Jefferson slave community. Jane Jefferson kept Little Sall as part of her slave holdings; she did not have to move to another plantation and a new community. Had she lived, she would have become Thomas's and stayed at Shadwell with her mother, some of her siblings, and her own children, Cyrus and Rachel. But Little Sall died in the service of the Jefferson child Elizabeth, a grown woman who may have lacked the judgment that put her and Little Sall in harm's way. They drowned together "while attempting to cross the Rivanna in a skiff" in the high water of the winter of 1774. Elizabeth was twenty-nine and Little Sall was twenty-two, although family traditions suggest that Elizabeth was mentally deficient. Little Sall may have been an adult but was not the master in this situation.[45]

Just as the historian chooses different categories in which to analyze and ask questions of artifacts, so, too, should the historian with the people whose lives she or he seeks to tell about. The people who lived on the home quarter were members of different communities at varying times. They lived at a center of African-American life on the plantation and probably a center of influence for African Americans in Albemarle County. They also moved in and out of the communities that their skills and jobs made them a part of: some were part of the Jefferson household, some were skilled craftsmen, some trained other slaves, some, it appears, trained their masters. By defining their community in different ways we necessarily reposition relationships among people, and the strategies they used to negotiate those relationships take on new meaning.[46]

Archaeology offers a view that the slaves who served the planter's household occupied a curious niche. Their lives were filled with fine material goods, and house slaves knew the manners to use fine wares properly—that made their masters look good. But the elite goods from the kitchen and home quarter sites belie the legal status of their users. Their small and even rustic house and cheek-by-jowl living conditions serve as reminders of the standard of living of most Virginians, slave or free, and connect them to the other slaves owned by the Jeffersons. Despite the pervasive material culture of their elite owners, the slaves at Shadwell retained some markers of a community outside the one defined by their masters. The close view of this group of people who worked for the Jeffersons indeed adds complexity to the story of Virginians who lived in slavery—and also to the story of those who owned them and lived around them. Reminders of their status as chattel were never far away.

Bequeathing

A few months before he died in the summer of 1757, Peter Jefferson wrote his will. The choices he made in the disposition of slaves reveal how he thought about them and their future relationships with his family. He knew his slaves well. He calculated what types of slaves various members of his family needed to fulfill their individual charges. He made three types of bequests of slaves in his will. First, Jane should choose her "sixth part of my Slaves," which she could then dispose of by deed or will "amongst & to such & so many of my Children as she shall think fit." Then Peter named a specific slave who would go to each daughter, with the provision that "if it shall happen that any of the slaves bequeathed to my Daughters as aforesd. die before they come to the possession of my said Daughters respectively then it is my Will that such & so many Females slaves of near the same age be set apart out of my Estate & Given to such Daugter or Daugters." Peter then chose individual slaves by name to go to his sons and specified that "all my Slaves not herein otherwise disposed of to be equally divided between my two Sons Thomas and Randolph, at such Time as my Son Thomas shall attain the Age of twenty one years."[47] Field hands were among the "slaves not herein otherwise disposed." Every slave whom Peter named lived on the home quarter of the plantation. Most of Jane's choices for her sixth of Peter's estate and the various slaves that Jane deeded to family members during her lifetime also lived on the home quarter. The Jeffersons' disbursement of their slaves begins a compelling story about the dynamics of plantation society on the home quarter and the value placed on particular slave families (see appendix, table 7).

The plantation management and the social obligations of the Jefferson family affected the people they owned. The lives of the Jefferson family and their slaves were inextricably linked; every change in the lives of the Jefferson family influenced the lives of their slaves. The ages and legal status of the Jeffersons, changes in numbers through birth and death or marital status, and their good or bad fortunes affected the fortunes of the people who served them, depended on them, and fulfilled duties in their personal and family lives as they could. Training for these roles—for both the servant and the master—began early.

Peter bequeathed by name nine slaves. His choices of the slaves he left to each of his children reveal his strategy for establishing the next generation of slaves and masters. Peter gave each Jefferson child, with two exceptions, a slave of the same sex who was slightly younger than her or himself. Each of these pairs then grew up together, one learning skills of domination, the other learning those of service. As Peter's son later observed: "the whole commerce between master and slave is a perpetual exercise of the most boisterous passions, the most unremitting despotism on the one part, and degrading submissions on the other." Lessons learned in childhood were deeply held and part of a slaveholding society. "The parent storms, the child looks on [and] puts on the same airs in the circle of smaller slaves, gives a loose to his worst of passions, and thus nursed, educated, and daily exercised in tyranny, cannot be but stamped by it with odious peculiarities." Some lessons in servitude were subtler. The special order for "Clothing for the Childrens Slaves" suggests that those slave children were well on their way to differential treatment and performed specialized roles in the plantation community at early ages.[48] Their future was part of their material landscape: their clothing and living arrangements advertised their roles and their future relationships, as well as the set of behaviors they and their child masters had to learn.

Peter intended that, on reaching their majority, each of his daughters would inherit a female slave just younger than herself. The eldest daughter, Jane, at seventeen when her father died, was given the choice of Cloe, who was about three in 1757, or Patt, who was about ten. Jane eventually chose Patt, who remained at Shadwell with her subsequent family until the unmarried Jane died there in 1765. Mary Jefferson, at sixteen, inherited Nan, Sall's daughter, who was about twelve. Daughter Elizabeth, who was thirteen, inherited Cate, who was between eight and ten years old. Eleven-year-old Martha inherited seven-year-old Rachel. In one exception to the pattern, daughter Lucy received a young slave girl and the girl's mother also; five-year-old Lucy inherited Cachina and her child Phebe. Phebe was two or three years old, while Cachina, possibly already trained as a house or personal servant, was also the mother of at least one daughter younger than Phebe. Anne Scott, at the age of two, inherited a girl named Eve, who was about the same age. Anne Scott's twin brother, Randolph, inherited two-year-old Peter, the son of Myrtilla.[49]

This strategy differed for Thomas, who, at the age of fourteen was left the skilled adult male Sawney, who was already trained in the ways of servitude. Sawney's job was to now teach his new young master his role in their newly intimate relationship. Sawney attained the highest valuation of any slave in Peter Jefferson's inventory, £57 10s. Sawney may have performed as a personal attendant to Peter Jefferson and had both the knowledge and skill to help young Thomas navigate new waters as Shadwell's master. Perhaps one test for a young Virginia gentleman was sorting out his strategies for domination over men like Sawney, who were both older and probably wiser but not fortunate enough to have been born free, white, and wealthy in colonial Virginia.

For Sawney, who certainly knew young Thomas as a boy, the task was to develop new strategies for ever so subtly training this young man, who in some ways was probably his ward as well as his master. Sawney needed to help the young Jefferson learn to be a master. If Sawney was the servant who traveled with Peter on his duties as a magistrate or burgess, Sawney knew his way around the local landscape and more distant places such as Williamsburg. Part of Sawney's value was his knowledge of things like shops where his master's wig could be repaired or someone who could tailor a new coat for him. His role was to grease the wheels that made his master seem a master of all things. Sawney was also an intimate link between the boy and his deceased father and was likely a conduit of advice and stories that Thomas could gain from no other source. There is no record of when Sawney died, but his name does not appear on slave lists that Thomas began keeping in 1774. By 1764 Jupiter became the trusted servant of Thomas, one from whom he borrowed money and sent on distant errands: a servant, it seems, who could be as an extra arm. Perhaps this relationship was acknowledged in 1771, when Thomas planned a burial ground at Monticello and included a place in a family temple for "the grave of a favorite and faithful servant."[50]

Peter's bequests also clearly favored certain families of slaves. Children often followed in their parents' professions, and slaves who earned rewards for being smart and obedient trained their children to be likewise. A slave born to parents who lived on the home quarter and had special skills was more likely than children of field hands to grow up to learn a skill and occupy a privileged place in the plantation community. Peter's assignments drew from three slave families: those of Sall the Elder, Cachina, and Myrtilla. It is entirely possible that these women were siblings or otherwise related, but there could be other reasons.

At Monticello, the Hemings family's light skin and blood ties to the Jeffersons ensured their privileged treatment as slaves with skills and household duties. The status of Sall's family echoes the place that the Hemingses held at Monticello; the Jeffersons went out of their way to acknowledge a single family in the most trusted and personal roles held by slaves on both plantations. The Jeffersons or their appraisers used the word "mulatto" to describe only three enslaved workers at Shadwell, and none were in Sall's known family. Two were men whom Peter Jefferson inherited from his father, Sawney and Sandy, both of whom had skills and privileges. Were these men Jeffersons also? Sawney was about the same age as Peter, and his position as Peter's servant suggests a close relationship built on trust and lifelong unspoken forms of communication. Sandy's discontent may suggest that he expected some similar arrangement. Sandy's birth year around 1735 coincides with the years that Peter Jefferson was carving out his landholdings and before he married. The other mulatto was the girl Rachel, who was born at Shadwell about 1750, indicating that a white man or man of mixed blood there or at Tuckahoe plantation was her father. Peter bequeathed Rachel to his daughter Martha, ensuring Rachel's career as house staff, perhaps because she was family or perhaps because she was light skinned and therefore seen as having special value. Shadwell had no noted families of mulattos, but interracial sex was certainly part of the landscape and affected household management.[51]

Jane's attention to slave families followed Peter's lead when she claimed her sixth portion of Peter's slaves in January 1760. She chose eleven individuals, including older slaves and one who had been born very recently (see appendix, table 5). Like the slaves whom Peter named in his bequests, all but two of Jane's choices lived at the home quarter and likely had domestic or craft skills and otherwise had close contact with the Jeffersons. Jane's list emphasized family relations; the eleven slaves represented only four or five families, possibly fewer if there were sibling relationships among parents. Jane's claim also included the loan to her of three slaves "to allow the Children were not divided." She specified "Myrtilla aged abt. 25 years Valued at £50 Phil 19 year old £45 Jupiter 16 year old £45," as slaves who needed to stay at Shadwell because their families were there.[52] The Jeffersons encouraged slave families and valued the guidance a slave parent gave to his or her own children. The Jeffersons also sought to pass on to their own children certain sets of skills and certain temperaments in their bondspeople. Clearly, Sall's family carried the traits that slave owners desired.

The enslaved workers chosen by name by Peter and Jane Jefferson to give to their children all had something in common in that they lived on the home quarter and they had experience as slaves very different from field hands at Shadwell and from most slaves in the Piedmont. Their position gave them a certain rank within the Shadwell community and probably across the region where they lived, among both black and white neighbors. They were from a few select families, whose progeny no doubt continued to hold status positions within their social circles, wherever they were. The status that Peter and Jane bestowed on certain of their slaves—even on two-year-olds—set those slaves on a trajectory that would ultimately send them to work in big houses on other plantations along the James River corridor, distant from home and kin. The importance of this to Jane and Peter Jefferson is reflected in the fact that the value of the nine slaves named in the original bequest was fully 11 percent of Peter's entire estate.[53]

New goods and new social rituals meant that not only wealthy, white practitioners but also their slaves needed education and training in the service and care these objects demanded. The increased specialization of wares, furnishings, and rooms required an increased specialization in the skills of enslaved workers. The Jeffersons' ability to entertain is best illustrated by the seating for twenty people in the dining room, including the pair of armchairs that suggests Jane and Peter presided at the table as host and hostess. In order to be used correctly—that is, show off the social prowess of their owners—the *table seating* required the presence of well-trained domestic servants and the *table setting* required skills of those same servants and of cooks to produce the dinner that showed off the serving wares. The style of dining and household management chosen by the Jeffersons meant that they needed to invest in workers whose roles were solely to support their lifestyle.

The Shadwell slaves who worked in the Jeffersons' house experienced life differently from the other plantation slaves. Even at the age of two, the slave children who grew up alongside the Jefferson children were acknowledged differently in the plantation ledgers. Their future was part of their material landscape: their clothing and living arrangements advertised their roles and their future relationships, as well as the sets of behaviors they and their child masters had to learn.

The increased material goods of the consumer revolution required investments that reverberated through the plantation. New standards for politeness required that people who wanted to use crisp white table linens, for instance, designate a slave or two who could be free of field or animal dirt when they worked with them (and maybe even add cleanly finished laundry rooms to plantation work spaces). The slaves who washed porcelain plates or silver forks under the eye of the plantation mistress needed fine motor skills and knowledge about these materials to perform their jobs. Hands calloused by hoes and stripping tobacco were not suited for drying delicate tea wares. Although specialized housework did not preclude slaves from also doing field work, it made it highly impractical for them to be involved in both domestic and field work on any regular basis. If cooks needed to produce multicourse meals that would show off the range of European cooking equipment and dining wares that the planters owned, the cook needed the facilities, the skills, and the time to do the work.

Jane and Peter Jefferson's investments in material goods, manners, and servants were not simply so they could enjoy a fashionable life at Shadwell. The slaves assigned to be personal servants to the Jefferson children had the role of carrying the culture of Shadwell to other plantations and teaching the next generations of slave children and their child masters how colonial Virginia worked. Although the enslaved people on the home quarter at Shadwell shared legal status and certain experiences with other people enslaved by the Jeffersons, the almost equal number of field workers who lived on the Jeffersons' outlying quarter farms had very different lives.

4 The Field Quarters: Slave Life and Field Work

Phillis

In 1757 Phillis, an enslaved black woman who was probably in her midforties, passed from one owner to another for at least the third time in her life. Peter Jefferson, her second owner, died in August that year, and Phillis may or may not have known that she was now part of an estate that would eventually be divided. Phillis was not one of the eight slaves chosen by Peter Jefferson in his will to attend one of his children. Instead she was among the anonymous slaves "not herein otherwise disposed of."[1] She may have known that, until the master's fourteen-year-old son turned twenty-one, she would likely continue to do the same work in the same place, with little change in her daily life. Or she may have heard that estates under the watch of executors who also had their own plantations to operate may not be the most predictable of places. As we shall see, she and two of her children had once been part of an estate whose fortunes were unsettled, and they would later hear of the death of a slave who was part of the Jeffersons' estate.

Peter Jefferson purchased Phillis and her two children, Dinah and Goliah, from his father's estate in 1732. Phillis, Dinah, and Goliah rejoined fellow slaves Farding and Pompey, whom Jefferson inherited when his father died the year before. It is likely that these slaves, and the rest of Peter Jefferson's growing slave community, lived on property at Fine Creek in Goochland County. A few years later, they all moved farther west on the north branch of the James River to land that Jefferson would name Shadwell, where Jefferson's own family would grow. Peter spread his sixty slaves across four sites at Shadwell and additional land he owned on the Fluvanna River, twenty miles to the south. By 1757 Phillis lived with nine other field hands, including her now-adult son: it is likely they lived on the south side of the Rivanna River on land that would later be named Monticello. Phillis and Goliah shared work, if not walls, with Tobey and Juno, and their children, Toby, Nanney, and Orange, and with Gill and Fany, whose first child would be born in 1760. Another adult woman Lucey also lived there. Phillis's daughter, Dinah, lived on another Shadwell quarter site with other field hands.

When Peter Jefferson died in 1757, the lives of this group probably were little changed, although they passed into the ownership of Jefferson's estate and its control by executors. Perhaps one of the strangest events of that year was when the estate appraisers came. The appraisers listed the slaves by name and perhaps announced the value assigned to each person standing there, exposed to this blunt face of chattel slavery and reminders of their mortality in the appraiser's judgment of their age and the promise of their physical ability. The appraisers called forth the three men, then the two boys, next the four women, and then the girl. Phillis and the senior Tobey shared either age or infirmity in 1757. Appraisers valued Phillis at £20 that year, when the average value of adult women on the plantation was £35. Tobey was valued at £25, when the average value of an adult male was almost £44. In fact, Tobey had the lowest valuation of any adult male on the plantation. His age is unknown, but he must have been at least twenty-eight, because he had been appraised as an adult in 1753 and had fathered two children by then.[2] His valuation in 1757 suggests that he may have been much older or suffered an injury that limited his ability to labor; it also highlights how many questions the documents leave us about these people.

These slaves continued to work year-round from their small quarter, which also housed the tools of their daily tasks: tending tobacco, clearing timber, feeding their group. Phillis and Tobey may have been the household members who stayed near the house to help with children, maintain tools, or otherwise support the more physical labors of their families who lived with them and nearby. Like all families, the slave families changed. Tobey, Juno, Toby Jr. and Nanney came to Shadwell in 1755 from nearby Orange County. Their son Orange was born at Shadwell between 1755 and 1757. Another daughter named Luna was born to them in 1758. Gill and Fany brought four children, Ned, Suckey, Frankey, and Gil Jr. into the household between 1760 and 1769. Changes from the outside came during the 1760s when Thomas Jefferson's claims to his patrimony shifted the center of his plantation from the north (Shadwell) side to the south (Monticello) side of the Rivanna River.

Peter Jefferson spread his slaves over five quarter sites. When sons Thomas and Randolph divided the slaves, roughly half of the slaves from each quarter went with each son. Goliah, Tobey and Juno and their son Toby, and Gill and Fany and their new family members lived on land now called Monticello. Nanney, Orange, and Lucey remained there or at Shadwell until their owners moved them to the lands that would become Randolph's on the Fluvanna River. Phillis had seen friends and kin come and go in her life. Sometime before 1757, Phillis saw her old companions from Fine Creek, Farding and Pompey, die or leave the plantation; they did not appear in Peter Jefferson's inventory. Phillis herself may have died before 1774. She was not in the lists kept by Thomas Jefferson when he came into ownership of his Shadwell legacy. If she lived, she changed hands again and became part of Randolph's Snowdon plantation in 1776. Phillis would have been in her midsixties by then, very old indeed by any eighteenth-century standards.[3]

Phillis experienced many changes in her world, sometimes because her owners moved her, sometimes because people moved around her. Although her work was primarily as an agricultural laborer, she probably also saw changes from the ubiquity of tobacco to the emergence of a grain economy. She may have spent her entire life on parts of plantations that were remote from public life, but she still may have recognized that when she moved to Shadwell it was remote from everything and that she was part of a growing and changing world. She would be part of the planter's efforts to remake the land to serve his commercial enterprise. Phillis helped turn forest into field, saw ancient Indian fields become farmland, watched as men built roads and wharfs to move crops. Documents and material evidence from Shadwell attest to some of the changes that slaves there experienced throughout their lives. The slaves' work may have been almost the same day in and day out for years. Then the Jeffersons divided land, reapportioned slaves, and remade long-standing patterns of work, social relationships, and even family. Historians, of necessity, have had to characterize broadly the general nature of field work on tobacco plantations or in other work, but the close view of the Shadwell slaves offers the opportunity to talk about how much planters' actions affected their slaves daily, yearly, and over the course of their lives.

The patterns of work and housing that the Jeffersons instituted illustrate a range of slave experiences. By 1757 the home quarter and some of the field quarters at Shadwell reflected the practices of established plantations such as were found in tidewater Virginia; in contrast, other field quarters suggested housing practices more often found in newly settled areas. In addition, the home quarter site of the plantation became a field quarter following the final dispersal of the Shadwell estate in the 1770s, and the use of the buildings and landscape changed to reflect later eighteenth-century ideas about keeping slaves.

Slave Lists: The Aggregate View

The Jeffersons' slaves occupied a world that we can explore through lists of slave names, the material organization of the plantation, and the labor systems of the plantation and surrounding county. The names of slaves who lived at Shadwell, from Peter Jefferson's probate inventory, a deed of Jane Jefferson to her son Thomas, the plantation account books, and Thomas Jefferson's later records, all contribute to "slave lists" for the plantation. Although the Jeffersons' papers give names to almost all of the Shadwell slaves, it is nearly impossible to get anything close to individual biographies for any of them. The slave population was a growing and changing thing, much like the plantation itself. Again, we begin with a moment in time, the "snapshot" of Shadwell made after Peter Jefferson's death in 1757, when his movable goods were inventoried and appraised for probate (see appendix, table 10). With the sixty slaves listed and the suggestion from material goods of slave housing and work, it becomes possible to move both backward and forward in time to describe these people's lives at Shadwell. Overall, the story is one of growth until the Jefferson children began to disperse their father's estate in the 1760s. What we know about the social organization of the Shadwell slave community comes to us primarily from documents left by these slaves' owners and does not tell us whether that organization was generated by the slaves or by those who owned them—or some of each.[4]

Peter Jefferson was the second-largest slaveholder in colonial Albemarle County. His probate inventory recorded 60 slaves on his plantation lands in 1757. The aggregate picture of these slaves—that is, their statistical measurement as a group—is a means to compare them to patterns of slaveholding across Albemarle County and elsewhere. Only 3 slaveholders in Albemarle County owned more than 50 slaves during the colonial period. Of 170 decedents whose estates were inventoried by the county, exactly half owned slaves. Of those 85 slave owners, 58 percent owned 5 or fewer individuals. The holdings of the 3 men with the most slaves, Robert Rose (62), Peter Jefferson (60), and Joshua Fry (51), comprised 22 percent of all slaves on Albemarle estates. In terms of estate value, these men represented the top 4 percent of slave owners, or the top 2 percent of all decedents during the colonial period. The 31 slaves on just the *home quarter* at Shadwell outnumbered the slaveholdings of 90 percent of Albemarle slave owners; only 5 slave owners held more than 27 people. Just the size of the Shadwell slave population afforded its members opportunities that few other slaves in the surrounding area had, such as friends and family—even extended family—close at hand. The size of the Jeffersons' slave population compares with tidewater plantations rather than those in the Piedmont, where estates with over 30 slaves were uncommon in the eighteenth century; most Piedmont slaves lived on plantations with 10 or fewer slaves.[5]

When he died, Peter Jefferson's investment in slaves equaled £1,805, a sum that of itself would make Peter merely the second instead of the wealthiest person in colonial Albemarle County. Measured in slaves alone, Peter was worth more than 99 percent of decedents in the county. Peter's slaves comprised 76 percent of the value of his estate, worth just over £2,399. The sixty slaves ranged in value from about £8 to £57 10s., with an average value of £30 1s. The male slave Sawney was the most valuable slave, at £57 10s, but female slaves totaled more than males. Females equaled a total of £944 10s., or 52 percent of the value of all slaves, and males equaled £858 10s., or 48 percent of the total value of slaves. In 1757 the Shadwell slaves ranged in age from newborn, in the case of five infants listed with their mothers, to at least one superannuated woman, Phillis. Age and a slave's value were closely associated (fig. 4.1). An individual's age, sex, and health affected his or her value, as seen by estate appraisers, who considered the skills a slave had, the labor he or she had the potential to perform, or the healthy children she might bear.[6]

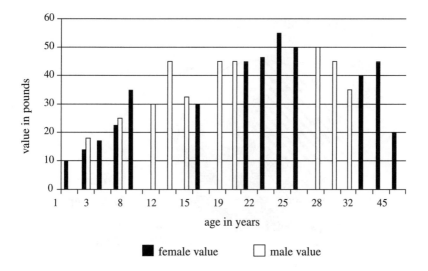

Figure 4.1. Plot of known ages versus known values for Shadwell slaves.

As a whole, the Jeffersons' slaves were physically healthy and had a reasonable chance, by eighteenth-century standards, to form families and have children who grew to adulthood. In 1757 one-fourth of the Shadwell slaves, or 15, were adult males, and just over 28 percent (17) were adult women (fig. 4.2). Nine boys made up the lowest percentage, 15 percent, while 19 girls made up the highest, at 31.5 percent. Overall, females outnumbered males 60 percent to 40 percent, offering males exceptionally good chances for creating a family within the Shadwell community. Among adults, this ratio was 1.13 women for each man, or 88 men per 100 women, a fairly close ratio, but still to the advantage of the men in terms of finding a partner. The ratio of adult women to men was closer to the parity found in tidewater and older counties than to the more newly established counties of the southside Piedmont. The 32 adults outnumbered the 28 children. In the abstract that meant that each child had 1.14 adults to learn from, while each adult woman could count 1.65 children. That figure is also closer to tidewater than Piedmont proportions. Based on the number of woman-child relationships that can be determined, families predominated at Shadwell. In general, the adult population of women was of childbearing age. Five women had infants listed with them in 1757. Most of the Shadwell slaves lived in households that had at least two generations within them; at least one had three generations.[7]

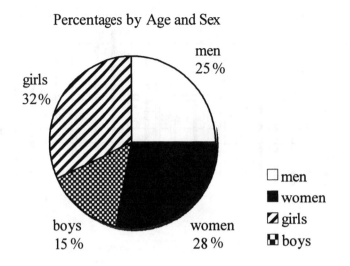

Percentages by Age and Sex

men
25%

girls
32%

boys
15%

women
28%

☐ men
■ women
▨ girls
⊞ boys

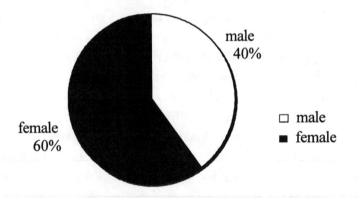

All Females: All Males

male
40%

female
60%

☐ male
■ female

Figure 4.2. Ratios of male to female slaves at Shadwell based on 1757 slave list.
AICWB, 2:45, 47.

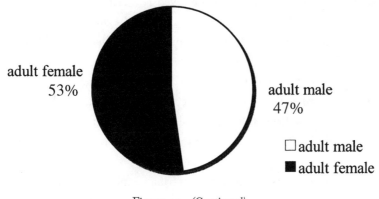

Figure 4.2. *(Continued)*

Fertility

Fertility patterns show that slaves at Shadwell had the benefits of a relatively healthy, stable environment. Twenty-eight children lived at Shadwell in 1757, and as many as fifteen of them were probably born in the 1750s. During the decade following Peter Jefferson's death, slave women at Shadwell gave birth to at least ten children. Women in labor—whether field or house slaves—received extra fortification in the form of spirits and sweeteners. Sometimes a local midwife attended births; sometimes other slaves must have aided. In 1758 midwives came four times and earned 10s. each visit. A midwife aided one birth in 1760, and in that year two slaves in labor were given a quart of brandy accompanied by a pound of sugar each. Another gave birth with the addition of only a pint of brandy, and others may have had molasses. The treatment of slave and free women in childbirth may have differed little, as the same midwives sometimes visited both populations.[8]

Known birth patterns of seven enslaved women born in the first half of the eighteenth century provide a measure of reproductive health on the plantation (see appendix, table 11). The seven women produced a total of forty-three children, an average of six births per woman. Two others had four children each; one woman had nine. The number of years each woman bore children ranged between nine and twenty-four, for an average of just over seventeen childbearing years. These women gave birth on average every 33.9 months, but the normalized average of five of the seven is 29.2 months. Except for Sall, they were all field hands, although Bellinda and Cate may have had other occupations during the Shadwell years because they lived on the home quarter site with skilled workers. Birth intervals among slaves reflect the patterns of a natural fertility population—that is, one in which lactation and conception were not artificially interrupted. Lactation, hard work, and diet all affected a woman's ability to bear children. The slave birth patterns contrast with those of Jane, whose fertility was affected by her means to have a wet nurse for her babies.[9]

Sall's role as wet nurse to the Jefferson babies explains her fertility. She bore children over twenty-four of her seventy-two years, but the intervals between pregnancies were long, on average 41 months, or 3.4 years. Some of her pregnancies coincide roughly with Jane's, and the impact of nursing Jefferson children in the intervals between her own children may have extended her amenorrhea (see appendix, table 12).[10] There is no similar explanation for the extended number of months between Nell's pregnancies, but the slave lists reveal only children who were alive when each census was taken. Nell's fertility may have been suppressed because of hard labor, extended nursing, or other natural causes—or she may have had children who did not survive infancy.

Although much of what can be said about the Jeffersons' slaves echoes patterns established in the tidewater, the quarter established on the Fluvanna River lands reflects practices of Piedmont slaveholding. At Snowdon, Jefferson moved fairly young slaves to new land to establish crops and families there. Peter purchased the bulk of the Fluvanna River lands in the 1750s and moved three men and three women there. The first child was born to this group in 1757, and others would produce children in coming years: they were at the early stages of their reproductive lives. Peter purchased some of these slaves not long before, and it is possible that some were African. The mid-eighteenth century saw the center of Virginia's African population shift from tidewater to west of the fall line, and with it dealers moved slave sales to the upper James River. In the 1750s, between a third and two-thirds of all slaves were African in some areas of the Piedmont. The names of the Snowdon group are more "outlandish" than other Shadwell slaves and may well reflect African origins. There is also a suggestion from the distribution of space and cooking implements that unrelated adults lived together at the Snowdon quarter, an arrangement that planters tended to favor during formative stages of settlement.[11]

An inventory list, however, represents a moment in time and does not tell the whole story; the slave population was always changing. Four slaves mentioned in Peter Jefferson's account book either died or, in one case, were sold before Peter's death; Farding and Pompey, the slaves Peter inherited, were two of these. A slave named Jupiter, who worked on the Shadwell mill in 1753, disappeared from the record. Presumably, Farding, Pompey, and Jupiter all died before 1757. In 1751 Peter sold a man named Jack to a Mr. Charles Clarke, and a man named Robin ran away from Snowdon in 1751. The slave Sandy was not listed in Peter's inventory, possibly because he had been leased out in 1757. In all, sixteen children newly appeared in the records between 1757 and 1770. Until the mid-1760s, when the Jefferson children began to claim their patrimony and move away, the biggest changes to slaves' lives were probably the effects of their own dynamic life cycles and families: people grew, married, had children, and died.[12]

Land and Labor: Organization of the Plantation

Peter Jefferson owned substantial quantities of land for planting. In his personal papers, Peter referred to his lands by location: "my lands on the Rivanna River" or "my lands on the Fluvanna River," occasionally by the name of an overseer, and in only one instance by a name for the land, although the Fry-Jefferson map refers to both "Shadwell" and "Snowdon" in 1751. Estate executor John Harvie used a mix of farm names and overseer names in his accounts to keep his records straight. He used Shadwell, Mountain Quarter, Snowdon, and North River, as well as names of overseers to keep his records for the Jefferson lands. Thomas Jefferson used another set of names for his land and fields, and it is not always possible to reconcile the names that the elder and the younger Jefferson and John Harvie assigned to the land. Planters divided their land into farms or quarters to facilitate organizing both crops and workers across large holdings. For Shadwell the records about the crops and about the workers tell us about the land divisions.[13]

The major divisions in the 1757 slave list represent three divisions of Peter Jefferson's plantations in terms of location, land, and labor organization. The three divisions were the home quarter at Shadwell, other Rivanna River land, and Snowdon (see appendix, table 13). The five subgroups within the three locations represent quarter sites that included the slaves' houses and domestic areas. Within the first two parts of the list, slaves appear four times in the order of men, then boys, women, and, last, girls, divisions that may represent households or another way of organizing domestic units. Quarter I was at Shadwell. Quarters II–IV were on other Rivanna River lands. The last group, Quarter V, listed the slaves who lived on Peter Jefferson's land on the Fluvanna River (Snowdon) and were inventoried separately from the body of Jefferson's estate. Other documentary material suggests that the quarter groups supported family ties as part of the organizational strategy for keeping slaves at Shadwell.[14]

The Jeffersons kept their slaves according to the codes of "enlightened" paternalism. By meeting society's minimum requirements for supplying their people with housing and clothes, the Jeffersons took on the appearance of "good" slave owners, whose attention to the physical care of their slaves partially obscured the fact that the owners were denying the bondspeople larger human rights. The Jeffersons invested in keeping their slaves, whether field or house labor, comfortable and presentable according to their station as defined by Virginia's slaveholding elite. In 1759 alone, the investment in "Clothing & Tools for the Negroes" totaled £62 8s. 8 3/4d., a sum greater than the net worth of 47 percent of all estates recorded in Albemarle County during the colonial period. This investment in capital inventory returned £188 4s. 3 3/4d., clear profit after payment to overseers and to overseers' wives for sewing, after purchasing fabric, blankets, and tools, after seeing the tobacco packed and shipped. The 1759 profit was greater than the value of 65 percent of all estates in colonial Albemarle.[15] Keeping this large slave force did not come cheaply, but it resulted in large profits for the planter.

Tobacco: Field Work

Tobacco dictated the material, seasonal, and social experiences of Virginia's planters and slaves. A single tobacco crop took more than a year from seed to shipping, with an intensive work schedule much of that time. Planters sowed seeds in nurseries during late December and early January. In late April through May the entire walking labor force—from small children to healthy elderly—worked to transplant seedlings to the fields. Children toted plants to the prepared hills, and adults carefully planted them. Both male and female slaves hoed weeds in summer, tending each field at least weekly. Skilled and experienced workers topped the plants before they produced seeds so that the plants would send all their nutrients to a dozen or so large leaves. Others removed the new leaves or suckers, and even children picked worms from the plants. Work crews cut and carted the crop in early fall and hung it to dry in the twenty-by-forty-foot-long tobacco houses near each field. Both women and men skilled at stripping leaves from stalks and removing stem fibers from the leaves worked long hours to prepare each leaf. By Christmas, workers "prized" or packed the crop into hogsheads to await shipment in the spring.[16] Field slaves at Shadwell also plowed, planted corn and grain crops, tended vegetable gardens, livestock, and orchard crops, and cleared new land as part of their regular tasks.

Much like the wares in the dining room in the Jeffersons' house, many of the agricultural tools at Shadwell showed a degree of specialization in their design and intended use that was rare in the eighteenth century. Peter's interest in experimenting with and exploring tools and methods of husbandry extended beyond farm implements to his bookshelf. The appraisers who recorded the farm tools at Shadwell noted particular details that suggest they were impressed by the range of special tools in their neighbor's outbuildings. Tobacco can be cultivated with a stick, but iron hoes are better. Different hoes—broad for weeding and narrow for hilling—made those jobs even more efficient, especially for a large-scale agricultural enterprise (fig. 4.3). The Jeffersons also had grubbing hoes for clearing land and foot hoes for weeding. Plows prepared fields for seed that was sown (as opposed to the nursery culture of tobacco). Peter had an English plow hoe (a type of plow) for work in heavier soils. The English plow hoe had a flat share that American planters reinvented as the shovel hoe (a trowel-shaped share replaced the flat share). He also had a Dutch (or hog) plow with an upright triangular share that could be used in lighter soils but may have had other uses in the heavier clay-based loam of the Piedmont. The plow hoe had applications in both grain and tobacco. It could cut furrows for small-grain seed, or it could be used for cross-marking a field before slaves hilled it for tobacco, thereby ensuring a regular—and efficient—use of the space. Thus African slaves used a European tool to aid their practice of an American Indian agricultural technique. The harrow hoe had an iron

Figure 4.3. Agricultural implements, from left: narrow ax, narrow spade, spade, grubbing hoe, broad hoe, narrow hoe. Photo by author, Collections courtesy The Colonial Williamsburg Foundation.

spike for breaking and combing the soil surface. A slave may have used the plows alone but probably plowed with draft animals. Peter's orderly and scientific management of his agricultural enterprise is reflected in the first few entries in his son's Garden Book, and Thomas Jefferson was and is certainly famous for his empirical approach to his plantation management.[17]

Overseers

Peter Jefferson and his estate after him employed a number of overseers who acted as intermediaries between the Jeffersons and their slaves. The 1763 list of "Negroes Cloths delivered out for Jefferson Estate" identified groups of slaves by their overseer or their location with such headings as "To Mrs. Jefferson," "To the Qur. at Snodon," and "To Matt: Moore." The slave Sawney was acknowledged by name, but otherwise an overseer represented the slaves to their owners—or to the estate's executor, John Harvie. In all, at least twelve overseers worked at Shadwell or Snowdon between 1747 and 1774. Some, such as

Martin Dawson, worked for the Jeffersons from as early as 1747 until at least 1760, providing continuity to both Dawson's life and those of the slaves who worked under him. In addition, other Dawsons also worked for the Jeffersons: Joseph from at least 1753 to 1761 and John, c. 1758–60. Peter Jefferson paid a carpenter "By his work on a Quarter 22 by 12 feet at Jos: Dawsons," evidence that Jefferson also thought of his land according to its overseers. The frequency of the Dawsons in the account books and the range of their activities suggest that they had a solid and productive role in the plantation. Martin Dawson supervised the Snowdon plantation. Joseph Dawson oversaw the plantations on the Rivanna River, with some exceptions. Fred Gillam oversaw the Shadwell tobacco crop from 1759 to 1761.[18]

The overseers ran specific tracts of land called "quarters" or "farms," but they also worked together at times. (For the probable distribution of slave and overseer labor during one year, see appendix, table 14). The North River land produced 40 percent of the estate's tobacco in 1759, using overseers and evidently slaves who normally lived and worked on other lands. This suggests that at least some slaves moved from property to property with some regularity during certain seasons. Planting tobacco seedlings in hills took many hands over days of intensive work, the plants demanded at least weekly attention during summer weeding, and long hours were required during the fall stripping. To produce the 1759 crop, Fred Gillam, Joseph Dawson, and William Gooch worked their usual quarter farms as well as the North River land.[19]

Other Hired Work

In addition to overseers, other hired workers lived at or visited Shadwell. John Moore worked for the Jeffersons from c. 1758 to 1770 and bore the title "steward" rather than overseer in both the executors' and Thomas Jefferson's records. At least some years Moore received a salary rather than a share of crops as payment. Moore engaged with the Jeffersons on levels other than simply as a hired hand. He contracted with Thomas in 1768 to level Monticello Mountain and served as an appraiser for the estates of Jane Jr. and Jane Sr. In addition to the family connections among the men who were overseers, some of their other family members worked for the Jeffersons. Matthew Moore's wife, Letitia, or "Letty," and William Gooch's wife, Lucy, sewed clothes for Jefferson slaves.[20] Tenant Peter Shepherd paid his rent with the money his wife, Eleanor, earned sewing clothes for Shadwell slaves.

As part of the plantation, Jefferson operated a toll mill at Shadwell, and a miller and his family lived there to run it and collect fees for grinding neighbors' grain. Various millers came, Robert Fry in 1757 and David Cook in 1758. The mill also brought craftsmen such as Francis Whilkill (also Whitehill), who did repair work on the mill, or Samuel Cobbs, who "work[ed] about the mill." George Dunkin and John Dunkin did carpentry work, including work on a tobacco house. Not all of the hired tradespeople were white. A "Negroe Carpenter" lent by Captain Charles Lewis worked at Shadwell for seventeen days in 1759. Jefferson slaves may have joined these hired workers as skilled hands or as labor. Slaves also may have made barrels for the mill—a number of coopering tools appear in Peter's inventory—but in some years barrels and casks were purchased or a cooper came to make barrels as needed.[21] Visiting workers offered the slaves an opportunity to hone their own skills or to learn new ones, as well as to make contacts outside the plantation.

Slave Life and Field Work

Details of the lives of field slaves come from a range of material, documentary, and social evidence. Although the documents imply that the slaves' domestic setting defined their social world, that may not have been the case in reality. Enslaved people had personal connections within and among their quarter sites and beyond the plantation. The incidence of related individuals within each quarter shows that the Jeffersons recognized their slaves' families, even though in most cases the documents reveal only the maternal line. Families in many cases determined how the Jeffersons managed their bondspeople and show in purchases, living and work arrangements, and distribution of slaves among Jefferson heirs. In some instances, slaves from different quarter areas formed families and had children, and then the children stayed with the mother, although as adults, some siblings lived on different sites. In some cases unrelated adults lived together because their families lived on other quarters.[22]

Both archaeological and documentary sources show that slaves belonging to wealthier masters generally fared better materially than other slaves or, indeed, most poorer white Virginians. Even at field quarters, slaves suffered from their owners' economic accidents and benefited to some degree from their success. Probate inventories offer only a skeletal image of what was in the slaves' environment, however. Generally when inventory appraisers visited slave houses, they listed only the movable goods that belonged to the planter, including tools, fireplace equipment, and possibly some furniture. Enslaved people owned things too, and these do not appear in probate inventories but sometimes emerge in the archaeological record or may be inferred from what is known about slaves' lives. All of the slaves had blankets and clothes given regularly as part of the Jeffersons' duty as slave owners: these appear in ration lists, not in inventories. Many slaves owned their own cooking tools, eating utensils, beds, chairs, or other furniture not part of the planter's regular distribution. They made things for themselves and purchased or traded for items to enhance their personal comfort or entertainment. Slaves had garden plots to grow produce and kept livestock such as chickens, which they used for their own food or for currency.[23]

The slaves who worked at Shadwell lived at a time when slaves' lives were changing as populations shifted from partially foreign to exclusively native-born in some parts of Virginia. In other parts, however, new slaves arrived with reinforcement of African language, naming patterns, religions, songs, stories, games, cookery, and craft traditions. Virginia-born slaves were more likely to speak English, have familiar (to the planter) English names, and have friends and relations nearby. Their living conditions changed because planters were changing their ideas about how to keep slaves properly, moving them from group to family-based houses. They saw tobacco culture giving way to grains and mixed crops, altering work patterns, tools, and commerce systems. And they experienced a time when their owners questioned government and ideas of freedom, and slaves received a call to steal away—some did. The Shadwell slaves retained a few vestiges of African traditions that reveal themselves in the material culture of the site, but they also used a variety of consumer goods that reflect the dominance of the British Empire in the Atlantic world. Indeed, the very presence of Africans in the Virginia Piedmont is an artifact of Atlantic trade networks.

The Jeffersons organized their slaves within quarters that roughly describe work details. For the purposes of this book, I have followed the organizational system implied by the Jefferson documents. Both documents and archaeology enable us to treat the home quarter residents as a distinct group within the whole. Although some workers on the home quarter performed field labor, unlike the outlying quarters, that was not the primary occupation of everyone there. Much less is known about the field quarters. Archaeologists excavated one site of an early quarter on present-day Monticello, but the locations of other field quarters remain unknown.[24] The physical organization of the slaves partly explains plantation work patterns. The quarter system acknowledged and perhaps encouraged the people there to form families within the slave community, but many of the social relationships transcended the boundaries of the physical and labor systems.

Field Quarters

Phillis, whom we met at the start of this chapter, lived in one of the field quarters along the Rivanna River. The field quarters were alike in some ways. The field slaves lived in small spaces they shared with their families and often with other unrelated people. The spaces where they slept and ate were also where they kept their tools. In every quarter, slaves had tools for working tobacco and for cooking. There was some difference between the other work they did at each quarter: some cleared timber, some plowed, others butchered animals.[25]

About half of Peter Jefferson's slaves—twenty-nine—lived in field quarters, in groups of five to ten people (fig. 4.4). The smallest of these groups, five, was most similar to the experience of enslaved people in colonial Albemarle: most slaves elsewhere in the county never lived among a quarter or even plantation population larger than five. There were at least two families of mothers and children in each quarter, sometimes with fathers present; sometimes fathers lived in other groups. There were families within each quarter group at Shadwell, as well as evidence that extended family was sometimes together. When Thomas and Randolph divided the field hands, some people from each quarter went with each brother; family was a greater determinant in dispersal than was the group identity of a work crew.

The smallest quarter group had two women and three girls, and represented two families (see appendix, table 15, Quarter II). Flora and her child Agey were together, and the other two girls, Moll and Ephey, were the daughters of either Flora or Sally, the other woman. The largest group had ten people, three men, two boys, four women, and one girl, in at least three family relationships, including one extended family (see appendix, table 15, Quarter III). Two other groups, one on the Rivanna lands and one on the Fluvanna lands,

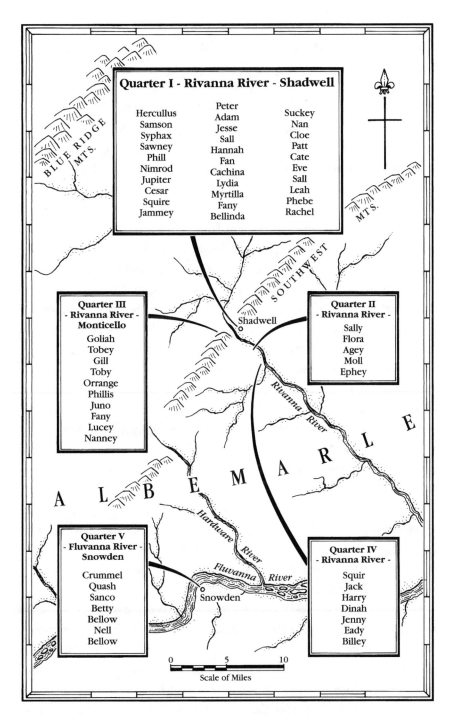

Quarter I - Rivanna River - Shadwell

Hercullus	Peter	Suckey
Samson	Adam	Nan
Syphax	Jesse	Cloe
Sawney	Sall	Patt
Phill	Hannah	Cate
Nimrod	Fan	Eve
Jupiter	Cachina	Sall
Cesar	Lydia	Leah
Squire	Myrtilla	Phebe
Jammey	Fany	Rachel
	Bellinda	

BLUE RIDGE MTS.

SOUTHWEST MTS.

Shadwell

Quarter III - Rivanna River - Monticello

Goliah
Tobey
Gill
Toby
Orrange
Phillis
Juno
Fany
Lucey
Nanney

Quarter II - Rivanna River -

Sally
Flora
Agey
Moll
Ephey

Rivanna River

A L B E M A R L E

Hardware River

Fluvanna River

Quarter V - Fluvanna River - Snowden

Crummel
Quash
Sanco
Betty
Bellow
Nell
Bellow

Snowden

Quarter IV - Rivanna River -

Squir
Jack
Harry
Dinah
Jenny
Eady
Billey

0   5   10
Scale of Miles

Figure 4.4. Map of Jefferson plantation and quarter sites.

had seven people each in 1757. The Rivanna group had two families from three men, two women, and two children, and also included people whose families lived in other quarters (see appendix, table 15, Quarter IV). Jack and Squire each fathered at least one child with Bellinda, who lived on the home quarter. The other adult, Harry, may have been the husband of Dinah or of Jenny, the women there. Girls Eady and Billsy belonged to one of these couples. Dinah was the sister of Goliah and daughter of Phillis, the older woman and her son listed who lived in the Monticello quarter (Quarter III). The Snowdon field quarter housed seven people, three men, three women, and one infant, a group that formed at least one family (see appendix, table 15, Quarter V).

The Jeffersons housed slaves near at least one domestic building that had built-in hearth equipment—pothooks—for cooking (see appendix, table 16), suggesting that one person out of the household cooked for the work group or that the group often cooked communally. Although there may have been other buildings on each site—even buildings with hearths that provided heat or the opportunity to cook with pots or pans set in the coals—the four pairs of pothooks may very well designate the only hearths and thus the only heated spaces among these four sites. By focusing the daily meal around a single hearth, the Jeffersons streamlined the work routine for field hands and eliminated the distractions of individuals preparing their own food. In spite of the evidence that the Jeffersons supported the family lives of their people, group meals denied people the satisfaction of feeding and providing for their families; the Jeffersons' system reinforced the work group and not the family unit. Most of the time, work crews ate single-pot meals that stewed most of the day over the fire. Slaves may well have owned their own cooking equipment and used their time off from field labor to cook for themselves and exercise family routines. The style of cooking done for themselves may have differed little from their workaday fare, as stewing in pots set in coals also reflected traditional African cooking methods.[26]

The locations of two field quarters remain unknown, but they were on one of the parcels of land along the Rivanna River, adjacent to Shadwell or Monticello. It is not known which of these sites the slaves from Quarters II or IV inhabited. One field site had a single building, which also housed tools for working tobacco—grubbing, weeding, and other hoes—and also falling axes and an ox yoke for clearing land between the demands of tobacco (see appendix, table 16,

Figure 4.5. Grindstone (about 9 inches diameter, 3/4 inch thick, with hole for square shaft at center). Grindstones were ubiquitous objects in the lives of field hands, whose maintenance of their metal tools was part of their almost daily work. This artifact was from the home quarter but illustrates part of slave life shared among the entire slave community. Courtesy Monticello/Thomas Jefferson Foundation, Inc.

Site A). A grindstone for maintaining tools and a spade for gardening suggest work that went on in or just around this small house. The spade may indicate that the slaves worked their own garden plots, or they may have had other plantation crops to tend. This house had a single pot and hooks for feeding the household. Another field quarter site may have had two houses or had a larger hearth for farm-related activities (see appendix, table 16, Site B). The group that lived there had grubbing hoes for tobacco work as well as tools for grain agriculture: a Dutch plow and two plow hoes. These slaves had a crosscut saw for work with lumber and a grindstone for tool maintenance (fig. 4.5). They also may have butchered, as indicated by stillyards (or steelyards) for weighing, "Beef Rope" (rope and pulley to hang a carcass?), and tight casks to hold liquids. Their household furniture included two pairs of pothooks, three pots, and two tin pans. If they rendered livestock, the pots and pans were part of plantation work and not only household fittings. There are no salting troughs listed as movable items in the inventory. This building or one at the plantation kitchen may have included a built-in trough for curing meats.[27]

Quarter III: Monticello

The second and largest field quarter was likely the land that would come to be called Monticello. Ten slaves lived there (see appendix, table 15, Quarter III, and table 16, Site C), overseen by Joseph Dawson. In 1753 a carpenter built "a Quarter 22 by 12 feet at Jos: Dawsons." This spare description fits the example of slave housing that contained two separate living spaces entered into from the outside, what we call a duplex (fig. 4.6). Each half, eleven by twelve feet, was about the size of a small house for many Virginians.[28] A central chimney provided heat to each side, although in this case only one side may have had a hearth. The single pair of pothooks as fireplace equipment indicates that a slave in one side of the house was thought of as the cook for the entire group. She had two pots, two tin pans, a frying pan, and a sifter to use in making their food. The other side of the house may have been warmed only by radiant heat from the rear wall of the chimney, or the second side may have had a hearth where occasional cooking was done right on the stones with unfixed equipment. This was the only field slave house in which the appraisers counted furniture, "2 old chairs," and ceramic dishes, "1 Dish & plate," items that would be considered amenities—that is, things beyond what is necessary—the only amenities in the quarter inventories.[29] But as in the home quarter, these slaves probably owned some pans and dishes of their own, which rounded out the basic tools they were provided.

The roughly even sex ratio within each quarter suggests that Jefferson slaves lived in family groups, although this may not fully describe their arrangement. Because slaves cooked communally for the larger group that occupied separate parts of one building, family groups may have shared space for sleeping. In 1757 at least three family relationships existed among the ten people in Quarter III: two couples, two parents with children, and three generations (see appendix, table 17). At least some people here shared quarters with other unrelated adults—the family unit and the household were not synonymous. Because the slave Phillis was elderly and Tobey Sr. was either elderly or infirm, the chairs provided by the Jeffersons enabled Phillis and Tobey to undertake handwork at the house, including cooking and maintaining tools. They probably watched the small children while parents worked. Nanney was about six, Toby Jr. about four, and Orange about two. When the appraisers came, Juno may have been pregnant with another daughter, Luna,

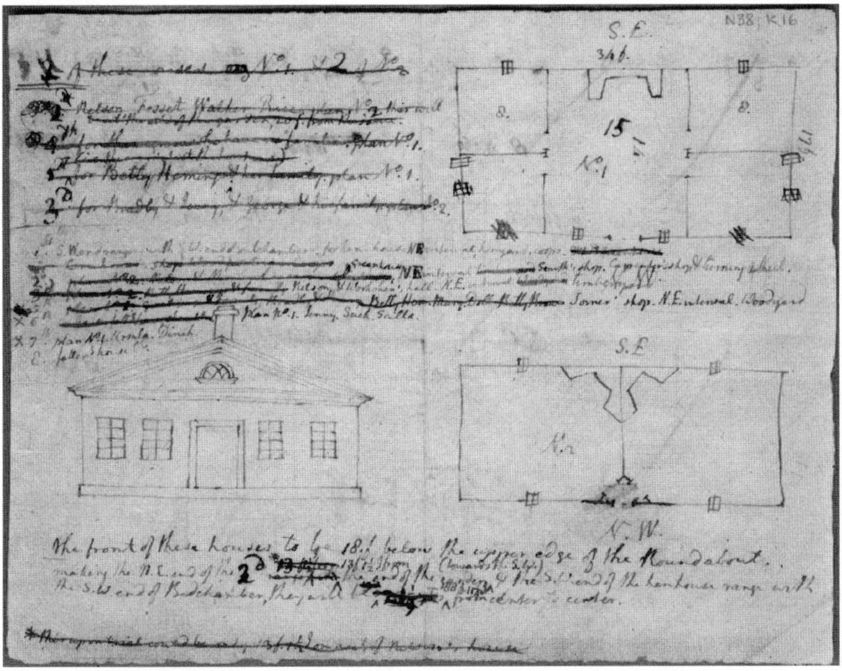

Figure 4.6. Thomas Jefferson's design for a duplex slave house at Monticello, c. 1778 (not built). Thomas's design shows a neat Neoclassical facade with a central doorway that gives way to two rooms, each heated by a corner fireplace in the single, central chimney.

Thomas noted that this plan was to serve two families. The illusion of private compartments is undone by the door that unceremoniously enters both spaces at once. Thomas's plan at 17 by 34 feet was larger than the quarter designated for Joseph Dawson's quarter at Shadwell, which was 22 by 12 feet (rooms were 289 and 139 square feet, outside dimension, respectively). Monticello: stone house (slave quarters), recto, September 1770, by Thomas Jefferson. N38; K16. Courtesy of the Massachusetts Historical Society.

who was born in 1758. Housemates Fany and Gill expanded the group with their children by 1760.

Like the slaves at the other field sites, those at the third quarter had a variety of hoes for tobacco culture. They had woodworking tools for clearing or rough carpentry, including narrow axes, iron wedges, a crosscut saw, and a handsaw. They had two grindstones for sharpening their cutting implements. Three rawhides may have been in production or related to tool care, or they may have been the product of hunting. These slaves kept a gun for pest control, hunting as one of their plantation jobs, or hunting for themselves as a way to supplement their rations. They made lead shot by their fireplace. The inventory did not include any harness fittings for draft animals, nor did it include any plows or harrows to indicate grain cultivation. The quarter was located just above a so-called Antient Field, a piece of land cleared earlier by Indians. They had land aplenty for planting.[30] When not tending tobacco, the slaves at the Monticello quarter harvested the forest for game, timber, and new fields.

The inventory does not list any spades for digging gardens, but the people here may very well have kept their own vegetable plots, perhaps with tools they made or owned themselves. Like people who lived across the river at Shadwell, they collected artifacts left behind by Native Americans. During their leisure or work time, the people on this quarter smoked tobacco using European-made, commercially sold pipes. They had other European ceramics for food preparation and storage, including plates and cups, forms not necessarily found in slave quarters and not required by people using African cooking methods, which relied mostly on bowl shapes. They used wine bottles for drinking or storage. They had small delft ointment pots and used either prepared medications mixed by an apothecary or reused the pots for their own salves (see fig. 3.6). Oyster shells may indicate "imported" foods here.[31] The archaeological record suggests that this field quarter had fairly direct access to goods from the home plantation or received supplies from the same sources; people used the same commercial wares on each site. The sparse rations listed in owner's accounts once again fail to describe the material record of slaves' lives.

The length of time the Quarter III slaves and Joseph Dawson worked together suggests the potential for stability during that period. Dawson worked for the Jeffersons over at least nine years from 1753 to 1761 and may have been part of a family that worked for the Jeffersons even longer. In 1759, Dawson and the six or seven adult workers there produced 11,111 pounds (eleven hogsheads) of tobacco on the thousand-acre Monticello tract. In addition, they combined forces with other Jefferson slaves and overseers from the Rivanna area to work the piece of land called North River, where they produced 29,353 pounds of the crop. It is not clear from the records whether the North River land was always tended in this manner. If that were an annual occurrence, these hands and others moved with some consistency between quarters to tend crops in both places. If these slaves worked more than one farm, their toils meant lots of travel and little leisure during those years.[32]

Quarter V: Snowdon—Problems of Distance

Because the Snowdon inventory was taken separately by Jefferson's associates in that part of the county, the slaves and the components of that plantation, the buildings, livestock, and tools, were grouped together, giving Snowdon the most specific documentary detail of any field quarter in the Jeffersons' holdings, although the site location remains unknown. Seven slaves—three men (Crummel, Sanco, and Quash), three women (Betty, Bellow, and Nell), and an infant (Bellow)—lived at Snowdon in 1757. At least one family formed among the six adults: Quash and Nell's baby Bellow had been born that year. Crummel came from Peter Randolph, purchased by Peter Jefferson in October 1750. He may have lived at Shadwell before moving to Jefferson's Fluvanna River land. At Snowdon the slaves lived in a single house where they shared a pair of pothooks and two pots and probably cooked and ate communally. Their house also sheltered their tools for tobacco—narrow hoes and broad hoes—and for grain—a plow, plowshares, and harrow hoes. The tool allotment matched the number of workers: six of each type of hoe for six adults, male and female counted together. The axes and wedges meant that slaves cleared land or chopped wood for fuel between crop work. They used the grindstone to keep their tools in working order. Additionally, "98 lbs old Iron" may indicate iron working at Snowdon, or else they stockpiled scrap to send to wherever else that work took place; the documents list no iron-working tools. Livestock at Snowdon included ninety-one hogs and twenty-two pigs, thirty-four head of cattle, and five horses. These slaves likely also had garden tools for their own use, cooking implements of their own, and clothing and bedding. At twenty miles' distance, the Snowdon slaves must have experienced the attentions and material culture of their wealthy owners far less than their colleagues at Monticello or Shadwell.[33]

In 1759 the plantation at Snowdon produced 18,076 pounds of tobacco, equal to 24 percent of the crop from all the Jefferson farms that year. Crummel, Quash, Sanco, Betty, Bellow, and Nell with overseer Martin Dawson picked, dried, and packed the crop into sixteen hogsheads that a visiting cooper made. In April 1760 Dawson arranged for the crop to be taken to Byrd's warehouse in Richmond. The hogsheads were both rolled and carried by water during their journey, which cost 16s. 6d. per hogshead, or £13 4s. total. Tobacco factor Mr. McCaul purchased fourteen of sixteen hogsheads from

Snowdon, and Dawson claimed the other two as his share of the crop, 2,257 pounds. Dawson's proceeds were £25 5d. In 1760 slaves at Snowdon also had a hand in producing corn, cider, and livestock sold from the plantation.[34]

Punishment

The only references to slave punishments were at Snowdon but undoubtedly reflect practice across the Jeffersons' holdings. The two incidents were representative of punishments used at the time and suggest that the Jeffersons treated and allowed their overseers to treat slaves according to what was commonly accepted among slaveholders. The use of corporal punishment at Snowdon may also be evidence of an immigrant population and overseers bent on training the newly enslaved. The Jeffersons or their employees used both whipping and collaring to control the people who worked under them. In 1751 a runaway named Robin "had on his Neck when he went away an Iron Collar." Robin may have been successful in his escape, since Peter Jefferson advertised as late as November for Robin, who had run away "May last," and the record is silent on any further mention of him. Jefferson described Robin as a Negro man, small, with crooked legs, about thirty years of age, who "speaks pretty good English." Robin took a gun when he ran. If slaves or free blacks with guns were commonplace around plantations, surely a slave in an iron collar carrying a gun would be an alarming sight; a slave being punished was not supposed to have access to weapons. Robin would need to get rid of the collar and use his English skills to work his way into obscurity. He may have had no particular training beyond agricultural work; none is mentioned in the advertisement. Jefferson noted that "Whoever brings him to me, shall be rewarded, according to Law."[35]

Distance from the home plantation had its problems and may have been part of the strategy employed by planters like the Jeffersons to break and control African people newly transported to rural Virginia. Sometime after 1764, when Thomas reached his majority, he began to redistribute the field slaves that he and Randolph were to divide according their father's will. Quash, Nell, Bellow, and Betty moved from Snowdon to Monticello. About twenty-one people moved from the Rivanna River lands to the Fluvanna River estate, land that Randolph would own when he turned twenty-one in 1776. For the most part, the brothers moved family groups, dividing the people from each of their father's quarters according to relationships the slaves had established.[36] Hannah and her daughter Fan were among ten slaves from the Shadwell home quarter who became Randolph's, along with eleven from other field quarters. Hannah may have left siblings at Shadwell, but she moved with her thirteen-year-old daughter and probably others in their family. She may have done field work or domestic work at Shadwell: she had lived in the somewhat privileged conditions of the home quarter there. The field quarter conditions and labor demands at Snowdon were no doubt an adjustment for her. During that decade the trusty Martin Dawson retired from the Jeffersons' employ, and a man named Isaac Bates succeeded him as overseer there. In 1770 Bates whipped Hannah to death. Thomas acted on his brother's behalf and brought suit against the cruel Bates.[37]

A number of circumstances contributed to the conditions in which Bates's violence occurred. Snowdon was on the periphery of the Jeffersons' attentions in 1770: it was distant physically, and its legal and administrative oversight was unsettled. Martin Dawson's long watch as overseer had ended. John Harvie's close watch as executor was over by 1765, and Harvie died in 1767. John Nicholas, another of Peter Jefferson's executors and who lived on the Fluvanna River near Snowdon, may have been watching over the estate there, and he may even have introduced Bates to the Jeffersons. Thomas, now a practicing lawyer, had not yet taken the reins as guardian of his younger siblings, but he had begun redistributing the slaves that he and Randolph inherited. When the house at Shadwell burned in February 1770, Thomas was focused on building his mountaintop home as his mother and siblings were rebuilding at Shadwell. So it was that the slaves were renegotiating social and work roles among themselves and with a new overseer when that overseer murdered Hannah. In November 1770, Jane gave Randolph a slave girl named Rachael, perhaps to make up for the economic loss Randolph suffered at the hand of Bates. Rachael, the daughter of Little Sall, may have been no older than two, perhaps too young to be frightened by the thought of taking the place of a murdered woman. Her mother, no doubt, was horrified. Whether Thomas's suit was successful—in dispensing justice or in quelling the fears of the slave families—remains unknown. Life at Snowdon must have fallen back into the usual rhythms of plantation life. By 1787 thirty-one adult slaves lived at Snowdon, a figure that suggests that patterns of birth and death had resumed normally.[38]

Beyond the Plantation

Life on a field quarter gives an overwhelming impression of everyday sameness, endless labor, and some degree of isolation, but many of the Jefferson slaves had their own connections beyond the plantation, places where kin, friends, or even immediate family lived (fig. 4.7). They knew plantation and town landscapes other than Shadwell. A few slaves came to Shadwell from other Virginia plantations, either through inheritance or purchase. Farding and Pompey came to Peter Jefferson by 1731. They lived on the Henrico or Goochland lands of Thomas Jefferson II until Peter acquired them, and maybe for some years following. If they lived as long as 1737, they surely moved to Shadwell with Peter Jefferson's household. Coworker and possible kinswoman Phillis and her children Dinah and Goliah joined them in 1732, when Peter purchased this family at his father's estate sale in Goochland County. Both Peter and Jane Jefferson's later attempts to keep slave families intact suggest that either Farding or Pompey may have been the husband of Phillis and father of Dinah and Goliah. The absence of Farding and Pompey from any of the 1750s documents suggests their deaths by then. Phillis, Dinah, and Goliah lived at Shadwell, and Goliah at least remained at Shadwell and Monticello during Thomas Jefferson's ownership. Dinah moved to Randolph's Buckingham County plantation, with other slaves from Shadwell. Phillis may have died by then.

Peter Jefferson purchased Tobey and Juno and their children Nanney and Toby Jr. at an Orange County estate sale in 1755. Previously, they lived among thirty-one slaves on the estate of Edward Spencer. When Tobey and Juno had their third child at Shadwell, they named him Orange, perhaps after the adult "Orange," with whom the parents lived at Spencer's. The young child became a link to the friend or family member whom the parents wanted to remember or even invoke in the next generation.[39]

Names connected people to others across time and space. A number of the Shadwell slaves may have been African. Seven slaves bore names that suggest African origin: Goliah, Gill, Crummel, Quash, Sanco, and two Bellows.[40] A number of classical and heroic names, the sort usually chosen by owners and not slaves, may indicate that another nine slaves were recent immigrants or children of recent immigrants. This list includes: Hercules, Samson, Nimrod, Syphax, Jupiter, Caesar, Cloe, Juno, and Phebe. Squire and Myrtilla might also fall into this historical category. Using classical names was not limited to

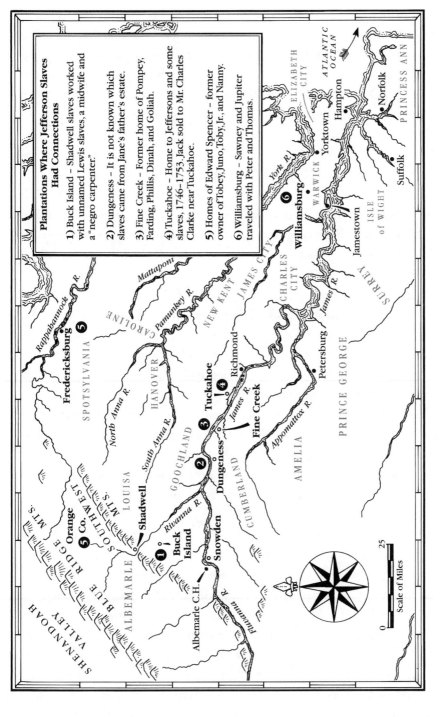

Plantations Where Jefferson Slaves Had Connections

1) Buck Island – Shadwell slaves worked with unnamed Lewis slaves, a midwife and a "negro carpenter."

2) Dungeness – It is not known which slaves came from Jane's father's estate.

3) Fine Creek – Former home of Pompey, Farding, Phillis, Dinah, and Goliah.

4) Tuckahoe – Home to Jeffersons and some slaves, 1746–1753. Jack sold to Mr. Charles Clarke near Tuckahoe.

5) Homes of Edward Spencer – former owner of Tobey, Juno, Toby, Jr., and Nanny.

6) Williamsburg – Sawney and Jupiter traveled with Peter and Thomas.

Figure 4.7. Map of plantations where Shadwell slaves had connections, before, during, or after their lives at Shadwell. See also fig. 7.1.

African immigrants, however. Bellinda and Squire had children born at Shadwell named Val and Minerva, but their other children had such English names as Suckey, Charlotte, and Sarah. Orange bore a name often assigned to Africans because of light skin color, but he was born in Virginia. Fourteen slaves had Old Testament names that their parents may have heard in church or meeting and chose for their children, although planters often chose some of these names for their slaves. Adam and Eve, for instance, were names sometimes given to the first slaves unloaded from a new cargo. Other Old Testament names at Shadwell included: Nimrod, Samson, Caesar, Jesse, Hannah, Lydia, Peter, Leah, Rachel, Dinah, Phillis, and Phil. Other names had English origins or were diminutives of familiar names, such as Suckey, Jammy, or Sall. The Shadwell slave community had no obvious felicity for naming their children after their white owners, the only coincidental name being Peter, a common name at that.[41]

Names were just one way that enslaved people reminded themselves of family and homes in other places. Some of the slaves who lived and worked at Shadwell experienced surprising mobility away from their Shadwell homes. Some had connections just as their masters did because they traveled around Virginia with the Jefferson family. Others had family and friends on plantations both near and far from Shadwell. Many shared in the visits of travelers or workers who spent time at the plantation. The slaves' material world reflects some of these cross-Virginia connections. Yet for some slaves, there is no evidence that they ever traveled beyond the plantation bounds, even remaining at "home" when the land passed from one generation to the next. Some stayed home and watched their friends and kin come and go.

A depiction of life on a field quarter usually conjures up images of physical remoteness from other groups of slaves and from planters, images of a rough-hewn life of near-subsistence. Much of the documentary record confirms that the Shadwell field quarters were simple physical settings oriented toward work. Within this setting, however, people were relatively healthy by eighteenth-century standards, both in terms of life expectancy and reproduction, despite the demands of their near-constant work. Although there is evidence that the Jeffersons respected and supported their slaves' own determination of family, the Jeffersons' ideas about plantation management also denied the people they held in bondage other aspects of family life, such as autonomy in housing and cookery. The precariousness of slave life was also measured at Shadwell, from seemingly stable working relationships with long-term overseers, to brutality and murder at the hands of an inexperienced hired man. Slaves created families, social structures, and community, but that could all be altered by their relationships to owners and overseers and the changing fortunes and demeanor of those individuals. The everyday, year-in and year-out agricultural work on the same site changed when the settlement of Peter Jefferson's estate divided long-standing households and neighborhoods. But, as we shall see, the connections that the Jeffersons' slaves had to one another and to land they worked continued to serve the Jeffersons long after no Jeffersons lived at Shadwell.

5 Plantation Business: Peter Jefferson at Home

When Peter Jefferson died, by his own request, his family buried him at Shadwell. Samuel Cobbs, a local carpenter, built a coffin for Jefferson, for which he was paid 10s. 6d. Cobbs worked on Jefferson's mill at Shadwell in previous years and also witnessed Jefferson's will when it was registered in the county will book. James Maury received £2 for speaking at Jefferson's funeral. The Reverend Maury was parson of Fredericksville Parish and became the tutor of young Thomas Jefferson (and, in 1763, the champion of "The Parson's Cause"). Captain Charles Lewis procured sugar for the funeral at the expense of £2 6s. Lewis was Jane and Peter's brother-in-law and had various family and business relationships with the Jeffersons. Someone in the household, probably the slave cook or housekeeper, followed Jane Jefferson's orders and used the sugar to produce between thirty-five and one hundred gallons of punch or other drink for guests who attended the funeral or stopped to pay their respects at Shadwell.[1] This event not only marked the end of Peter Jefferson's life: it also served to extend his largesse from beyond the grave to make yet one more statement about his family's ability its display its wealth and social prowess.

The funeral preparation was a microcosm of Peter Jefferson's life. Both involved the work of slaves, of skilled local craftsmen, of educated professionals, of high-ranking relatives and fellow officeholders, of his family, and of an unnamed populace who helped reinforce the intangible but coherent benefits and identity brought of status. Peter Jefferson's many business and personal alliances provide an interesting map of how one person's or family's associations connect him or her across a range of social and geographic settings. Just what was Peter Jefferson's business? He was a planter, and he was a surveyor. He served on the church vestry and had a family. He was a slave owner, mill owner, and public official. In short, he fulfilled varied roles that identified him publicly and professionally and ensured his own status and that of his family. His business, social, and family connections were almost one and the same.

Furthermore, Jefferson's involvements widely affected the community around him. His family's desire for fine consumer goods and clothes exposed others in the community to these things and provided work for neighbors who could sew, weave, or tailor. His agricultural investments supported the families of overseers, carpenters, wagoners, and canoemen, as well as one of the largest populations of slaves in colonial Albemarle County. His mill provided a service to small planters or farmers who could never have afforded the expense of such an enterprise, and so he affected the agricultural ecology and economy of the region. His ability to extend credit ensured that many of those around him were beholden to him. Jefferson invested in the new county seat, both in his service as a justice and as a landowner there who could lease a parcel for an ordinary to supply beds and drink and to profit from those who came to court. As a public official and perhaps as a friend, he hosted Native Americans traveling to Williamsburg for official business with the colonial government. These visits enlivened plantations and brought revenue to the owners of ordinaries and taverns along the way. His surveying and partnership in land companies not only changed the fortunes of his fellow investors but affected the lives of those living on and moving to land newly mapped and entered into the public consciousness. Peter Jefferson profited from his many and varied associations; that was the nature of his business.

The Gentry

Contemporaries remarked on the particular traits that identified Virginia's elite, and historians have pondered Virginia's colonial gentry since. Charles

Sydnor, among others, discussed the authority of the revolutionary generation as a product of the many and varied roles that young planters inherited from their powerful fathers. Eugene Genovese and others defined hegemonic power of paternalism, a system based on both absolute right and the ideals of Christian charity. Bertram Wyatt-Brown explored the culture of honor and how it defined gentility in the South. Timothy Breen examined the gentry as planters, whose common experience in tobacco production and debt laid the foundations of their culture. Rhys Isaac prompted consideration of the eighteenth-century idea of "liberality," the condition by which a gentleman was free from material worries, from the servitude of others, and from any question about his honor, as well as free to explore higher learning, all of which made him free to "undertake responsibilities in the community at large."[2] Peter Jefferson was one of the gentry, however we define them and measure their influence. Their power manifested itself in exchanges as mundane as buying shoes for slaves or selling corn, or as privileged as purchasing land with a bowl of punch. Peter Jefferson personified the connections through which gentry power spread and the social and material structure by which it was maintained. The social web only begins to suggest the endlessly overlapping realms of influence within colonial Virginia.

Peter Jefferson left no self-reflective letters or diary, no self-expression of his own determination, other than his last will and testament. The records he left are of business: of accounts charged and paid, of requests fulfilled, of shipments made. There are few entries that challenge the impression of successfully closing a transaction. We know this Jefferson from work *completed:* from maps he drew, from offices he served, from the family he fathered. The slaves on his plantation labored and reproduced. His wife bore a goodly number of children who survived childhood and grew up learning their lessons. Even though his children were all minors when he died, they successfully claimed their bequests and carried out their father's legacies. Jefferson's backwoods exploits fell into the category of brave adventure, not mishap, and became the foundation of family lore. The family tragedy of losing two infant sons was all too familiar in this era, and the fire that destroyed the family home occurred fourteen years after his death. All of this gives the impression of a very orderly world, and there is little evidence otherwise during Peter Jefferson's lifetime. About the only threat to this order came from being a slave owner, challenges to which show up at Shadwell in punitive acts such as forcing a slave to wear an iron collar and in acts of others who ran away. Contemporaries fretted about ungodly neighbors or the proximity of the French and their "Savage" allies, but Peter Jefferson did not leave such a record. His name is paired with other successful planters whose power came from their ability to deal equally in the realms of public service and private speculation. He pales only in comparison to his very famous son, the author of most of what we know about the father.[3]

Power

Peter Jefferson was charged with both extensive power and responsibility, and there is no evidence that he squandered either. Jefferson seemed to take these charges seriously, or at least there is little to contradict the record of his attention to both his privilege and his role in preserving it. Surely Peter Jefferson's power was to the detriment of many lives, including those of slaves owned by him and others and those of many Native Americans whose landscape forever changed after it was mapped and claimed by Jefferson and his colleagues. His role in the misfortunes of these two groups in particular is implicit in his place in this society whose structure defended the legal and property rights of Anglo-Virginians.[4] But Peter Jefferson also held and commanded power that he did not wield in any negative way that is evident from the existing documents. Rhys Isaac defined power as "the capability of determining the actions, even the destinies, of fellow members of society and is most generally institutionalized in the control of valued resources and the distribution of the products of labor."[5] The effect of a wealthy planter on the local economy had many implications for those of lesser means who lived nearby. Perhaps influence is a more subtle term for power in this sense. That Peter Jefferson's influence in early Albemarle County was broad is unarguable. That his power spread beyond local bounds is clear.

Peter Jefferson's power was manifest on many scales. Some of his power lay in his command of land and labor, capital resources that gave him direct say over people he owned, people he hired, and people affected by what he did with his real property. His wherewithal created markets were there had been none, demanded craftspeople where there had been wilderness, and required the participation of many in his neighborhood. More than just deference to a wealthy landowner, locals depended on Jefferson's success because it was part of their own economic landscape. Some of his power came from the associations he had with others like him, wealthy planters, slaveowners, and family members who enjoyed the benefits of each other's investments. It is hard to measure the social capital of Peter and his family and their many peers, but it is not hard to see the influence they had.

Economics

Peter Jefferson owned substantial quantities of land for planting, but he also invested in land that had a potential return for timber, copper, limestone, access to water power, resale to settlers, or even rent. He was a land speculator as much as he was a planter, and although the prominent land investments stand out, he had smaller, local investments with sizable returns.

Jefferson acted as landlord and collected rent for various uses of his property. This regularly included the Shadwell mill and also "the houses opposite to Albemarle Court House with 4 Acres of Land." Richard Murray leased and operated an ordinary near the county courthouse and collected tolls at the ferry landing during the late 1750s and early 1760s. He paid Jefferson £4 per year. Jefferson received rental income and Murray received profits from the sale of food, drink, and ferriage. This investment in making a new county illustrates Peter's ability to capitalize on his public role for personal gain; he helped form the local government in more ways than just deciding the law. The land he owned at the new county seat housed necessary functions of a courthouse town. Buildings on Jefferson's land offered people who traveled to court—including justices—a place to stay, as well as the conveniences of food, not to mention alcohol, a ubiquitous part of court day in colonial Virginia. The well-heeled, like Jefferson, built the infrastructure on which the new county would grow.[6]

Peter Jefferson's accounts reveal some of the smaller economic relationships between the plantation and the surrounding community. Women working in textile trades provided one source of supplies for Shadwell. They were paid in cash, exchange of goods, or credit. Eleanor Welsh knitted stockings for the Jefferson children, for which she received £1 1s. 3d. in 1762 and 15s. 9 d. in 1763. Another time an unnamed person was paid "1 pr. plaid hose . . . for making 3 shirts." Peter and Eleanor Shepherd rented land from Peter Jefferson, and although Jefferson recorded the account as Peter Shepherd's, it was Eleanor's work that paid the rent (see appendix, table 18).[7]

A Provider of Services

Peter Jefferson's mill at Shadwell illustrates the influence that he had locally as a purchaser of labor and services and as a provider of services. In many of these transactions, however, it is not the exchange of service—the milling—that stands out but the fact that the planter had available cash or could extend credit for goods bought or work performed. Credit, however, was a double-edged sword. Peter Jefferson made available to people things that they needed, such as grain from the mill or their poll taxes paid. But this meant also that people were indebted to the planter, and it appears that some never escaped the debtor side of Jefferson's ledger.

Wealthy planters in colonial Albemarle and elsewhere erected mills on their waterways. Mills provided income for the planters and a service to their neighbors, as well as jobs for slaves or hired labor as millers, carpenters, coopers, and those who transported the products. Neighbors could bring their grain crops to be ground for a price or a percentage of the grain, they could purchase storage for their grain from the coopers who worked alongside the mill, and they could avail themselves of the planter's wharf, water frontage, or access to road transportation. Private investment by planters in mills, wharves, and roads provided infrastructure that contributed to the public welfare. The credit side of Jefferson's ledger reveals one side of the story. The work on Jefferson's mill in 1753 earned carpenter John Biswell £5 5s. for forty-two days' work there and Jupiter and Samson, Jefferson's slaves who worked with Biswell, £1 3s. apiece for each of their twenty days' work there. Upkeep of the mill required hiring other skilled craftsmen. Two other carpenters, Francis Whilkill and Samuel Cobbs (who made Jefferson's coffin) both worked on the mill in 1756 and again later. Whether they worked together is unclear. Whilkill received £5 6s. for "26 1/2 day work on the Mill @ 4/." He returned in 1758 for "work repairing the mill," for which he received £3 11s. 3d. Jefferson paid Cobbs £10 4s. 4d. for unspecified work on the mill in 1756 and paid his estate 15s. for "Sund: Jobbs abt the Mill" in 1758.[8]

Robert Fry became the miller in 1756 at a salary of £5 per year. No doubt Fry owned a few tools of his own, but he lived in a house provided by Jefferson for the miller and his family and worked with Jefferson's equipment. Jefferson's investment in mill-related tools included four mill pecks and half-bushel, half-peck, and quarter-peck measures, valued at 7s. 9d. total. A pair of large marking irons, three hogsheads, five barrels, and four new bags (£2 8s. 6d. total) stood at the ready at the mill when the inventory was taken in 1757. Jefferson owned various tools that slaves or hired coopers used to make barrels, including narrow axes, a claw hammer, a broadax, and wedges. Slaves may have lived near the mill during times of work there. Shadwell housed three pairs of cart wheels (two of them old), six pairs of iron traces, eleven pairs of hames and collars, and cart boxes for transporting (total value £8 18s. 11d.), although much of this was likely used within the plantation only. At the mill also were three old spades, one broad hoe, and one grubbing hoe that may have been for the miller's family's own use for their garden. The inventory also listed thirteen worsted cotton petticoats, valued at £4 17s. 6d., on hand at the mill, listed with the new bags.[9] These may have been part of a new shipment to Jefferson's store kept elsewhere, or perhaps they were on hand to sell to farmers, who could come to Shadwell, mill their grain, and pick up something for their wives and daughters at home, all the while leaving yet more in Jefferson's coffers.

Jefferson's mill was a profitable venture, and it served Shadwell's own needs as well. In 1758 the mill made £36 5s. 5d., after subtracting £4 17s. 6d., the cost of feeding corn to hogs at Shadwell. The mill's products served as a kind of currency for the Jeffersons. The Jeffersons settled their accounts with tailors John Bell and George Twynman in both cash and grain. Benjamin Sneed, who schooled several of the Jefferson children, received grain from the mill, as did Manus Burger, a smith, and Hierom Gaines, who took up a stray horse for the estate. Even people with titles traded in corn. Captain John Grilles returned "To Cash Lent You to be paid in Corn @ 8/pBarrel." Although Jefferson usually entered the cash value of goods and services in his account books, very often the balance indicates that few actual pounds, shillings, or pence changed hands. Like elsewhere in the colonial world, any country's silver coin also had value, such as the 1723 Spanish real, cut to a one-quarter wedge, that emerged from excavation of the yard area on the slope just south of the Jefferson house (fig. 5.1). In 1758 David Cook became the miller, to receive £6 wages, against which were charged 5s. for a pair of shoes, his provision of meat and salt at £3 10s., and his levy and poll tax for the year at 9s. If

Figure 5.1. Spanish two reales coin,
silver, 1723, cut into one-fourth (above);
brass weight for pocket coin scale
(half-inch square) (below). Courtesy
Monticello/Thomas Jefferson
Foundation, Inc.

Cook did not use up the rest of his credit, he had a balance in his favor of £1 16s. at the end of the year.[10]

Credit and Patronage

John Biswell's relationship with Jefferson illustrates how Jefferson's influence was greater than simply being able to hire labor. In 1743 Biswell came to Saint James Parish (Goochland County) as an orphan. The court bound him to Thomas McDaniel, a carpenter, for three years to learn his trade. Jefferson paid both Biswell and McDaniel for work on William Randolph's Hall

Creek plantation while Jefferson was guardian of Randolph's estate. McDaniel performed unspecified carpentry work in 1746, and Biswell built a corn house in 1749. Biswell and McDaniel, like their employer, lived in Albemarle County following its division from Goochland in 1744. McDaniel did carpentry work there for Jefferson and transported tobacco for him. Biswell had an ongoing financial relationship with Jefferson.[11]

Whether Biswell needed money or Peter wanted to "sponsor" him and his trade, he was financially beholden to Jefferson. In his account book, Jefferson recorded Biswell's debts to him beginning in August 1752 and ending in November 1755. In a 1753 entry Jefferson recorded all of the money he owed Biswell for work. Jefferson's accounts with the carpenter Biswell reveal a range of transactions over four years. Some was cash value for services rendered: in all, Jefferson owed Biswell £49 7s. 5d. for a long list of work that included such things as "Hewing sills for Dwelling House £1," building tobacco houses, "getting and nailing on 400 sap shingles," "moving the stable," and providing shoe thread. In 1753 Jefferson recorded that Biswell owed him "9 Bushels of wheat (Borrow[e]d)," which Biswell returned as "9 ½ bushels of wheat . . . (borrowed)" in 1755. Biswell's debts to Jefferson, however, were greater: Biswell owed Jefferson £28 1s. 9d. more than his work, and Biswell's balance remained listed as "Acco[un]t to Settle" on a summary page of the account book. The debts included "To 6 ½ Bushels flower from the Mill" at 10s. in 1755; 4s. cash lent in 1752; whipsaw files; and two hogs. They also recorded that Jefferson paid accounts that Biswell had with other men. In a few entries Biswell owed Jefferson for a third party's patent fee or surveying fee, suggesting that Biswell occasionally acted as Jefferson's agent in collecting fees or carrying out surveyor's jobs. In August 1754 Jefferson paid Biswell to go to Winchester on some business that Jefferson had as executor of Joshua Fry's estate. Jefferson charged Fry's estate £2 12s. 6d. for Biswell's travels.[12]

Peter Jefferson's ability to extend credit can be interpreted in a number of ways. Jefferson had the wherewithal to offer cash or goods and perhaps take a loss if loans were not repaid. To Biswell's advantage, Jefferson's patronage may have offered him the opportunity to perform work that he might have been unable to get on his own. This may have been a stepping-stone for him to other jobs and enhanced skill as a craftsman. On the other hand, Biswell may have been "kept" by Jefferson, who could, because of Biswell's indebtedness to him, require him to do work that he did not want to do. The types of accounts suggest that Jefferson assigned Biswell to handle money and important errands, so the indebtedness did not breed mistrust. Biswell later became a landowner in Albemarle County. Whether Jefferson provided opportunity or used his wealth to control those around him is a matter of interpretation. A debt and credit relationship could be a tool or a measure of servitude.[13]

Jefferson's patronage went also to Francis West, a joiner of some skill. Jefferson engaged West for work at Tuckahoe and at Shadwell. The relationship began in January 1749/50 when Jefferson acknowledged a "Note of Hand" from West for £3 6s. 6d. On cashing this note for him or giving him this credit, the two men entered into a series of exchanges, according to their respective areas of expertise. Jefferson sold West fifty acres of land for £9 3s. 8d. and delivered the "Plot & Certificate" to him in September. Jefferson also sold West 632 pounds of pork for £4 5s. In return West made for Jefferson a substantial list of furniture worth £13 11s. 6d. Still, West owed Jefferson £3 11s. 8d. when their balances were figured. Jefferson also paid West to do some work for Randolph's Tuckahoe estate, work that included mending three tables (7s. 6d.) and for getting two shoe knives, for which he was paid 1s. 3d. West moved on and appears again in what had been southwestern Albemarle County doing both joinery and carpentry work for Nicholas Cabell at his plantation, Liberty Hall. West's work for Cabell included mending furniture, installing lath, flooring, roofing, dormers, and interior trim, fixing doors and locks, and getting a loom and warping box. The appraised value of West's work indicates its quality, and his range of abilities shows he was skilled in various media and flexible enough to work at different jobs. His family lived with him while he worked for Cabell, and perhaps he lived on the land purchased from Jefferson in 1750.[14] There is no telling what West's fortunes would have been had Peter Jefferson not hired him. The opportunity for showing his craft and the connections that Jefferson provided suggest that West was able to build on his credit and capitalize on his relationship with the planter. As a joiner, West's finer skills may have brought him more autonomy than Biswell had.

The Planter and the Local Economy

The hiring power of people like Jefferson may have brought people like West to remote areas. Joiners, tailors, dance masters, and music teachers needed income from other sources or a critical mass of patrons who could support their art. Many of these practitioners were itinerant, but still they needed clients. The material and social worlds of Shadwell support the argument for a socioeconomic rather than a diffusion idea about the spread of culture; that is, the money of rich planters caused culture to spread—people did not have to live near a metropolis to be involved in trade in fashionable goods and services. The Jeffersons provided access to goods and services that others around them would not otherwise have had. They exposed their neighbors to manners—both through material goods and through those they hired. They also provided work to other people, such as overseers and seamstresses, thereby helping create an economy for the local middling sort. Lois Carr and Lorena Walsh observe that diversification in agriculture encouraged home industries that were largely the domain of women.[15] At Shadwell this was not quite the case: Jane Jefferson, her slaves, and the family did not regularly produce slave clothing. The household industry that grew was for other women—wives of overseers and smaller planters—whose husbands worked for Peter Jefferson. The household craft of local women supported and was supported by Shadwell's prosperity.

The Jeffersons contributed to the local infrastructure and no doubt helped sustain the inland ports that grew along Chesapeake tributaries during the middle of the century. The Jeffersons' tobacco traveled by water and land to inland ports before heading across the Atlantic. Familiar watermen and carters transported the weed from plantation to port (fig. 5.2; see also appendix, table 14). The crop and the overseer represented Peter Jefferson to the agents at the inspection warehouses. The crop collected there represented Virginia to the colony's tobacco patrons overseas. Peter may well have accompanied his agents to the warehouses at various times, but his credit on the inspectors' books was what mattered. Tobacco connected the Jeffersons down the James River to the warehouses at the falls: Byrd's warehouse at Westham, Shocoes at Richmond. Tobacco also connected them to associates along the South Anna, Pamunkey, and York River corridors. Business with Crutchfield's, Page's, and Meriwether's warehouses on those rivers meant that families along this route would recognize the Jeffersons' reputation. Credit at multiple warehouses also meant that the Jeffersons could respond to different markets for their crop and choose which inspectors and rates they preferred in a given season.[16]

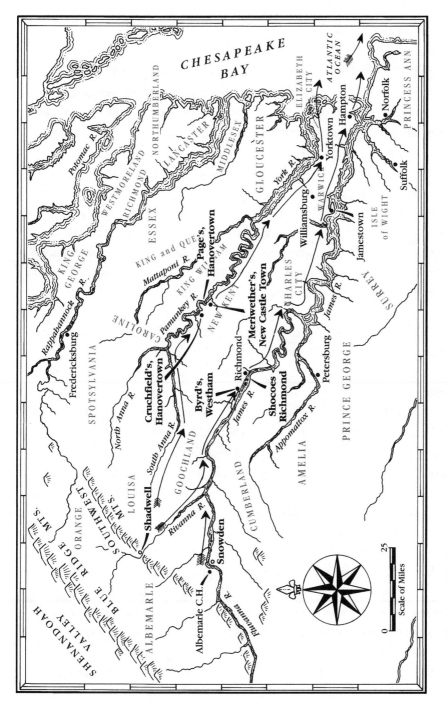

Figure 5.2. Jefferson's tobacco crop moved through different warehouses along the James and Pamunkey/York Rivers on its way to Atlantic shipping lanes.

Associations: Friends, Family, and Peers

The Jeffersons had a variety of economic relationships with people who performed skilled and unskilled labor. Beyond that, the social codes of Virginia's gentry required that Peter Jefferson and his peers respond to certain legal—and financial—responsibilities to each other.[17] Some of the business in which Peter Jefferson and his associates involved themselves was business—that is, commercial enterprise. But other contracts reveal obligations to family and friends that included such roles as executor of estates, guardian of minor children, and guiding each other's estates through appraisal for probate court. One of the ways the Jeffersons, their family, and their friends maintained their power was through public obligations that defined and preserved their estates and their families' positions in the community. These personal public obligations generated documents such as wills and account books that reveal a wealth of details about property and about the social and legal networks that connected family and friend.

The recording of wills and deeds was a legal function of county governments. Many people in colonial Virginia wrote wills to control how their property would be dispersed following their death. But many people also used their wills to designate who would maintain their property and manage their estates for minor children. The county court could designate neighbors and peers to these roles if someone died intestate, but for those in positions of power, protection of property preserved their families' authority from generation to generation. At the simplest level, a person writing a will designated as his or her executor a trusted family member or friend whose job it was to carry out the terms of the will. But often, as in the case of Peter Jefferson's will, executorship combined the ongoing guardianship of an estate with guardianship of minor children. In the event of a challenge to the will or a charge of debt against an estate, the executor was responsible for proving to the county court that the terms of the will were carried out. An executor could also be held responsible for debts of the estate. Thus, the executor often kept an account book for the guarded estate, and sometimes the account book became part of the court records.

Peter Jefferson wrote his will and signed it July 13, 1757, a little more than a month before he died. In his will he assembled a legal team of five high-powered men to serve as "Execrs. of this my last will & Testament & Guardian to all my Children." Three other men, not necessarily peers, witnessed Jefferson's signing of the will. At the October court, following Jefferson's death, one of the executors presented the will to the court, where the witnesses swore to its authenticity. Then, at the November court, the three executors who lived locally "made Oath According to Law[.] Certificate was granted them for Obtaining a Probat thereof in due Form giving security." They then hired the men who appraised the estate and made an inventory of Peter's movable goods.[18]

The witnesses to all these proceedings were acquaintances; John Bell, Edwin Hickman, and Samuel Cobbs, were all people who lived near Shadwell and had business there. Bell, a tailor, and Cobbs, the carpenter, were tradesmen. Hickman owned land adjacent to Shadwell and served as a county justice. The executors, however, were on an entirely different social scale and were people with a vested interest in the Jeffersons' ongoing welfare.

Executors

Thus did Peter Jefferson choose his legal team: "Finally I do appoint Constitu[t]e & Ordain The Honorable Peter Randolph Esq., Thomas Turpin the Elder, John Nicholas, Doctor Thomas Walker, & John Harvie Execrs. of this my last will & Testament & Guardian to all my Children." The demography of this small group is impressive. All were large land and slave owners. They were all burgesses, except Turpin, though he held office in three counties. John Nicholas could oversee Jefferson's interests from the local court, where he was clerk, to the highest reaches of colonial government, where his brother, Robert Carter Nicholas, was treasurer. Walker and Turpin were partners with Jefferson in the Loyal Land Company, and Nicholas and Harvie were investors with Jefferson in the speculative town of Beverley. Harvie also had a partnership with Jefferson for land "wherewith is immagined to be a Vein of Copper Oar." Randolph and Jefferson's accounts represent well over £1,000 of charges between the two, including the purchase by Jefferson of slaves from Randolph. Two of the executors were family: Randolph was Jane's first cousin, and Turpin was Jefferson's brother-in-law. Nicholas, Walker, and Harvie lived in Albemarle, but Randolph lived at Chatsworth in Henrico County, and although he surveyed for Albemarle, Turpin's primary residence was in Cumberland County. Four of the five executors—except Harvie—are represented on the Fry-Jefferson Map. In standing for Peter Jefferson following his death, any one of these men could command the attention and protection of Virginia's legal system, as well as secure Jefferson's heirs among their peers throughout Virginia.[19]

The executors promised to Peter Jefferson legal representation, guidance, and access to a network of relationships that paved the way for the young Jeffersons to take their places among the gentry. One of the first acts of the five executors was in November 1757, when they stood for the estate to complete a land transaction begun by Peter Jefferson. The local executors, Harvie, Nicholas, and Walker, involved themselves at different times in the day-to-day business of the Jeffersons' plantations and expenditures. Harvie and Walker lived near Shadwell, and Nicholas lived near Snowdon. The two who lived farther offered the young Jeffersons haven from home and, no doubt, lessons in the protocol of visiting.[20] Other help, in the form of visits and advising, shows how the older men guided the young.

The famous letter in which young Thomas Jefferson wrote to guardian John Harvie asking to attend the College of William and Mary was written after a visit at the house of another guardian, Peter Randolph. The letter reveals a number of the concerns an executor might have.

> Shadwell, Jan. 14, 1760.
>
> Sir—
>
> I was at Colo. Peter Randolph's about a Fortnight ago, and my Schooling falling into Discourse, he said he thought it would be to my Advantage to go to the College, and was desirous I should go, as indeed I am myself for several Reasons. In the first place as long as I stay at the Mountain, the Loss of one fourth of my Time is inevitable, by Company's coming here and detaining me from School. And likewise my Absence will in a great Measure, put a Stop to so much Company, and by that Means lessen the Expenses of the Estate in House-Keeping. And on the other Hand by going to the College, I shall get a more universal Acquaintance, which may hereafter be serviceable to me; and I suppose I can pursue my Studies in the Greek and Latin as well as there as here, and likewise learn something of the Mathematics. I shall be glad of your opinion.

Randolph and Jefferson discussed his schooling and his future plans and, probably, the formal mechanism for getting money to fund those plans, which was writing to John Harvie, the keeper of the estate accounts. Randolph helped Jefferson realize that lost time and housekeeping created debts, and Jefferson used these to appeal to Harvie's sense of economy. By "a more universal Acquaintance," Jefferson may have meant getting to know people or academic subjects: either interpretation has validity in the context of these two men. It is tempting to imagine as part of their discussion that Randolph referred to Williamsburg cousins Sir John or Beverley or Peyton, only to have the young Jefferson admit he had not met them since he was very young. Or the elder may have discovered lapses in the ability of the younger's schoolmasters. Either way, the system worked, and the older men guided their young charge to the place that was waiting for him.[21]

Executors' records provided estates with legal tools. Some accounts by John Harvie and Thomas Walker survive, and the other executors may have kept similar records. In effect the estate became three separate corporations with three different tasks: maintaining the plantation, protecting the livelihood of Jefferson's widow, Jane, and preserving the separate inheritance of each child. The accounts kept by Peter Jefferson's executors came back into play during the 1790s when Nicholas and the heirs of Jefferson and Walker sought to resolve some outstanding debts of Peter Jefferson that were magnified by the Revolution. The commitment of guardians and executors transcended generations. The status of friendship as expressed by the trust one person put in another in summoning the friend to service for one's estate was called to witness by Thomas Walker, unfortunately in a deposition against his once friend. He twice invoked executorship as evidence of their families' former trusting relationship. "My father was one of his fathers exr & his own guardian & advanced money for his education," and "All this time I held him first named in my will, as exct. Ignorant of every thing which had passed."[22] Clearly a relationship that had executorship at its foundation was understood to be almost intractable.

Just as Jefferson secured the power and prestige of peers through his will, Peter Jefferson's friends and family relied on him. Most famously, he was guardian of William Randolph's young children and moved the entire Jefferson family to Tuckahoe to complete his charge from his friend and Jane's cousin. But Peter appeared in other Randolph family wills, too. Isham Randolph named his wife, Jane Randolph, as executor. As guardian to his children he named Peter Jefferson, along with Isham's brothers William and Richard Randolph and his nephews William Jr. and Beverley Randolph. The estate of Shadwell kept company with Chatsworth, Curles, Tuckahoe, and

Tazewell Hall or Turkey Island in promising refuge to Isham's heirs. Peter's own father, Thomas Jefferson (II), named his son Peter sole executor of his will.[23]

Friends also called on Peter Jefferson to protect their estates. Joshua Fry named Jefferson an executor of his estate. In this role Jefferson made entries in his own account book as part of the public accounting of Fry's estate. Jefferson helped widow Mary Fry organize payment of taxes and collect outstanding surveyors' fees and tobacco notes.[24] Peter Jefferson, John Harvie, and John Nicholas gave bond to the court for Anne Rose for securities in administering the estate of her husband, Robert Rose.

Peter and his friends also stood for each other in legal and financial circumstances beyond estates. On September 16, 1735, Peter Jefferson recorded in court that William Randolph had power of attorney "to attend to all business."[25] This may have been before a surveying expedition that would put Jefferson in harm's way—it was during his years of active land acquisition—and Jefferson was not yet married with family to look after his business interests.

The executor-kept account books that arose from these arrangements often provide close detail of a plantation's workings for a few years. The account book was evidence of public duty—the executor's job was to help settle debts owed by and to the deceased—and some of the accounts kept by executors or executrices are the only record surviving about certain estates because the accounts became part of the court records. People who understood their own daily business did not necessarily keep books, or those books have disappeared with the passage of time and generations. But accounts kept for estates other than one's own have survived; in fact, the keeping of another's estate often prompted the closer accounting of one's own. Peter Jefferson kept plantation accounts before becoming William Randolph's executor, but what survives are accounts he compiled during those years and following. Randolph's accounts for Tuckahoe do not survive, but Jefferson's receipts for Tuckahoe tell us the names of overseers, plantations, and mills and offer some insight into the maintenance of Randolph's plantation. Jefferson may have kept more careful accounts for Shadwell during those years to monitor his own estate more closely while he was away from it. Jefferson's accounts, in general, deal with larger and commercial debts and contractual relationships. It is very different from John Harvie's accounting of Shadwell following Peter's death. Harvie's records provide a closer watch on crop yields, maintenance of people in the quarters, and small purchases than during Jefferson's years.[26]

Friends and Colleagues

Many of Peter Jefferson's friends were other officeholders and educated professionals. Among them were planters, surveyors, doctors, and clergy. They were people who traveled, purchased land and consumer goods, and read books. Their horizons were broad. The surveying fraternity shared not only the bonds that field work brought but also the intellectual problems of triangulation, mathematical calculation, and monetary speculation that connected them to others outside the profession. Jefferson and Fry worked with William Mayo, who had worked with William Byrd on his expedition along Virginia's boundary; indeed, Mayo is credited with giving Jefferson his training as a surveyor. Joshua Fry acknowledged the surveyors' bond that he and Jefferson had when he named Jefferson an executor of his estate and bequeathed to "my friend Col: Jefferson my surveying instruments." These may have included "1 sett of surveyors Instruments L3.10." and "1 case of surveyors pocket Instruments 1.11." listed among Fry's possessions. Their circle also included Robert Rose, for whom surveying was a part-time but active interest. In fact, when the Reverend Rose died, he was not out ministering to his flock but surveying Beverley Town with another friend, William Cabell.[27]

There is no record that Peter Jefferson traveled overseas, but he traveled widely in the colonies. He spanned Virginia, at least from the Virginia–North Carolina Line to the headwaters of the Potomac and to what he considered the branches of the Mississippi. He also spent time with many people who traveled abroad and certainly may have himself. His wife, Jane, was born in London to her Virginia-born, ocean-crossing, father, Isham Randolph, and her English mother, Jane Rogers. Peter's older brother Thomas (1700–1723) died aboard Randolph's ship *The Williamsburg* en route to Virginia from England. John Harvie was from Scotland, Fry was English-born and Oxford educated, and Fry's wife was one of Virginia's French Huguenot immigrants.[28]

The Jefferson circle included college professors and college presidents as well as authors of history books and maps. Fry taught mathematics at William and Mary before getting the college's approval for working on the map of Virginia with Jefferson. Jane's cousins included the Reverend William Stith, historian and president of the college. Peter's father-in-law hosted botanists John Bartram and Peter Collinson and supplied them with specimens and information on their travels through Virginia. Isham may even have sent Collinson to visit Peter Jefferson at Shadwell in the fall of 1738. Jefferson friends included also medical doctors Thomas Walker, George Gilmer, and Arthur Hopkins.[29]

Clergy

The Jeffersons also kept company with numerous clergymen, including Anglican ministers educated in Scotland, such as Rose, Douglas, and Maury, and in England, such as Stith. Jefferson's relationship with clergy was beyond his role as vestryman; the clergy, too, fall into the category of educated professionals. The clergy owned books, read in languages other than English, and often taught the planters' children. The clergy also needed the good graces of their politically powerful parishioners. As expected, Peter Jefferson served on the vestry in the parishes in which he resided. The established church played an administrative role in society and took care of the poor and collected tithes for maintenance of church property. As such, serving on the church vestry was a public role, rather than one having to do with religious conviction. The dozen vestrymen chosen to make decisions for the parish did not necessarily attend every service. A comment by the Reverend Devereux Jarratt in Bath Parish in 1763 reveals just that; at his first Sunday preaching at Butterwood church, he exclaimed, "Three or four of the vestry were then present." The vestry's job was administrative, not necessarily as spiritual leaders of the flock. The closest church to Shadwell was Mountain Chapel, built in the periphery of Saint James Parish in what would become Fredericksville Parish after 1744. As the county lines and population shifted, the parish boundaries changed around them: Peter served the old Saint James Northam Vestry, but Thomas served Fredericksville.[30]

During some of the years that the Jeffersons resided at Tuckahoe, Peter served on the vestry of Saint James Northam, where his life was already intertwined with some of his fellow vestrymen. Jefferson's friend William Randolph had been on the vestry and had been a burgess for Goochland County from 1742 to 1744. Two other vestrymen served as burgesses, and two were married to Randolphs. Vestryman Arthur Hopkins was a physician and among the richest men in Albemarle County when he died. He had witnessed Peter and Jane Jefferson's marriage bond in 1739. Jefferson, Hopkins, and Lewis all had residences in Albemarle and left the vestry when they removed from Goochland County; they all became leaders in the new county. In 1750 Jefferson was among the vestry who hired William Douglas as minister. Jefferson later arranged for his son Thomas to attend Douglas's Latin school and to board with him during the school year, which he did from 1752 to 1754 and maybe until 1757. Peter and Jane Jefferson's own children are not listed in Douglas's registry of baptisms, but Douglas baptized Peter and Jane's grandchildren who lived in that parish.[31]

The Reverend James Maury, who became rector of Fredericksville Parish in 1754, is best known as the teacher of Thomas Jefferson, but the link between Peter Jefferson and Maury extended back to at least 1748. Maury belonged to the Loyal Land Company, one of forty investors along with Thomas Walker, Peter Jefferson, and Joshua Fry. Maury married the niece of Thomas Walker, Peter's associate in various land speculation schemes, and Maury's daughter married one of Joshua Fry's sons. Thus, Maury's place among these surveyors was as family, friend, fellow investor, and professional, in short, that of a peer. Maury became Thomas Jefferson's teacher in 1758. The class included Dabney Carr, John Walker, and James Jr. and Matthew Maury, as well as James Madison, who later became bishop of Virginia. Clergy like Maury became important links in the cultural web of these young Virginians, but their personal relationships could be real and lasting. Thomas admired Maury's library and called him "a correct Classical scholar." Their friendship included the young Jefferson standing as a baptismal sponsor for Maury's son Abraham.[32]

Peter Jefferson also had a social relationship with Robert Rose. Their bond may have been professional, perhaps as pastor to flock, but they also shared interests as fellow surveyors, planters, readers, and Virginians. Jefferson did not live in Saint Anne's Parish, where Rose preached in the southern part of Albemarle, but he may have been concerned with the welfare of the parish as part of the county's general situation. Rose certainly shared an intellectual bond with surveyors and occasionally accompanied them on expeditions. He came to Virginia from England at the behest of Alexander Spotswood at Germanna, where he served as minister and as bookkeeper for the retired lieutenant governor. He performed the services of a doctor in the community and held substantial land and slaves. Rose was a fellow investor in the towns that Peter Jefferson surveyed. Rose bought four lots in the speculative Beverley Town (or Westham). But he did more than invest money: on March 7, 1750, Rose rode to Joshua Fry's "to make Him a visit and lay down Tye River in ye Map of Virginia." It is not known if Jefferson was with them for this work that took them into the following day. Jefferson may have been with his wife at Tuckahoe; Jane gave birth to a stillborn son there on March 9.[33]

Rose also experimented with refinements to the agricultural enterprise in which they all invested. He is credited with inventing the tobacco canoe, or "bateaux," that was used to transport hogsheads over the sometimes shallow drafts of the upper James River. After midcentury, both tobacco warehouses and ports of call for slave ships moved up the James to the head of deepwater navigation at Richmond. Above this settlement, water levels were less predictable. Carrying hogsheads by land was also problematic. A single hogshead could be rolled using a horse or two, hitched directly to the great barrel turned on its side. This was inefficient but effective if roads were in decent repair and not too muddy, a losing proposition during April, when most planters delivered their crops for inspection. A single hogshead could also be carried in a wagon, again, using two or more draft animals. Life in the upper regions required some adaptation, and Rose made some. He took the design of an Indian canoe, increased its length from sixteen to fifty or sixty feet, its width to four or five feet, and lashed two together for stability. This arrangement could carry up to nine hogsheads, lashed sideways across the gunwales. Rose's canoes first embarked in March 1748. James Maury commented, "For this great improvement in inland navigation, we mountaineers are indebted to the late Reverend and ingenious Mr. Rose."[34] Neither Rose nor Jefferson was passive in his agricultural pursuits. They experimented, developed, and invested, transforming the backcountry into part of the vibrant economic system of the colony.

Rose and Jefferson inhabited the same landscape. Rose dined with Jefferson at Shadwell, at Viewmont with Joshua Fry and John Harvie and Rose's brother John. Rose and Jefferson traveled together from Fry's to Tuckahoe, staying en route with John Bourke one night and Arthur Hopkins the next. He lodged with Jefferson, Fry, and William Stith at Albemarle Courthouse after a vestry meeting there. It is unclear whether the other men attended the vestry meeting or if they were at the courthouse on other business. John Harvie stood as a witness to Robert Rose's will, and Harvie and Jefferson, along with John Nicholas and Anne Rose, provided the bond that allowed Anne to obtain a probate inventory of her husband's estate. Peter Jefferson and Rose shared books, in at least one case, a volume of Enlightenment inquiry. Their common interests were practical, social, and intellectual, and many of their exchanges had to do with the men's active investment in the commonweal.[35]

Peter and Jane had social and family ties with the Reverend William Stith, Jane's first cousin. Both Jefferson and Stith were named executors of William Randolph's estate and guardians to Randolph's son. Stith had been master of the Grammar School at the College of William and Mary before moving to Henrico Parish as its pastor. Stith speculated in land with Jefferson's colleague William Mayo. In 1752 he moved back to the college to serve as president. There he replaced the Reverend William Dawson, who was also his brother-in-law. Like Peter, Stith tackled the intellectual problem of how to envision the whole of Virginia. Stith's contribution was his 1747 book *The History of the First Discovery and Settlement of Virginia*.[36]

The Jeffersons' family and friends also took them outside of the Established church. Brother-in-law Charles Lewis and his family were among the Dissenters of Albemarle County. The Lewises hosted visiting ministers that local Presbyterians requested from the nearby Presbytery of Hanover (County). The Lewises were among those of various faiths who signed the "Petition of Dissenters in Albemarle and Amherst Counties" that they submitted to the new government of the Commonwealth of Virginia in 1776 seeking no state support of any religion. Joshua Fry's wife was Huguenot, and their son Henry became a Baptist, whose evangelical fervor even drove him to convert the ballroom in his house to a room for preaching.[37]

As they came of age, the sons of prominent planters stepped into their places almost without pause. Young Thomas Mann Randolph became the Tuckahoe representative on the Saint James Northam vestry in December 1763, soon after he reached his majority. In 1767 young Thomas Jefferson joined the vestry of Fredericksville Parish, taking the place of John Harvie. Harvie and fellow vestryman Thomas Walker had both been executors of Peter's will and guardians and advisers to young Thomas. Seeing their charge take this important local office followed through on their duties to his father's estate. Fredericksville Parish served Albemarle County north of the Rivanna River. Almost immediately following the Shadwell fire, when Thomas Jefferson moved across the river to Monticello, he appeared on the vestry of Saint Anne's, the parish serving Albemarle south of the Rivanna. One gets the sense that young planters bore early entitlement to this office. The planters may have hired and befriended the clergy because the clergy were learned and had access to books and could teach some of the skills the planters' children needed. But the clergy also needed the planters. Influential planters could determine the fortunes of the local clergy by supporting them or denying their bids for re-hire, especially after the trials called the Parsons' Cause during the 1750s, which challenged who had authority to determine pay for the clergy: the Virginia Assembly or the bishop of London. The local glebe (the land given over to the church for the minister's use) represented a basic public commitment to the minister and the largesse of the vestry.[38]

Powerful Alliances

Peter Jefferson's many business and personal alliances provide an interesting map of how one person's associations connect him across a range of social and geographic settings. Peter Jefferson's status and influence in his personal, professional, business, and family relationships describe a man charged with extensive power and responsibility. The capital investments of Peter Jefferson and his peers affected and generally benefited the larger community of free laborers and small landowners around them while also establishing the economic systems that would encourage slavery as labor for the old system of tobacco and the growing diversified crops to come.

In discussing Peter Jefferson's many connections, we slip inexorably from the private to the public domain. His range of power through public office was ever-widening, yet the circle of associates included many of the same friends and relations no matter how high in office he rose. Peter Jefferson's friends were almost all planters and slave owners. They understood how to use their connections to protect their self-interest. In short, they were men of intellect and action, whose wealth, coupled with their system for supporting one another, made possible the liberality they enjoyed. Although they were alike in being men of property, the wealthiest were Virginia-born from a few familiar families—their connections were invaluable. Other colleagues were foreign-born and brought the fruits of their formal educations to the group.

They were related to one another in many ways—by blood and marriage, through their many roles as public servants, and by their private arrangements with each other. In short, beyond company kept as a burgess or plantation owner, Jefferson involved himself with people whose skills and intellect contributed to the welfare of the Jeffersons and to the growth of the colony. We will meet many of them again in chapter 6.

This close reading of plantation activities reveals the range of Peter Jefferson's business transactions across social strata. It shows how his wealth influenced the lives of many people, from giving them opportunities for work on his plantation to access to consumer goods or a place to grind and ship their corn. Historians such as T. H. Breen in *Tobacco Culture* have analyzed the debt relationship of wealthy planters to their overseas merchants. This study shows that planters like Peter Jefferson extended credit to people of all economic levels around him. Not only was there a whole other structure of debt among poorer Virginians, but the wealthy planters controlled that debt and hence the people who owed it. Entire households were involved in the economic relationship with the planter. Women's contributions to their household economies show in the exchange of their handwork to people like Jefferson. In fact, though his account book records debts in pounds, shillings, and pence, often the currency actually exchanged was sewing or corn or another product or service. People like the Jeffersons provided the economic opportunity and infrastructure that made it possible for others to move to newly settled areas.

That the Jeffersons associated with wealthy, influential Virginians is no surprise. It was in the interest of the gentry to look after each other's estates and heirs. The social and geographic range of Peter Jefferson's legal team suggests that the Jeffersons carefully calculated how various friends and family could best serve them after Peter's death. The geographic range over which they maintained close ties seems great and once again paints a picture of how powerful the gentry were, even from somewhere seemingly remote. Their vision for Virginia is the subject of the next chapter.

6 The Colony's Business: Peter Jefferson's Vantage

In 1757 Albemarle County lost one of its prominent citizens. Peter Jefferson held almost every title and elected office available in the county and the colony. From staking out an early settlement to sitting on the founding court to bringing the first members of prominent white and black families to the region, Peter Jefferson affected this world. Jefferson was part of the elite culture that already dominated Virginia in so many ways, and his contributions to both that culture and the colony continued from his location in the Piedmont. He prepared for his role as a public official growing up around other men who held these offices and reading books that helped him refine his practice. Success depended on Jefferson's association with other powerful people and families, but it also needed the support of legions of ordinary people—some of whom may not even have known they had a part in the story of someone like Jefferson.

A few artifacts from Shadwell illuminate Peter Jefferson's public roles and show how his activities required the participation of many people. The artifacts of Peter Jefferson's public life do not challenge the family hagiography that celebrated this master of land and horse, family and slave, wilderness and public office. The badges of Peter Jefferson's public service became relics in the year he died. The Peter Jefferson who wore a silver-hilted sword and carried a silver-hilted cutlass, who wore silver spurs to prod his horses and wielded pairs of brass-barreled pistols, left the mortal world, making room for this Jefferson's more famous son and heirs to create the mythical Peter Jefferson. The progenitor of a United States president who could purchase a piece of land for a bowl of punch was unusual in some ways, yet in many other ways he was very much like other elite Virginians of his time. He was influential as the wealthiest planter in the neighborhood, and his roles as businessman, surveyor, elected official, and representative of the Virginia colony contributed to local, regional, and colonial commonweal.

Historians know what men like Peter Jefferson did. We have their records from making laws, drawing maps, and keeping accounts. We know some of them from portraits, houses, gardens, letters, diaries, and even books they wrote. If material culture gives the historian an opportunity to find history and tell stories about people who had no voice in the official records, what do the artifacts of someone like Peter Jefferson tell us that we could not otherwise learn? What do they do other than help illustrate the images we have already? The material culture from Shadwell connects that place to many others, from European manufactories of consumer goods to Albemarle County, where slaves fashioned shoes or timbers for a millrace. Similarly, the objects that relate directly to Peter Jefferson's public roles connect him to people and places whose stories are less well known than his. That is the unique utility of his material culture. We can know him within a geographic and social range that puts other people and places in the same picture. Jefferson becomes part of larger social, cultural, and economic systems. The material culture of elite men enables us to explore the other people—some nameless, some rich, some poor—who helped reinforce their prominence.

Mapping

The most visible artifact of Peter Jefferson's public business was the map of Virginia that he and Joshua Fry surveyed. Peter's name is inextricably linked with that of Fry in what is probably Peter's second greatest legacy (after his oldest son), officially called *A Map of the Inhabited Part of Virginia Containing the whole Province of Maryland with Part of Pensilvania, New Jersey and North Carolina*. Most people then and now recognize its unofficial title, "The Fry-Jefferson Map of Virginia." Fry, Jefferson, and numerous unnamed contributors compiled the map from existing surveys and their own new work. The map is more than a document about Virginia's land features and political boundaries. It claims knowledge about territory beyond Virginia's bounds, some unseen by the mapmakers themselves, and it is a document of social connections and power.[1]

Peter is one of many surveyors whose professional name is linked with others. Surveying partnerships proved profitable, and the "genealogy" of the successful eighteenth-century surveyors is a powerful reminder of the value of making the right associations in this period of Virginia's expansion. The mapping projects also show how wide-ranging the surveyors' travels were (fig. 6.1). In 1737 Peter Jefferson worked with Robert Brooke of Essex County on a map of the Rappahannock River. Almost a decade later, in 1746, he worked with the son Robert Brooke on a map of the Northern Neck. Thus Jefferson was no stranger to the upper peninsula regions of the Chesapeake. The elder Brooke traveled with Alexander Spotswood and his Knights of the Golden Horseshoe, and surveyed the Potomac headwaters with William Mayo, a neighbor of Peter Jefferson's in Goochland County. The younger Brooke surveyed Mount Vernon for the Washingtons. In 1746 Jefferson held the post of surveyor to Joshua Fry, who was Virginia's commissioner on the expedition to draw a boundary between the claims of Virginia and Lord Fairfax's proprietary grant for the land between the Rappahannock and Potomac Rivers. The younger Brooke, Thomas Lewis, and Lunsford Lomax also served that expedition to the mountains in northwest Virginia. By 1749 commissioners Fry and Jefferson continued the Virginia–North Carolina dividing line, carrying west the boundary marked by William Byrd and William Mayo and others twenty years earlier (fig. 6.2).[2]

Two famous diaries of surveying expeditions, by William Byrd and by Thomas Lewis, define the various functions of commissioners, surveyors, and chain carriers, as well as the widely varying sleeping and eating accommodations along the way. Surveying cast the learned adventurer into nature and among all kinds of "lesser sorts," of European, African, and Indian extraction, many of whom seemed quite exotic to the Englishmen because of their living arrangements, accents, or diet. William Byrd supplied many uncharitable descriptions of North Carolinians, from the gentlemen commissioners to the householders along the way. Thomas Lewis rarely mentioned people outside the surveying party. In one instance, he and Colonel Jefferson "Went

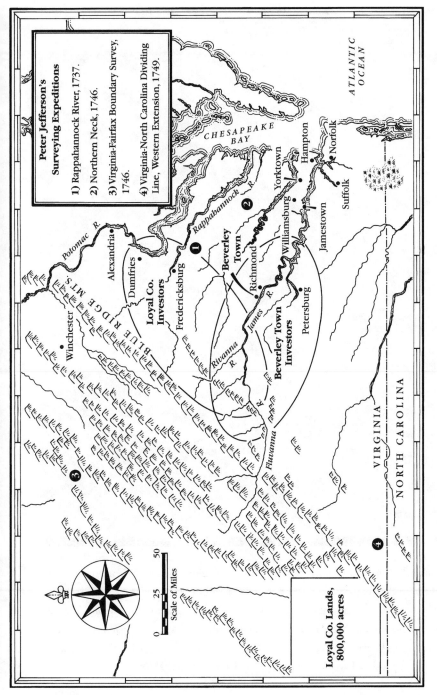

Figure 6.1. Peter Jefferson's surveying expeditions carried him across the colony: to the Northern Neck, into the northwest of Virginia, and to the Virginia–North Carolina dividing line (1–4). Oval diagrams show the relative location of homes of investors in Beverley/ Westham Town on the James River versus Loyal Land Company of eight hundred thousand acres on the southwest edge of the colony. Peter Jefferson, Joshua Fry, and John Harvie of Albemarle County were the only men engaged with both projects.

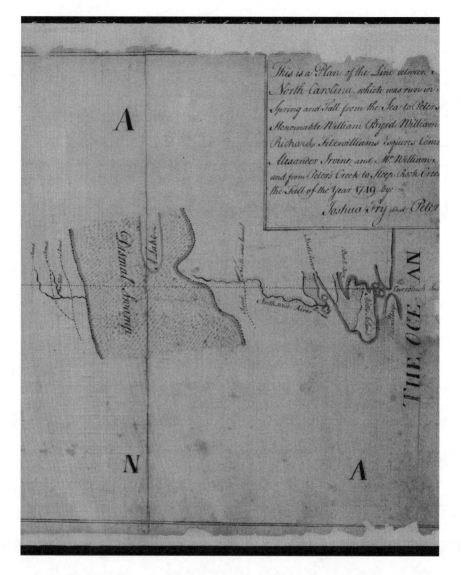

Figure 6.2. "This is a Plan of the Line between Virginia and North-Carolina, which was run in the Year 1728. in the Spring and the Fall from the Sea to Peter's Creek by the Honourable William Byrd William Dandridge and Richard Fitzwilliams Esquires Commissioners and Mr. Alexander Irvine and Mr. William Mayo Surveyors—and from Peter's Creek to Steep Rock Creek was continued in the Fall of the Year 1749 by Joshua Fry and Peter Jefferson." Courtesy Special Collections, University of Virginia Library.

Down the River to Discover Some Inhabitants that we might get Some provision." But the single "familey of poor Dutch people" could offer no supplies. Most of Lewis's journal focused on the mechanics of marking the trail and on the challenges of moving the entourage. Jefferson often had to find and pay people for carrying the chain and bringing provisions; his job involved not only maps and instruments but also dealing with people of all ranks.[3]

Peter Jefferson's wilderness exploits were the foundation of family lore, and even the family knew they compared to the adventures recorded by William Byrd. Sarah Randolph repeated stories she heard about her great-grandfather when he continued the Virginia–North Carolina line. The expedition had to fend off wild beasts and sleep in trees for safety. Men fainted for lack of food and sometimes had to eat raw flesh. But in the story, Jefferson's courage never failed, and they persevered and accomplished the task. Peter's self-reliance is echoed in Thomas Lewis's journal, where Jefferson rode out to engage with hunters they did not know or rode ahead to find a mark. The surveying fraternity shared the bonds that field work brings, and many of the stories that tied these men together were backwoods exploits.[4]

Although it is easiest to imagine Peter Jefferson in the outdoors, the contributions of his surveying were to Virginia's intellectual landscape. Thomas Jefferson called his father's map "the first map of Virginia which had ever been made, that of Captain Smith being merely a conjectural sketch." Thomas used the Fry and Jefferson map as the template for the map in *Notes on Virginia*. The son added information to the map to extend it north and west, and made minor corrections. The surveyor made a lasting intellectual and political contribution through his map, as well as through a legacy of family stories.[5]

Investments

Peter Jefferson held almost the full range of public office in colonial Virginia, and the list of Jefferson's offices is in itself impressive. But equally important to our story is how these offices provided opportunity for social and business contacts and how those contacts widened the geographic horizons within which the Jeffersons operated. For the wealthy, colonial Virginia was their oyster. Public office was a tool for maintaining the familiar structure of society; little did they want to change that. The vast lands beyond the legal boundaries of their county were where change would happen and where they could profit from it. True success in these endeavors needed more than the support of wealthy relatives, however; it needed a broader and deferential audience. One result of acting as county surveyor, collecting tithes, and paying bounties for wolf heads was that it ensured that local residents recognized Jefferson's name and position. He was their access to legal representation and remuneration. His prominence reinforced itself with his ability to pay neighbors for their skills and services, which he could use on his plantation and which he could engage in official capacity for such things as surveying parties and militia action.[6]

Jefferson made and maintained connections beyond the plantation bounds and well beyond the county limits. Through surveying and political duties, Peter joined the ranks of large land speculators in this expansive period of Virginia's history. In addition to his developed plantations, Jefferson invested in land with mineral resources, in schemes to develop a port town on the James River, and in the Loyal Land Company of Virginia. Although none of these plans came to full fruition, they represent a colonial world in which wealthy Virginians imagined almost limitless possibility.

Natural resources had potential to contribute to Virginians overseas trade. Peter had a partnership with John Harvie and others for two hundred acres of land in Albemarle County, "wherewith is immagined to be a Vein of Copper Oar." Jefferson's will ended his family's involvement with mining when he directed his executors to sell his interest in the land.[7] Men like Jefferson, Harvie, Byrd, and others had both the education and the desire to identify naturally occurring mineral or plant resources such as copper, limestone, slate, pine pitch, and even ginseng and to explore the possibility of exploiting them for international markets, often by forming companies to pool wealth and reduce individual risk.

Town Development

Peter was among a number of prominent Virginians who subscribed to lots in a speculative town on Beverley Randolph's Westham plantation, where Westham Creek joins the James River, just above Richmond (fig. 6.3). Various surveys of the town, called Beverley Town or Westham, survive, including two by Peter Jefferson. Beverley Randolph died in 1751 and he specified in his will "That part of Westham plantation to be laid off for a town, agreeable to

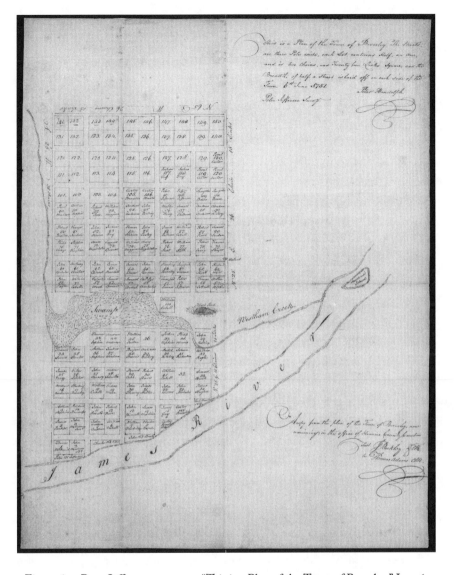

Figure 6.3. Peter Jefferson, surveyor, "This is a Plan of the Town of Beverley," June 6, 1751. Jefferson reserved lots 151 (above the "JA" along the river) and 107 and 108 (three blocks south and two blocks west of the upper-right corner of the town). Jefferson Papers, Courtesy Special Collections, University of Virginia Library.

my engagements with the subscribers, by my brother Peter, and that he sell and convey in fee simple to the subscribers." The plan was a basic grid, with some curvilinear elements to accommodate the swamp made by Westham Creek in the middle of town and the James River along its southern edge. The survey specified "The Streets are three pole wide, each Lot contains Half an Acre, and is two chains twenty four Links square."[8]

The goal of these towns was to collect shipments coming from upstream and inland and consolidate them for shipment down the James River. In 1750 Shocoes Creek was the westernmost inspection point on the James, and Westham or Beverley would have moved inspections five miles farther west, just above the falls. As part of thinking about economic return, Jefferson reserved for himself lot No. 57, which fronted on the James, "being the ferry lot." Perhaps Jefferson envisioned direct traffic from his ferry at Albemarle Courthouse to the one at Westham. Sixty miles west in Albemarle County, Robert Rose helped "promote a Subscription for lots at Westham" and helped lay out lots with William Cabell. Seventy-eight individuals signed up for 115 of the 156 lots. Many of the subscribers were surveyors, magistrates, and burgesses, and many were from Albemarle, Goochland, and Henrico Counties. Many were friends of Rose or Jefferson: the list echoes the social and political power of the James River corridor. Burgesses from Albemarle, Goochland, Henrico, Hanover, Caroline, and King and Queen Counties invested, and many bought more than one lot. Their aim was to develop a town that would service their region's needs, and if they personally profited, that was even better. Beyond issuing some deeds, Beverley Town was not realized.[9]

Loyal Land Company

Jefferson's attentions along the James River corridor did not prevent him from being involved elsewhere. His investments with the Loyal Land Company describe yet another social circle from an entirely different geographic region of the greater Piedmont. Peter Jefferson and Thomas Walker were involved financially in numerous joint land ventures. In 1748 the two, with Thomas and David Meriwether, obtained a grant for ten thousand acres of land on the New River. On July 12 that same year, forty combined investors including Walker and Jefferson formed the Loyal Land Company to administer and profit from a grant of eight hundred thousand acres in southwestern

Virginia. Their investment was part of the colonial enterprise of mapping and taming the wilderness to imprint the landscape with settlement of European (but not French) extraction.[10] As in much of Virginia's colonial project, individual investors would profit.

The investors, all family and friends of Thomas Walker, came from upper Albemarle County and across Louisa and Orange Counties to Fredericksburg. The names include Walker, Meriwether, Gilmer, and Thornton. The Loyal Land Company lists and the Beverley Town lists are surprisingly distinct (see fig. 6.1). Only three names appear on both rosters: Albemarle residents Peter Jefferson, Joshua Fry, and John Harvie.[11] Perhaps the two projects contrasted too much for most men. Developing infrastructure to tie their region into existing markets was a different process from looking outward to map and control distant and unseen lands. Perhaps men such as Jefferson, Fry, and Harvie were smart enough to spread their investments so that all risk was not tied to the same pool of resources. One wonders if the boundaries of the investors' social circles were as distinct.

The Public Jefferson

If you were to visit Shadwell as a friend of Peter Jefferson's, you would be impressed with a familiar and reassuring formality. As you approached the house, a black slave, perhaps in working clothes, perhaps in livery, would come to take your horse or show your own servant to the stables. As you dismounted you would hear children's voices, chickens, horses, and sawing on wood or hammering on metal or the sound of grindstones edging metal tools. You might notice the voices of black women and men singing as they worked or hear raucous laughter from beyond a fence across the yard. You would smell the wood fires that heated homes and notice the scent of roasting meat in the odors from the large chimney on the kitchen nearby. This was how a plantation should act, look, sound, and smell.

In the house you would be heartily entertained. A well-dressed black slave opened doors so that you and your host walked into the house unencumbered, through the passage to the dining room. After many courses of food and good conversation, perhaps followed by music played by your host's wife and children, you might leave the dining room for Peter's office. In this slightly darker room (there was no fireplace, after all), you would navigate the perimeter of the room looking at the maps on the walls: the Virginia map drawn by your host; a map of London with tiny streets, alleyways, and public squares—a reminder of your hostess's upbringing and of metropolitan life. Then you would look over the maps of the world—the globe, flattened and divided into four—the oceans, continents, and uncharted places. You would notice the books, perhaps even handle them. On the desk, their brass fittings and finished wood gleaming in the candlelight, lie the drafting tools that your host used to measure and draw. You might have a discussion of the science that tools of surveying could invoke, such as the mathematics of measuring latitude, tracking the sun and stars, or figuring how far it was from Greenwich, England, to Albemarle Courthouse. You might even discuss how your host's work that continued the dividing line at latitude 36 degrees, 30 minutes between Virginia and North Carolina sowed political good- or ill-will, depending on which side of the line your sympathies lay.[12] Just as the plantation and its people presented a well-ordered world with Peter Jefferson at its head, so too appeared that distant landscape controlled by transits and protractors, maps, and deeds. A finely engraved map can do that.

Peter's books, mathematical instruments, and maps created the intellectual apparatus for exploring, recording, and claiming ownership of the western parts of the colony. The maps and books not only announced Peter's profession and the Jeffersons' cosmopolitan view but also charted the bounds of England's legal and political system. Eighteenth-century liberal ideas positioned the British Empire as the true heir of ancient knowledge and successful champion of man in the natural and political world.[13]

The house contained images that invoked king and empire and informed even the illiterate visitor instantly that the Jeffersons were English Virginians. The Jeffersons owned a few GR jugs, blue and gray stoneware jugs made in the German Rhineland, often called Rhenish stoneware or Westerwald. The jugs had incised patterns and the cipher of George II (fig. 6.4). A large cast iron fireback in one of the fireplaces in the house echoed the GR jugs with a design of the royal arms of Britain's monarchy (fig. 6.5). Westerwald jugs and other drinking containers with these decorations were readily available throughout the eighteenth century, with decorations other than royal ciphers for the American market after 1776.[14]

Peter also had objects that sent messages of power and control of a different sort, but his symbols of military office were not on display in the house. Jefferson did not use his arms as the governor in Williamsburg did, a fanfare

Figure 6.4. King and empire at Shadwell: fragments of GR jug,
blue-and-gray Rhenish salt glaze stoneware jug with incised cipher
of George II. Fragments from multiple vessels from Shadwell;
whole jug, courtesy The Colonial Williamsburg Foundation,
image courtesy Monticello/Thomas Jefferson Foundation, Inc.

of bayonets and rifles, hanging on all the walls to impress at first glance. Peter locked his weaponry in a safe room. Perhaps this indicates that Jefferson,
unlike the governor, used his arms. No doubt, when he rode out bearing
sword, cutlass, spurs, pistols, and guns, Jefferson was an impressive figure
(see appendix, table 19). There was no mistaking his importance for those on
the receiving end of the message either. This presentation of his public role
would impress any who saw it, from his own family and slaves to locals hired
to carry the chain or asked to feed the expedition to backwoods squatters
from the Continent or the Highlands and to Native Americans. The medical
supplies kept with the weapons—a case of fleams (lancets) for bleeding an
ailing comrade—highlight the seriousness of these implements. Even if they
were thought of merely as tools, it was an impressive show.[15]

Figure 6.5. King and empire at Shadwell: reconstruction of fireback from cast-iron fragments found on site, with arms of Hanover kings. Reconstruction by Amy E. Grey, Courtesy Monticello/Thomas Jefferson Foundation, Inc.

Peter was one of twelve men who owned a sword in colonial Albemarle County; none of the other swords was silver. Like Jefferson, most sword owners kept their weapons out of the house. Fry's "1 reper or small sword" and its hanger were in his office, a space separate from the domestic rooms of his house. Others kept theirs near their saddles and riding equipment or in spaces with nondomestic items such as woodworking tools. In a few inventories, the swords lay or hung among household items. In the listing of the estate of Captain William Venable, his sword and belt followed a coffee mill and preceded a small desk. Bullet molds and a surveyor's compass lay nearby, as did parts to a loom. Captain Charles Lewis's sword was among a "looking glass gilted," and "15 queen china plates." One small section of William Witt's domestic scene was decorated thus: "1 pot & pot hooks . . . 1 violin . . . 1 whip saw and file . . . 1 gun . . . 1 pr of pistols holsters & sword . . . a parcel of wearing cloths." Even if Witt's possessions were in a closet or trunk, there was little distinction by function in their arrangement. It appears that unlike the governor, most people did not think of swords as trophies or decoration in early Virginia. A few owners brought them into the household, but most often they were kept with tools (perhaps they were sharpened on the same grindstones) or with riding equipment. Jefferson's may have been secured because they were silver and had intrinsic value in addition to their utility as weapons. This collection was worth more than the books in his library.[16]

Colonial Agents

Peter Jefferson entertained in his official capacity, opening his home to his peers, other Virginia gentry, and at least one Cherokee warrior, Outassetè (fig. 6.6). His public activities reflected the same frontier culture as his plantation, at once a statement about belonging to a larger British colonial project, yet revealing cross-cultural contacts and familiar exchange among colonists, slaves, and Indians. But just as the documents often show only the activities of wealthy white Virginians, so, too, follows the story of Native American activity in the Virginia Piedmont during this period; more than the most important warriors and chiefs passed through the colony. The archaeological record leads to the story that includes the others. At Shadwell excavators recovered a small quantity of Native American artifacts in both Anglo- and African-American contexts. These Indian materials, which occurred in both the context of the main house and the slave quarters, suggest that the entire population of Shadwell had contact with Indian peoples or had similar curiosity about bringing home their artifacts. More people than just Peter Jefferson and Outassetè made a connection.

Thomas Jefferson invoked the presence of Outassetè's visit to Shadwell when he wrote to his friend John Adams in 1812. The letter reveals the Virginian's youthful fascination with Indians, as well as the views of the mature statesman who could no longer be romantic about Native Americans. Jefferson leads us through this ethnographic inquiry.

> So much in answer to your enquiries concerning Indians, a people with whom, in the very early part of my life, I was very familiar, and acquired impressions of attachment & commiseration for them which have never been obliterated.

Figure 6.6. *Outassetè or Austenaco, Cherokee
man, Great Warrior, Commander in Chief of
the Cherokee Nation, 1762,* by Sir Joshua
Reynolds?, from *Royal Magazine,* copy in
National Anthropological Archives,
Library of Congress.

before the revolution they were in the habit of coming often & in great numbers to the seat of our government, where I was very much with them. I knew
much the great Outassetè, the warrior and orator of the Cherokees. he was
always the guest of my father, on his journies to & from Williamsburg. I was
in his camp when he made his great farewell oration to his people, the evening
before his departure for England. the moon was in full splendor, and to her he
seemed to address himself in his prayers for his own safety on the voyage, and
that of his people during his absence. his sounding voice, distinct articulation,
animated action, and the solemn silence of his people at their several fires,

filled me with awe & veneration, altho' I did not understand a word he uttered. that nation, consisting now of about 2,000. warriors, & the Creeks of about 3,000. are far advanced in civilisation. they have good Cabins, inclosed fields, large herds of cattle & hogs, spin & weave their own clothes of cotton, have smiths & other of the most necessary tradesmen, write & read, are on the increase in numbers, & a branch of Cherokees is now instituting a regular representative government. some other tribes were advancing in the same line. on those who have made any progress, English seductions will have no effect. But the backward will yield, & be thrown further back. these will relapse into barbarism & misery, lose numbers by war & want, and we shall be obliged to drive them with the beasts of the forest into the Stony mountains. they will be conquered however in Canada. the possession of that country secures our women and children for ever from the tomahawk & scalping knife, by removing those who excite them: and for this possession, orders I presume are issued by this time; taking for granted that the doors of Congress will re-open with a Declaration of war.[17]

What was the cultural frontier of Virginia in the mid-eighteenth century? The location of Shadwell seems unlikely for settlement by the regions' Monacan Indians, but Cherokees passed between the Valley of Virginia and Williamsburg with some regularity. The origins of the Indian artifacts recovered at Shadwell provide few clues to explain their provenience in the historic context. Further archaeological and documentary evidence for Indian, white, and black contact in this period answers more questions about what kind of frontier this was.

Archaeology has not yet offered a complete picture of the native peoples of the Central Virginia Piedmont. Monacan Indians occupied the Piedmont region until the late seventeenth century, when pressure from northern Indians forced their migration south, after which many eventually moved to Pennsylvania, leaving a few people here and there in Virginia and North Carolina. Indians settled along Virginia's rivers during the Late Archaic Period (2500–1000 BCE) and established towns, trade, and craft production such as pottery-making during the Woodland Period (1000 BCE–1600 CE). The Monacans built twelve known burial mounds in the region during their final era in the Piedmont and may have used the mounds for burial as late as the seventeenth century.[18]

The late 1730s to the 1770s coincides with the main settlement and occupation of the Shadwell site and also represents an era when the colonial government and southern Indians allied to use the other against its own enemy, other Indians or other Europeans. Pressures from northern Indians and changing trade patterns in the colonies pushed the Cherokees and Catawbas in particular into the arms (figurative and military) of the British in Virginia. The connections that the Cherokees had with the colonial government suggest that this group had the biggest impact on the central Virginia Piedmont. Cherokees were active in Virginia, but the documents make clear that Indians of all nations appeared in Williamsburg or at western treaty meetings. The exchange among the various European immigrants and Indians from across much of the eastern seaboard describes a complex cultural web in this period of Virginia history.

The dominant artifact pattern at Shadwell recalls the familiar objects and materials of gentry consumption in the middle of the eighteenth century. Despite the Eurocentric world that informed the family's consumer impulses and plantation landscape, Shadwell belied its frontier foundations. The road that took Jefferson's tobacco to market when the river was low carried Indians from the west to Williamsburg, just as it carried European traders beyond the mountains. The presence of a small number of Indian artifacts in excavations at Shadwell, both from the main dwelling house and from slave quarter contexts, prompts more questions of frontier contact. Though the land borders the Rivanna River, it sits well above the floodplain that characterizes other Late Woodland homesites and is an unlikely location for settlement by Monacan Indians. Though a small amount of quartz flake was recovered, suggesting onsite working of the material, no archaeological deposits indicated pre-European occupation of this piece of land.[19]

Shadwell's first European settlers and their African slaves may have collected Indian objects nearby, but Indian travelers along the road also traded and shared objects with both the white and black communities at Shadwell. Archaeological evidence augmented with the historical record of Indian travel in Virginia in the eighteenth century paints an intriguing picture of the possibilities of Indian, black, and white cultural exchange in this frontier world. Looking at artifact patterns on other Piedmont Indian sites provides a framework for establishing the origins of these objects, while the documentary record suggests that there is no easy explanation of how the objects got from their producers to the places where archaeologists found them.

The Artifacts

The Indian artifacts from Shadwell constitute a negligible percentage of the entire assemblage. The thirty-one objects are slightly less than one

one-thousandth of the whole collection, numbering more than 42,500 objects (fig. 6.7). But because the artifact pattern of the dominant culture is so clearly defined on this site, the few objects that fall outside this pattern are easy to identify. The analytical tool of "removing" the dominant culture from the landscape and studying what remains suggests two cultural influences other than European at Shadwell: African or African-American slaves and Native Americans.

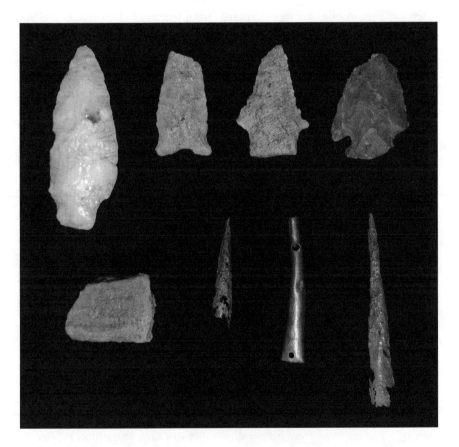

Figure 6.7. Native American artifacts from Shadwell. Projectile points (top row, left to right) of quartz, chert, argillite, and flint. Albemarle-type cord-impressed pottery (bottom left) and tinkling cones of rolled and pierced iron, brass, and iron. The largest point shown here is approximately 2 5/8 inches long.
Courtesy Monticello/Thomas Jefferson Foundation, Inc.

The Indian objects penetrated both the slave and free worlds at Shadwell, testimony that certain frontier experiences were commonly shared. The distribution of these thirty-one objects is fairly even across the major historic-period areas of occupation. Stone artifacts from the site include twenty-one projectile points and four other tools of flaked material, and at least two ground stone tools. Metal objects include one brass tinkling cone and two of iron. A single piece of cord-impressed pottery represents distinctive local Indian handiwork. The eleven sherds of colonoware may also represent Indian influences but have a closer correlation to pottery that was made by slaves on tidewater sites. A quartz scraper appeared from the cellar of the main dwelling house with other household objects, and four other pieces emerged near the house. The kitchen vicinity, a high-activity area of food production and storage and home for the slave cook, revealed five points and one iron cone. Around the slave quarter site, excavators recovered the other seventeen stone objects, two of the metal cones, and the pot sherd. One point was in the contents of the root cellar, a place where a slave might keep a precious object.[20]

Prehistoric Origins

Excavation of other Piedmont Indian sites provides a regional context for most of the stone objects and the potsherd. Archaeologists of mound sites attributed to Monacans report similar quartz and quarzite points and tools, and these materials occur abundantly in the region. These archaeologists also recover Albemarle-type pottery from the mounds, testament to the last period of precontact, when Woodland Indians established towns, potting traditions, and ossuary burial practices. Similar potsherds can still be found in river wash and plowed fields in the greater Piedmont area. But artifact groups from Indian mounds also include small numbers of stone points and tools made of nonlocal, usually western, material, indicating that Indians traded across the mountains and between tribes with some regularity. Of the twenty-six stone items from Shadwell, two are of distinctly nonlocal material, varieties of chert or flint that occur west of the mountains.[21] Thus, the pottery and all of the stone objects, regardless of origin in Piedmont or Shenandoah Valley Indian cultures, could have appeared at Shadwell in the prehistoric period.

The brass and iron tinkling cones also bear Monacan associations and symbolize the power held by the Monacans over other Virginia Indians because of Monacan proximity to copper resources, the cause of strained relations between the Powhatans and Monacans. If the presence of chert and flint tools at Shadwell represents Monacan contact with western Indians, the metal cones represent contact to the east. The evaluation of thirty-one Indian artifacts from this single site located between mountain gaps and seaward rivers establishes a network of distant trade associations well before European contact.[22] So the possibility exists that when Peter Jefferson brought his family and slaves to the Piedmont, they collected these curiosities during construction of their buildings, tobacco planting, or walking along the Rivanna.

Thomas Jefferson had a lifelong passion for collecting and researching the artifacts of other cultures. His *Notes on Virginia*, published in 1787, contains Jefferson's catalog of Indian demographics, languages, and history. When, as president, he commissioned Virginians Meriwether Lewis and William Clark to find the Northwest Passage, he also charged them to send back to him cultural artifacts, natural specimens, and botanical samples for his further documentation of the North American continent. In *Notes on Virginia*, he recalled that "thirty years before" he followed a group of Indians to a mound on the Rivanna River, where he watched them mourn.[23] Young Thomas Jefferson and his siblings become prime suspects for bringing home, and into the house, the artifacts of their native land's earlier inhabitants.

Historic Explanations

The historic record provides another perspective on cultural contact on the frontier, however; what whites and Indians wore, carried, and did on their travels points to other ways these Indian artifacts entered the plantation. Thomas Jefferson prompted the question of Indian and white social roles by describing the Indian warrior Outassetè as a guest of his father at Shadwell. Overnight accommodations of the white in the Indian world and the Indian in the white world suggest that, like other behaviors, the degree of comfort and privacy offered depended on the relative status of the visitor and his host in their own worlds and to each other. On occasion they camped together when traveling. Often, a party visiting the other's town on business pitched its own camp in the town or just outside its boundaries. When the meeting held high diplomatic value, the host offered a house in the town to the guest. Planters allowed passing Indians to camp on their land or in outbuildings, but little record remains of the sleeping arrangements made on plantations for Indian guests who were friends of the planters.

Travels in Backcountry

En route from Big Island at Holston to Chote in 1761, Henry Timberlake and two companions camped with seven or eight Cherokee hunters they happened upon. They shared the Indians' dinner of venison "dipped in bears oil, which served for sauce." Timberlake lay down to sleep next to an Indian on a large bearskin. He wrote that he "believes his companions did the same." The Indians shared both their food and bedding with the white woodland travelers. Though their camp included fewer than a dozen people, Timberlake was unsure of the accommodations given, or taken by, his interpreter and aide. Perhaps the Indians had their small shelters of skins on poles, obscuring Timberlake's view of his mates' sleeping arrangements, or perhaps they were spread through the woods. If Timberlake commented on sharing a bearskin because it was an unusual situation, the close quarters with the Indians were not unusual enough to engage his full attention to where the other white men slept.[24]

When they reached the Indian town, the chief Ostenaco gave Timberlake "a general invitation to his house, while I resided in the country." Whether the chief's language was symbolic or literal, the chief expected to offer an official emissary accommodations equivalent to his own, if not his own. Timberlake smoked, ate, drank, and celebrated with the Indians before seeking the quietude of King Kanagatucko's hothouse, but he was surrounded by crowds of Indians at his bedside. All the smoking and curious onlookers prevented much rest, but the bed provided little comfort for the white man. It was "composed of a few boards, spread with bear-skins, without any other covering," though the house was too hot for Timberlake's own blanket.[25]

Timberlake's mission of goodwill to the Cherokees afforded him a level of accommodation that was not automatic for all business transactions in Indian territory. At the 1752 Treaty of Loggs Town, the commissioners sent by Lieutenant Governor Dinwiddie, including Joshua Fry, Lunsford Lomax, and

James Patton, halted three miles from Shonassim's Town for preliminary peace rituals, which involved dismounting, smoking the calumet, and firing salutes with a small group of Delaware Indians. The Virginians pitched their camp on the riverbank, outside of town and upriver, and raised their colors. They later went to the town to be met by the cochiefs, who "dressed after the English Fashion, had Silver Breast Plates and a great deal of Wampum." The governor's commission heard an address by the chiefs that began, "You have come a long journey and have sweated a great deal."[26] The formality of the address echoed the literal and figurative limits placed on the Virginians' access to this Indian world. This was not a wholehearted embrace of brothers but a strategically regulated state occasion involving both protocol and formal distance.

Indian visits to the white man mirrored the white experience in the Indian camps. High-level visits demanded the presidential suite, while passersby were evaluated on a fairly personal level. A fairly large group of Indians— Jonnhaty, an Iroquois, with twenty-two Onondagas, and seven Oneidas— passed through the Valley of Virginia in 1742. They visited the Augusta County home of John McDowell, then camped nearby on a river for several days. Though the Indians' visit to McDowell was friendly, other residents of the valley felt it necessary to escort the group on their trip south, provoking frontier violence caused by misunderstanding and reactive reasoning. Similar white reaction resulted in the death of ten Indians in Augusta County in 1765. John Anderson allowed Nockonowe and nine Cherokees to spend the night in his barn, where his neighbors ambushed them in the morning.[27] Clearly, the hospitality of the trail offered by individuals did not represent how most backcountry residents felt about providing comfort to nonwhite travelers. Yet murdering guests was unusual enough that most references to Indian visits go into no great detail.

It was not only the valley residents who worried about Indians. In 1757 Peter Fontaine, safely ensconced at Westover in Charles City County—twenty-five miles from Williamsburg—reported: "Those of the Indians that call themselves our friends despise us, and in their march through our inhabited country, when going to our assistance, insult and annoy us. It is not above a month ago since a party of about a hundred and twenty Cherokees, in passing through Lunenburg, insulted people of all ranks." The Fontaine family paid close attention to how the English, the French, and their Indian allies fared in the backwoods.[28] The very idea of contact with Indians was too much for some white Virginians.

Indians in Piedmont and Tidewater

Plenty of records indicate that the Indians who came to town on business set up their own camps and established their separate cultural domain on a traveling scale. Outassetè camped with other Cherokees in Williamsburg the night before he sailed for England to meet George II. Jefferson described listening to this great orator *in his camp,* a place separate from the white world, even if the seventy or so Indians occupied the Palace Green. In 1751, when the Nottoways marched into town with a white flag for the Cherokees who had come to council, the two groups met "in the Market place . . . singing the Song of Peace." When the crowd became too great, the Indians went into the courthouse to meet. They exchanged wampum, heard orations, and smoked the peace pipe. They met later at "the Camp of the Cherrokees; where making a large Fire, they danced together round it."[29] The Indian activities that day illustrate a range of cultural interactions of the Indian in the white realm. The Indians sat with the executive council in the Governor's Palace, meeting the white man on his ground. They then met other Indians and used a convenient English public building for their own business. But the Indians celebrated in places staked out as their own. The Indians used the public spaces of the capital again in 1777, when Cherokees came to town to talk about running a boundary to prevent encroachment on Indian land. Following the talk, "they favoured the public with a dance on the green in front of the palace, where a considerable number of spectators, both male and female, were agreeably entertained."[30]

All Indian visits to Williamsburg, however, were not remarkable enough to make the news. The newspapers scarcely mentioned Indians at the college, and local Indians selling wares and produce appear only occasionally in account books. Fees paid "To the Indians for Earthen pans . . . o.2. 6.," and "To the Pamunkey Indians for Wild Fowl . . . 1.1. 6.," for the Governor's Palace kitchen suggest that Indians doing business in Williamsburg were neither unusual nor always of diplomatic importance. Clearly this colonial capital saw a variety of Indians from many nations in Virginia and beyond. Groups of Indians visiting Williamsburg on official business ranged in size from two

Cherokee deputies in August 1759 to a group of at least fifty-six, "King Blunt and thirty-three Tuscaroroes, seven Meherrins, two Saponies, thirteen Nottoways," who offered to join the English against the French in spring of 1757. An even larger gathering of Indians returned from the wars in Ohio in May 1757. Newspapers reported about one hundred Catawbas from Fort Cumberland arrived with two Shawnese scalps, followed a few days later by thirty Tuscaroras with another scalp.[31] No mention was made of where these troops billeted.

But official records do note that the governor provided a house for the visit of the Cherokee emperor and empress and their son in 1752. The emperor's address to Governor Dinwiddie began with formal treaty language that echoed how the Indians greeted the English at Loggs Town; he said they "had come through many Briers, Thickets, and great Waters" for this meeting. After the official presentations, the governor gave orders to entertain the emperor's family and attendants "with all necessaries." They then "returned to the House appointed to receive them." Although Dinwiddie clearly saw the protocol necessary for this visit of a head of state, he did not make the offer of "his house" that the Cherokee made to Timberlake in Tennessee. Perhaps the emperor's family lodged with one of Williamsburg's finest families, or perhaps they were given an adequate empty house equipped with government attendants and black slaves. The other Williamsburg residence that hosted an Indian belonged to Mr. Horrock, who invited Timberlake and Ostenaco (as Timberlake refers to Outassetè) to "sup with him at the College." It was here that Ostenaco saw a picture of the king and asked to go to England.[32]

Timberlake tells us that the Cherokees left their finery at home, leaving "their trinkets behind," when they went to war. But descriptions of Indians visiting Williamsburg and London indicate that Indians dressed and painted themselves when on official business. White men traveling to Indian towns or camps were met by the chiefs wearing some combination of English dress, breast plates, and wampum. The colonial government gave fine suits of clothes to Indian chiefs and emperors and their families, who asked for "some Cloathes proper for people in their Station." In 1746, the Cherokees received "blew cloth for a Suit of Cloaths and six double Breasted Coats and of Scarlet for a Suit and Callico for gowns for a Woman and Two children." In 1752, Ammoscossity returned to Tennessee with "a handsome Suit of Clothes for himself, his Empress and Son." Governor Dinwiddie sent "fine ruffled shirts" and plain shirts to the cochiefs of the Six Nations Iroquois at the Loggs Town treaty.[33] The Indians relinquished none of the important material symbols of their power yet embraced the visual impact of a fine gentleman's coat.

The colonial government required Indians traveling east of the Blue Ridge to carry a passport, and Indians on official business were often escorted across Virginia at the expense of the colony. The routes taken by Indian visitors to and from Williamsburg depended on their point of departure and destination as well as their escort. Staging for troops and supplies heading to Ohio in the 1750s took place in Winchester and Fredericksburg, suggesting travel routes north of Williamsburg and along the Rappahannock. Catawbas leaving the capital took the Jamestown ferry, traversing southside Virginia for home.[34]

Indians from the west, mostly Cherokees, passed through central Virginia. The usual route brought them from Tennessee, north into the Valley of Virginia, then east to Williamsburg. Some travelers undoubtedly used mountain gaps to the south and crossed Lunenburg County on their journey. But numerous groups came to the seat of Augusta County at Staunton, passing east through the pass named "Wood's Gap" or "Jarham's Gap" by the white settlers. Colonel James Patton of Augusta escorted Cherokees from his home near Staunton to Williamsburg and back in 1751. The colonial government paid Patton £50, as well as his expenses of £44 18s. 4 1/2d. An overly punctilious clerk recorded the tavern accounts for which he reimbursed Patton, which allows us to reconstruct just how much opportunity people in places like Shadwell had for interaction with these travelers.[35]

Patton and an interpreter traveled with a number of Cherokee chiefs, one of whom may have been Attakullakulla, or the Little Carpenter, eight of their councillors, and about thirty attendants. They left Williamsburg in mid-August, following the Chickahominy River to New Kent Court House (fig. 6.8). From there, they followed the Pamunkey River northwest, stopping at Page's Warehouse at Hanover Town and Hanover Court House. The next leg of the journey followed the westward path of the South Anna River, along which they stopped at Thomas Lankford's and Winston's Ordinary. In Albemarle County, they stayed with Thomas Walker at his home, Castle Hill. Following the Southwest Mountains to Secretary's Ford on the Rivanna, they passed over Peter Jefferson's land, perhaps stopping for refreshment or to greet old friends. They stayed at Ferrel's Ordinary before heading across the mountains via Woods Gap. Patton escorted them as far as Reed Creek, where they parted,

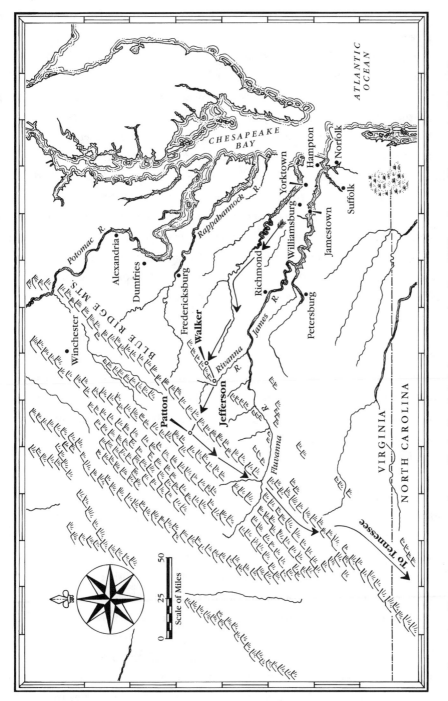

Figure 6.8. Native American travels near Shadwell included this route, taken from Williamsburg to Tennessee by Colonel Patton and a group of Cherokees, August–September 1751.

heading south to Tennessee. The accounts for the trip date its end on September 18, a journey of at least thirty days.[36]

Jefferson's letter to John Adams noted that Indian travels changed: "Before the Revolution, they were in the habit of coming often and in great numbers to the seat of the government, where I was very much with them." [37] About the time the Indians acculturated the Virginians, and vice versa, this brief moment of comradeship between the Indians and the English ended and westward expansion again pressured the homes of Indians bordering Virginia. This time, they could not use the French menace to entreat the English. And with the Revolution over, the former colonists turned back to their march across America and the Native Americans. Thomas Jefferson lamented their passing, but his new government took precedence in his affairs.

The Indians' impact on colonial society, measured through their visits and travels in Virginia, is evident in the language of newspaper accounts of these visits. The accounts of Indians in the *Virginia Gazette* reflected a growing awareness and interest in Indian activities during the late colonial period. Earlier "stories" consisted of a sentence or two, with no specific names of individuals, though the Indians were always categorized by tribe. A 1752 story read, in its entirety, "This week arriv'd in Town the Emperor of the Cherokee Nation, with his empress, to renew the Treaty of Friendship with this Government." Longer stories referred to the Indians as "Emperor," "men and women," and "warriors" but rarely used personal names, though the same text named the local theater manager. Of the *Gazettes* surveyed, one news story about Indians in 1765 used the anglicized names "Little Carpenter" and "Great Doctor," but not until 1777 did any Indian names other than tribes appear in the colonial press. The 1765 story, which mentioned "Oconostoto, the Little Carpenter, and the Pigeon," had an easy and friendly tone, referring to the Indians as "Forty Gentlemen and Ladies of the Cherokee nation."[38] Perhaps this change reflected the particular attitude of the different publishers of the *Virginia Gazette* over the years, or maybe the winds of war, but also the gradual ease of Virginians to some Indians during the short period in which they were compatriots.

Yet for all the commonalties between the Indians and the Virginians in this period, distinctions remained. Governor Dinwiddie offered his interpretation of Indian protocol to his commissioners to the Cherokee and Catawba treaty in 1755. He pointed out what the Indians expected in their peace ceremony and advised them to express love but not to promise any guns. The Indians needed equal coaching in their pursuit of diplomacy. Timberlake cautioned the Indians he escorted to London on how to act when meeting the king. He told Ostenaco not to offer the king his peace pipe nor to try to shake his hand.[39] Everyone involved in these two exchanges understood the other culture just enough to fear catastrophe from a small breach of basic manners.

Jefferson's reminiscence brings the Cherokee travelers to Shadwell and into the family home: "I knew much the great Outassetè, the warrior and orator of the Cherokees; he was always the guest of my father, on his journeys to and from Williamsburg." [40] Most likely, if they slept in the Jeffersons' house and not outside, Outassetè and some of his other warriors occupied the second downstairs chamber. The furniture in this room was almost as good as Peter and Jane's in the first chamber, though the fireplace was slightly smaller. If this room was the regular domain of some of the Jefferson children, they joined their brothers or sisters in one of the two heated bedrooms upstairs, making way for the guests. If the Jefferson's felt their visitors to be superior in status, then, in the English custom, Peter and Jane probably gave up their bed, the best in the house, to the best guest. Jefferson's old age memory of the Indian's visit implies some frequency of the event, and perhaps the second chamber always served as guest quarters. If the Indians used the beds, they found them as strange and uncomfortable as Timberlake found theirs. The Cherokees had their own hierarchy and clearly understood the white man's. Housing the chief in the best building and relegating his attendants to the surrounding dependencies appealed to both the Indians' and the planters' sense of propriety.

The rest of Outassetè's entourage probably slept in outbuildings or under the stars. Perhaps they joined the slave cook and her family in the kitchen building, other slave families in their small houses, or found room in the barns. In inclement weather, when the Indians built their small shelters, perhaps the plantation yard was dotted with Indian huts, campfires, and bearskins. The slaves who brought the Indians food probably traded with them and danced with them or shared songs around the fires, exchanging glass beads for copper pieces, buttons for wampum. Perhaps a slave showed the Indians the strange piece of pottery she found by the river, but the Indians were more interested in the stew roasting in the simple colono pot that she brought from the tidewater plantation where she was born. She may have shown them the white worked quartz from the plowed fields, and they may have given her an old chert arrowhead carried for good luck. The Indians' visit more than doubled the population of the plantation for a few days. It was a major event in the lives of all who resided there.

Thomas Jefferson, a small group of Indian artifacts, and the colonial records of Indian activities describe Outassetè at Shadwell, dining in the best room, wearing a bright blue coat, drinking cider with Peter Jefferson, Fry, Walker, Lomax, Patton, and Timberlake. Outassetè probably wore a European coat similar to Peter Jefferson's, though his adornment also included his tribal badges, gorget, and beaded garter. The reconstruction of Cherokee activities with their white counterparts in Virginia in this period clearly places the warrior and the surveyor in the same world, participating in many of the same rituals of colonial Virginia life. The shared material culture of late colonial contact meant that much of what Indians wore would be indistinguishable in the archaeological record from what whites and blacks wore.

As the material culture of famous men leads us to include more people in the discussion of how their worlds worked, we are also led to consider part of their material culture that is absent from the documents. Among Virginia's Indian neighbors, the protocol of visiting—in friendship or to carve out treaties—required the giving of gifts. Yet there are significantly few references to Native American–produced objects in eighteenth-century probate inventories. There is nothing listed in any Jefferson inventories as Indian, but that does not mean they received no tokens for their hospitality beyond the old arrowheads found at Shadwell. Estate appraisers may have thought so little of native goods that they did not even mention them. Indian items could be included as the Jeffersons' "2 Drest skins & some pieces soll Leather" in a storeroom or "2 raw hides & some tann'd Leather" in an outbuilding, but more likely, at least for the latter, these entries refer to supplies for the shoemaker, and the inventory listed his tools nearby. These leather and skin references did not mention decoration or origin, and none of these leather goods was in the house. Yet in Peter's office, in the passage, in hall or chamber, there must have been a skin, a headdress, a breastplate or pouch, a basket, or some other prizes of friendship. Albemarle County inventories include only six references to any item of native manufacture. Five people owned toma-hawks, which were listed with other weapons or tools. John Driver owned "1 indian pot," one of the few food vessels in his meager estate that totaled only £15 2s. 6d. If the inventories are correct, only one slave who lived in colonial Albemarle County was an Indian. If Indian objects were not rare, they were common enough to remain unmentioned.[41]

Ethnicity

The ethnohistory of Indian, planter, and slave contact in the mid-eighteenth century blurs distinctions between the ethnicity of the material worlds of these three groups. Indians maintained parts of their own ornament, such as breastplates, paint, and wampum, even as they requested ruffled shirts and coats with brass buttons. Their own ornaments reflected their Indian-ness to the white world, and maybe their white counterparts expected them to look a certain way. Their requests for fine European clothes do not suggest a desire to become English; they recognized the coats and shirts as status symbols that gave them another diplomatic tool in the white world. Timberlake noted the Indians' dress in his diary and said the "old people remember and praise an-cient days, before they were acquainted with the whites, when they had but little dress." He commented that the Indians' "dress is now become very much like the European; and indeed that of the men is gretly altered." Timberlake noticed that the Indians preferred some forms of European dress and wore it at home and that they were well aware that it changed their world.[42]

Standard archaeological categorization of various objects recovered at Shadwell allows us to label certain pieces as English, African, or Native Amer-ican, a distinction that may reflect only who made the objects. By the mid-eighteenth century in Virginia, these groups shared more objects that were the same than were different, yet these groups recognized the other's ethnic identity. Contemporary descriptions of visiting Indians reveal only a few orna-ments of native manufacture that would survive in the archaeological record as evidence of an Indian visit. Those same descriptions name many objects used by everyone in colonial Virginia.

The written record suggests that all these groups recognized status as an important part of identity. Each of these groups understood hierarchy within their own systems and appealed to each other's sense of rank as part of their interpersonal and diplomatic relations. The presence of brass buttons among slaves may indicate emulation of people who were free and wealthy, whether Indian or white. The lack of Indian trophies in household inventories may indicate the perceived worthlessness of these items in the English world. Even if status overshadowed ethnicity in this frontier environment—regardless of the fact that ethnicity often determined status—Indians used certain badges of their ethnic identity to reinforce their presence in the colonial world. Ethnic markers may have been more useful when one traveled as a visitor in another world than within one's own neighborhood.

The thirty-one Indian objects from Shadwell may have been relics of an earlier people at the time they were found and kept by slaves and planters there. The projectile points, stone tools, and tinklers were probably also relics of a past era to the Cherokees who carried guns and wore European clothes in the 1750s. Yet these same objects may have served well the Indians who visited Shadwell's residents and sought to charm their hosts by exchanging some distinct cultural artifact. Just as the use and ownership of objects changed, the use of ethnicity as a marker could change too. A stone projectile point, obsolete in its technology, still had cultural currency in colonial Virginia.

Outassetè and Peter Jefferson had many friends in common; they were at times part of the same social and political webs. Two of the commissioners who represented the crown at Loggs Town in 1751, Joshua Fry and Lunsford Lomax, were with Jefferson as part of the surveying crew that ran the Fairfax Line in 1747. Outassetè and Patton camped at Walker's; Walker lived near Jefferson and attended him as a physician in the last few months of his life. Dinwiddie wrote Jefferson in 1755 and 1756, charging him to send his militia to Patton's aid in the valley. The governor's letters to Patton assured him that help was on the way. John Harvie, executor of Peter Jefferson's estate, dined at Patton's house in 1751 before joining a mutual friend of them all, the parson Rose. Though Outassetè's name emerges from the history books, remembered for his oratory and humanity, other Indians traveled all his paths with him, dined in forests and plantation homes with him, and sailed to London with him (fig. 6.9). Just as Peter Jefferson lived as one of many settlers along the Blue Ridge, Outassetè was surely one of many remarkable natives who helped define the Virginia frontier. The names of these few provide the tools to write the history of the rest whose names remain unknown.[43]

Figure 6.9. London artists drew and painted the Cherokees who visited England with Henry Timberlake. *Three Cherokees Came Over from the Head of the River Savanna to London 1762*, George Bickham, London, c. 1765. Courtesy The Colonial Williamsburg Foundation.

Jefferson's Vantage

It is easier to list the business transactions in which Peter Jefferson involved himself than to describe the range of social relationships that grew alongside them. The impression of this part of Jefferson's world is almost as a men's club, a masculine place with highly specialized codes of interaction. The image of these powerful men, talking and drinking together at court day or seated at a member's table or around a surveying camp fire, is partly from legends retold by Thomas Jefferson and his siblings to their family. The chronology of Peter Jefferson's life also supports these stories, especially the visits of Fry, Rose, and Outassetè. The connections Jefferson had with other powerful men grew from exchanges made socially as well as in ledger books. Sarah Randolph reported the story told by Thomas Jefferson to one of his grandsons, who asked how the men of Peter Jefferson's day spent their time. Jefferson replied: "My father had a devoted friend, to whose house he would go, dine, spend the night, dine with him again in the second day, and return to Shadwell in the evening. His friend, in the course of a day or two, returned the visit, and spent the same length of time at his house. This occurred once every week; and thus, you see, they were together four days out of the seven."[44] This view is obviously romantic; the masculine bond, freely shared with certain leisure, with no interruptions from wives, children, or slaves, even the horses that brought them thus were subordinated to the idea of devoted male friendship.

The reality of these visits, in fact, involved the family and the whole apparatus of housekeeping—the personal slaves, servers, cooks, and horse grooms, as well as the burdens of spending time away from one's other obligations. Robert Rose revealed as much when after church one day he "returnd with some Company and [ate] a Batchelour's Dinner, my Wife & Daughter being gone to Col. Beverley's."[45] Dinner was not usual in the absence of his family. Possibly, it being Sunday and the family away, his house slaves had the day off and the men fixed their own food. At the least, Rose himself had to instruct the servants of the group's needs, and obviously this was novel to him. Rose also revealed that the women and children performed a similar visitation circuit. Sometimes Rose recorded meeting up with his wife and children on his visits to Joshua Fry or John Harvie.

The history of prominent white men has been known, recorded, and written. Historians also seek to tell the stories of women, slaves and free blacks, Native Americans, and the nameless multitudes who peopled early America. The lessons of social history, historical archaeology, and material culture studies have been instrumental in doing that. This close reading of a particular place and the family there brings together the histories of those many groups to make one story, and the story begins to reveal how many other actors helped shape the image of a man like Peter Jefferson in his time. Shaping that image for history would be the project of the next generation.

7 The Intangible Legacies: Creating and Keeping Family History

Peter and Jane Jefferson gave their children more than a comfortable home and financial legacies. They created and maintained professional, social, and family relationships that continued to provide a network of support for their heirs. They established, through documents, stories, and naming patterns, connections to generations past that would preserve intangible parts of their legacies for generations yet to come. Each generation of a family writes another chapter of the family history, whether its members choose to preserve and perpetuate the values and traditions of their ancestry or to reject traditions and fashion themselves anew. The Jeffersons clearly chose the former, connecting their past and their future through carefully staged presentations that provided each generation with knowledge about family that would further its members in the same worlds that their parents and grandparents had known.

This chapter is not meant to be hagiographic, taking at face value the words written by various family members that celebrate only their successes. Instead, I am taking the words as evidence of action. For instance, Thomas Jefferson wrote of his concern for Martha Carr when their sister Mary Bolling moved some distance away in 1787. He noted the relationship between his sisters, he acknowledged that Martha might feel a loss, and he cared to write about it at all. These were not thoughts he had to express nor even feel, yet there is evidence here that he did both. The Shadwell generation wrote letters and legal documents and acted in ways that show their concern and awareness of one another's successes and failures.

We have already visited many of the ways that activities at Shadwell played a role in training family members for their roles as adults. In this chapter we explore how many of these same activities reveal ways in which the Jeffersons maintained their family traditions. We have explored the didactic qualities of the Jeffersons' material world that taught lessons even to viewers who remained unaware that they were responding to the subtle messages of their surroundings. We have seen how the household skills of Jane Jefferson established her children for their lives as adults. We have witnessed the legal yoke of slavery that trained both servants and masters to their roles. We have measured the fruits of Peter Jefferson's alliances with family, friends, and associates. We will now visit the Shadwell generation as its members grow older, children marry, some die, and others step into roles as guardians of the family traditions. The legacies left are varied. They are as simple as a memory—a story told and retold—as complex an artifact as a family Bible bearing history in its birth and death records and in the symbolic value of its previous possession by an ancestor, or as genuine a declaration of devotion, as when a brother takes in a widowed sister.

Historian Daniel Blake Smith has called women the "guardians of the kin network."[1] Jane Jefferson performed many of the roles of such a guardian. Her kin, her family beyond Shadwell, provided a substantial portion of the social world that the young Jeffersons knew, and her family produced both friends and marriage partners for her children. She wrote family history in the form of genealogical notations that would become part of the formal mechanism for passing history from one generation to another. Above all, she played a role in establishing a family whose members showed deep concern and affection for one another. The willingness of the next generation to continue to act as such guardians reflects the successes of Jane and Peter's lessons. The Jefferson children watched their parents perform their public and private responsibilities to family and embraced these same roles when their time came.

Preserving and Creating Legacies: Wills, Genealogy, and Family

Peter and Jane Jefferson established legacies of property for their children. They gave their children slaves, land, money, and other items as they saw fair and fitting. For the children it was their passage to adulthood—on marrying or on reaching majority—that most often prompted the transfer of family wealth to them. The Jeffersons arranged these transfers to benefit both giver and receiver and to smooth the transitions for those who took on new responsibilities.

Peter and Jane set in place exacting instructions for the dispersal of their estates after their deaths. Their attention to legal and equitable arrangements likely provided a number of intangible advantages to the Jefferson children. Peter's will shows some of these. First, Peter's will maintained Jane and the family at Shadwell, providing continuity for both Jane and their children. Second, the legal details of his will ensured access for each heir to his or her money and property, with plenty of forethought about the consequences if a bequeathed slave or an heir should die before the distribution. Third, the will contained provisions to exclude heirs who might challenge their own or a sibling's right, quelling later protests and providing heirs with legal tools to resolve disputes. Peter's will explicitly stated that educating all the children was a priority and suggested which lands could be sold if there was a shortage of funds for this primary goal. Rather than limiting and controlling Jane's legal participation, Peter's appointment of executors may have given her freedom from worrying about plantation finances and enabled her closer attention to family concerns. After he returned to Albemarle as an adult, Thomas took over as executor of the Shadwell estate and refined the legal arrangements between his mother and siblings, the occupants of Shadwell—and himself, the would-be legal owner of the plantation. The established legal mechanisms worked in settling the estates of Jane Jr. and Elizabeth, who left only siblings as heirs. The seven surviving siblings divided Jane Jr.'s estate. Each of the siblings received £28 3s. 7 1/4d., or one-seventh of the £200 legacy, or would upon reaching majority in the case of Anna Scott and Randolph. The family was still settling Elizabeth's estate in 1790 when Thomas wrote to his brother to inform him he would receive £36 7s. 2d. from Elizabeth's estate.[2]

Jane's use of the estate following Peter's death shows timely and careful attention to Peter's wishes. She took deliberate care in charging the estate for certain costs, such as those for clothing for the "children's slaves." What have been interpreted by historians as cold and legalistic exchanges between Jane and her son Thomas are in fact their attempts to ensure that individual fortunes remained intact while Peter's estate underwrote the expenses of the minor children. Jane charged the estate for such small things as shoes, stockings, and tailoring for the children. Likewise, in his role as executor, Thomas charged the estate for personal items purchased for Lucy, Randolph, and Anna Scott, keeping their accounts separate from his own. Thomas made careful notes of leases for land and slaves from his mother during her days at Shadwell and when he leased Elizabeth's slave Cate from her.[3]

In 1790, thirty-three years after Peter Jefferson's death, Thomas defended his understanding of his father's will "that all my Family live & be maintained & my Children Educated out of the Profits of my Estate" until each child came of age. In the postwar years, when British creditors sought repayment of debts from their American colleagues, Thomas Walker and John Nicholas, two of Peter's executors, were called on to help settle an outstanding balance on the elder Jefferson's estate with the tobacco merchant Kippen and Company. Thomas Jefferson defended the charges and challenged Walker on the issue of "the maintenance of my sisters." Thomas presented two methods of calculating the valid expenses of the children: (1) "a statement of what they were actually" that would require an impossible knowledge of the accounts of Kippen and Company; or (2) an estimate by year that could be averaged "for every age from 11. to 21. years." Children under ten years of age were legally "infants." "Maintenance" and "board" were separate expenses for the estate. By an agreement of 1760 between Jane and the executors, she received money for board at the sum of £6 for the younger and £10 for the elder children. Thomas suggested averaging this at £8 for his settlement with Walker. Thomas reported that Walker had "confounded" the board of the sisters with "their cloathing &c." Jane "never cloathed them; the estate did that from the beginning to the end."[4] The seemingly petty accounts that Jane kept with executors John Harvie and then her son were part of the calculated mechanism for preserving individual fortunes.

Peter's will prescribed equitable legacies to each daughter and to each son, with the exception of his desk and bookcase, books, and mathematical instruments to his son Thomas. Peter may have felt that his oldest son would need these items most when he took over as family patriarch, or maybe he recognized the interest his son had in the activities served by these objects. Randolph was not yet two when his father wrote the will, so the decision to leave these objects to Thomas had nothing to do with any recognition that the younger son might not take to them.[5]

Jane's will differed in that she made bequests only to her unmarried children. She acknowledged the specific needs of those family members in their present lives. To Anna Scott and Randolph she bequeathed slaves, and to Elizabeth, who lived at home, Jane gave items for personal comfort—clothes and a bed. On three other occasions Jane deeded slaves to family members. In 1766 she gave Fany to Mary Bolling. In 1770 she deeded Lucy to Jane Barbara Carr and Rachel to Randolph. Although there is no easy explanation for why Jane gave slaves to Mary or Jane Carr when she did, the gift to Randolph was to replace Hannah, whom the Snowdon overseer killed in 1770.[6]

Marriage: Preservation of Family and Social Tool

The marriage partners of the Jefferson children allow us to discuss a number of different strategies for maintaining status and creating and preserving kin networks and social opportunity. Marriage was just one marker of adulthood for the Jefferson children. Of the eight children who reached adulthood, two daughters never married and one married late, a son married late, and two siblings married siblings who also were first cousins of the Jefferson children. Four of the Jefferson children—only one half—married in a timely fashion. Three daughters married at what would have been considered "on time," Mary at eighteen years of age, Martha at nineteen, and Lucy at sixteen. The youngest daughter, Anna Scott, married late, at the age of thirty-two. During the second half of the eighteenth century women married by about age twenty-two, a figure that had risen in correlation to higher population density and scarcity of land. Those same correlates pushed male marriage age higher also, from mid- to late twenties to later twenties when there was less nearby land available on which to establish themselves. Thomas married at age twenty-eight and Randolph at twenty-four.[7] The two Jefferson boys, however, came into substantial improved lands, ready labor in the form of slaves, and a network of willing associates on reaching their majority. That they did not marry early cannot be tied to their financial situations.

Two Jefferson daughters—Jane, who died at twenty-six, and Elizabeth, who died at twenty-nine—never married. The oldest daughter, Jane, extolled by her famous brother as lively and witty, even had a sizable dowry of £200 and an estate valued at £114 15s. 3d. in movable goods. Her estate included three slaves and did not include the value of her clothing. The fashionable state of her wardrobe as listed in her inventory after her death may indicate that she prepared for courtship and had every intention to marry. The value of Jane Jr.'s estate alone made her wealthier than 55 percent of all decedents in Albemarle County during the colonial period and, if her cash dowry was added, wealthier than 75 percent. The fact that the talented, lovely, and wealthy Jane did not marry may be an indictment on the Jeffersons' strategy of locating their family where they did. On the other hand, Elizabeth, who had similar personal wealth, may not have been a candidate for a wife owing to a mental deficiency, stories about which emerge in family lore.[8]

Distance

The Jefferson children found their marriage partners both near and far within Virginia. The three youngest Jefferson children, Lucy, Anna Scott, and Randolph, married nearby, within the range of 2 to 7 miles from home (fig. 7.1). Martha's partner, Dabney Carr, came from about 20 miles abroad but visited Shadwell often as a schoolmate of her brother. Mary's husband, John Bolling, lived about 35 miles hence, and Thomas's wife dwelt between 100 and 120 miles away, depending on whether she resided in Charles City County or Williamsburg when they courted. The associations between the families before the marriages reveal other trends. The two who married closest to home, Lucy and Randolph, married siblings who were first cousins of the Jeffersons. Randolph had boarded at the Lewises for schooling and thus knew his cousins well. Lucy shared the tutor Benjamin Sneed with her brother and their cousins but did not board away from home. This was the closest kin to Shadwell, and Jane probably relied quite a bit on her sister Mary and her husband, Charles Lewis, for both social interaction and family support. The children who married farthest from home gained more status from their spouses than those who stayed

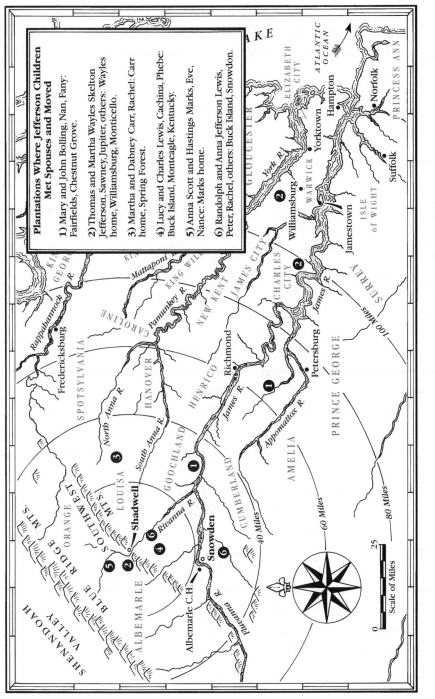

Figure 7.1. Plantations where Jefferson children met spouses and moved. The Jefferson children courted their spouses within 5 miles of home and as far away as 120 miles.

close, although each of the children faired reasonably well. Although the age of the children at first marriage might suggest some limitations to the Jeffersons' access to socializing events, the socially successful marriages that were distant argue that the Jeffersons were able to travel, to entertain, and to connect with people of their own station. The marriages of the Jefferson children indicate strategies for maintaining their place and a general "success" of each match to the Jeffersons' own status.[9]

Parents' Connections

The families of all but one of the children's spouses appeared in earlier exchanges with Peter Jefferson. Both John Bolling, who married Mary, and James Skelton, whose daughter-in-law would become Thomas's wife, subscribed to lots in the speculative town of Beverley that Peter Jefferson recorded in 1751. The families of Martha Wayles (Skelton) Jefferson had numerous opportunities for interaction with Peter.[10] The Bolling and Lewis families also appeared in Peter's account book, and John Carr, father of Dabney Carr, settled an account with Peter's estate in 1760. John Bolling's father's estate, Cobbs, appears on the Fry-Jefferson Map, and the elder Jefferson and elder Bolling were burgesses at the same time. Only Hastings Marks had no prior documented business with the senior Jeffersons, but he knew such other family associates as the Lewises at Buck Island and family friend Tucker Woodson, and his brothers held offices in Albemarle County. He had some minor interaction with Thomas Jefferson.[11]

The Jefferson children entered into adulthood with ready wealth and established places in society. Each Jefferson daughter entered the marriage market with a trained servant and a substantial dowry to add to the fortune of whatever husband she found and was thus extremely desirable as a bride. The two sons brought land and slaves; both daughters and sons brought education and social skills to the matches they made. Both daughters and sons brought the prestige of their father's public name and the many associates and relations of their father and their mother across Virginia. The children's marriage partners brought other wealth and connections, although many of them already were within the web that the Jeffersons occupied. Bolling, Carr, and the two Lewises came into their marriages especially well known to the family. Their alliances within the family to other than their own spouse speak of good relationships based on an intellectual and social affinity within this broadening cohort.

Status

Two sisters found husbands whose public profiles matched Peter Jefferson's and almost Thomas's. In 1760 Mary married John Bolling Jr. She was eighteen and he was twenty-three. There is no mention of where John and Mary courted, but their families clearly knew each other well. This was a triumphant match of families: both were children of burgesses; both came to the marriage with sizable fortunes. The Bollings and Mary's Randolph grandparents had neighboring lands in Goochland County. Bolling received Mary's portion of £200 and the slave Nan, valued at £55, from her father's estate the year they were married. The younger Bolling established himself in Goochland County at Fairfield. He was on the vestry of Saint James Northam, served as a county magistrate, was elected to the House of Burgesses from Goochland County, and served in the House of Delegates in 1778. Bolling shared interests with Thomas and presumably also with Mary, in the exchange of seeds and plants and breeding horses. They shared other associations: Bolling's duty as vestryman put him in the company of Thomas's close friend and cousin Thomas Mann Randolph.[12]

Martha's marriage to Dabney Carr rivaled that of Mary and John Bolling as the most triumphant match in terms of the public standing of the spouse. Carr was the son of Major John Carr and his wife, Barbara Overton Carr, of nearby Louisa County. Before Dabney's death at the age of thirty, he served as a burgess for Louisa County. His friendship with Thomas Jefferson is legendary. They studied together as boys and at college, shared books, and undertook the duties of similar public office.[13]

Thomas himself did not marry until relatively late in his life. His youthful crushes on women in his own social circle had remained unfulfilled, and he engaged seriously in his work at the bar and with politics before marrying. Perhaps only a widow who may have become a worldlier woman would do at this point for the partner of the sophisticated Jefferson, or perhaps an experienced woman could take lead of the shy Jefferson. Thomas was twenty-eight when he married the widow Martha Wayles Skelton; she was twenty-three. Her father, John Wayles, had been a lawyer and her first husband, Bathurst

Skelton, a colleague of Thomas's at the college. Thomas's wedding is the only one about which we know something of the festivities. His marriage to Martha took place at her father's house, The Forest, in Charles City County. Other Jefferson children's weddings were likely also held at the home of the bride. Thomas paid the Reverend William Coutts, rector of Martin's Brandon Parish, for officiating at his wedding, he paid a fiddler, and he made handsome tips to a long list of servants at Martha's father's home.[14]

Two siblings married within the same family, but whether this represents a triumph or failure of social engagement is a matter of speculation. Although it may indicate the seizing of social opportunity, it may also illustrate the limited field from which to choose. Lucy married her cousin Charles Lilburne Lewis in 1769 and took her inheritance, which included slaves Cachina and her daughter Phebe. They lived at Monteagle, part of Lewis's father's Buck Island estate, about five miles from Shadwell. Buck Island was the home of Mary Randolph and Charles Lewis Jr., sister and brother-in-law of Jane Randolph Jefferson. Lucy's husband was the brother of the woman who would eventually marry Lucy's brother Randolph. The proximity of Buck Island created close ties between the families there and at Shadwell. Marriage to cousins was a strategy for strengthening kin networks and keeping wealth within a family. The marriages of these two younger Jeffersons to their cousins occurred in 1769 and 1780, a time when there were more rather than fewer local opportunities for marriage outside the family: the population of Albemarle had almost doubled between Peter Jefferson's death and 1782.[15] Yet, with an aging mother, unstable crop prices, and a very busy brother instead of a father as their social representative beyond the home, perhaps the pool of worthy suitors seemed smaller to the youngest children.

The last sibling to marry was Anna Scott, Randolph's twin. Anna Scott's husband, Hastings Marks, lived about seven miles from Shadwell, near Thomas's Monticello holdings. Although Hastings did not hold public office, members of his family did. His brothers served as magistrates and sheriff, his brother John was on the county's central committee formed in 1775 to discuss the Revolution, and Hastings and John served in the Albemarle militia. Marks was also a family friend of the Lewises at Buck Island. Anna Scott and Hastings never had children (though Anna Scott's mother bore her last children at age thirty-five). Thomas was in Paris in 1787 when Hastings and Anna Scott married. It took some time for the news to reach him, but when it did, he wrote separate letters to the newlyweds offering wishes of joy and happiness and promising his support of their lives together. His letter to Hastings was also a formal introduction, since the two had only a passing acquaintance. Thomas claimed to "have good sense" of Marks's "good merit" from their neighborhood associates. In his letter to Hastings he also noted that Mr. Lewis had taken care of the business of seeing that Anna Scott's fortune was transferred to her husband.[16]

Martha Carr's letter to her brother informing him of Anna Scott's marriage contained cautions about Hastings, however. Anna Scott had lingered at the Lewises and married without consulting her sister Carr, with whom she had been living. Martha described Marks's life as "very Irregular" with "little or no fortune" but noted that he was "very capable of book keeping and has been of late extremely industrious." Martha added, "I find compassion added to my tenderness for her," as evidently the younger sister was nervous about invoking the older's disapproval.[17] Anna Scott's late marriage to a neighbor of unimpressive financial standing may be the clearest statement that family strategies for marrying well were not in place when she came of age. Her mother died the year she turned twenty-one, and her brothers and brothers-in-law were busy with political and military occupations.

Marriage Promises and Problems

The quality of the marriages themselves was something of which the Jefferson siblings were quite aware. Despite earlier indications of a warm relationship between brothers-in-law John Bolling and Thomas Jefferson, by the late 1790s Bolling's drinking problem became the topic of letters between family members. All hoped that John would treat Mary well enough and that Mary would bear the trials of an intemperate husband with patience. There were no comments that Bolling was physically abusive. Thomas used the occasion of Mary's complaints to offer what he called a "sermon" to his daughter on the duties of husbands and wives, stressing that "harmony in the marriage state is the very first object to be aimed at." The implication followed that Mary needed to learn to "leave [John] in quiet possession" of his views if she did not share those same views. Toleration was her wifely duty, according to her brother. The reservations that Martha may have had about Hastings Marks as Anna Scott's husband never resurfaced as a topic in family letters—at least not among those that still exist. But the many letters between Thomas and members of Lucy's family indicate that all the Jeffersons were aware of the inability of Charles Lilburne Lewis to be financially responsible or to instill such principles in his sons. On the other hand, in 1770 Thomas wrote of the household happiness of Dabney Carr, five years into his marriage with Martha. "He speaks, thinks, and dreams of nothing but his young son. This friend of ours . . . in a very small house, with a table, half a dozen chairs, and one or two servants, is the happiest man in the universe." Thomas admired Carr's situation and also his nature, which included the ability to take "every incident in life [and] render it a source of pleasure."[18] The siblings concerned themselves greatly when a sibling or sibling's spouse died: they offered company, accommodations, and words of heartfelt support. Keeping account of one another was among the important lessons that Jane and Peter had taught their children.

Kin Networks, Part I

In 1787 Thomas Jefferson wrote an affectionate and newsy letter to his sister Mary Bolling. He was in Paris responding to a letter that she wrote him with news about her family: he offered news of his daughters, who were then in France, and remarked on aging and the importance of family. In this letter Thomas expressed a number of sentiments about his relationships with siblings. "As I grow older," he wrote, "I love those most whom I loved first," and, "we often write seldomest to those whom we love most." He lamented the news that Mary and John Bolling were moving to Chestnut Grove, "as it will prevent my seeing you as often as would be practicable at Lickinghole." But Thomas took solace in the fact that Mary's son Jack moved into his inheritance at Lickinghole with his new family and would still accommodate the family's visits there. Thomas told Mary to extend his regard to "my nephews and n[ie]ces of your fire side." He ended his letter, "be assured of the sincere love with which I am, dear sister, your affectionate brother, Th: Jefferson."[19] There is ample evidence that the children of Peter and Jane Jefferson kept in close contact and regarded one another highly in the years after both elder Jeffersons were gone. Peter and Jane worked to build the Shadwell estate, the trained workforce, and the social and family relationships that the children inherited: that much we have already seen. The elder Jeffersons left not only a legacy of attention to legal details and knowledge of family history but a tradition of involved and affectionate communication.

The middle of the eighteenth century—when Jane and Peter created and nurtured their family—saw the growth of kin-based networks in Virginia. These networks often functioned locally for poorer folks and provided farther-ranging connections for the elite. Kin networks provided opportunity and support within a group as parents to children, as siblings, and as cousins and more-distant relations. The Jeffersons show that responsibility among kin underpinned many of their family's activities. Peter Jefferson appears to have had a fond relationship with his in-laws, Isham Randolph and Jane's Randolph cousins, for whom he served in various capacities as estate executor and guardian to children. Jane and Peter revealed their duty to cousins when they removed their entire family from Shadwell to Tuckahoe to help see the young Randolphs to adulthood. For Jane that meant company while her husband was away on some of his surveying expeditions: wives often stayed with relations when husbands were absent from the plantation. Visiting served both social needs and strengthened the kin-based web-building.[20]

Visits among family also reveal something about its intergenerational relationships. Peter and Jane Jefferson's children spent time at Shadwell with their own families during the years Jane still lived. The children of Mary and John Bolling and the children of Martha and Dabney Carr visited Shadwell and their grandmother there. Both Lucy and her husband, Charles Lewis, and Thomas and his wife, Martha Jefferson, lived nearby when they began their families and likely also brought them to Shadwell. There is not a record of Jane's mother, Jane Rogers Randolph, visiting with her grandchildren at Shadwell or at Dungeness, where she died in 1765; however, Jane Randolph persisted in family lore as "stern and strict" and must have been known by them. At least two of the Jefferson children returned to Shadwell during periods of extreme difficulty in their lives. Mary and John Bolling buried a child at Shadwell, and Martha and Dabney Carr were there when Dabney died in 1773.[21] The record does not tell us that Mary returned home for help nursing her sick child or that Martha and Dabney were there because of Dabney's illness, but we know they were there. Peter and Jane established a family that would know its extended members: grandparents, aunts, uncles, cousins, and they relied on one another well into later years.

That the Jefferson siblings visited one another shows the continued affection among them. Thomas called the 1787 news that Mary and John Bolling were leaving nearby Lickinghole to move to Chestnut Grove a "misfortune to myself." He went on to say, "It is still a greater loss to my sister Carr." Martha Carr, a widow living between Monticello and her own home in Goochland, relied on the companionship of this nearby sister more than Thomas did. Visits were news between the siblings and added social pressure to others to join in the visit. Thomas wrote to Randolph: "Our sister Marks arrived here last night and we shall be happy to see you also." In May 1813 Randolph told Thomas to tell "My sister Marks" that "We shall be extremely happy to see her hear" at Snowdon. In June Randolph wrote again and said that he and his wife expected Marks over the summer. Marks visited her twin again in April 1815, when she was well but he was "Extremely Week . . . and Scarce able to Walk." Her visit may have been to help Randolph and his wife during his illness. When Thomas returned from Paris in 1790, he worked his way home spending time with family and friends. His visits along the way included his siblings Martha at Spring Forest and Mary at Chestnut Grove, his niece Jane Carr and Wilson Miles Cary, the Eppes and Skipwith families, and Thomas Mann Randolph at Tuckahoe. His reacquaintance with kin clearly was important enough to him to delay his arriving at his beloved Monticello for a month after his ship landed at Norfolk. He could have made the journey in four to six days.[22]

Letters between the Jefferson siblings were filled with expressions of concern and affection. Their letters contained both family news and business: they wanted to know each other's children and have theirs known. They shared their complaints about health, aging, and raising children and marveled at becoming grandparents. They made substantive efforts to know one another's children and grandchildren. In a 1789 letter that Thomas wrote to Randolph, Thomas noted that his daughters asked to be remembered to Randolph and his wife, and Thomas inquired about Randolph's children, including "my namesake." Letters from his daughters told Thomas how his sisters fared. Ellen Randolph's letters to her grandfather included news about his sister's grandchildren.[23] Having their families know one another was important to the Jefferson siblings.

Their families also knew one another's in-laws, sometimes as neighbors, sometimes through the affinal network these marriages established. Thomas's daughter Mary stayed with her maternal aunt and uncle, Elizabeth and Francis Eppes, while Jefferson was in Paris in 1786. Visiting Eppington with Mary were her paternal aunts Martha Carr and Anna Scott Jefferson and Martha's daughter Polly Carr. Letters from Elizabeth Eppes to Thomas in Paris included news of Thomas's sisters' families. The Eppeses lived not far from Mary and John Bolling, and the Eppes and Bolling family lines intertwined on numerous occasions. Thomas's daughter Martha married within the Randolph family, which brought her in later years to Dungeness, the ancestral home of her grandmother.[24]

After marriage and raising children, the Jefferson siblings stood for one another in matters legal, financial, and familial well into their later years. Just as Peter Jefferson had stood as a witness or executor for family and such close friends as Isham Randolph and William Randolph, the next generation of Jeffersons and their spouses did the same. Hastings Marks was a witness for in-laws Charles Lewis and Isham Lewis. Thomas Jefferson was executor of estates for his mother, Charles Lewis, Hastings Marks, and his sister Elizabeth. Jane's 1766 deed of the slave Fany to daughter Mary Bolling was signed by her son-in-law Dabney Carr and family friend Patrick Henry Jr. Carr served as administrator of Jane Jr.'s estate. Thomas wrote a letter supporting his brother-in-law Charles Lewis's appointment to colonel of the county militia in 1781. Thomas wrote Randolph's will in 1808.[25] Thus, additions to the widening family circle served the public needs of its members in the same way that the immediate family had.

Support within the Jefferson family meant more than a legal relationship. The longer-established siblings looked after those following. Young Thomas stayed with the Bollings on his way to Shadwell from Williamsburg over Christmas 1762. He wrote to his friend John Page of rats and leaky roofs there and expressed his adolescent angst at being away from the gatherings of his cohorts in Williamsburg. In the years before her marriage at the late age of thirty-three, Anna Scott lived with her sister Mary at the Bollings' home in Goochland County. Anna Scott's older brother made sure her accounts were in order on numerous occasions when he visited or saw their brother-in-law John Bolling. Many of these associations that formed at young ages benefited the broad family network for generations.

Letters among family members show that the regard the Jefferson siblings had for one another during their early adult years extended into old age. The filial responsibility shown by Thomas to his family at Shadwell went well beyond his role as executor of his mother's estate. As a big brother he purchased personal items for his younger sisters, such as hair curls and stays for Lucy and Anna Scott. Into their later years they relied on their world-traveling brother to be their source of special items. He shopped for Lucy in Philadelphia in 1783. Before leaving for France in 1784, Thomas wrote to Anne Scott from Annapolis and invited her to "pass the hot season at Monticello" and noted that he would send her accessories from Europe, which he included in a packet to their sister Martha the following November.[26]

The Jefferson sisters and brothers inquired about one another when a spouse or child died. Thomas moved his sisters Martha and Anna Scott to Monticello during their widowhoods (fig. 7.2). Martha was with Thomas when his wife died, and Thomas went to Chestnut Grove to visit Mary just after her husband died. Mary commented to her father that the death of Polly Archer (Martha Bolling) was "afflicting to Aunt Bolling." They were aware and supportive during these momentous occasions.[27]

The Jefferson siblings inquired about one another's well being whether they were near or far. They also wrote numerous letters to their children and about

Figure 7.2. A silhouette representing the head and shoulders of Martha Jefferson Carr (1746–1811), Thomas Jefferson's sister, who lived at Monticello. Courtesy Monticello/Thomas Jefferson Foundation, Inc.

their children. They expressed love and affection and concern for happiness and education, and they worried when children moved away. In 1792, following the marriage of her daughter Lucy to Richard Terrell, Martha wrote her brother Thomas about her "distress and Anxiety of mind" at the thought of being "separated (perhaps forever) from an Affectionate and dutyfull Child," for the Terrells were moving to Kentucky. Thomas's daughter Martha echoed her aunt's concerns when she lamented to her father that "Aunt Carr will have only one of her children with her." Lucy wrote her brother Thomas of her happiness with her family in 1807, during a brief hiatus in the saga of the Lewis family's financial problems. When Lucy moved to Kentucky with her sons, Thomas's granddaughter observed, "I went to see [Aunt Lewis] before she set off. She appeared to be very much pleased with the thoughts of Living with her children."[28]

Just as their uncle Lewis had boarded and educated some of them, so, too, did Thomas for his nephews and nieces. Thomas raised and educated his sister Martha Carr's children, incorporating them into the everyday activities of his own family. When daughter Martha Jefferson [Randolph] recounted her youth, their names were included out of hand. She recalled "the time and attention [Thomas Jefferson bestowed] on our education—our cousins the Carrs and myself." Following his wife's death, he took "his children and his wards the Carrs," to be inoculated for smallpox. His interest was not just in their schooling, however; he was involved and aware of more details of their lives. In 1782 he noted of his Carr nieces that "the girls, three in number, are now become marriageable and of course require to be clothed more expensively than at any earlier period." In 1813 Thomas noted that James Lilburne, Randolph's son, had an interest in reading and offered to take him to live at Monticello to "improve his mind . . . to make him a very useful and respectable member of society." Randolph's sons sought their uncle's support in a suit against their stepmother in settling Randolph's estate. Letters to their uncle show that his investments in their education and well-being were fruitful: they included family news and reports of their reading and schooling, and solicited his advice on many topics. In short, they recognized those things that Thomas taught them as important and responded to him with proof that his lessons took hold in their lives. Successive generations connected the living with their ancestors. Family noted that Thomas Jefferson Randolph (Thomas's grandson) had the size and stature of Peter Jefferson.

Jeff Randolph's own mother worried that he had "enough of the Randolph character" to make her uneasy.[29]

Intellectual Affinity

After family, the topics that most engaged the Jefferson children, as evidenced by their letters, were plants and books. The siblings all seemed to share a love of plants and gardening. Many of their letters and accounts accompanied a seed or plant cutting, often invoking multiple generations and families in these exchanges. Anne Cary Randolph wrote to her grandfather about some Mignonett seed that her mother divided between "Mrs. Lewis Aunt Jane and herself," thereby sharing a plant between Thomas's sister Lucy Lewis, Thomas's son-in-law's sister, and Thomas's own daughter Martha. Letters between Thomas and John Bolling discussed agriculture and horse bloodlines. Thomas and Randolph exchanged the products of their plantations, and Thomas seemed to have an intimate working knowledge of Randolph's enterprise. The topics of correspondence between Thomas and Randolph remained domestic, however. The tone of Thomas's letters to his brother reveals a paternal relationship. Thomas offered Randolph all sorts of advice on planting, sheep dogs, and remedies for the younger's various ailments.[30]

The Jefferson siblings were also aware of one another's libraries. Thomas admired (and later inherited some of) Dabney Carr's books. Thomas's nephews solicited his advice on how to build their libraries. When Thomas was in Philadelphia and wished to acquire a copy of Catesby's *History of Carolina*, he knew that his brother-in-law John Bolling had a copy. Thomas asked his go-between, brother-in-law Francis Eppes, to induce Bolling to sell it, and suggested, "Perhaps you had better effect this by making the proposition to Mrs. Bolling. Of this your knowledge of the family will enable you to judge." Thomas included Francis Eppes and John Bolling in the distribution of his first printing of *Notes on Virginia*. Peter Carr solicited Thomas to purchase a Spanish dictionary for him in Paris, "as no such book is to be had, in any of the shops here."[31]

The expanded Jefferson family invested variously in the revolutionary activities that engaged the eldest son. Charles Lewis, Charles Lilburne Lewis, Randolph Jefferson, and Hastings Marks all served in the Albemarle militia, and all signed the Oath of Allegiance in Albemarle 1777. The father and son

Charles Lewis signed the 1776 "Petition of Dissenters in Albemarle and Amherst Counties," a request by non-Anglicans against the reestablishment of the Episcopal Church: the Lewises were Presbyterians. In 1777 Thomas, his brother Randolph, and brother-in-law-to-be Hastings Marks were among the subscribers to voluntarily support a local clergyman in the Calvinistical Reformed Church. Charles Lewis subscribed to the book of collected *American State Papers* in 1774, an effort at creating an archive of the nascent state. The Bollings' house, Fairfield, served to safeguard Jefferson's papers when they were removed from Richmond as the British army approached that city.[32] There were no Loyalists among the Jefferson siblings and spouses.

Rarely did the older Jefferson brother include the younger in news or philosophical discussions of state affairs that were the world Thomas inhabited, though other family members were occasionally privy to this information. In one letter to Randolph, Thomas acknowledged: "The occurrences of this part of the globe are of a nature to interest you so little that I have never made them the subject of a letter to you." He added that the time it took a letter to travel made news obsolete anyway. The statesman Jefferson shared news of international events with his brother-in-law Francis Eppes and occasionally with his daughters, who had traveled abroad with him.[33]

Although two of the siblings or their spouses became somewhat estranged from the family at different times, it appears that duty was served when it was needed. Both John Bolling and Charles Lewis had relationships with the other siblings that seemed to begin warm and later turned cold. Bolling's was caused by his drinking. Charles Lilburne Lewis died in 1831 in financial ruin, following a long tale of domestic problems and what his brother-in-law called "the shipwreck of the fortunes of his family." Although Thomas remained faithful in correspondence with his sister Lucy, his wariness of Lewis's financial duplicity was evident by 1792. The Lewises borrowed from Jefferson, from the Carrs, and from other in-laws. When a Lewis grandson requested financial assistance from Thomas, the dutiful uncle denied him money but offered to teach him surveying skills that would help him get a job—if he would come stay at Monticello for awhile.[34]

The ties among the Jefferson children reveal a commitment to both their responsibility to and their affection for one another. All this suggests the power of loving and engaged parents who knew the importance of raising children who would maintain family connections. Their parents showed them, through word and deed, that family, both immediate and near relations, enhanced the value of their own lives and careers. They recorded and taught their children about their family, not merely for taking credit for their ancestry, but to consciously build and expand on a resource that had real value for those who could keep it strong. Its strength proved itself many times in the post-Shadwell lives of the Jefferson family, even though its strength did not rest solely on other Jeffersons.

Kin Networks, Part II

As the Jeffersons cultivated their family trees along the James River basin, they also constructed a second girding of trees whose roots and branches intertwined with and underlay the first. Shadwell slaves moved with Jefferson children to new homes. They had ties to those who remained at Shadwell, and some had ties to previous homes. Their kin stretched along the same, and probably more, roads and waterways that connected the Jefferson family. The slaves who left with the Jefferson children had all occupied the home quarter at Shadwell, with the exception of the field hands whom Thomas and Randolph divided (see appendix, table 20). The members of the six or so families who lived together at Shadwell's center supplied the Jeffersons with their personal attendants and house servants. They took these skills to their new households, where they negotiated their roles with whatever slaves belonged to their owners' spouses. Thomas and Randolph split the remainder of their father's slaves after the initial distribution was completed. Each took about two dozen slaves to their respective plantations, where the slaves reestablished their work and family roles based on their new communities.[35] For the former slaves of Peter Jefferson, the largest concentrations of kin and familiar faces were now on one of the brother's plantations, some twenty miles apart.

The slaves who accompanied Jefferson children to new places brought, in their person, a bit of home with them. We speak of young gentry marrying and "setting up housekeeping," but as in so many other aspects of their privileged lives, they did not do this alone. They moved to their married households with staff who knew their preferences in food, in dress, in privacy, in entertaining. Thus Mary, Thomas, Martha, Lucy, Anna Scott, and Randolph took to their new homes someone who had known them all their lives. Nan and

Fany, Jupiter, Rachel, Cachina and daughters Phebe and Lydia, Eve, and Peter helped their masters with the novelty of setting up housekeeping. Young gentry relied on their slaves more than they realized. Jefferson's granddaughter Ellen Coolidge reflected on how disarming being attended by servants was, as well as just how much the well-tended gentry took for granted:

> When I was a girl, living in Virginia, I had an excellent lady's maid who did every thing for me. When I married and went to New England where every lady is her own maid, and waits upon herself, and dresses her own hair, I felt as if I should never be able to perform such Herculean tasks. Thirteen years of persevering effort, however, made these things so easy to me that I fancied I should never desire to be waited on again, or have a hireling intruding her useless services on the independence & privacy of my toilette. But it was a mistaken thought. In five minutes I had relapsed into old habits—allowed my maid to undress and put me to bed the night of my arrival, and now cannot stick a pin or smooth a hair without her. Will it take me, when I return to Boston, another thirteen years, if I live so long, to learn to take care of myself again? Heaven forefend![36]

The slaves reinforced continuity between households in their most basic performance of mundane tasks. The slaves also served the widening family network. Each was known on the plantation of the others, able to carry messages and property, money, and other slaves. The Jefferson children knew one another's slaves by name, and the slaves, in turn, knew the paths between and within the plantations. Isaac Jefferson, the slave of Thomas's whose memoirs were recorded, spoke with a casual familiarity about his owner's siblings: they were part of his world.[37]

When visitors to plantations tipped servants there—for looking after baggage, carriages, and horses, tending guest rooms, and other errands—they contributed to the idea that any planter was a master and any slave a servant. Thomas's accounts noted tips for "servants," to whom he sometimes referred as "valets," and he often used the individual slaves' names. These transactions greased the wheels of the master-servant dynamic between the visitor and a slave he or she did not own. They formalized the patriarchal relationship between a planter who expected to appear dignified—such as in the precision of his dress and livery—and a servant who could make that happen. Both traveler and slave benefited from cultivating a good relationship during visits, especially among family members who might visit often.[38]

When Mary left Shadwell for her life with John Bolling at Fairfield, Nan went with her. Nan was about eighteen, the same age as Mary, bequeathed to Mary by Peter Jefferson in his will. Nan brought her skills as a personal servant, her value as property, and her training to be subservient within a large population of other slaves who were family or simply neighbors. Nan left behind her kin network, which included her mother, Old Sall, and younger siblings. She would need to build new friendships and new alliances among the slaves and free people at her new home, and no doubt she offered a comforting continuity to the new mistress of Fairfield. After moving away, Nan may have accompanied the Bollings on their visits to Shadwell, where she could embrace her family and friends. Six years after her removal to Fairfield, Fany, another slave from "home," joined her. Fany was about nine years old and left her mother, Myrtilla, and brother Peter at Shadwell. Nan and Fany were not immediately related, but their mothers and siblings were among the slaves who stayed at Shadwell when Jane claimed her sixth portion in 1760. Both Nan and Fany came from the group of highly valued home quarter slaves, and their mothers may well have been related.[39]

The kith and kin of the slaves linked the plantations. As Nan and Fany went to Goochland County, Nan's mother and sisters stayed at Monticello. Fany left her mother at Monticello also, but her brother Peter went to Snowdon. Both Orange and Squire, who grew up at Shadwell and moved to Snowdon with Randolph, performed errands between Monticello and Snowdon, transporting seed, dogs, letters, cash, and other items between the two plantations. Orange's parents, Juno and Tobey, and his siblings, Toby Jr. and Luna, belonged to Thomas. Orange's wife, Dinah, and their children Sally and Lucy also belonged to Thomas. When Thomas sought to sell some slaves to pay off debts in 1792, he first offered Randolph the chance to find a buyer for Dinah and her family "in your neighborhood so as to unite her with [her husband]." Squire escorted Randolph's slave (simply referred to as "the girl" by the Jefferson men) who went to Monticello in 1813 to learn how to operate a spinning jenny from Thomas's skilled labor there. Siblings of Squire lived at Monticello, and childhood friends of both Orange and Squire lived there. The bonds that connected the slaves between the plantations were not lost on their owners. Letters between Thomas and Randolph often named which slave was carrying missives between the two brothers. The most trustworthy slaves, such as Randolph's Orange and Squire, could partake of social opportunities on their errands abroad.[40] They also enhanced the many ways the Jefferson kin networks supported the planter family's ongoing enterprises.

Leaving Shadwell could present an array of new experiences to a slave. The slaves undoubtedly understood whether they were leaving for a good home. John Bolling had not yet begun to drink when Nan and Fany left for Fairfield, and the Bolling wealth promised some degree of material comfort. Bolling's other slaves, thirty-one in number in 1786, likely offered the possibility of spouses and friends. On the other hand, it is easy to imagine the horror that Rachel's family faced when Jane Jefferson deeded her to Randolph, knowing she was replacing a slave who had been murdered by an overseer and would live twenty miles away. But some slaves came back. When Anna Scott moved to Monticello in her later years, her slaves moved there also. Her slave Nance moved back to a home she had known: Thomas chose her from his own slaves when he paid Anna Scott's marriage portion. Anna Scott's slaves entered Thomas Jefferson's farm rolls, and he arranged their care and their work.[41]

The lines of communication among plantations and the enslaved workers who lived on them also worked to the advantage of slaves. During the Revolution, Virginia's last colonial governor, Lord Dunmore, made an outright invitation to slaves to leave their rebel masters. Harry, a field hand, answered Dunmore's call in 1781 when General Cornwallis's army moved through central Virginia. Harry was old enough to have been an adult when Peter Jefferson died. He moved from Peter's ownership to Thomas's ownership, with no record of any change to where he lived or the field work he performed. But this constancy in his owners' records is misleading. Clearly Harry was aware of worlds beyond the Jeffersons' plantation lands, and when this opportunity arose, he recognized it as such. Thomas recorded his fate simply, "joined enemy," the last known note about Harry. He may have found new work with the now-alien British, or he may have died of disease like so many other slaves who joined the army camps. He may have, in fact, found freedom.[42]

The slaves who left Shadwell came to know new plantations where they forged new social alliances. But just as the Jefferson children maintained connections between their homes and families, there were opportunities for slaves to also keep in contact among the distant landscapes that descended from Shadwell. We are accustomed to discussing the networks of relationships that connected the kin networks of white families—especially certain white families—across Virginia. But every slave-owning Virginian who moved established the potential for another strand of a second network of black families. Not only did these networks undergird and make possible much of the visible success of slaveholding Virginians, but they also allowed enslaved people to maneuver with some autonomy through this same landscape. The networks of black families have the potential to illuminate connections we have not understood before. For many good reasons historians have written about colonial slave society as binary oppositions: field versus domestic labor, tobacco versus rice or sugar culture, or differences between blacks and whites or men and women, when in fact there are other types of relationships that can explain how these seemingly separate worlds and distant places worked in conjunction. A close look at the legal, social, and familial relationships among a group of enslaved African Virginians and how they overlay the relationships of their elite white owners begins to explain how these networks functioned. It is by now no surprise that the less-visible networks of black Virginians were holding up and making many parts of the whites' world possible, even as their very presence undermined it. In the documents the Jeffersons created to expressly record their lives and deaths, the people they owned are barely visible.

Changes on the Home Quarter

The slaves who remained at Shadwell in the era after all the Jeffersons left saw a different world from that they had known. Only five of the people who lived at Shadwell in 1757, when it belonged to Peter Jefferson, still lived there in 1777, when it was Thomas Jefferson's. By 1776, when Jane Jefferson died, Shadwell ceased to be the center of a plantation. Instead it became a satellite to the newer Monticello plantation. The benefits of the home quarter were no longer available to those slaves who remained at Shadwell; they now occupied the periphery. Archaeology reveals alterations to the plantation over the last part of the eighteenth century. The material culture of the quarter farm was indeed different from that of the home quarter. The plantation kitchen no longer augmented daily fare, and people no longer had the distractions—

nor the material wealth—of the big house as part of their daily routine. They did not use the spaces and buildings in the same ways. Instead of work patterns that orbited around the Jeffersons' house and tidily retracted to the somewhat private domestic spaces of kitchen and home quarter, the artifacts of daily living clustered broadly around the home quarter and now-former kitchen area, spilling slightly south over the ridge (fig. 7.3).

The use of each site became more superficial in the post–home quarter era. The large cellar at Building I did not experience any new deep deposits. There were no structural changes to the buildings and no new buildings erected; the former plantation kitchen now functioned the same as the other buildings on the quarter, as a house for field laborers. The people who lived at Shadwell worked in the field and slept in their houses, but perhaps new crops and new taskmasters ensured that they did not spend enough time in their houses to alter them. Despite the common activity now at the former kitchen and the quarter, the fence line in between remained, perhaps still keeping animals and gardens from active engagement with wildlife. The buildings and the landscape persisted, but they had grown old.[43]

The Monticello quarter farm was a different kind of plantation landscape, and a different kind of community resided there. Thomas Jefferson's rolls suggest that between about eleven and twenty-six enslaved workers lived at Shadwell during this last part of the eighteenth century. Because the entire plantation population worked as laborers, perhaps the social boundaries that encouraged contained local community activity were erased during this time. The quarter farm slaves lived in the kitchen building and on the home quarter site, and all of these slaves were now part of the same community during both work and leisure times. People may have cooked within households, or a slave cook may have used the kitchen to feed the quarter farm workforce, but her kitchen was no longer for the exclusive service of the Jeffersons, so her space could be included for the slaves' social use. The centers of local activity shifted to include a larger part of the plantation landscape.[44]

Yet another explanation may simply reflect the nature of survival in the archaeological record. The Shadwell slave quarters were fairly impermanent frame structures. They left no footprint, other than their cellar pits and heavy structural support members. They were not post-in-ground buildings, and may have been built on ground laid sills or piers, none of which survived the

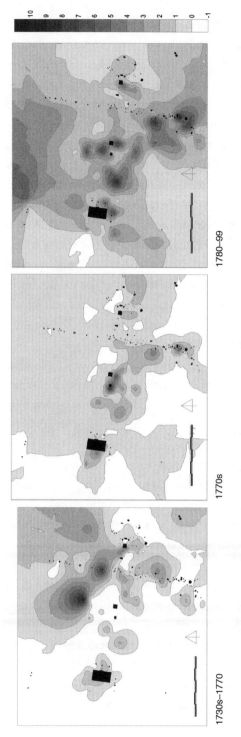

Figure 73. Surface distribution maps showing change in site use from middle of eighteenth century to early nineteenth century. Activity is primarily in a line east to west along the ridge during both the home plantation and quarter farm periods, with the heaviest concentration of wares on the slave quarter area. The quarter farm period saw heightened use of the area north of the kitchen and quarters. The slave quarters, kitchen buildings, fence lines, and probably Jane Jefferson's house disappeared by the nineteenth century. Tenants or farmers on the site in the early to mid-nineteenth century lived to the southwest of where the Jeffersons lived.

1730s–1770   1770s   1780–99

passing plow. It is also possible that they were built of log. It is hard to imagine that these buildings were not in need of some repair during the quarter farm period, having stood for at least a quarter century already. If the nature of repairs were all on aboveground members, and if the inhabitants of the buildings had no need to dig cooking pits or storage pits of any depth, then their active uses of the site remain invisible to us, or at least indistinguishable in the mixed context of the plowzone. Regardless, there is good evidence that the slaves who occupied the quarter site during the quarter farm period did not use the site in the same manner as when it was a home plantation.

The buildings and the fence lines that defined Peter Jefferson's Shadwell fell out of use or were removed about the turn of the nineteenth century (fig. 7.4). The archaeological date coincides with the documentary evidence that Thomas Jefferson removed his slaves to other plantations in the 1790s and leased the Shadwell lands to tenant farmers before giving Shadwell to his grandson. The extensive plowing of the Shadwell ridge may have begun shortly after 1813, when Thomas Jefferson Randolph became owner of the land. Early in the nineteenth century the Jeffersons' plantation and the Shadwell quarter farm were gone. All domestic activity on the eighteenth-century part of the plantation virtually ceased as Thomas Jefferson moved his slaves to his other holdings and passed the land to his heirs. New farming activity used the land differently, and for the next century the plow worked to cover up the remains of the earlier occupation. The Jeffersons' Shadwell became a place known only through family stories.

Figure 7.4. *Monticello and Montalto from Edgehill,* Russell Smith, 1844. This sketch shows Shadwell in the foreground. Smith marked Monticello "o" and put a "+" to mark "Birth Place of Jefferson." Thomas Jefferson's mill at Shadwell is visible along the river in the trees. Courtesy Monticello/Thomas Jefferson Foundation, Inc.

"Jane Jefferson—Her Booke"

In 1772, two years following the fire that destroyed the family home, Jane Jefferson took a Bible and inscribed in it the birth dates and birthplaces of each of her children (fig. 7.5). On the facing page she wrote "Jane Jefferson Her Booke—Sept. 6th { 1772" (fig. 7.6). In doing this, she followed a tradition of recording family history and inaugurated a book in which descendants would follow her example and ultimately invoke five generations—two centuries' worth—of people to remember. She may have reconstructed the contents of a document that was lost in the house fire, or she may have begun anew. Either way, she wished to provide a record of her family for her descendants. She chose to write her family history in a Bible, an object with meaning as a religious document, which also became an important family artifact because of its association with previous owners and for the notations inside it. The treatment of the book by Jane's heirs indicates that they valued it for all these reasons.

Other family members created similar working documents that recorded and preserved names, births, deaths, and marriages. Peter recorded the family of his friend and father-in-law, Isham Randolph, and his wife, Jane Rogers, on a sheet of paper. Peter also gave son Thomas a Prayer Book in which Thomas later copied his mother's genealogy and recorded his children with his wife, Martha. All of these documents—Jane's Bible, the paper Peter inscribed, and Thomas's Prayer Book—survive because first Thomas, then his daughter, and then her heirs kept and curated them. They are meaningful to this story of the Jeffersons because of both their content and their treatment as artifacts.[45]

What each person recorded and how she or he entered family history in these books invokes questions about both dating the records and about the events that prompted various Jeffersons to make these records. The action of writing the dates important to a family is a way of recording past events, but it also ensures that future generations will know the history: the act is for both the present and the future members of a family. The primary act of writing in these books stated ownership, however temporary and fleeting it was. Jane Jefferson wrote her name and the date in her Bible in 1772, four years before her death and the passing of the book to son Thomas. Thomas added his ownership marks in his mother's book after he had it rebound. Thomas's

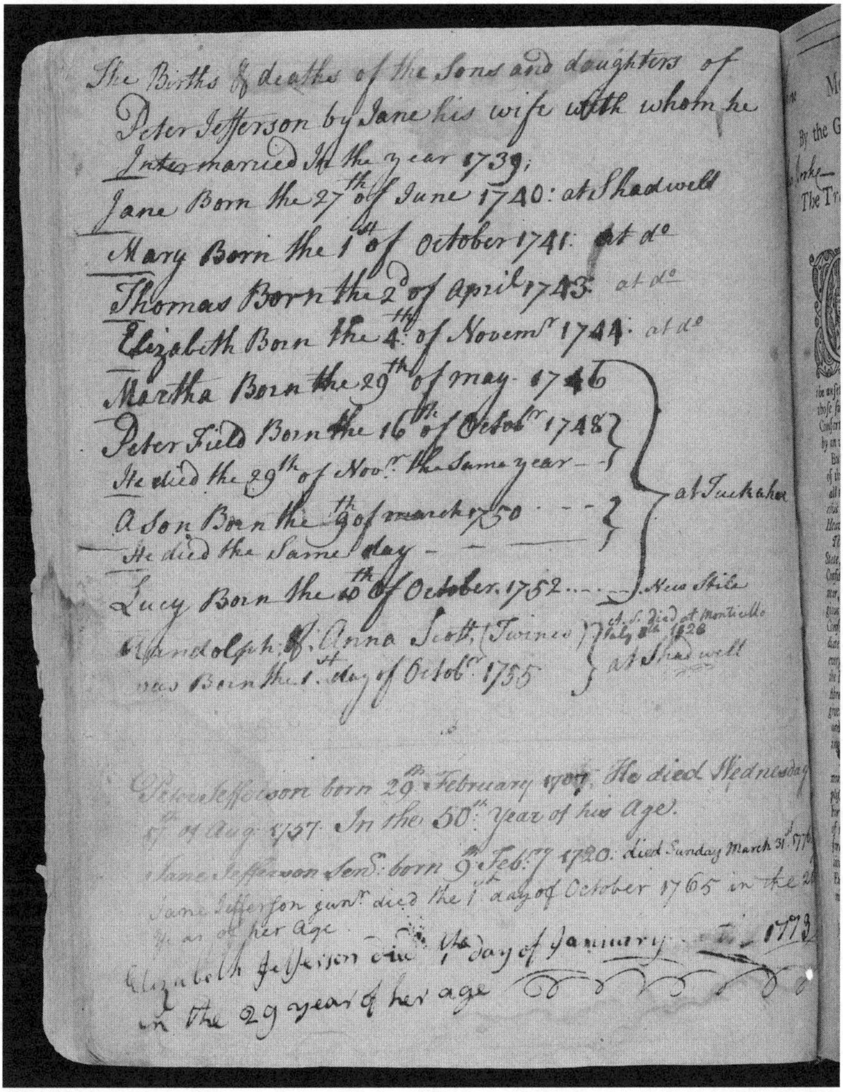
The Births & deaths of the Sons and daughters of
Peter Jefferson by Jane his wife with whom he
Intermarried In the year 1739;
Jane Born the 27th of June 1740: at Shadwell
Mary Born the 1st of October 1741: at do
Thomas Born the 2d of April 1743: at do
Elizabeth Born the 4th of Novemr 1744: at do
Martha Born the 29th of may 1746
Peter Field Born the 16th of Octobr 1748
He died the 29th of Novr the Same year
A Son Born the 9th of march 1750
He died the Same day
at Tuckahoe
Lucy Born the 10th of October 1752 ... New Stile
Randolph & Anna Scott (Twins) was Born the 1st day of Octobr 1755 at Shadwell
A. S. died at Monticello July 8th 1826
Peter Jefferson born 29th February 1707. He died Wednesday of Aug 1757 In the 50th year of his Age.
Jane Jefferson Senr born 9th Feb 1720. died Sunday March 31 1776
Jane Jefferson junr died the 1st day of October 1765 in the 2 year of her Age
Elizabeth Jefferson died 1 day of January 1773 in the 29 year of her age

Figure 7.5. Jane Jefferson's list of the family of Peter Jefferson and Jane Randolph. Jefferson Family, Bible. Courtesy Special Collections, University of Virginia Library.

heirs each added their names as they received the book. Various owners and their siblings made notes to update their generation's record.

Jane wrote her family history at one time from the perspective of her later years. Entries were not written as each child was born, or as two infant boys

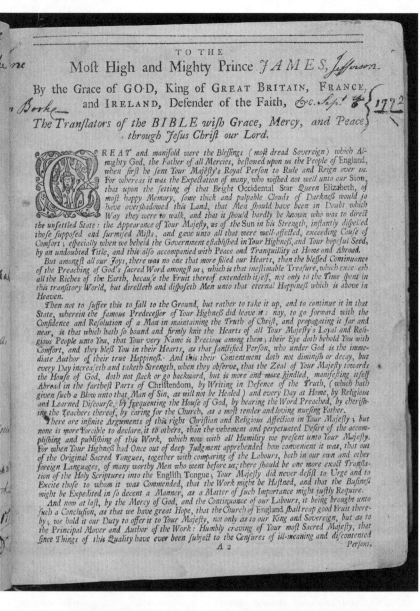

TO THE

Moſt High and Mighty Prince *JAMES,*

By the Grace of GO·D, King of GREAT BRITAIN, FRANCE, and IRELAND, Defender of the Faith, &c.

The Tranſlators of the BIBLE wiſh Grace, Mercy, and Peace, through Jeſus Chriſt our Lord.

REAT and manifold were the Bleſſings (moſt dread Sovereign) which Almighty God, the Father of all Mercies, beſtowed upon us the People of England, when firſt he ſent Your Majeſty's Royal Perſon to Rule and Reign over us. For whereas it was the Expectation of many, who wiſhed not well unto our Sion, that upon the ſetting of that Bright Occidental Star Queen Elizabeth, of moſt happy Memory, ſome thick and palpable Clouds of Darkneſs would ſo have overſhadowed this Land, that Men ſhould have been in Doubt which Way they were to walk, and that it ſhould hardly be known who was to direct the unſettled State: the Appearance of Your Majeſty, as of the Sun in his Strength, inſtantly diſpelled thoſe ſuppoſed and ſurmiſed Miſts, and gave unto all that were well-affected, exceeding Cauſe of Comfort; eſpecially when we beheld the Government eſtabliſhed in Your Highneſs, and Your hopeful Seed, by an undoubted Title, and this alſo accompanied with Peace and Tranquillity at Home and Abroad.

But amongſt all our Joys, there was no one that more filled our Hearts, than the bleſſed Continuance of the Preaching of God's ſacred Word amongſt us; which is that ineſtimable Treaſure, which excelleth all the Riches of the Earth, becauſe the Fruit thereof extendeth itſelf, not only to the Time ſpent in this tranſitory World, but directeth and diſpoſeth Men unto that eternal Happineſs which is above in Heaven.

Then not to ſuffer this to fall to the Ground, but rather to take it up, and to continue it in that State, wherein the famous Predeceſſor of Your Highneſs did leave it: nay, to go forward with the Confidence and Reſolution of a Man in maintaining the Truth of Chriſt, and propagating it far and near, is that which hath ſo bound and firmly knit the Hearts of all Your Majeſty's Loyal and Religious People unto You, that Your very Name is Precious among them; their Eye doth behold You with Comfort, and they bleſs You in their Hearts, as that ſanctified Perſon, who under God is the immediate Author of their true Happineſs. And this their Contentment doth not diminiſh or decay, but every Day increaſeth and taketh Strength, when they obſerve, that the Zeal of Your Majeſty towards the Houſe of God, doth not ſlack or go backward, but is more and more kindled, manifeſting itſelf Abroad in the fartheſt Parts of Chriſtendom, by Writing in Defence of the Truth, (which hath given ſuch a Blow unto that Man of Sin, as will not be Healed) and every Day at Home, by Religious and Learned Diſcourſe, by frequenting the Houſe of God, by hearing the Word Preached, by cheriſhing the Teachers thereof, by caring for the Church, as a moſt tender and loving nurſing Father.

There are infinite Arguments of this right Chriſtian and Religious Affection in Your Majeſty; but none is more forcible to declare it to others, than the vehement and perpetuated Deſire of the accompliſhing and publiſhing of this Work, which now with all Humility we preſent unto Your Majeſty. For when Your Highneſs had Once out of deep Judgment apprehended how convenient it was, that out of the Original Sacred Tongues, together with comparing of the Labours, both in our own and other foreign Languages, of many worthy Men who went before us; there ſhould be one more exact Tranſlation of the Holy Scriptures into the Engliſh Tongue; Your Majeſty did never deſiſt to Urge and to Excite thoſe to whom it was Commended, that the Work might be Haſtned, and that the Buſineſs might be Expedited in ſo decent a Manner, as a Matter of ſuch Importance might juſtly Require.

And now at laſt, by the Mercy of God, and the Continuance of our Labours, it being brought unto ſuch a Concluſion, as that we have great Hope, that the Church of England ſhall reap good Fruit thereby; we hold it our Duty to offer it to Your Majeſty, not only as to our King and Sovereign, but as to the Principal Mover and Author of the Work: Humbly craving of Your moſt Sacred Majeſty, that ſince Things of this Quality have ever been ſubject to the Cenſures of ill-meaning and diſcontented

A 2   Perſons,

Figure 7.6. "Jane Jefferson—Her Booke, Sept. 6th { 1772," Jefferson Family, Bible.
Courtesy Special Collections, University of Virginia Library.

died. Jane inscribed the words "New Style" after Lucy's 1752 birth date, further evidence that this was written by someone who was elderly in 1772 and
still more familiar with the previous calendar that was by then "old style" to
most people. Jane's list of her children with Peter used the same formula he
followed in recording the children of Isham and Jane Randolph. Jane entered
both the dates and places of her children's births: she bore the first four at
Shadwell, the next four at Tuckahoe, and the twins back at Shadwell. The
only deaths Jane recorded were for the two boys born at Tuckahoe who died
soon after birth. On his Randolph list, below the names of the children, Peter wrote the birth and death dates for Isham, that Isham was fifty-six years
old, and the birth date for his mother-in-law, Jane. Below her list Jane wrote
the birth and death dates for her husband and noted: "in the 50th: Year of his
Age." She wrote her own birth date below that.[46]

It fell to the next generation of Jeffersons to complete the records their
mother began. Below his mother's birth date, Thomas added the date of death
of his oldest sister, Jane, who had died in 1765. Randolph wrote the next line,
recording Elizabeth's death in January 1773 and adding some awkward curlicue-
like scrawls after his dutiful record, perhaps revealing his discomfort with
this role.[47] The penultimate addition to the page was Thomas Jefferson recording his mother's death, completing the line where his mother wrote her birth
date. The very last entry was by Martha Jefferson Randolph, who added the
tiny "A.S. died at Monticello July 8, 1828," on the line with Anna Scott's birth
record. Martha Jefferson Randolph and her descendants added marks of ownership to the book as it passed between generations.[48] The book carried Jane
Jefferson's words and her wishes for family attention to them across time.

Thomas's Prayer Book

Thomas Jefferson used his Prayer Book to record his family's important dates
and events (fig. 7.7). In 1753 Peter Jefferson gave a Prayer Book to his son
Thomas as the ten-year-old was to board away from home for school. Almost
twenty years later, when his daughter Martha was born in 1772, Thomas began using that Prayer Book to register the important events of his own family. With Martha's birth he began a record of his family on blank leaves in
the book (fig. 7.8). He did not follow quite the same formula that his parents
used, even when he copied their information. Most poignantly, his entries

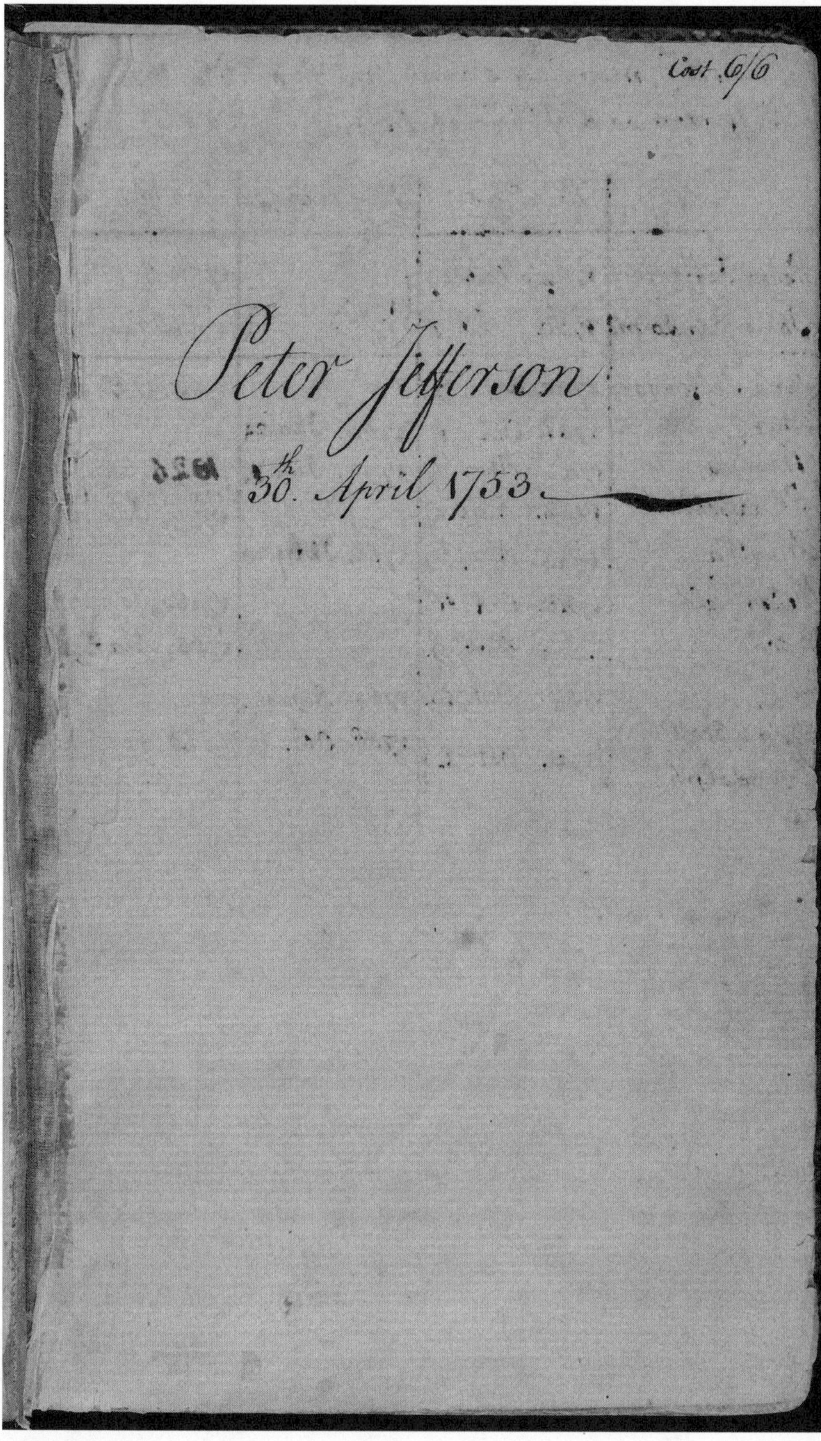

Figure 7.7. Peter Jefferson's signature in Thomas Jefferson's Prayer Book.
Courtesy Special Collections, University of Virginia Library.

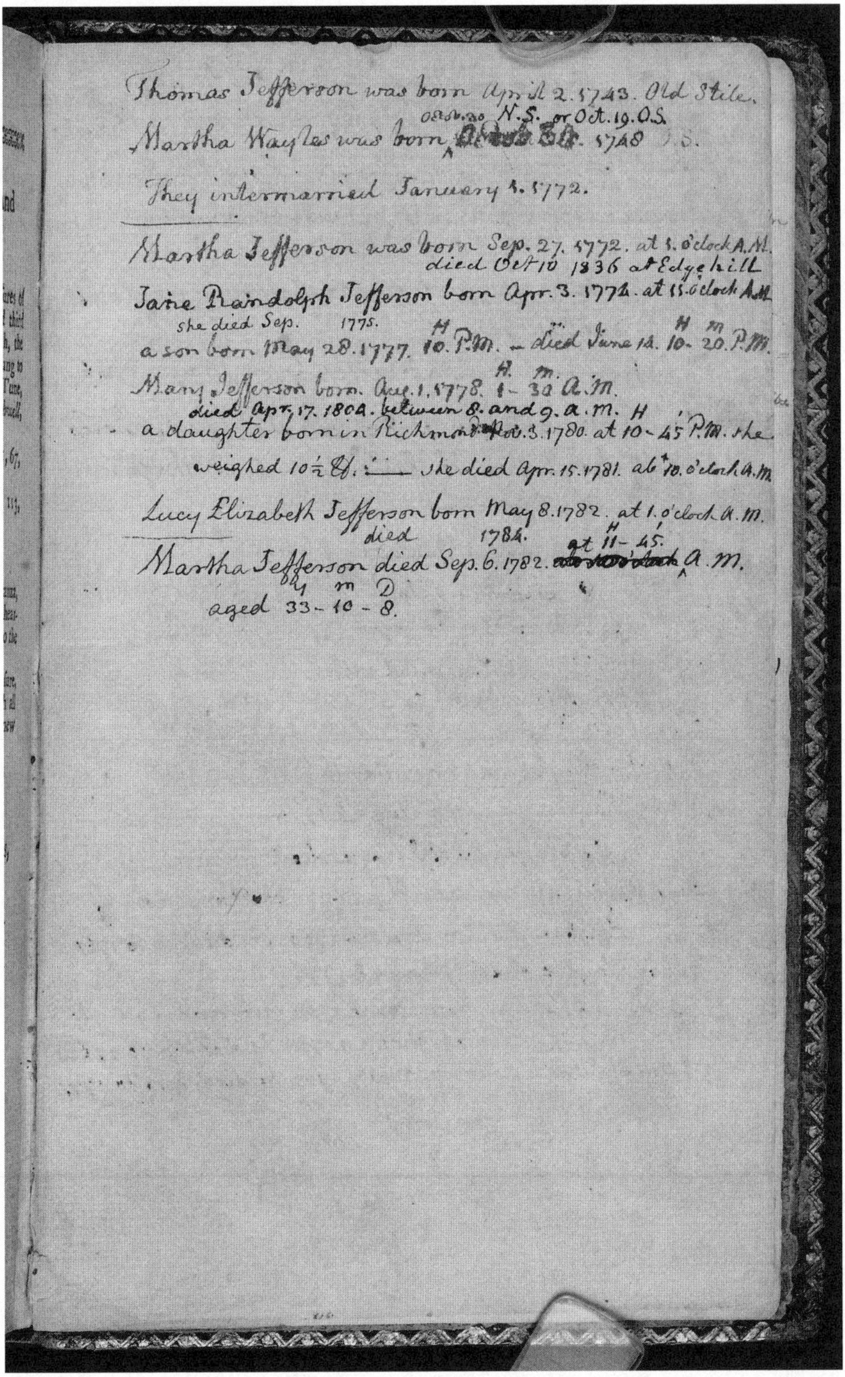

Thomas Jefferson was born April 2. 1743. Old Stile.
                      N.S. or Oct. 19. O.S.
Martha Wayles was born   1748

They intermarried January 1. 1772.

Martha Jefferson was born Sep. 27. 1772. at 1. o'clock A.M.
                died Oct 10 1836 at Edgehill

Jane Randolph Jefferson born Apr. 3. 1774. at 11. o'clock A.M.
she died Sep. 1775.
a son born May 28. 1777. 10. P.M. — died June 14. 10. 20. P.M.

Mary Jefferson born. Aug. 1. 1778. 1 – 30 A.M.
     died Apr. 17. 1804. between 8. and 9. A.M.
a daughter born in Richmond Nov. 3. 1780. at 10 – 45 P.M. she
    weighed 10½ ℔. ———— she died Apr. 15. 1781. at 10. o'clock A.M

Lucy Elizabeth Jefferson born May 8. 1782. at 1. o'clock A.M.
          died 1784. at 11 – 45.
Martha Jefferson died Sep. 6. 1782. A.M.
    aged 33 – 10 – 8.

Figure 7.8. Thomas Jeffersons' list of his children with his wife, Martha Wayles Skelton
Jefferson, in Thomas Jefferson's Prayer Book. Courtesy Special Collections,
University of Virginia Library.

about his family were written as they happened. Each entry about Thomas and Martha's children has an immediacy that no other pages have and to which only the pages with the births of his daughters' children come close. There are six separate lines that record the arrival dates and also the time each Jefferson child was born. Then, with the exception of daughter Martha, who outlived him, Jefferson recorded the deaths of his children and of their mother, including the time of day.[49]

He established the Prayer Book as the formal repository for the history of his and Martha's lives together by also inscribing the previous generation's names. On other pages in his Prayer Book he recorded Martha's parents' family and her first marriage. Then he recorded his parents' family's dates just as his mother did in her Bible, and perhaps he even copied his page from hers (fig. 7.9). He did this on or just after March 31, 1776, the day his mother died. Jefferson's daughter Martha added the dates of his and Anna Scott's deaths in 1826 and 1828, respectively, but the deaths of Thomas's siblings Mary (1804), Martha (1811), and Lucy (1810) were never recorded here. Anna Scott lived at Monticello after the death of her husband late in 1811, and so her death was more immediate to housemate Martha Randolph.[50]

For a time, Thomas was keeper of family records in both his mother's Bible and his Prayer Book. When his mother died, Thomas entered her date of death in it, completing the line that she began when she wrote her name and birthday. Her passing may have prompted him to then copy her history of the family into his own Prayer Book. His list of their family differs from hers in a number of ways. Jane recorded the locations of her children's births, and that it was Wednesday, August 17, 1757, when her husband died. Thomas dropped the locations but added the marriage dates of his siblings, part of their current instead of their past lives. When he wrote in her book, Thomas followed his mother's example and added her date of death and recorded that March 31, 1776, was a Sunday, but he did not enter the day of the week in his own book's record. In his own Prayer Book, Thomas recorded his birthday as April 2, 1743, the old-style calendar date, but did not designate old- and new-style dates as his mother did. He did, however, note that his birth date was old style on the page where he began the history of his life with his wife, Martha.

The Jefferson family had another Prayer Book at Shadwell that survived highly worn and well-thumbed. It is the only artifact that speaks of childhood in the Jefferson household. A young Randolph Jefferson used it for

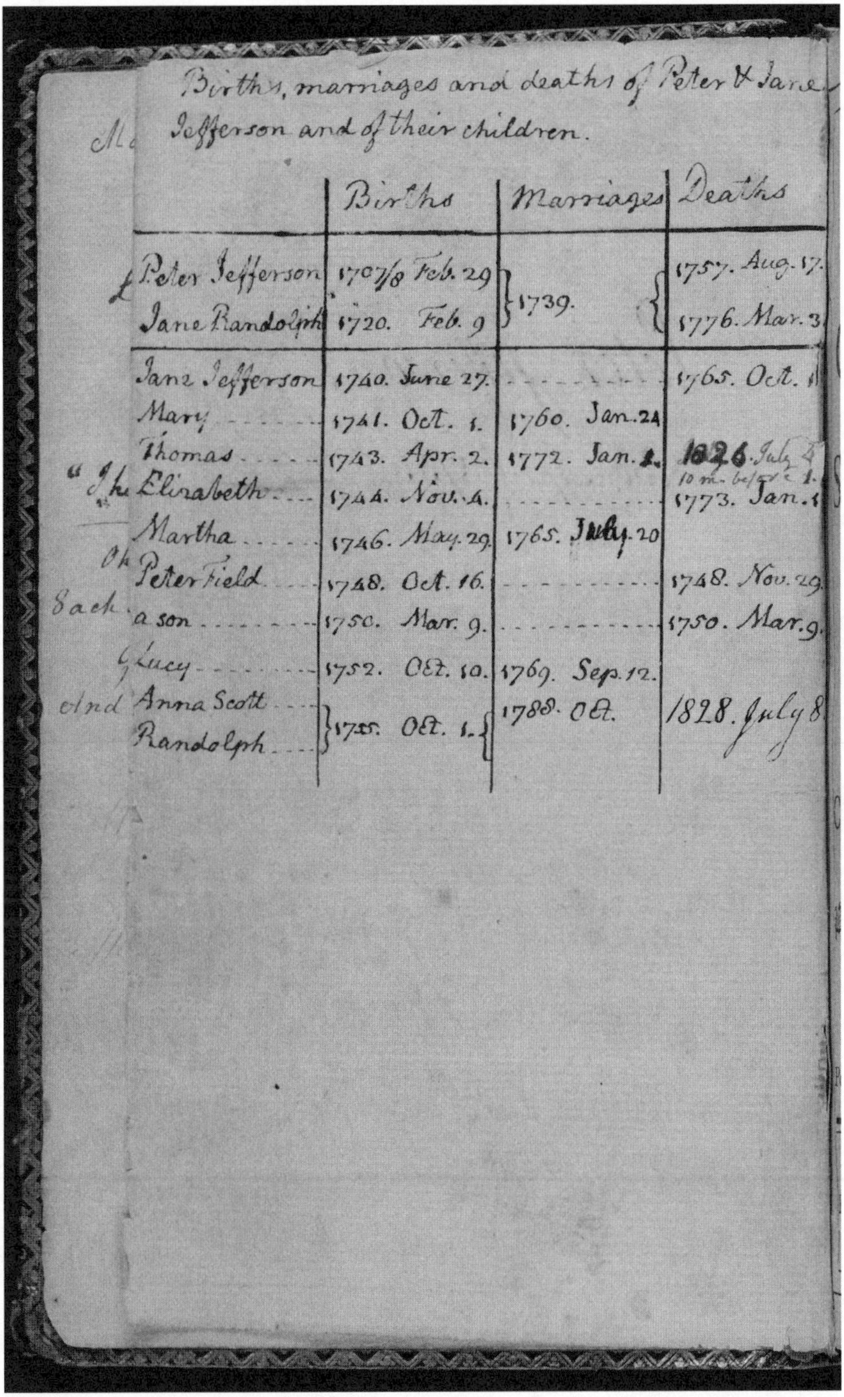

Births, marriages and deaths of Peter & Jane Jefferson and of their children.

	Births	Marriages	Deaths
Peter Jefferson	1707/8 Feb. 29	1739.	1757. Aug. 17.
Jane Randolph	1720. Feb. 9		1776. Mar. 3
Jane Jefferson	1740. June 27.	- - - - - - - -	1765. Oct. 1
Mary	1741. Oct. 1.	1760. Jan. 24	
Thomas	1743. Apr. 2.	1772. Jan. 1.	1826. July 4 10 m. before 1.
Elizabeth	1744. Nov. 4.	- - - - - - - -	1773. Jan. 1
Martha	1746. May 29	1765. July 20	
Peter Field	1748. Oct. 16.	- - - - - - - -	1748. Nov. 29
a son	1750. Mar. 9.	- - - - - - - -	1750. Mar. 9.
Lucy	1752. Oct. 10.	1769. Sep. 12.	
Anna Scott	1755. Oct. 1.	1788. Oct.	1828. July 8
Randolph			

Figure 7.9. Thomas Jefferson's list of his Shadwell family in Thomas Jefferson's Prayer Book. Courtesy Special Collections, University of Virginia Library.

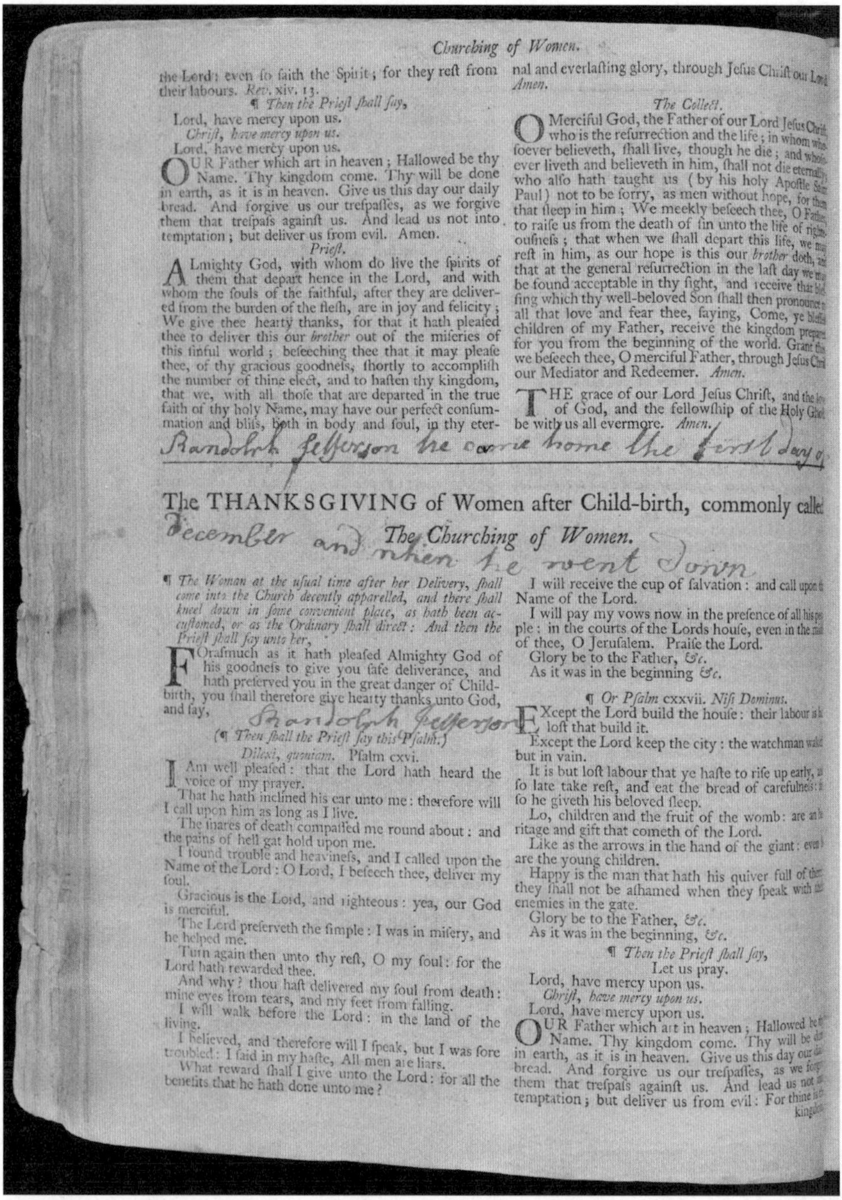

the Lord: even fo faith the Spirit; for they reft from their labours. *Rev.* xiv. 13.

¶ *Then the Priest shall say,*

Lord, have mercy upon us.

Christ, have mercy upon us.

Lord, have mercy upon us.

OUR Father which art in heaven; Hallowed be thy Name. Thy kingdom come. Thy will be done in earth, as it is in heaven. Give us this day our daily bread. And forgive us our trespasses, as we forgive them that trespass against us. And lead us not into temptation; but deliver us from evil. Amen.

Priest.

ALmighty God, with whom do live the spirits of them that depart hence in the Lord, and with whom the souls of the faithful, after they are delivered from the burden of the flesh, are in joy and felicity; We give thee hearty thanks, for that it hath pleased thee to deliver this our *brother* out of the miseries of this sinful world; beseeching thee that it may please thee, of thy gracious goodness, shortly to accomplish the number of thine elect, and to hasten thy kingdom, that we, with all those that are departed in the true faith of thy holy Name, may have our perfect consummation and bliss, both in body and soul, in the eter-

nal and everlasting glory, through Jesus Christ our Lord. Amen.

The Collect.

O Merciful God, the Father of our Lord Jesus Christ, who is the resurrection and the life; in whom whosoever believeth, shall live, though he die; and whosoever liveth and believeth in him, shall not die eternally; who also hath taught us (by his holy Apostle Saint Paul) not to be sorry, as men without hope, for them that sleep in him; We meekly beseech thee, O Father, to raise us from the death of sin unto the life of righteousness; that when we shall depart this life, we may rest in him, as our hope is this our *brother* doth, and that at the general resurrection in the last day we may be found acceptable in thy sight, and receive that blessing which thy well-beloved Son shall then pronounce to all that love and fear thee, saying, Come, ye blessed children of my Father, receive the kingdom prepared for you from the beginning of the world. Grant this, we beseech thee, O merciful Father, through Jesus Christ our Mediator and Redeemer. Amen.

THE grace of our Lord Jesus Christ, and the love of God, and the fellowship of the Holy Ghost, be with us all evermore. Amen.

Randolph Jefferson he came home the first day of

The THANKSGIVING of Women after Child-birth, commonly called

December and The Churching of Women. *when he went down*

¶ *The Woman at the usual time after her Delivery, shall come into the Church decently apparelled, and there shall kneel down in some convenient place, as hath been accustomed, or as the Ordinary shall direct: And then the Priest shall say unto her,*

FOrasmuch as it hath pleased Almighty God of his goodness to give you safe deliverance, and hath preserved you in the great danger of Childbirth, you shall therefore give hearty thanks unto God, and say, *Randolph Jefferson*

¶ *Then shall the Priest say this Psalm:*

Dilexi, quoniam. Psalm cxvi.

I Am well pleased: that the Lord hath heard the voice of my prayer.

That he hath inclined his ear unto me: therefore will I call upon him as long as I live.

The snares of death compassed me round about: and the pains of hell gat hold upon me.

I found trouble and heaviness, and I called upon the Name of the Lord: O Lord, I beseech thee, deliver my soul.

Gracious is the Lord, and righteous: yea, our God is merciful.

The Lord preserveth the simple: I was in misery, and he helped me.

Turn again then unto thy rest, O my soul: for the Lord hath rewarded thee.

And why? thou hast delivered my soul from death: mine eyes from tears, and my feet from falling.

I will walk before the Lord: in the land of the living.

I believed, and therefore will I speak, but I was sore troubled: I said in my haste, All men are liars.

What reward shall I give unto the Lord: for all the benefits that he hath done unto me?

I will receive the cup of salvation: and call upon the Name of the Lord.

I will pay my vows now in the presence of all his people: in the courts of the Lords house, even in the midst of thee, O Jerusalem. Praise the Lord.

Glory be to the Father, &c.

As it was in the beginning, &c.

¶ *Or Psalm* cxxvii. *Nisi Dominus.*

EXcept the Lord build the house: their labour is but lost that build it.

Except the Lord keep the city: the watchman waketh but in vain.

It is but lost labour that ye haste to rise up early, and so late take rest, and eat the bread of carefulness: for so he giveth his beloved sleep.

Lo, children and the fruit of the womb: are an heritage and gift that cometh of the Lord.

Like as the arrows in the hand of the giant: even so are the young children.

Happy is the man that hath his quiver full of them: they shall not be ashamed when they speak with their enemies in the gate.

Glory be to the Father, &c.

As it was in the beginning, &c.

¶ *Then the Priest shall say,*

Let us pray.

Lord, have mercy upon us.

Christ, have mercy upon us.

Lord, have mercy upon us.

OUR Father which art in heaven; Hallowed be thy Name. Thy kingdom come. Thy will be done in earth, as it is in heaven. Give us this day our daily bread. And forgive us our trespasses, as we forgive them that trespass against us. And lead us not into temptation; but deliver us from evil: For thine is the kingdom

Figure 7.10. Randolph Jefferson's writing practice. Jefferson Family, Bible.
Courtesy Special Collections, University of Virginia Library.

writing practice. It bears his repeated sentences and scribbles practicing script with a pen on various pages, including a sort of test inscribing "Randolph" and "Jefferson" near the top of the first page in the manner that other, older, family members showed their ownership of books (fig. 7.10). These are not the scribbles of a young child (Randolph was two when his father died) but may be the post-fire grammar exercises of a fourteen-year-old boy. This Prayer Book was in the Shadwell house during Randolph's later schoolboy days.[51] In October 1771, at age sixteen, he left for the College of William and Mary. Randolph's notes do not preclude the book from being at Shadwell before Peter Jefferson's death, but they do put its active presence in the household about the time of or just after the house fire.

Jane, the Historian

The history that Jane Jefferson wrote for her family confirms details of Thomas Jefferson's early years. Biographers of Thomas Jefferson have known from his own autobiography that he was born at Shadwell, in what is now Albemarle County, Virginia. The birthplaces of Jefferson's two older sisters and when the family moved to Shadwell and, later, to Tuckahoe and back to Shadwell, have been long-standing questions. When Henry Randall cited Thomas's Prayer Book in his biography of Jefferson, he said nothing about the birthplaces of Jefferson's siblings. The University of Virginia acquired the Bible with Jane's inscriptions in 1954, so it was not available to Randall or to Marie Kimball or Dumas Malone for their influential biographies of Thomas Jefferson; they, too, cited Thomas's Prayer Book. In Thomas's *Autobiography* he wrote of his father: "He was the third or fourth settler, about the year 1737, of the part of the country in which I live." Malone dismissed this date out of hand as being too early. Jane's inscription tells us that she and Peter indeed had moved to Shadwell by June 27, 1740, when Jane Jr. was born there, and probably they moved some months before June to avoid traveling late in Jane's pregnancy. Perhaps they came within days of their marriage on October 3, 1739. The family moved to Tuckahoe in time for Jane to give birth to Martha there on May 29, 1746. They returned to Shadwell following the birth of Lucy in October 1752. The activities in Peter Jefferson's account book suggest that August 1753 marked their return home. The archaeological record supports Jane Jefferson's written history.[52]

Not only are the details of family movements important, but the inscription also casts new light on Jane Jefferson and her role as a keeper of family history. The historiography of Jane Randolph Jefferson has not included an image of a woman who carefully ensured knowledge as part of her family's legacies. Her son Thomas followed as steward of her book and the history it held. He saw that it was rebound and maintained. He not only kept the book but also fulfilled the duty of completing the family history in it. Jane's Bible and his Prayer Book were in his library on his death, and about two months later his daughter Martha claimed them and continued their legacy as important family artifacts. She then chose to ensure that the family history dispersed among her heirs through the books. Two subsequent generations wrote their names in the volume, and its 1861 owner copied out Bible verses in it. Their descendants valued the book enough as an artifact, with Jefferson connections no less, to give it to the University of Virginia's growing Jefferson collection.[53] Jane Jefferson's Booke provides new details about who in the Jefferson family were writers of history, keepers of books, and designers of ways to pass knowledge from the long dead to the living to the not yet born.

Death and Remembrance

In 1771 Thomas wrote plans for a graveyard at the back of his Memorandum Book. In this emotionally wrought essay he composed an epitaph for his sister Jane, who had died six years before at the age of twenty-six. Jane was a favorite of Thomas's, and memories of his sister colored his perceptions of the world well past her death and into his final years. He recalled her singing voice—even in "extreme old age" he said, "often in church some sacred air which her sweet voice had made familiar to him in youth recalled to him sweet visions of his sister." Thomas passed stories about her to his daughters and his grandchildren, and even their children heard of the delightful Jane, who was "the pride and ornament of her house."[54] The powerful bonds between this brother and sister transcended time. In his life Thomas Jefferson composed three epitaphs of exalted scale: for his sister Jane, for his boyhood friend and brother-in-law Dabney Carr, and for his own wife, Martha Jefferson.

Thomas envisioned a graveyard as part of his plans for his house and grounds at Monticello. This act of establishing a burial ground and thinking about his favorite sister's place in it connected the old home and the new, just as it connected the living and the dead. Thomas noted that his brother-in-law John Bolling had planted cedar trees at Shadwell near the grave of one of his children there, and cedars figure prominently in Thomas's plans for the Monticello burial ground. Thomas's specification for "one half to the use of my own family; the other of strangers, servants &c." is the only acknowledgment of any Jeffersons that their slaves might share the same commemorative landscape. The timing of Thomas Jefferson's thoughts about a burial ground is intriguing. Entered following a legal account on December 21, 1771, they are on the eve of his marriage, January 1, 1772, a mere ten days later. Perhaps the excitement about changing his household brought on this reverie about the home he was creating and the people in his childhood home who were important to him. His companion Martha would never meet his companion Jane.

The Jeffersons regarded the formality of funerals as part of their duty to both the living and the dead. They established a family burial ground at Shadwell for the immediate and extended family's use there. The family burial ground occupies a small knoll southwest of the main house, now planted in cedars, with many unmarked graves and others marked with fieldstones. On his 1799 survey of farm fields at Shadwell, Thomas labeled the graveyard area "cedars" and indicated that it was not part of the cultivated land there (see fig. 1.2). Burials that likely occurred at Shadwell include Peter Jefferson, an unnamed Bolling child, Jane Jr., Dabney Carr, Elizabeth and the slave called Little Sall, who died with her, and other slaves and colleagues who died while at Shadwell and whose names are lost to time. There are no gravestones with inscriptions for anyone who was buried at Shadwell.[55]

We have already visited Peter Jefferson's funeral and how it required participation from the various parts of the Jeffersons' social world. Fewer details are available regarding other family funerals. There are no records of Isham Randolph's funeral—he was buried at Turkey Island—but his epitaph remains. Isham was remembered as a gentleman, "steady of heart" to "justice probity & honour" and "meriting an universal esteem." There is no record of where the family buried Jane Rogers Randolph. The Shadwell generation left no stone epitaphs until Thomas developed his Monticello burial ground. To the memory of a lost child, John and Mary Bolling planted trees, investing also in improving the landscape of the Shadwell burial ground. There is no record of Jane Jr.'s cause of death, burial, or funeral in 1765, only her brother's idealized memorial six years later. He wrote in Latin, "Ah, Joanna, best of all girls. Ah, torn away from the bloom of vigorous age. May the earth be light upon you. Farewell, forever and ever." Perhaps he always wished to improve on the circumstances of the Shadwell burial ground. Jane's inscription echoes an epitaph written by the poet William Shenstone, and literary sources remained an important source for other memorials Thomas composed.[56]

Thomas's ideas for a burial ground would be put to use eight years after his sister Jane's death. Thomas began his graveyard at Monticello in May 1773 following the death of Dabney Carr. Carr died while he and Martha were visiting Shadwell. Thomas returned from Williamsburg and moved Carr's body to the mountaintop according to their boyhood pact that whoever survived would bury the other beneath their favorite oak tree on Monticello Mountain. Thomas's emotionally wrought inscription for Carr's grave marker reads:

> Here lie the remains of Dabney Carr
> Son of John and Barbara Carr of Louis County, Va.
> Intermarried July 20, 1765, with Martha Jefferson,
> Daughter of Peter and Jane Randolph Jefferson
> Born October 26, 1743—Died May 16, 1773, at Charlottesville, Va.
>
> Lamented Shade!
> Whom every gift of heaven profusely blest,
> A temper winning mild, nor pity softer,
> Nor was truth more bright; Constant in doing
> Well, he neither sought nor shunned applause,
> No bashful merit sighed near him neglected;
> Sympathising he wiped off the tear from sorrow's clouded eye
> And with kindly hand taught her heart to smile.
> To his virtue, good sense, learning and friendship,
> This stone is dedicated by Thomas Jefferson,
> Who of all men loved him most.[57]

Thomas's draft also included directions for a copper plate to be fixed to a tree at the foot of Carr's grave that would read:

> Still shall thy grave with rising flowers be dressed
> And the green turf lie lightly on thy breast;
> There shall the morn her earliest tears bestow,
> There the first roses of the year shall blow,
> While angels with their silver wings o'ershade
> The ground now sacred by thy reliques made.[58]

Except for a sermon by the Reverend Charles Clay, there is no mention of whether Carr's funeral included public fanfare or the dispensing of drink to kin, slaves, and visitors. It is also unclear whether Clay spoke at Carr's interment at Shadwell or at Monticello.

The Jeffersons expected formal preaching at their funerals but often hired clergy who were friends rather than the local parish minister. Reverend and tutor James Maury spoke at Peter Jefferson's funeral in Maury's Fredericksville Parish. Thomas paid Charles Clay for "[preaching] Mr. Carr's funeral Sermon." Clay was rector of Saint Anne's Parish in Albemarle and a lifelong friend of Thomas's. The family chose him over the Reverend William Douglas, the rector of Carr's home parish, Saint James Northam, who had baptized Carr's children there. Clay also preached at the funerals of Elizabeth in 1774 and Jane in 1776, although Elizabeth and Jane lived in Fredericksville Parish, not Clay's Saint Anne's. Jane, like Dabney, was laid to rest at Monticello, in Clay's parish. There is no record to suggest that Elizabeth was buried other than at Shadwell, even though Thomas had begun his Monticello graveyard the year before her death. Thomas took on the paternal role of arranging funerals for his nearby family members. When Martha Jefferson Carr died at Monticello in 1811, Thomas hired Charles Wingfield to officiate at the funeral. Wingfield was related by marriage to the Jeffersons. As he lay dying, Thomas thought he heard someone mention the Reverend Mr. Hatch, rector of the Episcopal church Thomas attended. Thomas remarked, "I have no objection to see him, as a kind and good neighbor," which his grandson knew to mean that Thomas did not care to be attended by a clergyman. In the end, Hatch presided over Thomas's burial.[59]

Thomas Jefferson began the Monticello graveyard to honor his companion Dabney Carr. Carr was joined by Jane Jefferson three years later. Jane died in the morning on March 31, 1776, and Thomas chose to bury her at Monticello rather than at Shadwell. Her son Thomas wrote to his friend William Randolph later that spring that his mother—also Randolph's aunt—died "after an illness of not more than an hour. We suppose it to have been apoplectic." To his mother's memory, Thomas erected a stone inscribed: "Jane Randolph, wife of Peter Jefferson. Born in London 1720—Died at Monticello 1776." Thomas distilled her life down to these simple and important bits of information. Her birth name was Randolph and she had been the wife of Peter Jefferson. She was born in London and she died at Monticello. Thus her identity as a wife and the name of her husband bonded her life to his. Her birth overseas—and in the capital of commerce and power—must have been important to her or to Thomas for him to decide it was one of the compelling parts of her identity, more important, in fact, than the month and day of her birth and death. That she died at Monticello may mean that she lived with her son during her final days or that Thomas now considered Shadwell part of Monticello or that he considered his mother part of his Monticello family. The Reverend Clay preached the half-hour sermon at her burial on April 6 in the Monticello graveyard, and Thomas joined two loved ones from his past to his future at Monticello.[60]

Death was a time for family to support one another, and the Jeffersons did, with the participation of the entire household. When Dabney Carr died, Thomas invited his sister Martha and her children to live at Monticello, which they did from time to time. Martha Carr and Elizabeth Eppes (Martha Jefferson's half-sister) were with Thomas when his wife, Martha Jefferson, died. Thomas's sister figures prominently in the deathbed scene as the one strong enough to shepherd the inconsolable Thomas during his grief. "A moment before the closing scene, he was led from the room in a state of insensibility by his sister, Mrs. Carr, who, with great difficulty, got him into the library, where he fainted." Martha Carr and Elizabeth Eppes "remained constantly with him for some weeks," as did daughter Martha, who wrote of her father's reaction to his wife's death. In addition to the sisters, the bedside was tended and visited by others who knew Martha Jefferson as family: Betty Brown; Sally, Critta, and Betty Hemings; and Nance and Ursula, who had come to the Jeffersons from John Wayles.[61] The grief of the household seems to have eclipsed any record of Martha Jefferson's funeral, which may have been as private as Thomas kept their correspondence.

Martha Carr died in the early fall 1811 of "a wasting complaint which has for two or three years been gaining upon her." Thomas's epitaph to his sister was in the form of a letter to Randolph. He wrote: "She had the happiness, and it is a great one, of seeing all her children become worthy and respectable members of society and enjoying the esteem of all." Randolph replied that he was "extremly sorry to hear of My sisters death and Would of bin over but it was not raly in My power but it is What we may all expect to come to either later or sooner." Martha Carr was probably closest of the surviving siblings to her brother Thomas, and he showed real interest in her and in the lives of her children. Thomas buried his sister with her husband, Dabney, and inscribed her grave stone simply, "Martha Jefferson, Wife of Dabney Carr, Born May 29, 1746—Died Sept. 3, 1811." Evidently her role as wife of her brother's best friend was more important to her identity, at least in her brother's eyes, than where she was born, lived, or died, her parents, or the children she bore.[62]

When Hastings Marks died in 1812, Thomas reported in a letter to Randolph that he "sent for our sister as soon as she could leave that neighborhood." Anna Scott came to Monticello but remained in "very low health . . . scarcely able to walk about the house." She lived at Monticello the rest of her life, well loved, despite occasional complaints from great-nieces and nephews that she meddled in their business. Shortly before his death, Thomas added a codicil to his will recommending his daughter Martha look after "my wellbeloved sister, Anne Scott," he added, "[I] trust confidently that from affection to her, as well as for my sake, she will never let her want a comfort." Martha Randolph took her grandmother's Bible and added, "A.S. died at Monticello," and the date, and she added the date to the record her father started in his Prayer Book.[63] Anna Scott, the last of the Shadwell generation, was not buried at Monticello, however, and perhaps joined her husband at whatever family or church cemetery contained his grave.

Three other siblings were also buried elsewhere. Mary Bolling died in 1804, and she may have been buried with John at Chestnut Grove or one of the other family plantations. Lucy died in Kentucky in 1810 and was buried on her son's plantation there. Her family reported to Thomas Jefferson of their "iraparable loss" of the "best of mothers, and sister. Her remains was entered the twenty eighth on a high emmenence, in view of that majestic river the Ohio." Randolph's death brought his twin sister, Anna Scott, and likely his brother to Snowdon for his final illness, death, and burial there in 1815.[64] There are no other details about their funerals.

Thomas Jefferson, who composed epitaphs for friends and family, also designed his own burial marker and the inscription that was to go on it. He specified that his marker should "be of the coarse stone of which my columns are made, that no one might be tempted hereafter to destroy it for the value of the materials." The simple forms would also deter vandals: "a plain die or cube of three feet without any mouldings, surmounted by an obelisk of six feet height, each of a single stone." The obelisk would bear a listing of three of his triumphs, "not a word more."

Here was buried
Thomas Jefferson,
Author of the Declaration of American Independence,
Of the Statute of Virginia for Religious Freedom,
And Father of the University of Virginia.

The die would read: "Born April 2, 1743, O.S.—Died July 4, 1826." Thomas used old-style dates on one other burial marker, that of his wife. Her gravestone read, "Martha Jefferson, Daughter of John Wayles and Martha Eppes, Born October 19th, 1748, O.S., Intermarried with Thomas Jefferson, January 1st, 1772, Torn from him by death September 6th, 1782."[65] Specifying "O.S." here is even more curious in that her October birth date was unaffected by the change made to the calendar in 1752. Thomas did not use old style for any of the other dates that fell before 1752, such as Dabney Carr's, also in October, his sister Martha's, in May 1746, or his mother's, where he put simply the year of her birth. Perhaps it was an attempt to evoke more history in the inscription of a date; perhaps it was Thomas's attempt to summon eleven more days to his and his wife's lives.

Family members Jefferson Randolph, Nicholas P. Trist, and Martha Jefferson Randolph, his servant Burwell, and possibly slaves Joe Fosset and John Hemings attended Thomas at his deathbed. Thomas requested that his burial be private, "without parade," and his family made no public invitations. He was buried July 5, 1826, borne from his house by slaves, accompanied by family to the Monticello graveyard. A friend who visited Monticello on July 4 wrote to his wife nearby, "His remains will be buried tomorrow at 5 o'clock P.M. No invitations will be given, all coming will be welcome at the grave." The Reverend Hatch performed the rites of the Episcopal Church at his interment, which was attended by students from the University of Virginia and many neighbors who came to pay their respects.[66]

Jane and Peter Jefferson created many legacies within their Shadwell household. In addition to material goods, land, and slaves, the parents gave their children a long list of intangible legacies. The family connections that the Jeffersons created made a lasting impression on the younger Jeffersons. There is undeniable evidence that the Jefferson children learned to care for, support, and love one another, despite alcoholism or financial problems, and in addition to intellectual interests they shared. They learned to maintain family rituals that were important and to keep family history. The intertwined lives of the Jefferson children and the people they owned also served to enhance the family connections of the Jeffersons. The familiarity of the slaves with their owners' families and plantations contributed to the planters' success, just as owners used knowledge of their slaves' kin networks to leverage advantages for the plantation.

The Jeffersons and their African-American slaves spread across Virginia, as their parents' generation had, taking their turns at replicating the cultural patterns they inherited. Patterns are useful, however, because they define not only what fits but also what does not. Just as artifacts have disproportionately greater value when they fall outside expected patterns, our story of life at Shadwell turns on unusual occurrences because they catch our attention. The means by which people defined both white and black family and community over great distance and passing time help explain Virginia's eighteenth-century plantation culture, as well as more universal elements of human behavior. Yet despite the dominance of patterns that enlarge our understanding of how colonial Virginia worked, we also find challenges to that. The compelling actions of runaway slaves, for instance, create trajectories away from the primary narrative of the planter's success and open the way for stories that redefine and reshape our understanding of how many people in colonial Virginia merely tolerated the gentry's dominance. While we marvel at the details that fit the picture we thought we were making, the declarations of independence from that become even more intriguing.

8 Thomas Jefferson's Shadwell Stories: Family and Slavery

Thomas Jefferson's early years have been called the lacuna of Jefferson studies.[1] This book is about all the people at Shadwell, yet Thomas Jefferson is its start and endpoint (fig. 8.1). Shadwell both alters and reinforces what historians have written about Thomas Jefferson, his character, and who he became as a result of the formal and informal education he received during his early years. Material evidence and close rereading of documents demand reassessment of many of the myths surrounding the early Jeffersons. Some myths can be retired directly based on new information while other foundation myths remain useful because they still explain history in ways that make sense to their particular audiences. Both the facts of these stories and their uses are important to the history and historiography of the Jefferson family and the ongoing conversations among Jefferson scholars. This study adds a tangible connection to the early years of Thomas Jefferson and his boyhood home. Even historians who do not specialize in material culture have been swayed by the visual impact of Tuckahoe or Westover and other standing eighteenth-century buildings used by contemporaries of Peter and Jane Jefferson. It has been hard to imagine the Jeffersons in these houses as peers without an equally impressive home of their own. Shadwell was that home.

Figure 8.1. Thomas Jefferson by John Trumbull,
1787–1788. Courtesy Monticello/Thomas Jefferson
Foundation, Inc.

Thomas Jefferson's meticulous record keeping once again displays its seemingly infinite value as familiar documents shed new light on old subjects. This
study of Shadwell, all the Jefferson siblings and relations, and the slaves
working there is weighted by the accounts kept by Thomas Jefferson because
his records provide so many details about late eighteenth-century life. But
what does the Shadwell material reveal about him? Archaeology at Shadwell
recovered a multitude of everyday objects whose cumulative effect is an image of place and people—of culture—that has everything to do with explain-
ing Thomas Jefferson. Our fascination with Jefferson lies in trying to understand
the intellectual capacity that shaped a nation and world history and also allowed him to be a connoisseur of so many things that remain interesting to us
today: books, wine, horticulture, architecture, languages, as the list goes. The
finely appointed house, expert servants, and attentive parents enabled the natural inquisitiveness of the son. Jefferson also embodied something unimagi-
nable for us today—an exploiter of enslaved humans, both those laboring in
distant fields and also those dressing, washing, and caressing him. Shadwell

taught Jefferson that a well-ordered landscape and a well-ordered household freed him for exercises of the mind.

In this study of Thomas Jefferson's family, he becomes one of many talented, well-trained gentry youth—instead of the exception. By making him part of the pattern, the other family members become actors instead of mere backdrops for their famous son and brother. In fact, the only biographical attention paid to any of Jefferson's siblings was the book *Thomas Jefferson and His Unknown Brother*, in which the younger was compared to the older, with the assessment that Randolph sadly lacked his older brother's abilities. However, Randolph held local titles and offices, and his children married well. He hardly compared poorly among other Virginia gentry. Had he been someone else's brother, he might at least have gotten his name in the title of the only book about him.[2]

Jefferson studies began almost immediately after his death in 1826. George Tucker's *Life of Thomas Jefferson* was first, in 1837, followed in 1858 by Henry S. Randall's *The Life of Thomas Jefferson*. Sarah N. Randolph added family and home to the political and public stories with *The Domestic Life of Thomas Jefferson* in 1871. The interest in Jefferson by biographers during the nineteenth century caused the family to examine their stories, as well as their attics and trunks for memorabilia. Jefferson's heirs made some new discoveries about their ancestry during this period; in fact, they expressed surprise at some of the revelations of their research. Randall recounts the heirs opening a trunk of papers at Edgehill (home of grandson Thomas Jefferson Randolph). They discovered then that Peter Jefferson had been a colonel and a burgess. That had not been part of the family lore; in fact, they wondered if Thomas Jefferson knew these things about his father. He did, of course, but the younger Jefferson had chosen to tell a different kind of story about his father.[3]

Until now, the sparse lines about Thomas Jefferson's early years in his *Autobiography* have stood out as the few bits of information about Jane and Peter Jefferson and their Shadwell home, yet Thomas's scant words sowed the seeds of many Jefferson myths. Some of Thomas's remarks have been taken as gospel, others dismissed. This study of Shadwell requires reflection on Thomas's own words yet again. The word "neglected" that Thomas used to describe his father's education has been quoted by almost every biographer, yet in the context of colonial Virginia, Peter performed as well as any other gentry and better than most. Thomas may have been comparing his father to his own experience or reinforcing the distinction between academic and home learning for some younger family member who was recalcitrant about school. Peter was among many gentry and burgesses whose schooling took place at home or with a tutor. Peter was no more self-made than Thomas.[4]

Jefferson inherited two sets of stories about his father. The set the family repeated depicted Peter as physically capable and mentally resourceful. Peter Jefferson's children, grandchildren, and great-grandchildren heard about Peter Jefferson the backwoods adventurer, whose feats of strength bested wild animals and treacherous terrain; these were stories for children that Thomas heard as a boy and that he retold to younger family members. In his literary analysis of Jefferson's writing, Jay Fliegelman sees Jefferson's description of the Cherokee Outassetè visiting Peter Jefferson as "addressing, mourning, and ennobling" his father's death by following the mention of his father with the Indian's great oration.[5] Thomas's own stories about his lost friendship with Dabney Carr echoed the separate and idealized masculine world that emboldened the tales about Peter Jefferson. Young Jefferson came away from his schooling abroad with his legendary friendship with Dabney Carr, his future brother-in-law and the first of his loved ones to be buried at Monticello. The hours Jefferson and Carr spent exploring the woods and mountains near Shadwell recall the story that Thomas later told about Peter Jefferson and a friend, spending four days out of seven in close camaraderie, dining and drinking at each other's homes in succession.[6] Thomas Jefferson associated his father with a nostalgic past that included wilderness exploits, noble Indians, and exclusive male friendships.

A subtler storyline told of the Peter Jefferson whose careful planning ensured his heirs' place in the world. The counterpoint to the adventure yarns were lessons about careful execution of legal and social offices. In these stories, the Jeffersons triumph not because of physical strength of themselves or others but because the elder Jefferson engaged professionals as executors, guardians, and schoolmasters to act on his behalf. In addition to the legal team that his father established in his will, the younger Jefferson invoked proxies for his father, men of standing who were capable in specific roles. In the breath after claiming, "at 14 years of age, the whole care & direction of myself was thrown on myself entirely," Jefferson told his grandson to always act as would gain approval from men such as those whom the school-age Jefferson looked to for guidance, men like William Small, George Wythe, and

Peyton Randolph.[7] Peter's family had the right relatives and he made sure they knew the right people.

Peter also made sure his son knew another professional who could show him how to present himself in the masculine world of the Virginia gentry. Sawney, Peter's, then Thomas's, manservant, was among the younger Jefferson's most intimate teachers, able to guide the young master in all sorts of subtle and crucial ways. The enslaved men and women at Shadwell helped raise Jefferson. Sawney was among the steady adult hands that taught him personal grooming and comportment necessary to a man of his station. Sawney's job was the detail work that made the young Jefferson appear competent. The masculine stories that Thomas chose to portray his father were part of the lessons of physical prowess and social ability that he was expected to master, and mastery of Sawney was part of those lessons as well. When Sawney died, Jefferson's most intimate physical link to his father was gone. Sawney may have been the intended servant honored in Jefferson's idealized plans for the burial ground at Monticello that included "the grave of a favorite and faithful servant." The legacy of this relationship was Jupiter, the boy slave who grew up at Shadwell as part of the Jefferson household and became indispensable to Thomas as his manservant after Sawney died. When Jupiter died in 1799, Jefferson lamented that his death left a "void," although Jefferson called it both "a void in my domestic arrangements" and "a void in my administration." Jupiter, whom Jefferson knew well enough to have him carry Jefferson's "Draft of Instructions to the Virginia Delegates in the Continental Congress" (which became "A Summary View of the Rights of British America") from Monticello to Williamsburg when Jefferson was sick, filled both public and private offices for his owner.[8] Sawney and Jupiter helped raise Thomas Jefferson.

The Jeffersons and the enslaved men, women, boys, and girls on their plantations experienced life together: birth, childhood, adolescence, marriage and parenthood, maturity, physical failing, sickness, death. Sall and other women who tended Thomas as nurses stood him on his feet and guided him through childish fears and taught him that physical comfort could come from any number of people with any skin color. Young gentry and slave children were at times playmates, sharing adventures, challenges, and taunts, including those of adolescent boys and girls on the verge of sexual awakening. Surely this was among early tests of domination over girls and other boys by white boys, and of self-control or extreme frustration by black boys. Jefferson, like many gentry boys, boarded with schoolmasters at other plantations. Young planters practiced formal scholarship and the skills of record keeping and also socialized as a cohort that would one day take seats on the vestry, courts, and assemblies. The history of slave society also acknowledges the informal lessons that were part of this, where planters' sons visited the slave quarters and exercised their power on both willing and unwilling partners there.[9] Jefferson had no choice that his relationship with slaves began at his birth; however, historians have mistakenly portrayed him as a passive actor in this chapter of his story until he inherited the Wayles patrimony of the slaves and debt that came to define him at Monticello. Jefferson practiced and made choices about the nature of his relationship with enslaved people from a young age.

One of Jefferson's most famous stories about childhood in Virginia bears new scrutiny here. Jefferson's caution about the effects of slavery on slave owners looms larger and larger as the image of his childhood home becomes clearer with the realities of teaching all the young slaves and masters there. Some historians have observed that Jefferson sought most of all to avoid conflict within his home and personal relationships. Yet Jefferson described a culture reared on conflict in *Notes on Virginia*, when he tells us that children were steeped in their parents' "unremitting despotism" over family slaves. Demonstrations of violence were usual and produced the desired effect: "The parent storms, the child looks on [and] puts on the same airs in the circle of smaller slaves, gives a loose to his worst of passions, and thus nursed, educated, and daily exercised in tyranny." We know about the collaring, whipping, and beating of slaves at Shadwell and Snowdon because they produced unusual responses in a few instances: runaways, a murder. The everyday violence and petty subjugation did not enter the written record.[10]

In *Notes on Virginia*, Jefferson recognized the tyranny and despotism of slaveholders as "odious peculiarities." Peculiar to what? Surely he does not mean to imply that brutality in slaveholding Virginia was rare. Did he mean that it made white people behave differently than how the gentry engaged one another in their regular commerce? Or, since *Notes on Virginia* was his response to a Frenchman's inquiry, did he understand that the behavior of slaveholders was peculiar within the context of polite or humane behavior as understood by Europeans who would read this as the identifying feature of manners in Virginia? Is this Jefferson's admission of guilt where he who could position the rights of British Americans as natural rights understood violence against slaves as peculiar? If Jefferson invoked "peculiarity" as property belonging to an individual (an alternate definition), again "odious peculiarities" acknowledged that slavery brought out the worst in any slave owner by challenging the owner's self-control—the opposite of gentry behavior. In another overt lesson in self-control, Jefferson cautioned his grandson to consider how participation in such vices as horseracing and gambling might reflect on his standing among gentlemen; Jefferson did not, in that lesson, caution his grandson to be likewise careful in how he treated his slaves. Jefferson chose the actions of slave owners as a characteristic to indict himself on the international stage, but he seemed to not want or need to teach it through written missives to his progeny, who were Virginians.[11] Yet even as Jefferson understood that Virginia's slaveholding was a distinct culture, this was his culture. Both the violence and the comforts of slavery were customary to him. Raising Jeffersons meant teaching children that two-year-olds owned other two-year-olds and also made sure that the same young gentry found reassurance in being groomed, taught, reprimanded, and feared by their black slaves.

Granddaughter Ellen reported that Jefferson's "affections were cultivated in the midst of an attached and united family," yet the family relationships have been questioned over and over, especially by academic historians. Jefferson's letter, in which he wrote, "As I grow older, I love those most whom I loved first," and "we often write seldomest to those whom we love most," has been quoted often by historians writing about Thomas's family relationships with his wife, daughters, and grandchildren. It has not, however, been used to argue evidence of a warm relationship with his own siblings, even though Jefferson wrote the letter quoted here to his sister Mary. Jefferson's notion of family often extended beyond the immediate, nuclear group; most famously, Jefferson's "family" encompassed the slaves he owned, and Jefferson also romanticized households that included both related and unrelated people.

Despite Jefferson's stories that idealized male friendships, he also idealized family life and often described a household teeming with family, friends, kin, and the implied presence of slaves. At Shadwell and elsewhere, these social groups coexisted by design; one was not a rejection of the other in Jefferson's Virginia. Jefferson also had "imagined households," which Rhys Isaac has explored through the literary circles and stories told and kept at Monticello. Some of these households could never be realized, such as one that included his dead sister Jane, for instance, in conversation with his charming new wife. These household circles fulfilled a number of roles in Jefferson's Virginia, as he related to his brother-in-law: "A lively and lasting sense of filial duty is more effectually impressed on the mind of a son or daughter by reading King Lear, than by all the dry volumes of ethics and divinity that ever were written." In that same letter describing a perfect collection and setting for a library and literary conversations, he conceded that the "lessons of the day" might even be lost to "Musick, Chess, or the merriments of our family companions," and that the family companions included friends and friends' wives.[12] The Jefferson households had intellectual, entertainment, and social value as places of formal and informal learning.

Family was important to Jefferson, which invites reconsideration of what some historians have taken as his denigrating views about genealogy and his mother's family. Thomas invested time and effort in copying and maintaining records of early family (even those of his wife's first husband). Current events when Jefferson was writing his *Autobiography* were more likely the source for his cautionary comments about ancestor worship. During the early nineteenth century, when Jefferson retired from public service, he found himself still under the scrutiny of political enemies, among them his own Randolph cousins. John Randolph of Roanoke accused Jefferson of mishandling money during his presidency and blamed Jefferson for what Randolph thought was an unfortunate leveling of the social order following the Revolution. The dispute between John Randolph and Thomas Jefferson was public and bitter. The Randolph connections, John notwithstanding, served the Jeffersons well. They were the same family—not different ones. Thomas's mother, grandfather, sons-in-law, and grandchildren bore the name. There is no compelling event in his early years to make association with Randolphs anything but fruitful. Jefferson's seeming denial of the importance of ancestry was accompanied by a response that indicates he had thought about his own quite a bit. Earlier in Jefferson's life, on his marriage, he queried a friend about acquiring a family coat of arms and acknowledged that ancestry might be useful. He also commented with ease that his father's family came from Wales and that there were Jeffersons in Virginia for at least a century before him.[13]

Another story is not Thomas Jefferson's at all but that of historians who write about him. How does the mid-twentieth-century story that Jefferson did not get on well with his mother serve the historians who created it and who choose to repeat it? Stories that bear retelling turn on conflict. In order to make Jefferson the flawed defender of natural rights, historians have chosen their Jefferson carefully. Jefferson claimed that family was important to him, and historians accept that to write about his brief, happy marriage. Historians also celebrate the widower-father's role in the sweet but coercive relationship that Jefferson had with his daughters. Many historians also like to think that Jefferson exercised self-discipline in dealing with the more than six hundred people he enslaved and that he faced very difficult choices that "required" him to remain a slave owner. In creating the hero Jefferson, what better place to find conflict than in something over which Jefferson had no control? By naming his mother as the problem in this flawed-but-otherwise-idyllic world, historians chose an apolitical, nonracial actor to carry the interpretive weight of conflict in the story of home. In her important work on how historians have treated the history of Sally Hemings and Thomas Jefferson, legal scholar and historian Annette Gordon-Reed challenged historians to reevaluate how they use historical evidence to make claims about past events. To the list of "truths" too easily accepted because they make a good story, add the twentieth-century myth that Thomas Jefferson did not like his mother. The mother story is about the discomforts of twentieth- (and now, twenty-first-) century historians. By repairing Jane to this picture and recasting Jefferson's home and family life as an almost materially and socially perfect world, historians in search of conflict will need to explain Jefferson's childhood differently. His home life enabled the liberality in which Jefferson's biggest challenges were the intellectual ideas of his time. The real and obvious conflict, then, lies with Jefferson as a slaveholder and charges him as more profoundly aware and responsible for his own role with racial slavery.[14]

There is evidence for intellectual influence on the Jefferson children from both their mother and their father. Jane's family enjoyed horticulture and the company of botanists; Peter kept company with mathematicians. Both parents read and wrote. Jane's influences have been ignored for the sake of historiographical fashion. It is time for the potential of her abilities to be restored. Shadwell was Thomas Jefferson's patrimony, a deed to real property. But the real legacy was far greater and came from both parents. This study of the Jeffersons reveals the active role of Peter and Jane Jefferson in establishing in their children the strong social and family connections that would ensure them of every advantage they needed during their adult lives. They came to the counter with preapproved credit and, they came to the table without question of their belonging. Doors stood open to them across Virginia, and probably well beyond; slaves at plantations far and wide readily accepted their tips and showed them into familiar dining rooms—from Shadwell to the seat of Virginia's royal governor.

The artifacts, books, and maps at Shadwell defined connections across Virginia and between Virginia and the Americas, London, and the world. The book collections tied English law, letters, and landscape to ancient and classical times and asserted the ongoing correctness of a liberal republican view of man's paramount place in nature and society. The Jeffersons were among colonial Virginians whose reading drank heartily at the font of Whig history and belles lettres. The intellectual landscape at Shadwell shows that the Jeffersons' lives were filled with a degree of certainty about legal rights, accepted behaviors, and social position. This sense of entitlement helped them move through the world with assurance. The Jeffersons occupied a frontier, but not the frontier of Frederick Jackson Turner, where lack of government invited creative and egalitarian solutions to problems of individuals and communities. The Jeffersons faced the frontier knowing that they had the military and legal authority of the British Empire behind them. They were certain of their power.

Peter and Jane Jefferson planned Shadwell to replicate culture and expand empire, not to move away from it. It was not—at least not for the Jeffersons and other gentry—a frontier that proposed any kind of separatist alternative to British Virginia. The romance of America's later frontier thesis of hearty individualism was never part of Shadwell's well-ordered, well-connected world. Peter and Jane Jefferson ensured that their children knew the benefits and comforts of gentry Virginia; they conquered worlds through books and maps, land companies and patents. Although all the Jeffersons had some experience with the physical work of the plantation, they always owned people and paid others to labor for them. Peter and sons Thomas and Randolph rode, surveyed, and kept account books. Jane and the daughters planned, entertained, and trained the next generation to this estate. If the Jeffersons had been less than gentry, Thomas's earliest garden book entries would not reveal the amazing luxury of a young man measuring and documenting the spring peas; if the garden book existed at all, it would have been about tobacco. Jefferson's peas do not make him a farmer, except perhaps in his own self-image.[15]

But the peas are part of stories from Shadwell that this family knew how to hold the world in wonder, to find fascination with ancient found objects, to marvel at the horticultural magic of the vegetable and fruit gardens, to imagine faraway and unknown lands from books and maps, and to celebrate the cunning and strength of Englishmen hacking through wilderness in order to tame it for the public weal. Jefferson displayed both sides of this upbringing many times in ways that seem both fascinating and horrifying today. Jefferson had the ability, for instance, to marvel at the cultural practices of American Indians, even inviting them to sit for portraits when they visited him during his presidency. He could document their language and artifacts, then turn to discuss their extermination because their land-use practices clashed with his.[16] The Jeffersons' observations of nature bolstered their eighteenth-century view of the world that positioned their British social and legal authority at the pinnacle of the natural order of things.

The plantation culture of Virginia was also at odds with Jefferson's ideal agrarian republic. Virginia's colonial economic and social power lay not in farmers but in producers of a staple crop that fed an intercontinental network of merchant houses and highly regulated international trade. Not only was tobacco damaging to the land and those who used it, but it meant that planters were merely workers in someone else's economic engine; the planters were to the merchants what the slaves were to the planters. Jefferson understood both the economic shackles and the opportunities that this system created. Perhaps Jefferson's self-fashioning as a farmer who decried tobacco because of its extractive properties was a fiction meant to deny his dependence on both the mercantile system and the labor system that underlay his fortunes. Jefferson was unyielding in his defense of an agrarian republican new nation, yet Jefferson the slaveholder undermined the very ideal.[17]

The undeniable story is that Jefferson depended on African-American slaves his entire life. The liberality that allowed men like Peter Jefferson to spend time on concerns of commonwealth was because his own labor as head of a household was replaced by the labor of many. The enslaved residents of the household cooked, dressed, arranged, packed, washed, and nursed the Jeffersons, which meant that the Jeffersons could read or study law. The physical comforts and luxuries were possible because of people kept as slaves. Jefferson was aware of this and aware of the system of deliberate subjugation that he wrote of in *Notes on Virginia*. He was not proud of that Virginia, yet he could not imagine life any other way.

In the early twenty-first century the founding generation serves a different purpose for us than it did a century ago. Historians who study the personal lives of founders—homes, family, education, friendships—do so not to glorify their subjects but to understand the contexts that produced them. In part by making the founders human we help create a landscape of possibility that people born today—citizens defined differently than how the founders defined citizens—have the educational opportunity, protection of law, and civic responsibility to exercise the promises the founders made. But as other historians have found when proving that in many ways Jefferson was just like us, we come again to the fact that he was not. In spite of the profound moral problems that bound Jefferson in slavery's grip, he still had the intellectual capacity and ability to imagine the world anew made from claims of self-evident truths, inalienable rights, of legal, civil, and personal equality. Why did Thomas Jefferson choose to risk this world that seemingly held nothing but comfort for him? What remains the marvel of this exercise, wherein Jefferson is completely naturalized within Virginia gentry culture, was how he made the leap to an intellectual and legal position that conceived the rights of man differently. Slaves made possible the home where Jefferson could be so schooled, practiced, and acculturated to his legal rights that he could recognize when those rights were threatened. Thomas Jefferson's move to Monticello continued stories begun at Shadwell, where most of what was Virginian about Jefferson continued with little change, even as Jefferson's ideas began to transform the culture that raised him.

Appendix: Tables

Table 1. Peter Jefferson's books by general subject, percentage
of number of volumes, and percentage of total cost

	volumes (%)	cost (%)
legal	22	18.0
history	18	43.0
natural philosophy	2	1.5
practical	6	1.6
religious	6	10.0
popular culture/literature	39	27.0
miscellaneous	6	0.8
(history and literature)	(57)	(68)

Note: Number of volumes = 49; total cost = £16 17s. 9d.

Source: AlCWB, 2:41.

Table 2. Inventory of books in Peter Jefferson's library, 1757, by category (spelling and titles as written)

	pages	size	£	s.	d.
Legal (5 titles, 11 volumes)					
Solomons state trials	6v[a]	f	1	6	0
Nelsons office of a Justice	619	8vo		15	0
Scriveners guide 2 vols	432	8vo		8	0
Virginia Justice	364	8vo		3	6
Laws of Virga.	184[b]	6 11/16		7	6
History (5 titles, 9 volumes)					
Rapins Hist. of England 2v & 2v Cont.	5 v	f	6	0	0
Oglvies Discription of America	674	f		15	0
The present state of great Britain	274[c]	8vo		3	0
a secret History of Queen Annes Ministers	71	7 1/16		1	8
Ansons Voyage round the World	356	8vo		4	0
Natural Philosophy (1 title, 1 volume)					
Trents Astronomy	[d]			5	0
Practical (2 titles, 3 volumes)					
the London & Country brewer	332	8vo		3	0
Switszers husbander, 2 vols.	363	8vo		2	6
Religious (3 titles, 3 volumes)					
1 Quarto bible w[t] Book of Common Prayer		4to	1	5	0
a Large Prayer book		4to[e]		8	1
Bishop of sodor & mans Instructions for indians	271	6 11/16		2	0
Popular culture/literature (4 periodicals, 19 volumes)		4to	4	5	6
Spect[r] 9V					
Tattler 5V					
Gaurd[n] 2V					

(*Continued*)

Table 2. (*continued*)

	pages	size	£	s.	d.
Addisⁿ Work 3 V					
Three old Books		d		3	0

Notes:

[a] The 1730 publication of Salmon's State Trials had 6 volumes, it is unclear how many of these PJ owned. This column has number of text pages or volumes.

[b] Robert Beverley's 1722 *Laws of Virginia* had 184 pages. It is possible this could also be the collection of British laws for the colonies printed by John Nicholson in 1704.

[c] Various editions have from 274 to 529 pages.

[d] Unknown, see text.

[e] I have assumed that large here means quarto.

Source: AlCWB, 2:41.

Table 3. Peter Jefferson N[ote] One. A bale of goods arrived for the Jeffersons in November 1760 aboard *The Planter.* The bale contained seven kinds of cloth, including Irish and German fabric, English-made Monmouth caps, knives, two sizes of nails, sickles, German steel, and salt. The entry also shows the cost of the goods and the duties and insurance paid on the bale.

[Nov.] 25 × Rece.d from Messrs. Farrell & Co of Bristol Merchts. Bill of Lading & Invoice of Goods by the Planter Capt. Randolph

        Viz.

PI N.1 a Bale packcloth packing &c:	. 9.	
94 yds. Cotton at 1/. is 94/. 97 yds. Plains 15 1/2 is 121/10 1/2	10.15.10 1/2	
2 ps. Stript Duffle £9.17., 2 doz monon.th Caps 37/	11.14.	
6 [?] bro. thread 12/ 31 ys. Stripd Cotton at 1/6 is 46/6	2.18. 6	
2 doz Butchers knives	. 4.	
24, 24, 23, 18 is 89 yds. 7/8 Irish Linen No. 5 at 1/2	5. 3.10	
25 yds. 4/4 Do. at 2/3 is 56/3, 26 yds Do. N.14 at 2/11 is 75/10	<u>6.12. 1</u>	37.17.3 1/2
2 a Truss Viz 100, 93, 96 is 289 Ells Ozna at 6 1/4	9.18.8 1/4	
8 Ells Hissens [at] 9	. 6.	10.4.8 1/4
3 a Cask 12 M 8d. nails 49/. 12 M 10d. Do. 60/ Cask 2/	5.11.	
4 a Bundle 1 1/2 doz Sickles . . . at 8/	.12.	
5 a Bundle German Steel 8.2.4 . . . at 56/	<u>1.10.</u>	7.13.
6 Jacks & lying at 22 d. [?] 24 Bush Salt at 8		<u>1. 7.</u>
		£57. 1.11
Paid Fees in Entry Town Duty Shipping &c	13. 4.	
Primage Paid	.6. 6	
Counts 2 pr prbs. on £58.1.9	1. 9. 1	
Premium on £67.10 Insured at 7 Guineas pr Ct.}		
Policy 1/6 Counts.[?] 8/9 }	<u>5. 7. 6</u>	<u>7.16. 5</u>
		£64.18. 4

Source: PJ Estate, 1759–1763, 3.

Table 4. Birth information of Jane Jefferson's children, her age at their birth, estimated date of conception, and time from last birth to next conception

Year	Date	Birthplace	Child	Jane's age	Conception date estimated[a]	Duration since last birth in:		
						Days	Months[b]	Years
1740	6/27	Shadwell	d. Jane born	20.5	10/4/1739			
1741	10/1	Shadwell	d. Mary born	21.5	1/7/1741	194	6.5	
1743	4/2	Shadwell	s. Thomas born	22	7/9/1742	281	9.4	
1744	11/4	Shadwell	d. Elizabeth born	24.8	2/11/1744	315	10.5	
1746	5/29	Tuckahoe	d. Martha born	26.3	9/4/1745	304	10.1	
1748	10/16	Tuckahoe	s. Peter Field born	28.5	3/7/1748	647	21.6	1.8
1748	11/29	Tuckahoe	s. Peter Field died	28.8				
1750	3/9	Tuckahoe	s. born	30	6/15/1749	242	8.1	
1750	3/9	Tuckahoe	s. died	30				
1752	10/10	Tuckahoe	d. Lucy born	32.5	1/5/1752	667	22.2	1.8
1755	10/1	Shadwell	s. Randolph born	35.5	1/7/1755	819	27.3	2.2
1755	10/1	Shadwell	d. Anna Scott born	35.5	1/7/1755	819	27.3	2.2

Notes:
[a] Assumes an average 267-day gestation period.
[b] Average 30 days.

Table 5. Jane's sixth part of the Shadwell slaves and the family groups among them

---

1760 Janr. 5 ×

Pursuant to the Will of Peter Jefferson & at the Request of his Widow Jane Jefferson divided the Slaves belonging to the said Estate & allowed her her Share being one Sixth part Viz

Squire aged abt.	30 years Valued at	£60	
Sampson	30	35	
Sall	35	45	
Cain[Lucinda?] her Child		10	
Belinda	23	55	
Suckey her Child		14	
Casar	12	45	
Little Salley	8	35	
Fanny Myrtillas Child		14	
Jesse	5	25	
Aggey	3	17	355. .

Note that the following Slaves being lent to Mrs. Jefferson to allow the Children were not divided Viz Myrtilla aged abt. 25 years Valued at £50 Phil 19 year old £45 Jupiter 16 year old £45   90—

Families among the eleven slaves Jane chose in 1760:

Sall	Belinda m. Squire	(Myrtilla)
Lucinda	Suckey	Fanny
Casar		(Peter)
Little Salley		
(Jupiter)		

Undetermined relationships:
Sampson
Jesse
Aggey
(Phil)

Note: Names in parentheses are slaves not owned by Jane but still on the plantation and also belonging to these families. Myrtilla's son Peter belonged to Randolph, who was still at home, which may be why Jane requested that Myrtilla stay.

Source: PJ Estate, 1759–1763, 10.

Table 6. Naming patterns of the grandchildren of Jane and Peter Jefferson

Mary and John Bolling	Thomas and Martha Jefferson	Martha and Dabney Carr	Lucy and Charles Lewis	Randolph and: 1. Anna Jefferson 2. Mitchie Pryor
Martha	Martha	Jane Barbara	Randolph	1. Isham Randolph
John	Jane Randolph	Lucy	Jane Jefferson	1. Thomas
Edward	Son	Mary	Isham	1. Field
Archibald	Mary	Peter	Charles	1. Robert Lewis
Mary	Daughter	Samuel	Anna Marks	1. James Lilburn
Robert	Lucy Elizabeth	Dabney	Elizabeth	1. Anna Scott
Jane	Lucy Elizabeth		Martha Ann Cary	
Thomas			Lucy	2. John
Ann			Mary	
			Lilburne	

Table 7. Shadwell home quarter by family group, 1757[a]

Mothers and known children

Sall (the elder)	Hannah	*Cachina*	*Myrtilla*	*Bellinda*
Nan[b]	Fan	*Lydia*	*Fany*	(m. Squire)
Jupiter		*Phebe*	*Peter*	Suckey
Caesar				Squire
Sall				
Cate				

Unassigned men	Unassigned boys	Unassigned girls
Hercules	Jammey	*Cloe*
Samson	Adam	*Patt*
Syphax	*Jesse*	*Eve*
Sawney (Sall?)		Leah
Phill (Moll)		*Rachel*
Nimrod		

Notes:

[a] Names in italics indicate slaves bequeathed by Peter to one of the Jefferson children or by Jane when she claimed her portion of Peter's estate. Names in parentheses are known spouses who did not live on the home quarter. Unassigned means that I have not found direct evidence to which family a person belonged.

[b] Nan was counted among the adult women, but she was also the daughter of Sall.

Source: AlCWB, 2:45.

Table 8. Kitchen inventory from 1757 probate record
(spelling as written)

	s.	d.
1 old Oznaburg tablecloth	1	6
3 Large & 2 small Pewter Dishes	15	9
1 Pr Large Kitchen HandIrons	30	7
1 old D: Oven, Pewter dish, Pat: pans &c @	6	0
4 Tubs & 4 Pails	16	0
two copper Kettles	6	10
2 Iron spits	9	0
2 frying pans & Grid Iron	4	6
2 Iron pot racks	22	6
4 pots & 3 pr pot Hooks	55	0
1 bed & Covering	45	0
2 old Tables	3	6
2 brushes	1	0
2 old chairs & 1 pr scissors	2	0
A meal bag, 2 bedsteads & 2 barrels	11	6
1 Cleaver	1	6
10 light cask	25	0
old Lumber	2	6
1 cask	5	0
4 meal bags	11	6

Source: AlCWB, 2:43.

Table 9. Clothing made 1762 (above) and clothing delivered 1763 (below) (spelling as written)

Acct. of Negroes Cloths made for the Estate this year Viz

1762 Decr.	Shirts	Suits	Wools	Wos	Childrens	Childrens	Linen
By Martha Harvie	1		6	12	7		1.2.10
Nelly Shepherd	2	6	1		7	28	.14.6
Mary Spiers	4	4			0[?]	0[?]	.4.
Lucy Gorge	8	8	1	1	1		
Letty Moore	4	4	1		2	1	

Paid for Cutting the Negroes Cloths to Mrs. Harvie . 9.

Delivered to Mrs. Jefferson Cloths for Chloe & 8 yds Cotton 13 Ozna. 2m. hose

Deld. to the Overseers Cloths for all the Negroes & 5 Blankets to yr. No. River

Accot. of Negroes Cloths delivered out for Jeffersons Estate

1763 Novr.	Shirts	Suits	Mens Wollen	Wos Wollen	Small Shirts	Frock	hose	Cotton	Ozna	Thread
To Mrs. Jefferson		2		1				13 yds	20½ Ells	14#
To the Qur. at Snodon	6	6	3	3	8	4	6			14
To Matt: Moore	8	9[3?]	4	4	12	6	8			1/2
William Gooch	6	6	3	3	8[?]	4	5			14
Geo. Gillespy	4	4	2	2	4	2	5			14
To Sawney							1	4 ½	6	

Source: PJ Estate, 1759–1763, 1.

Table 10. Slaves and their values (in pounds and shillings), 1757, as listed in Peter Jefferson's inventory (spelling as written)

Hercullus	35.	Sally	37.10.
Samson	45.	Flora her Child Agey	47.10.
Syphax	45.	Moll a Girl	27.10.
Sawney	57.10.	Ephey a Girl	17.10.
Phill	30.	Goliah	50.
Nimrod	45.	Tobey	25.
Jupiter	32.10.	Gill	45.
Cesar	30.	Toby a boy	18.
Squire a boy	27.10.	Orrange a boy	13.
J ammey	25.	Phillis	20.
Peter	17.10.	Juno	27.10.
Adam	15.	Fany	35.
Jesse	17.10.	Lucey	40.
Sall	40.	Nanney a Girl	15.
Hannah & her Child Fan	45.	Squir	50.
Cachina & her C Lydia	40.	Jack	45.
Myrtilla and her C Fany	47.10.	Harry	35.
Bellinda & her C Suckey	45.	Dinah	35.
Nan	35.	Jenny	30.
Cloe	15.	Eady	25.
Patt	30.	Billey	_25._
Cate	27.10.	1 Negro Fellow Crummel	L50.
Eve	20.[?]	1 Negro Quash	55.
Sall a Girl	22.10.	1 Negro Sanco	50.
Leah	25.	1 Negro Wench betty	40.
Phebe	16.	1 Negro Bellow	40.
Rachel	_27.10._	1 Negro Nell	40.
		1 Negro Child Bellow	8.

Source: AICWB, 2:45, 47.

Table 11. Birth records of eight women from Shadwell

Name	Dates[a]	Children (N)[b]	Age range of reproductive years, if known	Fertile years (N)	Average months between pregnancies (N)
Sall (Elder)	c. 1725–1797	7	16–40	24	41
Fany	1736–1802	4	24–33	9	27
Juno[c]	Before 1735–1801	4	—	9	27
Nell	Before 1741–?	5	—	21	50
Cate	1747–after 1819	6	29–48[d]	19	38
Bellinda	1739–1808	8	18–38	20	30
Moll	1749–1811	9	19–37	18	24
AVERAGE		6	—	17	34
Jane Jefferson	1720–1776	10	19–35	16	19

Notes:

[a] Dates are approximate. Dates of Juno and Nell are based on an assumption that each was at least 16 years old at the birth of her first child.

[b] Number of births recorded. There may have been other children who died or other pregnancies not recorded.

[c] Juno was excused from labor because of age or infirmity by 1774.

[d] Cate's age seems high, but multiple documents by Thomas Jefferson record the dates of her and her children's births.

Sources: AlCWB, 2:45, 47; FB, 21, 22, 28; Files LCS; "Jefferson Family, Bible"; PJ Estate, 1759–1763, 10.

Table 12. Comparison of birth years of Sall's and Jane's children

Year	Sall's births	Jane's births
1740		Jane Jr.
1741	Nan	Mary
1743	Jupiter	Thomas
1744		Elizabeth
1746		Martha
1747	Cate	
1748	Caesar	Peter Field (died)
1750		son (died)
1752	Sall	Lucy
1755		Anna Scott and Randolph
1760	Lucinda	
1765	Simon	

Table 13. Shadwell slaves listed by quarter (I–V) and sex, from 1757 inventory

	Men	Boys	Women	Girls	Total	Quarter
I	6	7	6	12	31	home quarter, Shadwell
II			2	3	5	(location undetermined)
III	3	2	4	1	10	Monticello(?)
IV	3		2	2	7	(location undetermined)
V	3		3	1	7	Snowdon
Total	15	9	17	19	60	

Source: AlCWB, 2:45, 47.

Table 14. Jefferson lands, tobacco yields, slaves, and overseers based on 1760 returns from the 1759 crop. John Harvie's lists for 1760 are the most complete for any year of the plantation's operation.

Land[a]	Acres	1759 tobacco (lbs.)	Total yield (%)	Tobacco/ acre[b] (lbs.)	Quarter	Adult field slaves[e]	Tobacco lbs./ field slave [e]	Overseer(s)
Shadwell	400	4,999	7	12.5	I	(3–4)	(1,500)	Fred Gillam
Monticello	1,000	11,111	15	11.1	III	7	1,587	Joseph Dawson
Pantops	650	10,444	14	11.0	II/IV?	2 + 5	1,492	Joseph Dawson
Portobello	150							Joseph Dawson
Tufton	150							Joseph Dawson
Pouncey's	(300)[c]							Joseph Dawson
Snowdon	2,050	18,076	24	8.8	V	6	3,013	Martin Dawson
North River	2,769 est.	29,353	40		I–IV?	(18–20 est.)	(1,500)	Joseph Dawson, William Gooch, and Fred Gillam
Totals/ averages	7,169	73,983	100	10.9[d]		(25)	(3,000)	

(continued)

Table 14. (*continued*)

Notes:

[a] This list uses the names that Thomas Jefferson assigned to the properties; we do not know what Peter Jefferson called them.

[b] Tobacco/acre is a raw estimate based on the total property acreage, including any noncultivated land and acreage for domestic uses.

[c] Pouncey's is not included in acreage for tobacco because it is referred to as a woodlot. *FB*, 331.

[d] This figure is the average tobacco/acre based on the four figures in the column above and was used to estimate the acreage for the North River land based on its tobacco yield. The total land estimate was 7,169 acres used for tobacco, or 7,469 for all uses, including Pouncey's. Peter Jefferson paid rents on 7,080 acres in Albemarle County in 1754 (Peter Jefferson Account Book, 22). Dumas Malone did not think that Jefferson owned the North River land, an assessment that he supported with John Harvie's record of a 1757 quitrent payment for 4,375 acres, but which was a partial payment. Multiple payments for rents were spread over multiple years, making the total hard to isolate. Jefferson clearly had some ownership of the North River land, since it produced 40 percent of his 1759 tobacco crop. PJ Estate, 1757–1765, esp. 7, 19, 23, 34; Malone, *Jefferson*, 1:435.

[e] The figures in parentheses in these two columns are generated from the other information in this table. I use the figure of about 3,000 lbs tobacco per adult field slave from the self-contained Snowdon quarter (V) as the maximal work load. The figures of approximately half that for sites II, III, IV suggest that workers on those quarters had another half work load they could spend on the North River property. Using 1,500 lbs/worker generates each number of workers required for Quarter I (first row, Shadwell), and for North River (eighth row). The North River tract would require about 20 workers to produce the 1759 crop, the equivalent of the combined workers from quarters I, II, III, and IV.

Source: PJ Estate, 1757–1765, 7, 19, 23, 34.

Table 15. Residents of field quarters, grouped by family where possible, 1757[a]

Rivanna River Quarter Farms (II, III, and IV)			Fluvanna River (V)
Quarter II	Quarter III (Monticello)	Quarter IV	Quarter V (Snowdon)
5 people (2 women, 3 girls)	10 people (3 men, 2 boys, 4 women, 1 girl)	7 people (3 men, 2 women, 2 girls)	7 people (3 men, 3 women, 1 girl)
Sally	Gill+Fany	Squire [m. Belinda (QI)]	Crummel
Flora her Child			
Agey			
Moll a Girl		Jack	Quash
		Harry	Nell
Ephey a Girl	Phillis +Goliah		Child Bellow[a]
		Dinah (mother Phillis and brother Goliah [QIII])	
	Tobey		Sanco
	Juno		Betty
	Nanney a Girl	Jenny	
	Toby a boy	Eady	Bellow
	Orrange a boy		
		Billey	
	Lucey		

Note:
[a] Quarter I is the home quarter, the subject of chapter 3.
Source: AICWB, 2:45, 47.

Table 16. Field quarter inventory, 1757 (spelling as written)[a]

Site A (Quarter IV?)	Site B (Quarter II?)	Site C Quarter III (Monticello)	Quarter V Snowdon
1 Oxyoke	1 Dutch Plow	4 broad hoes	98 ^{lbs} old Iron
2 falling axes	2 Plow hoes	6 Hilling hoes	6 Br° Hoes
3 Grubbing hoes	1 old + cut saw	3 Narrow axes	5 Nar° axes
5 Ft: Hoes	3 Grubbing hoes @	2 old chairs	3 Iron Wedges
3 Weeding hoes	1 Grindstone	4 Hilling hoes @	1 Grind stone
a Grind stone	2 tight casks	2 Narrow axes	3 Harrow Hoes
1 spade	1 p^r stillyards &	4 broad hoes	1 Plow
1 pot and hooks	Beef Rope	1 p^r Iron wedges	1 Iron Pot &
1 M:	3 Potts & 2 p^r	1 + cut saw	Hooks
	pot hooks	1 Handsaw	1 I pot
	2 Tin pans @	1 Gun	
		2 pots & 1 p^r pot hook	
		2 tin pans	
		1 Dish & plate	
		1 frying pan	
		2[?] sifters	
		1 Grindstone	
		3 Rawhides	
		1 Grindstone	

Note:

[a]The correspondence of adults and tools argues for the 7 people (5 adults) from Quarter IV to work at Site A and the 5 people (2 adults) from Quarter II to work with the tools listed at Site B (see table 15, Residents of field quarters).

Source: AICWB, 2:46–47.

Table 17. Quarter III slave list, by families, 1757

Family 1	Family 2	Family 3	Family 4
Phillis, mother	Tobey, husband	Gill, husband	Lucey[a]
Goliah, adult son	Juno, wife	Fany, wife	
	Nanney, daughter	(4 children not yet born)	
	Toby, son		
	Orrange, son		

Note:
[a] Relationship not known.

Source: AlCWB, 2:45.

Table 18. Account of Jefferson Estate with Peter Shepherd, 1761, showing Eleanor Shepherd's contribution to her family's economy

Peter Shepherd	Dr.	Cr.
To his Rent for the Present year	1. .	
To cash pd. his Wife		2.6
By his Wifes work for making 46 Shirts & Shifts out of Dam } sisyrd[?] Linen @ 8 Each }		1.10.8
By Do for 15 Small Do 4		. 5.
By Do. for 10 Do. delivered when returned 4		. 3.4
By Do. for making 8 Cotton Frocks 6		. 4.
By Do. for 6 Frocks + 1 little Jacket & Breeches when returned to Cash	1. 4.	
	2. 6.6	2. 6.6
Cash	Dr.	
To pd. for making 13 mens & 12 Suits of Wos. Wollen Cloths @ $\frac{1}{3}$	1.11.3	
To cutting out the Linen Cloths	. 5.	
To paid Peter Shepherd	1. 4.	

Source: PJ Estate, 1759–1763, 1.

Table 19. Inventory of Peter Jefferson's weapons, kept in a storeroom or strong room at Shadwell (spelling as written)

	£	s.	d.
1 Gun @	2	10	0
1 Gun	1	5	0
1 Pr Brass barrel'd pistols		15	0
1 Pr Brass barrel'd pistols	1	15	
1 silver Hilted sword	3		
1 silver Hilted Cutlass	3		
1 bayonet		3	0
a pr files		7	6
A parcel of sword belts & Double Girth		6	0
1 silver Watch	5		
1 pr silver spurs @	2	10	0
12 Dozn Razors, a hone & Case flemes		10	0
Total	20	1	6

Source: AlCWB 2:43.

Table 20. Division of slaves from 1757 list
to Thomas and Randolph[a]

Quarter	Thomas	Randolph
I	11	10
II	2	3
III	6	4
IV	3	4
VI	4	3
Totals	26	24

Note:

[a] The figures include slaves bequeathed by Peter and deeded
to them by Jane.

Abbreviations and Archival Sources

Abbreviations

AlCOB	Albemarle County Order Book
AlCDB	Albemarle County Deed Book
AlCWB	Albemarle County Will Book
Autobiography	"Autobiography of Thomas Jefferson," in *The Life and Selected Writings of Thomas Jefferson*, edited by Adrienne Koch and William Peden (New York: Modern Library, 1944)
Beverley Town	Plat of the Town of Beverley [also spelled Beverly, aka Westham], Henrico County, surveyed by Peter Jefferson, June 6, 1751, Edgehill-Randolph Papers, ViU
Brother	Bernard Mayo, ed., *Thomas Jefferson and His Unknown Brother* (Charlottesville: University of Virginia Press, 1981)
CSmH	Henry E. Huntington Library, San Marino, California
CWF	Colonial Williamsburg Foundation
DLC	Library of Congress, Washington, D.C.
EEBO	Early English Books Online
ESTC	English Short Title Catalog
Family Letters	Edwin M. Betts and James Adam Bear Jr., *The Family Letters of Thomas Jefferson* (Charlottesville: University of Virginia Press, 1986)
FB	Edwin M. Betts, ed., *Thomas Jefferson's Farm Book* (Charlottesville: University of Virginia Press, 1987)

File LCS	Files on slaves kept by Lucia Stanton, Monticello Research Department
Fithian, *Journal*	Fithian, Philip Vickers, *Journal and Letters of Philip Vickers Fithian: A Plantation Tutor of the Old Dominion, 1773–1774,* edited by Hunter Dickinson Farish (Williamsburg, Va.: Colonial Williamsburg, 1957)
Fry-Jefferson Map	Joshua Fry and Peter Jefferson, *A Map of the Inhabited Part of Virginia . . .* (1751)
GB	Edwin M. Betts, ed., *Thomas Jefferson's Garden Book* (Philadelphia: American Philosophical Society, 1944)
Jefferson Family, Bible	Jefferson Family, Bible, 1752–1861, acc. no. 4726, ViU
Jefferson, "Memoirs"	Isaac Jefferson, "Memoirs of a Monticello Slave," in *Jefferson at Monticello,* ed. James A. Bear Jr. (Charlottesville: University of Virginia Press, 1967)
Jefferson, *Notes*	Thomas Jefferson, *Notes on the State of Virginia* [1787], edited by William Peden (New York: Norton, 1982)
JJ	Jane Jefferson
Kern, "Report on a Burial Ground"	Susan A. Kern, "A Report on Archaeological Investigation of a Burial Ground at Shadwell, Virginia, 1992–1993," ms., TJMF, 1994
Kern, "Report on Shadwell"	Susan A. Kern, "Report on Archaeological Investigations at Shadwell, Albemarle County, Virginia, 1991–1995," ms., TJMF, 1996
L&B	Andrew A. Lipscomb and Albert E. Bergh, eds., *Writings of Thomas Jefferson,* 20 vols. (Washington, D.C.: Thomas Jefferson Memorial Association of the United States, 1904–5)
LCB	Douglas L. Wilson, ed., *Jefferson's Literary Commonplace Book,* The Papers of Thomas Jefferson, 2nd Ser. (Princeton, N.J.: Princeton University Press, 1989)
Malone, *Jefferson*	Dumas Malone, *Jefferson and His Time,* 6 vols. (New York: Little, Brown, 1948–81)
MB	James A. Bear Jr. and Lucia C. Stanton, eds., *Jefferson's Memorandum Books* (Princeton, N.J.: Princeton University Press, 1997)
MHi	Massachusetts Historical Society, Boston
MJR	Martha Jefferson Randolph
Neiman, "Shadwell Quarter"	Artifact inventory made February 7, 2000, of excavations at Monticello directed by Fraser Neiman on a site called "Shadwell Quarter" or "Early Farm Quarter" to distinguish the Shadwell-era site from other sites at Monticello

Papers	Julian P. Boyd, Charles T. Cullen, John Catanzariti, Barbara B. Oberg, eds., *The Papers of Thomas Jefferson*, 36 vols. to date (Princeton, N.J.: Princeton University Press, 1950–)
Papers, Retirement Series	J. Jefferson Looney, ed., *The Papers of Thomas Jefferson, Retirement Series*, 6 vols. to date (Princeton, N.J.: Princeton University Press, 2005–)
PJ	Peter Jefferson
PJ Estate, 1728–1758	Peter Jefferson Account Book, 1744–1757, CSmH [NB: numbers given are folios]
PJ Estate, 1757–1765	John Harvie Accounts (of Peter Jefferson Estate), 1757–1765, CSmH
PJ Estate, 1759–1763	The Estate of PJ to J. Harvie, 1759-1763, Albemarle County Court Records, loose pages in collections of MHi
PJ Estate, 1760–1761	Estate of Colo. PJ dece'd in Account with John Harvie, Albemarle County Will Book 2, 1752–1785, 83-87
Randall, *Jefferson*	Henry S. Randall, *The Life of Thomas Jefferson*, 3 vols. (New York: Derby and Jackson, 1858)
Randolph, *Domestic Life*	Sarah N. Randolph, *The Domestic Life of Thomas Jefferson* (New York: Harper, 1871)
RJ	Randolph Jefferson
Rose, *Diary*	Ralph Emmett Fall, ed., *The Diary of Robert Rose* (Falls Church, Va.: McClure Press, 1977)
SJL	Summary of Journal Letters, Thomas Jefferson's record of letters written and sent, entries included in Boyd, *Papers*
TJ	Thomas Jefferson
TJF	Thomas Jefferson Foundation
TJMF	Thomas Jefferson Memorial Foundation
ViU	University of Virginia, Charlottesville
VMHB	*Virginia Magazine of History and Biography*
WMQ	*William and Mary Quarterly*
Woods, *Albemarle*	Edgar S. Woods, *Albemarle County in Virginia* (Charlottesville, Va.: Michie, 1901)

Archival Sources

Albemarle County, Virginia, Court Records

Deed Book 2, 1758–1761
Deed Book 3, 1761–1764
Deed Book 4, 1764–1768
Deed Book 5, 1768–1772

Deed Book 6, 1772–1776
Deed Book 7, 1776–1782
Order Book, 1744–1748
Order Book, 1783–1785
Surveyors Book 1, 1744–1755
Surveyors Book 2, 1756–1790
Will Book 2, 1752–1785
     Estate of Colo. PJ dece'd in Account with John Harvie, 83–87
     Jane (Randolph) Jefferson Inventory, 1777, 356
     Jane (Randolph) Jefferson Will, n.d., 367
     Jane Jefferson Jr. Inventory, 1768, 227
     Peter Jefferson Inventory, 1758, 41–47
     Peter Jefferson Will, 1757, 32–34
Will Book 3, 1785–1798
Wills and Deeds, No. 1, 1748–1752

Alderman Library, University of Virginia, Charlottesville (ViU)

Cabell Papers, box 1, 1727–1776, acc. no. 5084
Church of England, *Book of Common Prayer . . .* (Oxford, 1752), with alternate titles
   "Thomas Jefferson's Prayer book" or "Jefferson's Prayer book," Special Collections,
   call no.: A 1752.C87
Edgehill-Randolph Papers
Ellen Wayles Coolidge Letterbook
Gilmer-Skipwith Papers
Jefferson Family, Bible, 1752–1861, acc. no. 4726
Jefferson Papers of the University of Virginia
Joshua Fry and Peter Jefferson. *A Map of the Inhabited Part of Virginia . . .* , 1751
Papers of the Carr and Terrell Families
Trist Burke Family Papers

Colonial Williamsburg Foundation, Williamsburg, Virginia (CWF)

Education and Research Database Material Record
Gallow, Liz, "Preliminary Analysis of the 1798 Tax Record in Maryland," Department
   of Architectural Research, Spring 2004
Marshman, William, "Dayly Account of Expenses [at the Governor's Palace]," Mar. 3,
   Nov. 9, 1769, extract, files of Research Department
York County Records

Goochland County, Virginia, Court Records

Deed Book 2, 1734–1736
Deed Book 3, 1737-1742
Deed Book 4, 1741-1745
       Isham Randolph, will, 110–111
Deed Book 5, 1745–1749
Deed Book 8, 1759–1765
Order Book, 1741–1744
Record Book 2
Wills, 1742–1749
Wills and Deeds, 1728–1736

Henrico County, Virginia, Court Records

Wills and Deeds, 1725–1737
Wills and Deeds, 1750–1767

Huntington Library, San Marino, California (CSmH)

Account Book of the Estate of Peter Jefferson, 1728–1759 (bulk 1743-1758)
Account Book of the Estate of Peter Jefferson, 1757–1765
Thomas Jefferson, Surveys of Shadwell, 1799–1806

Library of Congress, Washington, D.C. (DLC)

National Anthropological Archives

Massachusetts Historical Society, Boston (MHi)

Coolidge Collection of Thomas Jefferson Papers
Thomas Jefferson Papers: An Electronic Archive

Orange County, Virginia, Court Records

Orange County Deed Book 2
Will Book 2, 1748–1778

Philadelphia Museum of Art

Fiske Kimball Papers

Thomas Jefferson Birthplace Memorial Park Commission (TJBMPC), papers,
ViU

Thomas Jefferson Foundation (TJF/TJMF), papers, Charlottesville

Archaeology Department, records and collections
Johnson, Floyd, Interview
Research Department Files

University of North Carolina–Chapel Hill

Trist Papers

Virginia Historical Society

Clay Family, Papers, 1769-1951 (bulk 1769-1869), Section 2

Notes

Introduction

1. "To the Inhabitants of Albemarle County, in Virginia," *Papers, Retirement Series,* 1:102.

2. Shadwell and Monticello are adjacent and were part of the same tract of land that TJ inherited from his father. The TJF (formerly TJMF), which operates Monticello, owns both properties today.

3. Artifacts, field records, and related materials are in the collections of the Monticello Archaeology Department, under whose labor Shadwell was excavated from 1991 to 1995. See also Kern, "Report on Shadwell," and Kern, "Report on a Burial Ground."

4. William M. Thornton, "Who Was Thomas Jefferson?" Address delivered before the Virginia State Bar Association, Aug. 12, 1909 (Richmond, Va.: n.p., 1909), 10. Merrill D. Peterson, *The Jefferson Image in the American Mind* (New York: Oxford University Press, 1960), 244–50, 418–20. Marie Kimball, *Jefferson: The Road to Glory, 1743 to 1776* (New York: Coward-McCann, 1943), esp. Prologue and chap. 1; Malone, *Jefferson,* 1:chaps. 1–2; Fiske Kimball, "In Search of Jefferson's Birthplace," *VMHB* 51 (1943): 312–25.

5. For the comment about the Palladian plan, see Fiske Kimball to Shadwell project architect, c. 1954, interview with Floyd E. Johnson, FAIA, August 1996. See also Kimball Papers, Philadelphia Museum of Art. Kimball, "In Search of Jefferson's Birthplace," 324 (quotations 319, 325); Malone, *Jefferson,* 1:1:27; Peterson, *Jefferson Image,* esp. 324, chaps. 5 and 7; and Jack McLaughlin, *Jefferson and Monticello: The Biography of a Builder* (New York: Henry Holt, 1988), 39–40.

6. Jan Lewis, *The Pursuit of Happiness: Family and Values in Jefferson's Virginia* (New York: Cambridge University Press, 1985), 1–3 (quotation 3); Noble E. Cunningham Jr., *In Pursuit of Reason: The Life of Thomas Jefferson* (Baton Rouge: Louisiana State University Press, 1987), 1; Willard Sterne Randall, *Thomas Jefferson: A Life* (New York: Henry Holt, 1993), 12, 14–15, 17; Andrew Burstein, *The Inner Jefferson: Portrait of a Grieving Optimist* (Charlottesville: University of Virginia Press, 1995), 12–15 (citation 12); Joseph J. Ellis, *American Sphinx: The Character of Thomas Jefferson* (New York: Knopf, 1997), 26 (citation 402); Norman K. Risjord, *Thomas Jefferson* (Madison, Wis.: Madison House, 1994), 3.

Fawn M. Brodie pursued the oppositional line set up by William Thornton, in Brodie, *Thomas Jefferson: An Intimate History* (New York: Bantam, 1974), esp. chap. 2. Other authors for the popular audience, Page Smith and Elizabeth Langhorne, find utility in the story of a self-made man who had important friendships and married up. Neither describes Shadwell. Page Smith, *Jefferson: A Revealing Biography* (New York: American Heritage, 1976), 7–9; Elizabeth Langhorne, *Monticello: A Family Story* (Chapel Hill, N.C.: Algonquin Books, 1989), 1–2. This is by no means an exhaustive survey but represents the threads of interpretation. The same range of interpretation is found in children's literature on TJ.

Chapter 1. The House

1. When PJ died, Albemarle County was a frontier of settlement and a politically and socially immature region; its political center relocated in 1761, and its final boundaries were determined in 1777. PJ charged the county "To 5 day Going 5 days Returning" for traveling from Shadwell to the House of Burgesses, a trip that may have been by carriage and certainly with attendants. PJ Estate, 1728–1758, 37. Robert Rose recorded a three-day journey between Albemarle Courthouse and Tuckahoe, still only halfway to Williamsburg. Rose, *Diary*, 60. Except for its wealthiest residents, most people in Albemarle had limited access to markets. For various definitions of frontier, see Gregory H. Nobles, "Breaking into the Backcountry: New Approaches to the Early American Frontier, 1750–1800," *WMQ*, 3rd ser., 46 (1989): 641–70. For the effects of shopkeepers on local tastes, see Ann Smart Martin, *Buying into the World of Goods: Early Consumers in Backcountry Virginia* (Baltimore: Johns Hopkins University Press, 2008). For a discussion of the market accessibility model of the frontier, see John Solomon Otto, *The Southern Frontiers, 1607–1860: The Agricultural Evolution of the Colonial and Antebellum South* (Westport, Conn.: Greenwood, 1989), esp. 1–8, 24–26.

2. In eighteenth-century *VG* advertisements, 84 percent of houses that listed dimensions had fewer than a thousand square feet of living space, and more than half had fewer than six hundred square feet. Ninety percent were built of wood or were wood with masonry features, such as a chimney or foundation. Camille Wells, "The Planter's Prospect: Houses, Outbuildings, and Rural Landscapes in Eighteenth-Century Virginia," *Winterthur Portfolio* 28, no. 1 (1993): 1–31, esp. table 6, fig. 9. But the 1798 Federal Direct Tax

for three counties in Maryland (few tax lists exist for Virginia) show that the advertisements were skewed toward the wealthy. Tax records reveal that between 80 and 90 percent of property owners lived in houses that were eight hundred square feet or smaller at the end of the eighteenth century. Mean house size in square feet in Anne Arundel Co. was 591 (n=567), Prince George's Co. was 618 (n=126), and Baltimore Co. 509 (n=331), and the percentage of houses with fewer than eight hundred square feet were 80.8 percent, 81 percent, and 89.4 percent, respectively. Liz Gallow, "Preliminary Analysis of the 1798 Tax Record in Maryland," ms. report, Department of Architectural Research, CWF, Spring 2004.

Other scholars who add to the contextual historiography include: Lois Green Carr and Lorena S. Walsh, "Changing Lifestyles and Consumer Behavior in the Colonial Chesapeake," in *Of Consuming Interests: The Style of Life in the Eighteenth Century*, ed. Cary Carson, Ronald Hoffman, and Peter J. Albert (Charlottesville: University of Virginia Press, 1994), 59–166; Cary Carson, "The Consumer Revolution in Colonial British America: Why Demand?" in *Of Consuming Interests*, ed. Carson, Hoffman, and Albert, 483–697; Dell Upton, "Vernacular Domestic Architecture in Eighteenth-Century Virginia," in *Common Places: Readings in American Vernacular Architecture*, ed. Upton and John Michael Vlach (Athens: University of Georgia Press, 1986), 315–35; Upton, "White and Black Landscapes in Eighteenth-Century Virginia," in *Material Life in America, 1600–1860*, ed. Robert Blair St. George (Boston: Northeastern University Press, 1988), 357–69; Lorena S. Walsh, "Urban Amenities and Rural Sufficiency: Living Standards and Consumer Behavior in the Colonial Chesapeake, 1643–1777," *Journal of Economic History* 43, no. 1 (1993): 109–17; Mark R. Wenger, "The Central Passage in Virginia: Evolution of an Eighteenth-Century Living Space," in *Perspectives in Vernacular Architecture*, vol. 2, ed. Camille Wells (Columbia: University of Missouri Press, 1986), 137–49; and Wenger, "The Dining Room in Early Virginia," in *Perspectives in Vernacular Architecture*, vol. 3, ed. Thomas Carter and Bernard L. Herman (Columbia: University of Missouri Press, 1989), 149–59.

3. For the defining elements of gentry culture, see Rhys Isaac, *The Transformation of Virginia, 1740–1790* (Chapel Hill: University of North Carolina Press, 1982); and Allan Kulikoff, *Tobacco and Slaves: The Development of Southern Cultures in the Chesapeake, 1680–1800* (Chapel Hill: University of North Carolina Press, 1986).

There are few studies of the Piedmont, and fewer still that include or compare both the tidewater and the Piedmont. Those in the forefront have focused on the movement of slaves and slavery from tidewater west. On the Piedmont, see Kulikoff, *Tobacco and Slaves;* Philip D. Morgan, "Slave Life in Piedmont Virginia, 1720–1800," in *Colonial Chesapeake Society*, ed. Lois Green Carr, Morgan, and Jean B. Russo (Chapel Hill: University of North Carolina Press, 1988), 433–84; Morgan and Michael L. Nicholls, "Slaves in Piedmont Virginia, 1720–1790," *WMQ*, 3rd ser., 46 (1989): 211–51; and Nicholls, "Piedmont Plantations and Farms: Transplanting Tidewater Traditions?" *Magazine of Albemarle County History* 49 (1991): 1–17. See also S. Edward Ayres, "Albemarle County, Virginia, 1744–1770: An Economic, Political, and Social Analysis" (M.A. thesis, University of Virginia, 1968). There are no intact Piedmont buildings as early as Shadwell, and little archaeology falls in the same period; recent archaeological work at James Madison's Montpelier in Orange County, Virginia, however, has the potential to furnish some material for comparison of early settlers who were well-off.

Backcountry studies generally concentrate on Virginia's Shenandoah Valley region, although the Southside (Piedmont south of the James River) has been included in a few. On the backcountry, see Carl Bridenbaugh, *Myths and Realities: Societies of the Colonial South* (Baton Rouge: Louisiana State University Press, 1952); and Albert H. Tillson Jr., "The Southern Backcountry: A Survey of Current Research," *VMHB* 98 (1990): 387–422. See also Warren R. Hofstra, "The Virginia Backcountry in the Eighteenth Century: The Question of Origins and the Issue of Outcomes," *VMHB* 101 (1993): 485–508; Turk McCleskey, "Rich Land, Poor Prospects: Real Estate and the Formation of a Social Elite in Augusta County, Virginia, 1738–1770," *VMHB* 98 (1990): 449–86; and Michael Lee Nicholls, "Origins of the Virginia Southside, 1703–1753 : A Social and Economic Study" (Ph.D. diss., College of William and Mary, 1972).

4. John Hammond Moore determined that the rough frontier was gone by the end of the Revolution. See *Albemarle: Jefferson's County, 1727–1976* (Charlottesville: University of Virginia Press, 1976), 85. Peter Fontaine quotations in James Fontaine, *Memoirs of a Huguenot Family* (1852; reprint ed., New York: Putnam, 1907), 337, 342; Maury quotation in Rose, *Diary*, 251, n. 545. See also William Byrd, *Histories of the Dividing Line betwixt Virginia and North Carolina, with Introduction and Notes by William K. Boyd*, introduction by Percy G. Adams (New York: Dover, 1967). Devereux Jarratt, *The Life of the Reverend Devereux Jarratt: An Autobiography*, foreword by David L. Holmes, The William Bradford Collection, series ed. Barbara Brown Zikmund (Cleveland: Pilgrim Press, 1995), 14. On the nineteenth-century historiography, see Ellen Wayles Coolidge Letterbook, 1856–1858, ViU 9090, 38–584, 1–4. See also Malone, *Jefferson*, 1:4, 33; and Randall, *Jefferson*, 1:11–12. For the career of TJ as a "child of the frontier," see Peterson, *Jefferson Image*, 248–49, 324–25, 418–19, 454. Malone thought the 1737 date that TJ said his father moved to Shadwell was too early, based on the rough condition of the region. See Autobiography, 4; and Malone, *Jefferson*, 1:18, n. 39.

5. Autobiography, 4. Albemarle County formed from the western part of Goochland County in 1744. Goochland County Record Book 2, 202; Goochland County Deed Book 3, 1737–1742, pt. 2, 535. For reconstruction of the Jefferson land deeds, see Marie Kimball, *Jefferson: The Road to Glory, 1743 to 1776* (New York: Coward-McCann, 1943), 17–18, 309–11; Malone, *Jefferson*, 1:17–18, 28, 31, 435–39; and Mary Jo Miles, "Slave Life at Shadwell, 1741–1799" (M.A. thesis, Oakland University, 1992), 4–5, 7–9. For the movements of the family, see "Jefferson Family, Bible."

6. PJ's grandfather Thomas Jefferson (TJ I, d. 1698) left a substantial estate that listed a number of amenities signaling elevated status, including table and bed linens, pewter, plantation tools and livestock, and a large quantity of furniture, including five "rusha" leather chairs, ten other chairs, three feather and one other beds, three tables, two

couches, thirty pewter plates (twenty-four new and six old), and twelve "new alchymy" spoons plus eleven old ones. His estate totaled £97 16s. 6 1/2p., without slaves. He owned slaves and had at least one indentured servant, but the list is incomplete. Among his endeavors other than planting he owned speculative land in Yorktown, which he evidently did not build on. He was prominent enough for a public funeral that included mourning rings and the serving of a mutton, and he was buried in a coffin. TJ I's wife was Mary Branch, whose father, Christopher, was a justice in Charles City County; TJ I was an executor of Branch's estate. TJ I certainly had money and important associates. Charles E. Hatch Jr., *Yorktown's Main Street* (Denver, Colo.: U.S. Department of the Interior, 1974), 35. For TJ I's inventory (no will exists), see Henrico County Wills and Deeds, 1697–1704, 114, printed in *VMHB* 1 (1893–94): 08–212; and *VMHB* 23 (1915): 173.

Captain Thomas Jefferson (TJ II, 1677–1731), son of TJ I, left his son Peter a number of items that signaled wealth or prescribed social behaviors, including slaves, clothes, six silver spoons, two feather beds, a table cloth and six napkins, six leather chairs (possibly the ones TJ II received from his father in 1698), and a couch and two tables. The couch "in the hall" and "two tables there" offer a clue that PJ's boyhood home had more than one room with seating furniture. This hall was likely where William Byrd came to drink persico and dine on roast beef with the captain as part of a day of mustering. TJ II visited with Byrd and Colonel Benjamin Harrison and others at times that did not revolve around public duty, and he witnessed legal documents with future in-law Isham Randolph: his associates in matters both legal and social were other gentry. TJ II had the wherewithal to act as undertaker to build a chapel in Varina Parish (Henrico Co.) in 1723 and invest in a mill. He was sheriff and justice of the peace for Henrico, owned a racehorse, and had land investments. He and Captain Henry Randolph chose each other as guardians for their minor children. Peter's mother, Mary Field, was the daughter of Peter Field, a burgess for Henrico, and Judith Soane, widow of Henry Randolph and daughter of Henry Soane, who was speaker of the House of Burgesses. Like PJ, with one exception, his siblings fared well in marriages to people of property and titles. PJ's brother Thomas (1700–1723) died aboard Isham Randolph's ship *The Williamsburg* on a voyage to Virginia. In his will Isham Randolph appointed his nephew Beverley Randolph and PJ guardians to his children. Louis B. Wright and Marion Tinling, eds., *William Byrd of Virginia: The London Diary (1717–1721) and Other Writings* (New York: Oxford University Press, 1958), 411–12; Louis B. Wright and Marion Tinling, eds., *The Secret Diary of William Byrd of Westover, 1709–1712* (Richmond, Va.: Dietz, 1941), 414, 486; Henrico County Court Records, 1677–1699, 181, in *VMHB* 2 (1894–95): 296–98. For TJ II's will (no inventory exists), see Henrico County Wills and Deeds, 1725–1737, 293; and Henrico County Wills and Deeds, 1725–1737, 31. Bishop William Meade, *Old Churches, Ministers, and Families of Virginia*, 2 vols. (1857; reprint ed., Baltimore: Genealogical Publishing, 1995), 440. Prince George County Records printed in *VMHB* 4 (1897): 277. For Isham Randolph's will, Goochland County Deed Book 4, 1741–1745, 110–11.

7. Autobiography, 3.

8. Edmund Berkeley and Dorothy Smith Berkeley, eds., *The Correspondence of John Bartram, 1734–1777* (Gainesville: University Press of Florida, 1992), 84, 102. Goochland Deed Book 2, 1734–1736, 259; for a portrait of Isham Randolph, see *VMHB* 34 (1926): opp. 183. TJ's granddaughters reported that JJ was agreeable, intelligent, lively, cheerful, and humorous and that she was fond of writing letters and wrote readily and well. Randall, *Jefferson*, 1:16–17. See also Kimball, *Road to Glory*, 16; Malone, *Jefferson*, 1:14–17; PJ Estate, 1757–1765; PJ Estate, 1759–1763. The historiography of JJ is revisited in chap. 2.

9. The Jeffersons moved to fulfill the wishes of PJ's friend—and JJ's first cousin—William Randolph, who in a codicil to his will requested that his friend PJ and family come live in his house, Tuckahoe, in eastern Goochland County, and raise his son Thomas Mann Randolph to majority. In part because Tuckahoe still stands, historians have relied on it for statements about architectural influence on the young TJ. Goochland County Deed Book 5, 1745–1749, 73–76; "Jefferson Family, Bible." Activity at Shadwell during these years included business and social occasions; see Rose, *Diary*, 33; and AlCOB, 1744–1748, 139, 231–32, 254, 332, 365. Payment for work on the house ranged over three years from 1750 to 1753; PJ Estate, 1728–1758, 26, 36. To date, archaeology has located only a few of the buildings and landscape features that supported this sizable plantation. For agricultural investments, see AlCWB, 2:41–48; and *GB*, 1–14.

10. PJ was the wealthiest decedent in colonial Albemarle of estates that were valued. Ten decedents (6 percent, n=143) had estates valued at more than £1,000; PJ's was more than twice that, at £2,399 0s. 6 1/2d. PJ was the second largest slaveholder in the county and one of only three slaveholders who owned more than fifty slaves. Fifty-one percent of decedents (n=162 [this figure includes estates that were not valued and thus not included in the number above]) owned slaves, and 55 percent of slaveholders (n=83) owned one to five individuals. PJ also served as sheriff, justice, and surveyor in Goochland before the forming of Albemarle County. AlCWB, vols. 1, 2:esp. 41–48.

11. TJ wrote to John Page following the fire and lamented the loss "of every pa[per I] had in the world, and almost every book." He estimated the value of the books at £200 sterling, and wished all he had lost were the money. *Papers*, 1:35 (quotation, 34).

The probate inventories offer "snapshots" that show the plantation at particular moments, especially the comprehensive 1757 list of PJ's estate. Artifacts and account book entries provide both confirmation of and counterpoint to the inventories. JJ lived at Shadwell for six years following the fire until her death. Her house stood over the western portion of what had been her house with PJ. It was decidedly smaller but fashionably furnished. After she died, her two minor children lived with siblings. See also Kern, "Report on Shadwell."

12. Shadwell was a landmark near milepost 12 as measured from the mountains back to the east. PJ became surveyor of this road in 1734, when it was still called the Mountain Road. Nathaniel Mason Pawlett and Howard H. Newlon Jr., *The Route of the Three Notch'd Road: A Preliminary Report*, rev. ed. (Charlottesville: Virginia Transportation Research Council, 1980), 9.

The brief list of buildings here includes only the mid-eighteenth-century domestic remains. The nineteenth- and twentieth-century Shadwell occupants also left archaeological remains; see Kern, "Report on Shadwell."

13. A pole, the surveyor's unit of measurement, equals sixteen and a half feet. Garden organization is in *GB*, 1–14, and subsequent entries show TJ's use of beds and rows as the defining element of the vegetable gardens at Monticello. Dial post is in PJ Estate, 1728–1758, 36. Will Rieley, landscape architect and historian at the University of Virginia, helped decipher the landscape plan.

14. Upton, "Domestic Vernacular Architecture," 318–25; Wenger, "Central Passage," 137–39. The 1757 slave list indicates that thirty-one slaves lived on the main quarter site and kitchen area at the plantation center near the Jeffersons' house. Twenty-two slaves lived in outlying quarters at Shadwell, and seven people lived on PJ's Fluvanna River lands, called Snowdon. AlCWB, 2:41–48. Slaves and slave life at Shadwell are explored more fully in chaps. 3 and 4.

15. Rhys Isaac explores the stories, songs, and activities that formed common experiences at plantations like Shadwell. He proposes that TJ was driven to formally "deny the African part of his upbringing" in his later attitudes toward African Americans because of this early intimacy. Rhys Isaac, "The First Monticello," in *Jeffersonian Legacies*, ed. Peter S. Onuf (Charlottesville: University of Virginia Press, 1993), 77–108, esp. 79–81 (citation, 100–101). See also Mechal Sobel, *The World They Made Together: Black and White Values in Eighteenth-Century Virginia* (Princeton, N.J.: Princeton University Press, 1987), esp. chap. 10, 132–34. The granddaughters' story about the fiddle is recounted in Randall, *Jefferson*, 1:59. Isaac Jefferson, "Memoirs of a Monticello Slave," in *Jefferson at Monticello*, ed. James A. Bear Jr. (Charlottesville: University of Virginia Press, 1967), 3–24 (citation 22). Even TJ's daughters and granddaughters, who grew up in the highly regulated spaces of Monticello, remembered the songs and music of the slaves there; see Lucia Stanton, "'Those Who Labor for My Happiness': Thomas Jefferson and His Slaves," in *Jeffersonian Legacies*, ed. Onuf, 147–80, esp. 166–67. Annette Gordon-Reed's analysis of the roles and relationships among the Hemingses, the Wayles, and then the Jeffersons at Monticello explores the ways we must envision people of different status, sex, and race who spend their lives together on plantations. Gordon-Reed, *The Hemingses of Monticello: An American Family* (New York: Norton, 2008).

16. The first house may have been as small as 601 square feet on the ground floor, if it occupied only the space marked by the brick cellar; evidence of rebuilding of the west wall of the cellar, however, suggests that the house may have been larger than the cellar footprint. Kern, "Report on Shadwell," 54–65.

17. PJ Estate, 1728–1758, 36; Randall, *Jefferson*, 1:2; TJ surveys, 1799–1800, HM 9379–5, HM 9379–4, CSmH; and N198 verso, N233, MHi. The conjectural dimensions of the house are 32 1/2 by 50 feet, or 1,625 square feet.

18. Randall, *Jefferson*, 1:2. Randall uses "hall" in the nineteenth-century fashion, as in, "hall way," what would have been "passage" in the eighteenth century. PJ's probate inventory

does not name the rooms in the house. I refer to them by their most likely names based on the nature of the furnishings in each room and according to the patterns observed in eighteenth-century Virginia probate inventories. The early 1750s renovations added the dining room and its substantial furnishings, which altered the functional relationship of the spaces in the house. The passage may have been added at this time or converted from an existing space. The first house probably had two or three rooms on the ground floor, and the main entrance may have been directly into one of these rooms instead of into a passage that buffered inner living spaces from the outdoors. The porch added in the 1750s united the old and new parts of the house and framed the entrance that now opened to the passage flanked by imposing rooms. The 1750 furniture order confirms that the social function of the rooms was updated with the architectural plan. JJ's first cousin Peyton Randolph added the dining room to his Williamsburg house in the later 1750s. See Carl R. Lounsbury, *An Illustrated Glossary of Early Southern Architecture and Landscape* (New York: Oxford University Press, 1994); Upton, "Domestic Vernacular Architecture," 323–24; Wenger, "Central Passage"; and Wenger, "Dining Room," 153–55.

19. AlCWB, 2:42–43. On table manners and utensils, see Barbara G. Carson, *Ambitious Appetites: Dining, Behavior, and Patterns of Consumption in Federal Washington* (Washington, D.C.: American Institute of Architects Press, 1990), esp. 25–57, 59–70.

20. For the purposes of these settings, I have made "minimum vessel counts" for each activity. The inventory specifies eight china cups and saucers, four glass teacups and six saucers, and "a parcel of white stone tea Ware." Thus eight and four indicate twelve minimum at a setting, and the white stone tea ware suggests at least two additional services, for a minimum total of fourteen. AlCWB, 2:42. Estate appraisers valued healthy adult slaves between £30 and £57 10s. Children ranged from £8 to £27. Boys Peter and Jesse, and Ephey, a girl, each cost £17 10s., the same as the silver coffee service. AlCWB, 2:42, 45. Captain Charles Lewis, JJ's brother-in-law, obtained the sugar for the funeral. PJ Estate, 1757–1765, 5.

21. Carr and Walsh, "Changing Lifestyles," tables 1–6, 11; Carson, "Consumer Revolution," 590–91; Walsh, "Urban Amenities," table 1; Wenger, "Dining Room," 150–53; PJ Estate, 1728–1758, 26; AlCWB, 2:42. Shadwell was not just well furnished but fashionably so, as indicated by the shape, material, and matched sets of objects and by the behaviors they imply, such as the oval tables, matching side chairs and armchairs; the various matching sets of dining wares that specified certain foods or courses at a meal and the ability to prepare carefully cooked and seasoned dishes; the substantial tea and coffee service; a list of clothing, including pumps and sacks and gowns of lutestring and India chintz; and items to aid in personal hygiene, such as dressing tables and a closestool. These details of form allow consideration of an object's fashionability, which offers an additional level of information than Carr and Walsh's amenities index, which measures the *incidence* of a particular item to gauge broader shifts across a population.

22. The four harrateen upholstered chairs had a combined value of 50s., and the closestool was valued at 18s. The parlor tables compared less favorably than those in the hall.

The two oval parlor tables cost 35s., or 17s. 6d. each, compared with values of 26s. to more than £1 1/2 for any table in the hall. The tea table in the hall was valued at 26s. Those in the parlor were 20s. and a mere 7s. each. The parlor chairs were 9 1/2s. each, and the hall chairs were 10s. each. AlCWB, 2:41–48.

Other items that represent traditionally female-centered production include a book on brewing, kept in the office, and in the parlor, candle molds, the only craft item to occur in both JJ's and PJ's inventories. AlCWB, 2:41–42, 356.

The accepted use of major circulatory spaces—such as the passage—by slaves changed by the beginning of the nineteenth century, when house plans were more likely to include lateral passages, secondary stairs, and side doors to hide servants as they moved through houses.

23. Harrateen was a worsted wool fabric polished and imprinted with wavy or watery patterns. The cloth was usually a deep, rich red, green, yellow, or blue, and though it is not specified in these documents, the chairs and bed probably matched in color. See Florence M. Montgomery, *Textiles in America, 1650–1870* (New York: Norton, 1984). For a definition of harrateen, see 35, 256. For Montgomery's assessment of matching materials within rooms based on upholsterer's bills, advertisements, and inventories, see 58. For candlesticks, see AlCWB, 2:42.

24. I have added seven volumes to forty-two that are usually cited for PJ's library holdings. The additional volumes come from understanding physical descriptions of three titles. Thomas Salmon published the second edition of *A Complete Collection of State-Trials* as six volumes in 1730. This is most likely the edition available to PJ. The title had been counted as a single volume. The 1719 edition had five volumes, and editions after 1776 had eleven volumes. The appraised value suggests that PJ owned more than one volume. The second addition to the total number of books is one volume to "Rapins Hist. of England 2v & 2v Cont," which has been counted as four, but in which the fifth volume, known as "Mr. Tindal's continuation," is indicated by the appraiser's abbreviation. The third addition is a second volume to Switzer's "Husbander," a two-volume work that had been counted as one. I have put *State-Trials* in the legal category, though it could also occupy a place in the history column; the categories and sorting of titles here are of my making.

On many of the bibliographic entries I include a call or catalog number for a library. Some of my information about the physical attributes of a title (size, pages, volumes) comes from the catalog records.

AlCWB, 2:41. On Thomas Salmon, *A Complete Collection of State-Trials* (London, 1730 and other years), see EEBO; see also DLC no. 33008748. On Rapin, see Rapin de Thoyras, *The History of England Written in French by Mr. Rapin de Thoyras; Translated into English, with Additional Notes, by N. Tindal* . . . (London, 1743–51). See also Rockefeller cat. no. DA30.R3.

On the Shadwell libraries, see William Peden, "Some Notes Concerning Thomas Jefferson's Libraries," *WMQ*, 3rd ser., 1 (1944): 265–72, esp. 267–68. For a summary of Virginia library holdings, see William S. Simpson Jr., "A Comparison of the Libraries of

Seven Colonial Virginians, 1754–1789," *Journal of Library History* 9, no. 1 (1974): 54–65, esp. 58–59. For TJ's loss in the house fire, see TJ to John Page, Feb. 21, 1770, *Papers*, 1:34. A few of TJ's books did survive the fire. See also *LCB*.

The titles of JJ's and Jane Jr.'s books are unspecified. AlCWB, 2:227, 356. I discuss the family Bibles and prayer books in chap. 7.

25. Thomas Salmon, *A Complete Collection of State-Trials, and Proceedings for High-Treason, and Other Crimes and Misdemeanours . . .* , 2nd ed. (London, 1730), DLC no. 33008748. Nicholas Covert, *The Scrivener's Guide: Being Choice and Approved Forms of Precedents of All Sorts of Business Now in Use and Practice . . .* (London, 1740 and other years), DLC no. 17016670. Robert Beverley, *An Abridgement of the Publick Laws of Virginia, in Force and Use, June 10, 1720; To Which Is Added, for the Ease of the Justices and Military Officers, &C., Precedents of All Matters to Be Issued by Them, Peculiar to Those Laws and Varying from the Precedents in England* (London, 1722 and other years), Swem cat. no. KFV2430.A34.

William Nelson, *The Office and Authority of a Justice of Peace . . .* , 4th ed. (London, 1711), DLC no. 68049479. George Webb, *The Office and Authority of a Justice of Peace . . . and Adapted to the Constitution and Practice of Virginia* (Williamsburg, 1736), Rockefeller cat. no. KFV2930.Wf 1736a.

26. William Ellis, *The London and Country Brewer . . .* (London, 1744 and other years), Rockefeller cat. no. TB569.L66. *The Practical Husbandman* contained Switzer's defense of Virgil's advice on horticulture in light of Jethro Tull's attack against Virgil's Georgics as a useful guide for agriculture. According to Frans De Bruyn, Switzer embraced Virgil's classical ideals and horticultural methods, while Tull tried to move the debate from horticulture to agriculture by questioning whether Virgil's poetry was the appropriate vehicle to discuss the mundane aspects of planting. See De Bruyn, "Reading Virgil's Georgics as a Scientific Text: The Eighteenth-Century Debate between Jethro Tull and Stephen Switzer," *ELH* 71 (Fall 2004): 661–89. Stephen Switzer, *The Practical Husbandman and Planter: Or, Observations on the Ancient and Modern Husbandry, Planting and Gardening; . . .* , 2 vols. (London, 1733–34), ViU cat. no. F229.C28 Z9.P73. See also Switzer, *Ichnographia Rustica: Or, The Nobleman, Gentleman, and Gardener's Recreation*, 3 vols. (London, 1742 and other years); *The Practical Fruit-Gardener* (London, 1731 and other years); and *The Practical Kitchen Gardiner* (London, 1727).

27. Richard Beale Davis categorizes most of these history books as Whig history—that is, full of the republican values that glorified and promoted liberal thought within the bounds of England's legal and political system. See Davis, *Intellectual Life in the Colonial South, 1585–1763*, 3 vols. (Knoxville: University of Tennessee Press, 1978), for holdings by other Virginians, esp. 1:524–73; on the Whiggishness of available history books, esp. 1:495, 537, 593. Thoyras, *History of England*. Edward Chamberlayne, *Magnæ Britanniæ Notitia: Or, The Present State of Great-Britain; with Diverse Remarks upon the Ancient State Thereof . . .* (London, 1755 and other years), DLC no. 46037569. John Ogilby, *America: Being the Latest, and Most Accurate Description of the New World . . .* (London, 1700 and other years), Swem cat. no. AC1.E2. Richard Walter, *A Voyage Round the World: In the*

Years MDCCXL, I, II, III, IV, by Geoge Anson . . . (London, 1756 and other years), Rocke-feller cat. no. G420.A5 1756. Daniel Defoe, *The Secret History of the White-Staff: Being an Account of Affairs under the Conduct of Some Late Ministers, and of What Might Probably Have Happened if Her Majesty Had Not Died* (London, 1714), Swem cat. no. DA496 1714.D38.

28. Searches of "Trent" and "Astronomy" in library catalogs and databases such as EEBO and ESTC have not helped identify this book. The unidentified "Three old Books" have even less prestige, at 1s. each; AlCWB, 2:41.

29. On TJ's preferred book size, see E. Millicent Sowerby, "Thomas Jefferson and His Library," Bibliographical Society of America, *Papers*, 50 (1956): 219. The designations "octavo," "quarto," and "folio" refer to how many times a full sheet of paper was folded to make a book and do not designate specific sizes in the eighteenth century, because the size of the full sheet was not standard. For TJ's specifications for his reading desk, see *MB*, 18.

30. Salmon, title page to *State Trials;* Ogilby, title page to *America;* Walter, title page to *Voyage.*

31. Rapin, title page to *History of England*, also 33, 132, various pls.; AlCWB, 2:41, 44.

32. For Rose's comment and a description of the book, see Rose, *Diary*, 3:112, n. 10. On Virginia libraries, see Davis, *Intellectual Life*, 510. Sir Thomas Browne, *Pseudodoxia Epidemica; Enquiries into Very Many Commonly Received Tenets and Commonly Presumed Truths* (1658), table of contents for books 3, 4, 6, 7, EEBO.

33. On PJ's reading, see Randall, *Jefferson*, 1:14. I cannot confirm Randall's report that PJ's volume of Shakespeare still existed in the 1850s when Randall wrote his biog-raphy. On the influence of these books, see Davis, *Intellectual Life*, 1364–65; also *The Guardian*, ed. John Calhoun Stephens (Lexington: University Press of Kentucky, 1982), introduction.

34. For beds and desks, see AlCWB, 2:41–42. For dance, see PJ Estate, 1757–1765, 4; and PJ Estate, 1759–1763, 26. Lois Carr and Lorena Walsh chose twelve items to measure changes in amenities. These are: (1) coarse earthenware and (2) bed or table linens, for basic convenience and sanitation; (3) table knives, (4) forks, and (5) fine earthenware, for refinements in convenience and elegance at the table; (6) spices and cookery tools for variety and elaboration of food; books, (7) religious and (8) secular, for educational and leisure pursuits; and objects of luxury, such as (9) wigs, (10) timepieces, (11) pictures, and (12) silver. Carr and Walsh, "Changing Lifestyles," 69, for definition of categories, and tables 1–6. Based on the Carr and Walsh figures from table 6, "Incidence of selected con-sumer items, York Co. (urban)," over the years 1745–67, showing the percentage of dece-dents with the richest estates (more than £491) who owned each of twelve particular items, the Jeffersons would have compared as favorably in Virginia's biggest city as they did in Albemarle.

35. AlCWB, 2:43–45; PJ Estate, 1757–1765, 20, 36, 42; PJ Estate, 1759–1763, 1–3.

36. Others who lived near the Jeffersons did not welcome Native Americans. In 1756 neighbors in Louisa County called the news of Indians allied with the French within

seventy-five miles "terrifying" and commented that "no doubt [the Indians'] numbers were greatly augmented by our fears." "Letters of Francis Jerdone," *WMQ*, 1st ser., 16 (1907): 127–28.

Historian Ann Smart Martin explores the role of merchants as arbiters of fashion and supply in *Buying into the World of Goods*. She reports a rural-urban dichotomy in consumption of ceramics that was greater for both the middling and lower sorts than for the elite and notes that it becomes more marked toward the end of the eighteenth century. See Martin, "'Fashionable Sugar Dishes, Latest Fashion Ware': The Creamware Revolution in the Eighteenth-Century Chesapeake," in *Historical Archaeology of the Chesapeake*, ed. Paul A. Shackel and Barbara J. Little (Washington, D.C.: Smithsonian Institution Press, 1994), 169–87, esp. 179–83.

For other men like Jefferson, see, e.g., Archibald Henderson, "Dr. Thomas Walker and the Loyal Company of Virginia," *Proceedings of the American Antiquarian Society*, n.s., 41 (1931): 77–123. For the importance of these professionals in the formation and growth of Virginia, see Sarah S. Hughes, *Surveyors and Statesmen: Land Measuring in Colonial Virginia* (Richmond, Va.: Virginia Surveyors Foundation and Virginia Association of Surveyors, 1979).

Jack Greene argues that people sought visible symbols of improvement as they moved. Landscape historian Barbara Sarudy suggests that fences, garden walls, and hedges demarcated civilized space from wilderness and gave settlers a feeling of security within safe, familiar bounds. Jack P. Greene, *Imperatives, Behaviors, and Identities: Essays in Early American Cultural History* (Charlottesville: University of Virginia Press, 1992), 193; Barbara Wells Sarudy, *Gardens and Gardening in the Chesapeake, 1700–1805* (Baltimore: Johns Hopkins University Press, 1998), 45, 150.

37. Jefferson biographers have assumed that both distance from Williamsburg and Shadwell's rural location, if not near "wilderness," prescribed a necessarily simpler life. Andrew Burstein, *The Inner Jefferson: Portrait of a Grieving Optimist* (Charlottesville: University of Virginia Press, 1995), esp. 12–18; Cunningham, *Life of Thomas Jefferson*, 1–2; Malone, *Jefferson*, 1:chaps. 1–2, esp. 30, 33. The assumption that towns defined culture and that distance from a town was necessarily equal to distance from culture is the reason many historians of the Chesapeake have to first define the region's settlement pattern and lack of towns, and perhaps contrast the relation of people to towns in New England or in Europe. See, e.g., Isaac, *Transformation of Virginia*, 13–17; Kevin P. Kelly, "'In Dispers'd Country Plantations': Settlement Patterns in Seventeenth-Century Surry County, Virginia," in *The Chesapeake in the Seventeenth Century: Essays on Anglo-American Society*, ed. Thad W. Tate and David L. Ammerman (New York: W. W. Norton, 1979), 183–205; Darrett B. Rutman and Anita H. Rutman, *A Place in Time: Middlesex County, Virginia, 1650–1750* (New York: W. W. Norton, 1984), esp. 19–25, 47. For Francis West, see PJ Estate, 1728–1758, 7; and Cabell Papers, box 1, 1727–1776, acc. no. 5084, ViU.

Lois Carr and Lorena Walsh find that proximity to an urban area did not mean that a county had more amenities. In fact, their study of four Chesapeake counties shows that entirely rural counties ranked higher on mean amenities scores and mean value of consumer durables than rural parts of counties with urban centers. Carr and Walsh, "Changing Lifestyles," 102–3.

Chapter 2. The Household

1. AlCWB, 2:41–48.

2. This study of JJ, and of everyone at Shadwell, is grounded in the particulars to Shadwell. My analysis is based on action—what people wrote; what they owned, purchased, made, kept, used; and the relationships they had with others around them at Shadwell and the other places they went. Secondary works on women in eighteenth-century Virginia are useful for comparison in the most general way, and statistics provide a counterpoint for comparing demographic data. The more prescriptive women's studies are of limited use. I refuse to see all the action here as either dictated by or limited by the patriarchal structure of society, and I make no claims that JJ occupied a "golden age" for women or that her "agency" made her a strong or unusual woman for her time. There are no halo-laden images of JJ as "motherhood," but there are actions that suggest she was revered for a job well done.

3. AlCWB, 2:32–34.

4. "Jefferson Family, Bible." *VMHB* 26 (1918): 324. In Williamsburg the Randolphs may have stayed with Isham's brother John at Tazewell Hall or with his sister Mary Stith and her husband, John. Elizabeth's actual date and location of birth were not recorded in the Bible record. The number of places JJ lived becomes nine if she moved to Monticello before she died (more below); see "Jefferson Family, Bible." For the myriad Randolph homes and intermarriages, see Johnathan Daniels, *The Randolphs of Virginia* (Garden City, N.Y.: Doubleday, 1972), esp. genealogical charts at end of book; *Genealogies of Virginia Families from the William and Mary College Quarterly Historical Magazine,* indexed by Judith McGhan, 5 vols. (Baltimore: Genealogical Publishing, 1982), 4:226–55; John W. Pritchett, *Southside Virginia Genealogies* (Baltimore: Genealogical Publishing, 2007). It is unlikely that JJ remembered much about Shadwell in London, which was a bustling wharfside neighborhood of mixed seafaring trades and houses of prosperous merchants. Michael Power, "Shadwell: The Development of a London Suburban Community in the Seventeenth Century," *London Journal* 4, no. 1 (1978): 29–46.

5. "Jefferson Family, Bible."

6. TJ to Mary Jefferson, May 30, 1791, in *Family Letters,* 83–84.

7. Allan Kulikoff, *Tobacco and Slaves: The Development of Southern Cultures in the Chesapeake, 1680–1800* (Chapel Hill: University of North Carolina Press, 1986), 49–50, 54–55.

8. Pregnant women were commonplace on the landscape. The tutor Philip Fithian described how the girls among his young charges stuffed their gowns to play at being pregnant. Philip Morgan found an average of 28 months between births among slaves. Hunter Dickinson Farish, ed., *Journal and Letters of Philip Vickers Fithian: A Plantation*

Tutor of the Old Dominion, 1773–1774 (1957; reprint ed., Charlottesville: University of Virginia Press, 1968), 193; Kulikoff, *Tobacco and Slaves,* 57; Morgan, *Slave Counterpoint: Black Culture in the Eighteenth-Century Chesapeake and Lowcountry* (Chapel Hill: University of North Carolina Press, 1998), table 21, 92.

9. Standard deviation = 7.22, n=20. Beverly I. Strassmann and John H. Warner, "Predictors of Fecundability and Conception Waits among the Dogon of Mali," *American Journal of Physical Anthropology* 105 (1998): 171, 176.

10. On nursing, see Catherine Clinton, *The Plantation Mistress: Woman's World in the Old South* (New York: Pantheon, 1982), 154. If JJ had averaged the 30-month birth rate that Kulikoff found, she and PJ would have had 7.13 children in their years together. They were married 17.8 years, or 214 months. In 1768 Martha and Dabney Carr had twins, Lucy and Mary, although it appears only Lucy survived childhood. Douglas, *Register,* 168.

11. Fithian, *Journal,* 39. Catherine Clinton presents evidence that elite women nursed their own babies in the eighteenth century and more likely used a nurse by the middle of the nineteenth century. Clinton, *Plantation Mistress,* 155. Marylynn Salmon finds other trends when women—especially elite women—nursed their own babies. They were more likely to do so toward the end of the eighteenth century. Coincidental with the time JJ was bearing children, William Cadogan's 1748 treatise on the benefits of breastfeeding one's own babies influenced many elite women to do this themselves. Before this treatise, which also celebrated the benefits of colostrum to newborns, many elite women had their babies nursed by others until their milk came in, which very often did not happen because their bodies lacked the stimulation of the first nursing. Marylynn Salmon, "The Cultural Significance of Breastfeeding and Infant Care in Early Modern England and America," *Journal of Social History* 28, no. 2 (1994): 8, 10–12.

12. Jefferson, "Memoirs," 3, 123, n. 2.

13. Doctor Gilmer (d. 1796) practiced medicine in Williamsburg before moving to Albemarle. By 1780 he advertised his apothecary as being in Charlottesville. His fee book lists twenty-five entries for JJ from 1771 to 1774: fifteen of those were visits, four times for slaves, and one was for a "Miss Jefferson" (could be Elizabeth or Anna Scott). Dr. George Gilmer's Feebook, 1767, 1771–1775, Gilmer-Skipwith Papers, Mss 6145, ViU. PJ Estate, 1728–1758, 53–55; *VG,* June 27, 1755; *VG,* Richmond, Aug. 16, 1780. On JJ's will, see AlCWB, 2:367; "Jane Jefferson's Slaves Deeded to Thomas Jefferson, September 29, 1773," *FB,* 8–9; also *MB,* 346; and "Jefferson Family, Bible." Randall, *Jefferson,* 1:17; Randolph, *Domestic Life,* 7. See also Kern, "Report on Shadwell," app. 3.

14. *MB,* 415 and n. 76.

15. The Bollings lived at Fairfields in Goochland County. In 1785 they moved to Chestnut Grove in Chesterfield County; *MB,* n. 32. The Shadwell burial ground is indeed covered with cedars today. See also Kern, "Report on a Burial Ground." AlCDB, 4:234.

16. AlCWB, 2: 227, 233. PJ Estate, 1757–1765, 3b, 34, 43.

17. AlCWB, 2:-227, 233. TJ's granddaughters comment on "carrying the keys": MJR to Virginia Jefferson Randolph, Dec. 27, 1821, Trist Papers, University of North Carolina–Chapel Hill. I thank Ann Lucas for this reference.

18. *MB*, 251, 369. Jane Jr. died in 1765, but her estate inventory was dated 1768. AlCWB, 2:227, 233.

19. Marie Kimball, *Jefferson: The Road to Glory, 1743 to 1776* (New York: Coward-McCann, 1943), chap. 3; Malone, *Jefferson*, 1:21–22.

20. PJ Estate, 1757–1765, and PJ Estate, 1759–1763, in *Brother*, 2–3.

21. TJ settled the account between Clay and Carr's estate in March 1774. *MB*, Mar. 7, 1774, 370–71. Martha and her six children moved to Monticello in 1781. They were back at Spring Forest in 1790. *GB*, nn. 41–42; *MB*, n. 21, 340, 523, 748.

22. Among stories that one Jefferson daughter was mentally unstable or deficient, the stronger tradition is that Elizabeth was the weak link. This story appeared in a letter from Wilson Miles Cary to Sarah N. Randolph, n.d., Collection of Mrs. Mary Kirk Moyer, Geneva, N.Y., cited in *MB*, n. 370. But TJ's biographer Sarah Randolph reported that one sister "was rather deficient in intellect," and later claimed that to be Anna Scott. Randolph, *Domestic Life*, 39, 135; *MB*, 370–371.

23. *MB*, 144, 438.

24. In May 1768 TJ contracted with John Moore to level 250 square feet for a house at Monticello. *MB*, xlv, 76.

25. Papers of the Trist, Randolph and Burke Families [manuscript], 1721–1969, acc. no. 10487, box 2, ViU.

26. AlCWB, 2:356.

27. AlCWB, 2:41–48, 227, 233, 356.

28. Jane Jr.'s estate is AlCWB, 2:227. The bequest was not the reason her clothing was eliminated from her estate inventory. The cherrywood desk and bookcase that PJ willed to TJ was appraised with all the other goods he owned. Statistic from AlCWB, vols. 1, 2.

29. Ellen Wayles Coolidge Letterbook, 1856–1858, ViU 9090, 38–584, 36. Both Betty Leviner at Colonial Williamsburg and Susan Borchardt at Gunston Hall have noted in their ongoing analyses of probate inventories the pattern of not listing musical instruments. Personal communication, 2001. On the violin, violincello, and spinet, see *MB*, 29. In Albemarle, five men owned fiddles or violins, and one owned a flute (although this could be a food-related object). Of these six, all but two owned slaves, and all but one had estates over £100 that included at least a few amenities. AlCWB, 1:22–24; AlCWB, 2:20, 26, 105, 141, 181–84.

30. JJ's rank at number 19 is greater than 87 percent of all decedents, n=143. Mary Fry's inventory included only better furniture and specialized cooking equipment and no slaves, livestock, or work tools, suggesting that her retirement was just that. Mary's husband, Joshua Fry, was the tenth wealthiest decedent in Albemarle in this period. AlCWB, vols. 1, 2:esp. 300 for Fry inventory.

31. PJ Estate, 1757–1765, 42. More details of the slave children and Jefferson children are in chap. 3.

32. PJ Estate, 1759–1763, 10.

33. On tailors, see PJ Estate, 1757–1765, 20, 23, 28, 36. For Jane Jr.'s clothing, see AlCWB, 2:227, I thank Linda Baumgarten, curator of textiles at Colonial Williamsburg, for her help in understanding this list of garments. On clothing before marriage, see TJ to Overton Carr, Mar. 16, 1782, *Papers,* 4:166–67. On JJ's bequest, see AlCWB, 2:367.

34. Clothing related artifacts include: SW437A, which had a cut brass buckle that was double pierced on the cross piece for sewing on clothing, and SW213B, which contained a cast alloy buckle that had been silvered. Kern, "Report on Shadwell," app. 6. On TJ's purchase of curls, see *MB,* 32. For dressing tables, see PJ Estate, 1728–1758, 14; and AlCWB, 2:41–48.

35. On his niece's clothing, see TJ to Overton Carr, Mar. 16, 1782, in *Papers,* 4:166–67. On the veil for Martha, see TJ to MJR, Apr. 17, 24, 1791, in *Family Letters,* 78, 79.

36. Wool in dirt was unwashed wool. On the wool and wheel from TJ, see *MB,* 406 and n. 36, 415. On sheep, see AlCWB, 2:44, 356. Pattey was a nickname for Martha. On her wheel, see PJ Estate, 1757–1765, 36. AlCWB, 2:356.

These women owned their own tools for a polite hobby rather than as an integral part of the domestic economy, which may explain why these implements were not represented in PJ's list of property. There is no evidence that JJ and her daughters needed to earn additional income following PJ's death. Roughly 43 percent (61 of 143) of colonial Albemarle inventories included spinning wheels, and 59 of the 61 owners were male; PJ Estate, 1757–1765, 36; AlCWB, vols. 1, 2:esp. 227, for Jane Jr.'s estate. PJ Estate, 1757–1765, 4; PJ Estate, 1759–1763, 26.

37. Fithian, *Journal,* 189. MJR to TJ, June 19, 1801, in *Family Letters,* 205. Kern, "Report on Shadwell," app. 6.

38. JJ's inventory is AlCWB, 2:356. For the delivery of rum, TJ paid Will, a slave wagoner who belonged to a Mr. Matthews. Shipments from J. Smith may have been empty bottles. Whether he suspected someone en route of theft or whether this was his standard procedure, TJ carefully recorded the number of bottles present, broken, or missing in each hamper from Smith. Lisbon wine was generally a white table wine. *MB,* 28, 30, 148–49. On wine at Monticello, see Ellen Wayles Randolph to TJ, Oct. 20, 1808, in *Family Letters,* 352–53. The Jeffersons did not own a still.

39. AlCWB, 2:41–48, 356. The appraised values in JJ's inventory are not the highly inflated values that came during the Revolution. There is no date when the appraisers made her inventory, just when the clerk entered it into the court records, and she is among the last year of prerevolutionary values that show up in Albemarle inventories. The inventories entered in the years following JJ's show inflation, such as that of her brother-in-law, Charles Lewis, in 1779, in which, for instance, the values assigned to slave children range from £300 to £500.

40. AlCWB, 2:41–48, 356.

41. AlCWB, 2:41–48, 356. See entries for 1766, 1767, and 1768 in *GB*, 1–14.

42. Indenture between George Dudley and Isham Randolph, Goochland Deed Book 2, 1734–1736, 259, in *WMQ*, 1st ser., 5 (1896): 109–10.

John Bartram reported traveling up the north branch of the James River to "a Gentlemans house where my good friend Isham recommended me." Bartram's description of the landscape suggests a situation much like Shadwell and the view from Monticello Mountain. The gentleman's house was "at ye foot of ye mountain [he] entertained us civily I rose early this morning a little before day with a design to go up to ye top of ye mountain (which is allways my constant practice in all my travails after plants to rise as soon as it light & search all about before breakfast for I cant aford to loos any time) it being about one mile & half & light moon shine I got up to ye top just before ye sun rose where I had ye fines prospect of ye largest Landskip that ever my eyes beheld A grand view from ye east to ye south & south west all ye land of virginia as far as sight could reach all seemed as even as ye sea I seemed to bid adieu to all ye pleasant entertainments of virginia & conversations after I had observed ye sun to rise upon this wide horizon I descended down ye mountain & got my breakfast & parted with my host." Edmund Berkeley and Dorothy Smith Berkeley, eds., *The Correspondence of John Bartram, 1734–1777* (Gainesville: University Press of Florida, 1992), 99, 102–3, 119–20, 228.

43. There are extant letters written by all of the Jefferson siblings except Jane and Elizabeth. These letters have not been published in any comprehensive volume, unless written to TJ and are included in the Jefferson *Papers* series or in *Brother*. Others are cited in part in works as various as Randolph, *Domestic Life*, and Daniel Blake Smith, *Inside the Great House: Planter Family Life in Eighteenth-Century Chesapeake Society* (Ithaca, NY: Cornell University Press, 1980). Although further study is needed, it appears that the older siblings all have a better command of language and are more likely to use standardized spellings than the three youngest siblings. It may reflect the social status to which each married or the attention that each had at home during schooling that may have been more rigorous for the older children than for the younger. PJ Estate, 1757–1765.

44. For schooling years and costs, see PJ Estate, 1757–1765. For values of goods at Shadwell, see AlCWB, 2:41–48; Phillis was likely at least forty-three years old when she was valued at £20 in 1757.

45. AlCWB, 2:22–34, 367. PJ Estate, 1757–1765, 31.

46. Statistically, the two cellars are holes in the data. Because they had been cleared of debris, there are few or no artifacts in these locations relative to the plowzone data from across entire site. Kern, "Report on Shadwell," esp. 52–53, 59, 65–66, and app. 3.

47. AlCWB, 2:41–48, 356.

48. JJ's inventory includes mention of sugar, coffee, and tea. PJ's inventory includes no foodstuffs.

49. JJ owned "2 doz. Earthen plates & 1 bowl 10/." At twenty-five units (two dozen plus one), each plate or the bowl is worth .4s., or 4.8d. A comparable value for creamware can be found in the estate of Anthony Hay, keeper of the Raleigh Tavern, whose "139 Queens China plates 57/6"were worth .41s. each, or 4.9d. "The estate of Anthony Hay, Williamsburg, Jan. 21, 1771," York County, Wills and Inventories, no. 22 (1771–83), 19, reprinted in Graham Hood, ed., "Inventories of Four Eighteenth-Century Houses in the Historic Area of Williamsburg" (Colonial Williamsburg pamphlet, n.d.), 20–23. See also Ann Smart Martin, "'Fashionable Sugar Dishes, Latest Fashion Ware': The Creamware Revolution in the Eighteenth-Century Chesapeake," in *Historical Archaeology of the Chesapeake*, ed. Paul A. Shackel and Barbara J. Little (Washington, D.C.: Smithsonian, 1994), 169–87.

50. Merrill D. Peterson, *The Jefferson Image in the American Mind* (New York: Oxford University Press, 1960), 248, 418. The TJMF purchased Monticello to open as a museum and "shrine" in 1923. William M. Thornton, "Who Was Thomas Jefferson?" Address delivered before the Virginia State Bar Association, Aug. 12, 1909 (Richmond, Va.: n.p., 1909), 13. Kimball, *Road to Glory*. For the context in which Marie Kimball's book was received, see Carl Becker's glowing review in *American Historical Review* 49 (1943): 109–11. The backwoods versus aristocrat was a popular Colonial Revival theme and showed up in such works as David Lloyd's film *The Howards of Virginia*. One scene shows the [male] patriot's mother, a proud woman sitting in the shadows in her rocking chair, keeping distant from the excited talk and rustic activities of the rest of the family around their cabin.

51. See the *Oxford English Dictionary* for the career of the word "frigid" in regards to sexual interest and its twentieth-century connotation as a "problem" that was particularly female. John Dos Passos, *The Head and Heart of Thomas Jefferson* (Garden City, N.Y.: Doubleday, 1954), 75–76. On page 76 Dos Passos entered part of Jane Jr.'s inventory as the entirety of her mother's.

52. Kenneth A. Lockridge, *On the Sources of Patriarchal Rage: The Commonplace Books of William Byrd and Thomas Jefferson and the Gendering of Power in the Eighteenth Century* (New York: New York University Press, 1992), 69–70, 75, 80, 121, 8–9. Lockridge credits Fawn Brodie with the germ of this interpretation and Jack McLaughlin with the interpretation of the literary notebooks. Brodie, *Jefferson;* McLaughlin goes on to say that by building his own home, TJ could create a "womblike place of warmth, comfort, and love." McLaughlin, *Jefferson and Monticello: The Biography of a Builder* (New York: Henry Holt, 1988), 46–51. Andrew Burstein's claim that TJ rejected JJ in how he located her burial in the Monticello graveyard is undone by simple chronology and the fact that his plan was never executed. Burstein, *The Inner Jefferson: Portrait of a Grieving Optimist* (Charlottesville: University of Virginia Press, 1995), 262–63. On TJ's burial ground plan, see *MB*, 245–50, 246n54.

53. Randall, *Jefferson*, 1:16–17; Coolidge Letterbook, 1–3; Randolph, *Domestic Life*, 7.

54. *MB*, 415, 444.

Chapter 3. The Home Quarter

1. For a biography of Jupiter, see Lucia Stanton, *Free Some Day: The African-American Families of Monticello* (Charlottesville, Va.: TJF, 2000), 19–27.

2. AlCWB, 2:32–34. Recent work that traces former slaves into their careers as freed men and women finds that people who had positions of prestige within the plantation often became the civic, business, and religious leaders in communities of free blacks. Although this is a nineteenth-century model, it may show that a person's innate intelligence and ability to perform skilled and dependable work served him or her both in and out of slavery and would have been recognized and put to use by slave owners. See, e.g., Annette Gordon-Reed, *The Hemingses of Monticello: An American Family* (New York: Norton, 2008), esp. 489–96, 521–30; and Lucia Stanton, "'Those Who Labor for My Happiness': Thomas Jefferson and His Slaves," in *Jeffersonian Legacies,* ed. Peter S. Onuf (Charlottesville: University of Virginia Press, 1993), 170–71.

3. See fig. 4.4; also *FB,* 30.

4. I have made the conclusion that the buildings here were frame based on PJ's attention to their orientation in the landscape and the high quantity of wrought nails in the vicinity of the kitchen. There were, however, no physical remains of the walls or foundations to indicate the size of the buildings. In addition, a high quantity of window glass indicates windows and that the buildings were decently appointed. The objects in the kitchen come from both the inventory and from archaeology. See Kern, "Report on Shadwell."

Unfortunately, even though there is a concentration of evidence for the home quarter, it is still impossible to put most individuals in specific roles and in specific places.

I have made the assumption that the cook was female, based on the most likely use of labor resources. It is possible, however, that the cook was male, as TJ chose to maintain at Monticello. The adult females in 1757 were Sall, Nan, Hannah, Cachina, Myrtilla, and Bellinda. AlCWB, 2:43.

Two latch plates (SW15 and SW94) for boxes or other locked containers may have served purposes similar to the cellar, either to protect kitchen stores from wandering or giving the cook and her family a place to secure their possessions.

5. List of tools is from AlCWB, 2:43; for the uses of them, see Mary Randolph, *The Virginia House-Wife,* ed. Karen Hess (Columbia: University of South Carolina Press, 1984). Archaeology recovered a wide variety of utilitarian food preparation and storage vessels, as well as iron implements and cookware. The kitchen area was excavated in the 1940s and 1950s, but the record of those excavations is not stratigraphic; so I have analyzed the entire assemblage for the area as plowzone. See the introduction for a discussion of plowzone sites. Because of the complete excavation of this area in the 1950s and its subsequent rebuilding with modern materials as part of the 1960s site interpretation, there was no opportunity for soil analysis of the brick-lined cellar that might have indicated its use. Kern, "Report on Shadwell."

At Monticello the path between the kitchen and the vegetable garden is direct. PJ's landscape seems as if it, too, would have made such work connections clear, although archaeological testing did not turn up garden evidence on the sunny south slope of the ridge below the kitchen. The lack of positive evidence for the garden in this location does not confirm that it was not here, however.

For the role of women and slaves in processing pork, see Catherine Clinton, *The Plantation Mistress: Woman's World in the Old South* (New York: Pantheon, 1982), esp. 16, 23–24. Artifacts are listed in Kern, "Report on Shadwell." See Randolph *Virginia House-Wife*, for curing, salting, or preserving meats, vegetables, and fruit.

6. There are no plants of specifically African origin listed in the early pages of TJ's Garden Book, although it is entirely possible that slaves grew these in their own gardens and some found their way into the Jeffersons' food. The style in which the cook prepared certain foods may well have reflected her African heritage. See Hess, in Randolph, *Virginia House-Wife*, xxix–xxxi.

Much of the tableware and many of the utensils appeared in the inventory with the contents of the Jefferson dwelling house, suggesting that there, and not the kitchen, was their appropriate place when not in use; Kern, "Report on Shadwell," 81, apps. 2, 3.

The more precious wares probably never left the Jefferson house parlor or were removed only to be washed in the kitchen under the direct supervision of a Jefferson or a most trusted house servant. At Monticello, for instance, MJR wrote to her father about things she had to lock up when a responsible person was not in residence and TJ's enslaved butler Burwell oversaw storing wine in various vessels in the wine cellar there. MJR to TJ, Jan. 16, 1791, Ellen Wayles Randolph to TJ, Oct. 20, 1808, in *Family Letters*, 68, 352–53. See also chap. 1.

7. On Shadwell gardens, see *GB*, 4–6, 12. TJ assigned one or two slave women to cook for the entire work group during the wheat harvest. *FB*, 46.

8. On controlling access to goods, see MJR to TJ, Jan. 16, 1791, in *Family Letters*, 68.

Robert Rose wrote of bringing home some company and ate "a Batchelour's Dinner, my Wife & Daughter being gone." Whether he got out the food they ate or summoned a slave to do so, they had a different type of meal than would have been planned had the women been home; Rose's slaves did not plan the meal. Rose, *Diary*. See also chap. 6.

Archaeological evidence from Mulberry Row at Monticello illustrates that slaves who lived close to or who had a family connection in the plantation kitchen acquired better cuts of meat than what historians generally expect to find in slave quarters based on documentary evidence. Historians have interpreted in a number of ways the slaves' acquisition of controlled goods, such as meat that was reserved for planters. Slaves' interest and success in augmenting their diets may be evidence of individual and group creativity in using all available resources, including cast-offs from the big house or kitchen. It may also be evidence of "resistance" to the slave system, and indeed there are accounts that slaves impertinently questioned whether eating their master's pig, for instance, was stealing, since the pig nourished the worker, thereby strengthening the master's investment.

See faunal (animal bone) analyses by Diana Crader of the Monticello archaeological assemblage in the reports by William Kelso and by Kelso and Douglas Sanford. They are summarized in William M. Kelso, *Archaeology at Monticello*, Monticello Monograph Series (Chapel Hill: University of North Carolina Press for the TJF, 2002), 68–70, 93–97. See also Joanne Bowen, "Foodways in the Eighteenth-Century Chesapeake," in *The Archaeology of Eighteenth-Century Virginia*, ed. Theodore R. Reinhart (Richmond: Archeological Society of Virginia, 1996). On slave morality and the difference between stealing and taking, see Eugene D. Genovese, *Roll, Jordan, Roll: The World the Slaves Made* (New York: Pantheon, 1974), 602–3. The 1940s and 1950s excavations in the area of the Shadwell kitchen did not save bone material in a way that could be analyzed except in plowzone distribution studies. See Kern, "Report on Shadwell," 31–32.

9. A common query posed by archaeologists is whether artifacts relating to particular groups of people reflect native or adapted versions of their culture. There are a few sites and contemporary references where slave houses reflected African building practices or ornamentation. Although there is no archaeological evidence of ornamentation for the buildings that housed slaves at Shadwell, the evidence of their orientation suggests that these quarters were a product of PJ's Anglo-Virginian ideas about buildings and the plantation landscape. The use of the living space, however, provided an opportunity for self-expression by the slaves who lived there. See, e.g., Genovese, *Roll, Jordan, Roll*, 529–30; William M. Kelso, *Kingsmill Plantations, 1619–1800: Archaeology of Country Life in Colonial Virginia* (Charlottesville, Va.: Distributed for WMK Press by the University of Virginia Press, 2003), 27–28; and Philip D. Morgan, *Slave Counterpoint: Black Culture in the Eighteenth-Century Chesapeake and Lowcountry* (Chapel Hill: University of North Carolina Press, 1998), 118–20.

10. The archaeological details of the features related to this building are: the large clay-walled cellar (SW99, SW351E-R) measures roughly six and a half feet square and reaches about three and a half to four feet below modern grade. About eight feet east of the east side of the cellar, an oblong feature (SW362F, H) (two by five feet) was the pit for the hearth, and the two large postholes just north and south (SW327J, K and SW364M, N, respectively) of this pit mark post supports for a chimney structure. Roland Robbins excavated most of the cellar in 1955 as a single deposit—that is, he did not record the stratigraphic and hence chronological deposition of artifacts in the feature. A few early layers survived the 1950s work and were recorded stratigraphically. For specific details, see Kern, "Report on Shadwell"; Seth Mallios, "A Ceramic Analysis of 1954–5 Excavation Unit 99/1991 Excavation Unit 351 at Shadwell," ms., TJMF, 1994. ("Feature" is the name archaeologists give to any soil disturbance—a hole, layer, or deposit that can be identified as distinct from another layer. Excavation may indicate that the feature was a posthole, a well, an animal burrow, etc.)

The building may have measured as long as eighteen to twenty feet on the exterior if there were reasonable space for flooring on all sides of the large cellar pit and the four-and-a-half-foot-deep chimney structure is included in the overall length. It is possible that the building was log construction, but the quantity of wrought nails suggests otherwise, though there were not as many nails around Buildings I and II as there were around the kitchen buildings.

Recent work by Garrett Fesler has recognized the relationship between the type and number of subfloor pits and slave housing practices. At the Utopia site in James City County, earlier plantation housing put people in single-sex, gang-style arrangements, and in these buildings archaeologists discovered many small subfloor pits that served the separate storage needs of many individuals. Later period housing revealed that slave families used only one or sometimes two larger pits for the group. Garrett Randall Fesler, "From Houses to Homes: An Archaeological Case Study of Household Formation at the Utopia Slave Quarter, ca. 1675–1775" (Ph.D. diss., University of Virginia, 2004), esp. 280–350.

The south chimney support postmold contains a single wire nail that confirms the building's destruction by the nineteenth century and probably reflects the gradual filling of the postmold by plowing. See Kern, "Report on Shadwell."

11. The sill was excavated in 1991 as SW341E. The postholes were about a foot in diameter, and their centers were about three feet apart. The postholes were filled with brick rubble to a depth of about fifteen inches. The rubble sill was slightly more than six inches wide, and extended to a depth of only two and a half inches, much shallower than the postholes. The rubble from the sill seemed to cap the postholes, and the three parts appeared as one distinct feature on the surface. There were no postmolds evident in the fill, but the fill was rubbly. It is possible that Building II was log. Mulberry Row at Monticello shows that even the most planned plantation landscape could display a variety of materials and construction methods. There were fewer nails around Building II, as shown in the distribution maps, although the distributions of window glass show pretty consistent patterns around each of the buildings on the quarter and the kitchen area. See Kern, "Report on Shadwell."

12. These posts were features SW364F, G, H, J, L, P. Enclosures such as this are associated with a number of slave sites. Their interpretation is best illustrated by the reconstruction of a quarter by the CWF at Carter's Grove; see Edward A. Chappell, "Reconstructed Slave Quarter at Carter's Grove," in Charles Brownell, Calder Loth, William Rasmussen, and Richard Wilson, *The Making of Virginia Architecture* (Richmond: Virginia Museum of Fine Arts, 1992), 432–33; and Lorena S. Walsh, *From Calabar to Carter's Grove: The History of a Virginia Slave Community* (Charlottesville: University of Virginia Press, 1997), 181–82. The cooking pit was feature SW330H, J.

13. The fence described as part of the landscape plan here delineated only the western side of the quarter area. Excavations north, south, and east of the activity yard did not uncover fences; however, many kinds of enclosures do not leave archaeological footprints, and in fact, evidence for split-rail fences is rare. The one at Shadwell left its mark because of the pairs of staves that locked each intersection of rails in place.

14. See SW722B, C, K in Kern, "Report on Shadwell."

15. On slave rations, see *FB,* 163; and Morgan, *Slave Counterpoint,* 134–45. Generally, an archaeologist would save bone and other animal material and have a faunal analyst or faunal archaeologist assess the type of animals, grades of meats, and butchering or even cooking methods indicated by the collection. Most of the kitchen area and part of the quarter site (the cellar of Building I) were excavated in the 1950s work of Roland Robbins. The bone material was kept without regard to stratigraphy, and some degraded in storage. In short, faunal analysis was not done with the material recovered in the 1950s, as there was no way of knowing how complete the sample was or even if there was a datable context for the assemblage, except to make a general statement about diet. On pothooks, see AlCWB, 2:41–48.

16. See SW339A. At Monticello, TJ used incentives of an extra pot or a crocus bed (a mattress covered with the coarse fabric called crocus) to slaves who married at "home," and he rewarded craftsmen with suits "of red or blue." It is possible that PJ and JJ used similar incentives. TJ to Jeremiah Goodman, Jan. 6, 1815, *GB,* 540; Jefferson, "Memoirs," 23.

17. The cooking pit was SW330H, J. The pit was roughly circular with a surface diameter of about two and a half feet and a depth of eighteen to twenty-four inches. These measurements are estimates because the feature only appeared below plowzone. The rock was about nine inches in diameter and two inches thick. See Kern, "Report on Shadwell" and field notes. It is hard not to think of the social aspects of a present-day barbeque or gathering around someone's grill.

18. See Kern, "Report on Shadwell," especially app. 2.

19. William Kelso called findings on slave quarters at Kingsmill and Monticello a "representative sampling of whatever the owner had on hand"; see Kelso, *Archaeology at Monticello,* 88–100; *Kingsmill,* quotation 205; and Monticello Archaeology Collections. Lorena Walsh proposes that an internal slave economy for goods emerged just before rather than after the American Revolution in older tidewater areas. Shadwell evidence supports Walsh's chronology and extends the region, as does much of the Shadwell evidence for whites. Slaves at Shadwell experienced a world of goods more like that on large plantations near urban centers than most small plantations and farms in the Piedmont. Walsh, *Calabar to Carter's Grove,* 182–86, 307, n. 17.

The consumption of ceramics by slave and free members of plantation communities has been explored in different ways by archaeologists, who focus variously on the attributes of objects, the status of objects, or the relations of the people who use the objects. On ceramics as status in nineteenth-century Georgia, see William Hampton Adams and Sarah Jane Boling, "Status and Ceramics for Planters and Slaves on Three Georgia Coastal Plantations," *Approaches to Material Culture Research for Historical Archaeologists,* comp. George L. Miller, Olive R. Jones, Lester A. Ross, and Teresita Majewski (California, Pa.: Society for Historical Archaeology, 1991), 59–86. Charles E. Orser Jr. proposes a relation-based analysis in "Artifacts, Networks, and Plantations: Toward a Further Understanding of the Social Aspects of Material Culture," in *Historical Archaeology and the Study of American*

Culture, ed. Lu Ann De Cunzo and Bernard L. Herman (Winterthur, Del.: Henry Francis Du Pont Winterthur Museum, 1996), 233–56.

20. The Shadwell collection represents a well-off family at an advanced stage in its lifecycle; PJ's and JJ's ages afforded them time to acquire things and replace items broken or lost. A younger couple, an unmarried person, or a poorer person may not acquire or replace possessions that marked once-in-a-lifetime events such as marriage. Authors who have considered the meaning of objects in the waning years of their fashion include Cary Carson, "The Consumer Revolution in Colonial British America: Why Demand?" in *Of Consuming Interests,* ed. Cary Carson, Ronald Hoffman, and Peter J. Albert (Charlottesville: University of Virginia Press, 1994); Bernard L. Herman, "Multiple Materials, Multiple Meanings: The Fortunes of Thomas Mendenhall," *Winterthur Portfolio* 19, no. 1 (1984): 67–86; and Ann Smart Martin, "The Role of Pewter as Missing Artifact: Consumer Attitudes toward Tableware in Late Eighteenth-Century Virginia," in *Approaches to Material Culture Research for Historical Archaeologists,* comp. George L. Miller et al. (California, Pa.: Society for Historical Archaeology, 1991); Barbara Carson considers the varied scales of new consumer goods in *Ambitious Appetites: Dining, Behavior, and Patterns of Consumption in Federal Washington* (Washington, D.C.: American Institute of Architects Press, 1990). Sidney W. Mintz probes the fashions behind certain foods in *Sweetness and Power: The Place of Sugar in Modern History* (New York: Viking, 1985), esp. 121–22.

See also Grant McCracken, *Culture and Consumption: New Approaches to the Symbolic Character of Consumer Goods and Activities* (Bloomington: Indiana University Press, 1988), 14; and Neil McKendrick, "Commercialization and the Economy," in *The Birth of a Consumer Society: The Commoditization of Eighteenth-Century England,* ed. McKendrick, John Brewer, and J. H. Plumb (Bloomington: Indiana University Press, 1982), 9–13.

21. Archaeologists must consider both how an object was used in the past and how it got to the place where it was found.

22. Archaeologists found pots made for drugs and salve at Shadwell in the kitchen area and the quarter site and at the quarter site at Monticello. See Kern, "Report on Shadwell"; and Neiman, "Shadwell Quarter." The Pasteur and Galt Apothecary in Williamsburg kept stocks of English delft salve pots for the medications they mixed and sold. It is possible that doctors in the Piedmont also had stocks of pots for mixing preparations for their patients, although these doctors may have purchased theirs from a commercial apothecary such as Pasteur and Galt or may even have purchased patent medicines made abroad. By 1780 George Gilmer sold medicine in Charlottesville (see chap. 2). I thank Robin Kipps, supervisor of the Pasteur and Galt Apothecary at Colonial Williamsburg for sharing her knowledge of the drug jar trade with me. Delftware apothecary jars were made in Holland, but most that appear on Anglo sites were made in and around London. Ivor Noël Hume, *A Guide to Artifacts of Colonial America* (New York: Knopf, 1970), 203.

Glass pharmaceutical containers appear in the same areas as the delft: in the Shadwell kitchen and quarter and at the Monticello quarter. A single piece of glass also came from the Jefferson house, the only medicinally related artifact from that site. See chap. 2; Kern, "Report on Shadwell"; and Neiman, "Shadwell Quarter."

23. PJ Estate, 1728–1758, 9, 17, 23. This is probably the same Mrs. Eliza. Lewis, who also sewed clothes for Shadwell slaves. PJ Estate, 1757–1765, 36, 41; PJ Estate, 1759–1763, 2. Dr. George Gilmer's Feebook 1767, 1771–1775, Gilmer-Skipwith Papers, Mss 6145, ViU. AlCWB, 2:43.

24. Stanton, *Free Some Day*, 26–32; Stanton, "Those Who Labor," 168. Marylynn Salmon, "The Cultural Significance of Breastfeeding and Infant Care in Early Modern England and America," *Journal of Social History* 28, no. 2 (1994): 9.

25. The name colonoware, or colono Indian ware, was given to coarse-fired earthenware when archaeologists in America in the 1960s recognized that European forms had been hand made from locally found materials. Observers assigned their manufacture to Native Americans whose pot-making traditions changed to reflect Anglo-Indian markets. The classic example is an Indian-made chamber pot—a European object made using Native American technology. During the following decades when archaeologists began to study slave sites, they debated whether planters bought rustic pots from Indians to give to slaves or whether the pots indicated that slaves traded with Indians. Then in the 1980s archaeologists realized that many colono pots reflected African potting traditions and likely were made by slaves who fired local clay right in their hearths or in fire pits, although other archaeologists argue that many colono pots are too technologically sophisticated to be made in simple fires. The discovery that many pots bear incisions of cosmograms ties them to West African religious practices, perhaps as their sole purpose. Colonoware became rarer following the Revolution, when slaves were more likely to be American-born and to obtain inexpensive ceramics from their owners. For a summary of research on colonoware, see Leland Ferguson, *Uncommon Ground: Archaeology and Early African America, 1650–1800* (Washington, D.C.: Smithsonian Institution Press, 1992), 6–7, chap. 4, esp. 116–17; and Barbara Heath, "Temper, Temper: Recent Scholarship on Colonoware in Eighteenth-Century Virginia," in *The Archaeology of Eighteenth-Century Virginia*, ed. Theodore R. Reinhart (Richmond: Archeological Society of Virginia, 1996), 149–175. For other African and African-American folk traditions about pots, see Anne Elizabeth Yentsch, *A Chesapeake Family and Their Slaves: A Study in Historical Archaeology* (Cambridge: Cambridge University Press, 1994), 205–10, 321–28.

26. There are many broad discussions of the appeal that Christianity, especially evangelical Christianity, had for slaves and poor people generally. See, e.g., Genovese, *Roll, Jordan, Roll*, bk. 2, pt. 1; Rhys Isaac, *The Transformation of Virginia, 1740–1790* (Chapel Hill: University of North Carolina Press, 1982), esp. 68, 161–77; Lawrence W. Levine, *Black Culture and Black Consciousness: Afro-American Folk Thought from Slavery to Freedom* (New York: Oxford University Press, 1977), esp. chap. 1; Donald G. Mathews, *Religion in the Old South* (Chicago: University of Chicago Press, 1977); Morgan, "Slave Life in Piedmont Virginia," esp. 472–79; Albert J. Raboteau, *Slave Religion: The "Invisible Institution" in the Antebellum South* (New York: Oxford University Press, 1978), esp. chaps. 5 and 6;

Mechal Sobel, *Trabelin' On: The Slave Journey to an Afro-Baptist Faith* (Princeton, N.J.: Princeton University Press, 1988); and Sobel, *The World They Made Together: Black and White Values in Eighteenth-Century Virginia* (Princeton, N.J.: Princeton University Press, 1987), pt. 3.

27. These descriptions of clothes from the Shadwell account books rely heavily on the work of Linda Baumgarten, who defines all these items in her article and discusses the range of what planters distributed. See Baumgarten, "'Clothes for the People': Slave Clothing in Early Virginia," *Journal of Early Southern Decorative Arts* 14 (1988): 26–70. The Shadwell rations were very like the clothing rations that TJ made at Monticello. See *FB*, various.

28. That Shadwell slave children received different weights of clothing was at variance of the oft-nakedness of slave children elsewhere. Monmouth caps were knitted wool caps without a wide brim, made in Monmouth, England. Blankets came from England, Scotland, or Wales, from factories that manufactured inexpensive woven woolen cloth. Plaid was a woven woolen cloth (unpatterned) that was sewn into stockings that were very different from fashionable knitted stockings. Many of these goods came directly to the Jeffersons, shipped from merchants, such as Messers. Farrell and Co. of Bristol, with the exception of the blankets bought in Virginia one year. See Baumgarten, "Clothes for the People," esp. "Glossary of Fabric and Clothing Terms," 45, 48, 50, 62–66; PJ Estate, 1757–1765; PJ Estate, 1759–1763, country quotation, 3.

29. PJ Estate, 1759–1763, 1.

30. PJ Estate, 1728–1758, 9, 11, 19, 22. Sawney's hire was during the years that TJ boarded with the Reverend James Maury. PJ Estate, 1757–1765, 38, 45; PJ Estate, 1759–1763, 3.

31. PJ Estate, 1759–1763, 3.

32. PJ Estate, 1759–1763, 1. On livery, see also Carson, *Ambitious Appetites*, 94–95, 192.

33. There was no mention of any pants or breeches for male children in the field hand lists. Linda Baumgarten makes the point that most slave clothes used the same types of fabrics. Status was indicated by the cut, ornamentation, and style of garments. Baumgarten, "Clothes for the People," esp. 57–58. The clothing corresponds to the list of people whom JJ kept as her sixth portion. It is possible that JJ's clothing list represents only their house clothing—it is only one set—and that they might have received other clothes for work outside the house from the regular distribution lists. PJ Estate, 1757–1765, 42; PJ Estate, 1759–1763, 1, 2.

34. See Barbara J. Heath, "Buttons, Beads and Buckles: Self-Definition within the Bounds of Slavery," in *Historical Archaeology, Identity Formation, and the Interpretation of Ethnicity,* ed. Maria Franklin and Garrett Fesler (Richmond, Va.: Colonial Williamsburg Foundation, 1999), 47–69. See also chap. 1.

35. PJ Estate, 1728–1758, 19. Sawney was hired out for six months in 1759, perhaps because his new young master was away at school and he would not be put to field work. Sandy was not included in PJ's inventory, so it is not known where he lived, but since he

was skilled, he was likely on the home quarter. He sold grass seed to TJ in 1768. He ran away in 1769 and was sold to Colonel Charles Lewis in 1773. PJ Estate, 1757–1765, 28; *MB*, 79, n. 79. There are many other skills we can reasonably expect to find on a plantation this size, such as ironworking, tinsmithing, and cart making. I have listed here only the trades indicated by the documents or the archaeological record. Skills relating to sewing are discussed with clothing, above; and skills relating to cooking are explored in the section on the plantation kitchen, above. See chap. 1 on TJ II's horses.

36. *VG*, Purdie and Dixon, Sept. 7, 1769.

37. PJ Estate, 1728–1758, 19. PJ Estate, 1757–1765, 28, 36; PJ Estate, 1759–1763, 1. Sept. 7, 1769, printed from *VG*, Purdie and Dixon, Sept. 14, 1769, reprinted in *Papers*, 1:33. See also chap. 6.

38. PJ Estate, 1757–1765, 25. Randall, *Jefferson*, 1:11. PJ Estate, 1728–1758, 15. See also chap. 7. The slaves at Monticello had a song that invoked Tuckahoe. As written, it is anachronistic to our period and may have come from slaves who knew Tuckahoe because of TJ's daughter's marriage to Thomas Mann Randolph of Tuckahoe. The song was called "Old Colonel Tom": "While old Colonel Tom lived and prospered, / There was nothing but joy at Tuckahoe. / Now that old Colonel Tom is dead and gone, / No more joy for us at Tuckahoe." TJ's daughter Martha reported that this song was about her father-in-law, Thomas Mann Randolph Sr., whom the Shadwell slaves knew only as a young man. Still the song may have been based on an earlier tradition. Elizabeth Langhorne, "Black Music and Tales from Jefferson's Monticello," *Folklore and Folklife in Virginia* 1 (1979): 60–67.

39. TJ used both spellings; *MB*, 13, n. 623. Unfortunately, there are no local store accounts for African Americans in Albemarle County during the colonial period. Ann Smart Martin has analyzed the buying habits of African-American slaves; see Martin, *Buying into the World of Goods: : Early Consumers in Backcountry Virginia* (Baltimore: Johns Hopkins University Press, 2008), esp. 173–93.

40. The pipe made of local stone called Candler Phyllite was from layer SW363E. Steatite is a more familiar local stone for carving and shaping pipes. The laminate structure of Candler Phyllite explains why the stone split during carving. I thank geologists Stephen Clement and C. Rick Berquist for their help in identifying local stones.

41. Tobacco pipes made of white ball clay had long stems that broke off in one-inch to two-inch segments. The stem sections predominate archaeologically, with occasional pipe bowls.

42. M. Drake Patten, "Mankala and Minkisi: Possible Evidence of African American Folk Beliefs and Practices," *African-American Archaeology* 6 (1992): 5–7. The slate was from SW363E. For interpretation of collections of buttons, see Elizabeth Grzymala Jordan, "'Unrelenting Toil': Expanding Archaeological Interpretations of the Female Slave Experience," *Slavery and Abolition* 26 (2005): 217–32; Heath, "Buttons, Beads and Buckles"; and William M. Kelso and Douglas Sanford et al., "Monticello Black History/Craft Life Archaeological Project, 1984–1985, Progress Report," ms., TJMF, 1985.

43. The group of Native American artifacts is explored at length in chap. 6.

44. *MB*, 79; *Papers*, 1:33; *VG*, Purdie and Dixon, Sept. 14, 1769, reprinted in *Papers*, 1:33.

45. Sall's name was recorded as Sall, "Little Sal," and "Little Salley." I have chosen to call her "Little Sall" to distinguish her from her mother as the Jefferson documents do. Cyrus was born 1772, and Rachel about 1768. JJ deeded Rachel to RJ following the death of RJ's slave Hannah at Snowdon. *FB*, 8–9; *MB*, 462. See also chap. 4.

On Little Sall's death, see *MB*, 370–71, n. 370; TJ & JJ Acct., 1763–1778. See also chaps. 3 and 7. The Shadwell burial ground received Jefferson family members who died during the eighteenth century. It is entirely possible that slaves at Shadwell buried their dead on this spot, too, or they may have had their own plot on yet another promontory above the river. See Kern, "Report on a Burial Ground."

46. The dual nature of slave life required by this material culture reading of Shadwell fits W. E. B. DuBois's description of black Americans as having a "double-consciousness . . . two unreconciled strivings; two warring ideals" from the "sense of always looking at one's self through the eyes of others." W. E. B. DuBois, *The Souls of Black Folk* (1903; reprint ed., New York: Penguin, 1989), 5.

47. PJ also carefully outlined that if JJ failed to write a deed or will for her slaves, or if a daughter died while unmarried, those slaves became part of the estate to be divided by TJ and RJ. AlCWB, 2:32–34.

48. Quotation from Jefferson, *Notes*, 162. The separate charge for clothing also kept accounts from PJ's and JJ's estates separate. See chap. 7.

49. AlCWB, 2:32–34.

50. The average value of adult male slaves at Shadwell was just less than £44, see above. Jupiter was born at Shadwell in the same year as TJ, 1743. His mother was likely Sall (the Elder). I have speculated that Sawney was Jupiter's father and that Jupiter carried on a family profession, but in that case Jupiter (and Sall's other children) should appear in records as mulatto like Sawney and he never does. *MB*, see index for Jupiter. Jupiter is the subject of a substantial portion of recent work on Monticello slaves, see Lucia Stanton, *Free Some Day*, esp. 19–27. On the graveyard, see *GB*, 25.

51. Gordon-Reed, *Hemingses of Monticello*, esp. 55, 77–90. Among the important questions that follow Gordon-Reed's work is whether or not the status of slave families within a plantation can be used as an indicator of sexual relations between black and white families there.

52. JJ's "sixth" was very close to both that portion of PJ's slaves in monetary value, as well as in number of individuals, if one counts children born between 1757 and 1760—there were at least five. PJ's slaves in the inventory totaled £1,820, one-sixth of that is £303. The inventory listed sixty slaves; one-sixth equals ten. JJ's sixth was valued £355, or eleven individuals, but clearly included new births in the mention of Lucinda, Sall's daughter. TJ's Farm Book names at least four more slaves born during this period. These three all went to TJ eventually. See *FB;* and PJ Estate, 1759–1763, 10.

53. In 1757 the nine slaves named in PJ's will had a combined value of £270, equal to 11 percent of the estate total of £2,399 5d., or 15 percent of the total value of all slaves, £1,820.

Chapter 4. The Field Quarters

1. AlCWB, 2:32–34.

2. Phillis's age is based on the assumption that she was about sixteen when her first child was born and that two years passed before the birth of her second child. I have used sixteen as the beginning of adulthood for males since they were considered titheable (taxed as adult labor) then, and sixteen is a reasonable starting point for reproductive history. "Tobey" is also spelled "Toby" in other documents. Orange County Deed Book 2, 181–83. Almost all of the Shadwell documents, including JJ's 1776 inventory, reflect values for slaves and property unaffected by the dramatic inflation of the later 1770s.

3. AlCWB, 2:45; *FB,* 5; PJ Estate, 1728–1758, 17. The evidence for which slaves RJ inherited is primarily negative. There are no known surviving farm rolls by RJ if in fact he made any. A few of RJ's slaves are mentioned by name in correspondence with TJ. If a slave is not on TJ's 1774 slave list, I have presumed that slave went to RJ, unless that slave, like Phillis, was older and may well have died before then. See esp. *FB,* 5–21. On old age, see Allan Kulikoff, *Tobacco and Slaves: The Development of Southern Cultures in the Chesapeake, 1680–1800* (Chapel Hill: University of North Carolina Press, 1986), 60–63.

4. For the purposes of this study I use "Shadwell" as a synonym for the entire agricultural enterprise of PJ. Where I am referring to the plot of four hundred acres on the Rivanna River, I use "Shadwell tract" or otherwise make it clear that I am talking about just that land, since PJ used a quarter farm system and thought about his landholdings as somewhat independent entities. The same goes for "Monticello": the word refers to TJ's entire plantation, or just the home quarter within his or his father's larger plantation system. Although it is anachronistic to do so, I have used the TJ-era farm names to refer to those same tracts when they were under his father's ownership. There is little record of how PJ referred to his land, and using the familiar TJ names is the way to write them that is clearest.

PJ and, later, TJ used a quarter farm system where the plantation was divided into smaller agricultural units that each had domestic facilities—houses and work areas—for both the slave and hired people who lived and worked that piece of land. I use the word "quarter" here as both quarter group—the five distinct groups of people within the plantation labor population—and as a particular site where workers were quartered.

5. The number of slave owners is based on probate inventories and represents only those slave owners who died during the colonial period and whose estates were ordered into probate by the court. The number of estates (n=170) and slave holders (n=85) differs from the number of inventories used in wealth calculations in chapter 1 (n= 165) because the wealth figures use only inventories in which the goods were assigned monetary values. Slaveholding figures include a number of estates that listed slaves but that did not have appraised values assigned to the slaves or other goods.

Rose owned 62 slaves in Albemarle County and another 41 in other counties (total 103). A few other slaveholders owned slaves in more than one county. Since my purpose here is to explore the experience of the Shadwell slaves, I am using only the Albemarle County figures in the statistics in this chapter; see AlCWB, vols. 1, 2.

In Albemarle County, 76 percent of slaves lived with ten or fewer cohorts. Morgan and Nicholls find that the disparity between most measures of slave life in the Piedmont and the tidewater evened out toward the end of the eighteenth century. The Shadwell figures suggest that slaves on larger plantations had greater stability earlier. See AlCWB, vols. 1, 2. For Piedmont statistics, see Philip D. Morgan and Michael L. Nicholls, "Slaves in Piedmont Virginia, 1720–1790," *WMQ*, 3rd ser., 46 (1989): 238–41.

6. The figure £1,805 is obtained by adding the values of all sixty slaves listed in the inventory: the subtotals are £1,522 for Shadwell and £283 for Snowdon. The subtotal for the Shadwell slaves in the inventory is listed as £1,537, which is off by £15 from the above figure. The discrepancy may be a math error on the part of the recorder or the result of a miswritten figure when the inventory was copied into the county will book. For the statistics of slave values within the group I have used the corrected figure of £1,805. In wealth statistics for the county I have used the written inventory total of £2,399 5d. The statistical difference is negligible. See chap. 1 for wealth statistics on colonial Albemarle. N=165, counting estates that were inventoried and for which values were assigned during the colonial period. AlCWB, vols. 1, 2.

The lowest individual value at Shadwell was £8, assigned to the child Bellow (or Bella); however, five infants were assigned a value with their mothers and not an individual value. AlCWB, 2:41–48.

7. Piedmont counties tended to have higher ratios of women to men. In older counties Morgan and Nicholls found ratios about even (Orange and Prince Edward) and more than 150 women to 100 men (Goochland), whereas in new counties ratios were higher, c. 1757: 115 (Amelia), 140 (Chesterfield and Spotsylvania), and more than 150 (Lunenburg). Fewer than two to one children to women were found in the tidewater versus more than two to one westward. See Morgan and Nicholls, "Slaves in Piedmont Virginia," 222, 230–32, esp. figs. 4, 5.

8. Midwife Jane Hammock was mentioned by name only in 1762. Mrs. Gaines, a midwife hired by TJ in the 1770s, helped deliver babies for TJ's wife, Martha, and for Nell, a slave. *MB*, 447, 468; PJ Estate, 1757–1765, 5, 26, 36, 37; PJ Estate, 1728–1758, 10.

9. These seven women all became the property of TJ, which is why there are records of their lives after Shadwell. They may not be representative of the entire Shadwell population including the slaves that went to RJ, but there are not records that continue the history of the other slaves. The normalized average of 29.2 months between births throws out the figures for Sall and Nell since they are so far from the other averages. Studies of natural fertility populations find an average duration of postpartum amenorrhea (the period during which ovulation is suppressed) at 20.1 months. Standard deviation = 7.22, n=20. Beverly I. Strassmann and John H. Warner, "Predictors of Fecundability and Conception Waits among the Dogon of Mali," *American Journal of Physical Anthropology* 105 (1998): 171, 176. Allan Kulikoff found that white women in the second half of the eigh-

teenth century had an average of 6.9 children and had a birth about every 30 months. Philip Morgan found that on average, slaves gave birth every 28 months and were about eighteen years old at first conception. Kulikoff, *Tobacco and Slaves,* 57, table 2, 60; Philip D. Morgan, *Slave Counterpoint: Black Culture in the Eighteenth-Century Chesapeake and Lowcountry* (Chapel Hill: University of North Carolina Press, 1998), 89, table 21, 92.

10. This coincidence may also reflect the travel schedules of their husbands, as it is likely that Sawney, PJ's valet, was the father of Sall's children.

11. Morgan and Nicholls find that "planters singled out young slaves when they opened up quarters further west." Morgan and Nicholls report 1755 figures for the percentage of adult slaves who were African as 59 percent in Amelia County and 37 percent in Chesterfield County. "Slaves in Piedmont Virginia," 215–17, table 4, 220, 224. Morgan, *Slave Counterpoint,* 104–5.

12. On Farding and Pompey, see Henrico County Records, 1725–37, 293. On Jupiter, see PJ Estate, 1728–1758, 19. Jack cost £45 3s., and Clarke still owed PJ £21 14s. 7 1/2d. when PJ died. Clarke may have lived in the vicinity of Tuckahoe because PJ purchased from Clarke such small manufactured items as basins, pins, brushes, shirt buttons, and beeswax, some of it for the Randolph family at Tuckahoe. PJ also paid Clarke "By drawing one Map of Virginia 1 1/2 pistole," and for making beer. PJ Estate, 1728–1758, 15, 51, 54. On Robin, see *VG,* Hunter, Nov. 7, 1751, no. 45.

TJ's undated accounts, 1764–1775, include the entry, "To hire for Sandy from my father's death 1757 to Dec. 31, 1762 5–1/2 years @ £18"; *Papers,* 1:33. Thus, Sandy was owned by PJ in 1757 but leased by whom? TJ was a minor and not in a legal position to lease a slave, unless one of the executors arranged it.

TJ contracted to clear land for his famous home on the top of Monticello Mountain in 1768 but did not move there until November 1770. Some of PJ's slaves already lived on the land that would be called Monticello. TJ's 1774 slave lists show slaves at Monticello and Shadwell (and elsewhere), but it is not known when he moved people to quarters higher on Monticello Mountain, where he would build his house. Some of RJ's slaves moved from Shadwell to Snowdon by 1770. See *FB,* 5–21; *GB,* esp. 12, 16–18; and *MB,* xlv–xlvi, 177.

13. I use "Shadwell" to indicate Jefferson's entire agricultural enterprise—that is, his entire plantation holdings. The land comprising the home quarter is also called Shadwell, and I use "Shadwell site" or "Shadwell tract" or "Shadwell quarter" when I am referring only to that piece of land. I use TJ's field and land names freely in this section because they are the most precise about specific properties as we know them today. Shadwell and Snowdon are the only names both TJ and Harvie used. Where PJ or Harvie's citation is apt, I use that name. Certain properties, North River among them, I have been unable to locate.

There is not a definitive answer to how much land PJ actually owned. Marie Kimball cataloged PJ's land acquisitions and patents: more than 25,000 acres passed under his eye, if only his portions of joint ventures are added. With other investors PJ speculated in at least 71,770 acres of land. Neither of these figures includes the 800,000 acres granted (but not realized) to the Loyal Land Company. Archibald Henderson, "Dr. Thomas Walker and the Loyal Company of Virginia," *Proceedings of the American Antiquarian Society*, n.s., 41 (1931): 88; Kimball, *Jefferson: The Road to Glory, 1743 to 1776* (New York: Coward-McCann, 1943), 309–11; see also chap. 4. PJ referred to "New Quarter" in 1753. AlCWB, 2:32–34; PJ Estate, 1728–1758, 19.

The Harvie accounts are more detailed than PJ's accounts for PJ's plantation, just as PJ's accounts for William Randolph's plantation have very specific detail. Executors were more careful with unfamiliar records and accounting that had to be made clear to the court as part of the public record. The Harvie accounts for Shadwell have greater detail about crop yields and clothing for slaves, for instance, than PJ's records. I have assumed that the operations of the plantation changed little during the period of executorship.

14. Other Rivanna River land includes what became Monticello and the rest of TJ's patrimony. Inventory appraisers entered subtotal lines that marked these three divisions. AlCWB, 2:45, 48.

The labels Quarters I–V are my own way of distinguishing the groups in the list. For consistency in this study, I have used "quarter" to refer to the five groups of slaves as indicated by the 1757 inventory. I have used "quarter site" or "site" for the domestic area that included houses or yards. I have used "house" or "building" in talking about the structures in which the slaves lived.

I designated each individual as adult or child according to three criteria when a person's age was not given in any other documents: (1) location within the inventory list; (2) the occasional specification of "a boy" or "a girl" following a person's name; and (3) the valuation given by the appraisers. Unless the appraisers specified, I decided a person was probably an adult male if they were listed at over £32, although some boys were valued at just under £33. Adult women generally were valued at over £30, and girls generally under that figure. Exceptions within these criteria are sometimes accountable to advanced age or infirmity.

In addition to the groupings made in PJ's will and inventory, a few lists that indicate relationships survive from JJ's years as plantation mistress. In addition, TJ's extensive Farm Book lists provide information about family relationships among the slaves who remained at Shadwell or Monticello. A bit of negative evidence can be gained from those missing from the Farm Book, in suggesting which slaves went to RJ's estate when he and his older brother divided the Shadwell slaves as per their father's directions. There are few post-Shadwell references to RJ's slaves by name, however, and nothing to tell us who may have died before the brothers divided the estate. Although it may seem naive to pair up the adult male and female slaves into "families," the fairly even sex ratio and the distribution of the adults among the quarters suggests that this is a valid means of describing their social structure.

15. N=165; see AlCWB, vols. 1, 2.

16. At least four tobacco houses measure twenty by forty feet, of log construction. PJ Estate, 1728–1758, 19. T. H. Breen, *Tobacco Culture: The Mentality of the Great Tidewater Planters on the Eve of Revolution* (Princeton, N.J.: Princeton University Press, 1985), 46–53; *FB*, 256; Arthur Pierce Middleton, *Tobacco Coast: A Maritime History of Chesapeake Bay in the Colonial Era* (1953; reprint ed., Baltimore: Johns Hopkins University Press, 1984), 111–15.

17. See chap. 1 on Switzer's *Practical Husbandman*. PJ's hoes were also distinguished by the shape of the shaft to which they would be attached as either round eyed or ax eyed. Ivor Noël Hume's study of eighteenth-century Virginia found only hoes with round eyes. Many colonial Albemarle inventories list just "hoes," and if they specify type, most identify hilling (or narrow) and weeding (or broad). Next most often listed are grubbing hoes, used to create fields after trees were removed from an area. A few other planters had more specialized hoes, including one that had "garden [hoe]" distinguished from "old hoes" (presumably old hoes were tobacco hoes). AlCWB, vols. 1, 2:citation 416–17; Noël Hume, *A Guide to Artifacts of Colonial America* (New York: Knopf, 1970), 275.

I am indebted to Wayne Randolph of the Rural Trades Division, CWF, for his help identifying the tools in the Jefferson inventory. His observation is that this is fairly early usage of specialized tool terminology and range of types. Personal communication, Aug. 1, 2002. See also Peter H. Cousins, *Hog Plow and Sith: Cultural Aspects of Early Agricultural Technology* (Dearborn, Mich.: Greenfield Village and Henry Ford Museum, 1973).

TJ, surprisingly, was less specific about hoes in his Farm Book notes, lumping them into a count, "18 hoes," although in his section called: "Aphorisms, Observations, Facts in husbandry," TJ describes both weeding and grubbing activities with hoes. His interest, though, was not in the tool, but in gauging the amount of work that could be done by a group of laborers. *FB*, 54, 64; also *GB*.

18. On the clothing distribution, see PJ Estate, 1757–1765, 1. The relationships between the Dawsons are unclear. Martin Dawson may or may not have been the father of the Martin Dawson who became one of the earliest Baptist preachers in Albemarle in 1774. About the same time another Martin Dawson became a prominent merchant in the Rivanna River town of Milton. The Martin Dawson who served as an inventory appraiser in 1762 signed with his mark. AlCWB, 2:140; Edgar Woods, *Albemarle County in Virginia* (Charlottesville, Va.: Michie, 1901), 176–77. For work at Jos. Dawsons, see PJ Estate, 1728–1758, 19. Other overseers are mentioned in PJ Estate, 1759–1763.

19. This apparent use of work crews tending tobacco on more than one piece of land has not been explored and brings up many questions about work and home life that may be very different from labor models usually used to discuss slave life in this period.

20. Matthew had an older brother John who may have been the John Moore working for the Jeffersons. Matthew and Letitia Moore owned land near the Albemarle border with Louisa County that they sold in 1774 to the Reverend Maury. PJ Estate, 1759–1763, 1, 4; Woods, *Albemarle*, 284.

21. PJ Estate, 1757–1765, 25, 27, 38; PJ Estate, 1728–1758, 20; PJ Estate, 1759–1763, 10.

22. In the Piedmont plantations he studied, Kulikoff found that large numbers of un-related men lived together and only 40 percent of women lived with their husbands. He also found that slaves tended to seek spouses outside their own quarters. Kulikoff, *Tobacco and Slaves*, 371–74.

23. Planters used the word "peculium" to refer to goods owned by a slave, including furniture, clothing, bedding, cookware, and even crops or livestock the slave raised. Pe-culium was a Roman law concept that acknowledged that people who were owned could also own things and that those things did not belong to the master. One year, because he planted tobacco, TJ said his slaves should not grow tobacco "as the peculium," since "there is no other way of drawing a line between what is theirs & mine"; *FB*, 269. TJ's slaves received material incentives such as his offer that women could "earn" a crocus bed (a mattress covered in a coarse, burlap-like material) or a pot by marrying another slave within the plantation; *GB*, 540.

Archaeology on Mulberry Row at Monticello has provided a catalog of objects that contrast what the Monticello slaves owned and what TJ provided. William M. Kelso, *Archaeology at Monticello*, Monticello Monograph Series (Chapel Hill: Distributed for the TJF by the University of North Carolina Press, 2002); see also archaeology reports by Kelso, "A Report on the Archaeological Excavations at Monticello (1979–1981)," ms., TJMF, 1982; William M. Kelso and Douglas Sanford et al., "Monticello Black History/ Craft Life Archaeological Project, 1984–1985, Progress Report," ms., TJMF, 1985; and Kelso and Sanford, "A Report on the Archaeological Excavations at Monticello, Char-lottesville, Virginia, 1982–83," ms., TJMF, 1984. Lucia C. Stanton, *Slavery at Monticello*, Monticello Monograph Series (Chapel Hill: Distributed for the TJF by the University of North Carolina Press, 1993), 38.

24. The documentary evidence and the archaeological evidence for the five quarters are not parallel, and any discussion of them necessarily involves talking around the many gaps in the information available for each site. The home quarter has the benefit of ar-chaeological detail for part of the residential and work sites. But although some occupa-tions can be identified from the assemblage, in only a few instances can a particular slave be tied to a particular occupation. For the Snowdon plantation, the 1757 inventory tells us which slaves and which tools were there, a nice correspondence of people and things, but that allows only a generalized picture of the place because the site remains unknown. There is strong evidence of which tools in the inventory and which slaves may have been on the farm that became Monticello, and there is some archaeology to round out that picture. Two other groups of people and two lists of tools are left floating, offering some suggestions of the bigger patterns of life but infuriatingly brief in their detail.

25. Historians tend to divide slave housing as either dormitory-style housing for work-ers of a single sex (also called gang housing), or single-family housing. Historians often equate the shift from the first to the second type as a product of changes in labor systems because of the change from a tobacco-based to a grain-based economy. The ratio of peo-ple to spaces in the Shadwell field quarters suggests another variation. Many of the slaves

lived as families but shared the space with other unrelated individuals or with other families. The fact that family took precedence at Shadwell did not mean that families lived in their own spaces. There may have been some spaces reserved for unmarried adult men, but group houses most likely included families and members of both sexes. William M. Kelso, *Kingsmill Plantations, 1619–1800: Archaeology of Country Life in Colonial Virginia* (Charlottesville, Va.: Distributed for WMK Press by the University of Virginia Press, 2003), 28–30; Morgan, *Slave Counterpoint,* 104–9.

26. I have used pothooks as the marker for field quarter buildings in the 1757 inventory. Pothooks were the only architectural fitting in the inventory for the field sites. For general trends of slave diet and stewing, see Joanne Bowen, "Foodways in the Eighteenth-Century Chesapeake," in *The Archaeology of Eighteenth-Century Virginia,* ed. Theodore R. Reinhart (Richmond: Archeological Society of Virginia, 1996), 87–130; Diana C. Crader," The Zooarchaeology of the Storehouse and the Dry Well at Monticello," *American Antiquity* 49 (1984): 542–58; Crader, "Faunal Remains from Slave Quarter Sites at Monticello, Charlottesville, Virginia," *ArchaoZoologia* 3 (1989): 229–36; Crader, "Slave Diet at Monticello," *American Antiquity* 55 (1990): 690–717; also Crader, unpublished reports in collections of Monticello Archaeology Department; Leland Ferguson, *Uncommon Ground: Archaeology and Early African America, 1650–1800* (Washington, D.C.: Smithsonian Institution Press, 1992), 93–107; and Morgan, *Slave Counterpoint,* 137.

27. It is tempting to put group II (five people who are women and children) with less cooking equipment at site A and group II (seven people) at site B. If the plow leans toward men's work, then the tools may suggest gender roles and confirm this, but people and tools may have moved around with the seasonality of work.

28. When TJ and RJ divided the slaves, six of this group formed the core of TJ's Monticello slave force. Enough of the physical evidence at the site coincides with the documentary evidence about overseers that I feel I can discuss this group of people living at this place. See PJ Estate, 1728–1758, 19, for building instructions.

29. Excavation here under the direction of Fraser Neiman uncovered evidence of a building occupied roughly 1750–70, marked by a small cluster of cobbles of sandstone and greenstone and a few brick fragments, similar to hearth foundations found on other Monticello sites. The chimney was probably wood and the building frame or log construction. Derek Wheeler, Leslie McFaden, and Fraser D. Neiman, "The Early Farm Quarter at Monticello," Paper presented at the Society for Historical Archaeology Annual Conference, Salt Lake City, Utah, January 1999, 3.

Although pothooks has worked for my "marker" of the slave spaces in the inventory, this third field quarter site may be contrary to that pattern. The inventory for this site repeats tools in two separate groups: four broad hoes, six hilling hoes, and three narrow axes; then four hilling hoes, two narrow axes, and four broad hoes, suggesting that the appraisers entered two different spaces when making their list. Multiple pots and pans and grindstones also support the idea that this site accommodated larger numbers who perhaps ate and worked separately at times. Cooking to feed this group may have gone on in only one of the spaces. If the second side was unheated, it is possible that slaves crowded into one side to sleep during cold seasons, but the fireplace wall probably offered a fair degree of comfort during the winter, as well as discomfort during the summer. AlCWB, 2:41–48. For definitions of amenities and the class of objects listed under convenience, see Lois Green Carr and Lorena S. Walsh, "Changing Lifestyles and Consumer Behaviors in the Colonial Chesapeake," in *Of Consuming Interests: The Style of Life in the Eighteenth Century,* ed. Cary Carson, Ronald Hoffman, and Peter J. Albert (Charlottesville: University of Virginia Press, 1994), 69.

30. Evidence of firearms in slave houses has been found at Monticello, Mount Vernon, and other plantations in the Chesapeake. See also Morgan, *Slave Counterpoint,* 138–39. The shot comes from Neiman, "Shadwell Quarter." Ancient Field was a name often given to Indian fields that planters used. For TJ references, see *FB,* 45, 69.

31. For artifacts, see Neiman, "Shadwell Quarter." The interpretation of these artifacts is my own. More work needs to be done on establishing the relationship between this set of artifacts and those excavated at Shadwell. I thank Fraser Neiman for sharing preliminary data with me.

32. Other Dawsons worked as overseers on other quarters. The relationships among Martin, Joseph, and John Dawson are not known.

33. PJ Estate, 1728–1758, 14. The demographics of this group suggest the pattern found by Morgan and Nicholls that recently imported slaves to the Piedmont tended to be younger and reflected the fairly even sex ratio of midcentury slave cargoes. The presence of a single infant among these six men and women suggests that family formation was in its early stages here. Morgan and Nicholls, "Slaves in Piedmont Virginia," 220–21. PJ owned some land on the Fluvanna River before 1750. Malone uses 1754 for the purchase date of the Snowdon tract; however, the name Snowdon is on the 1751 map of Virginia. If TJ was correct in his autobiography that his father named the land for the family's ancestral home in Wales, then PJ owned and named Snowdon before 1751. Malone, *Jefferson,* 1:437; Autobiography, 4.

There is no information about what other buildings or activities took place at Snowdon. There may not have been a plantation house until RJ claimed his land there in 1776, but overseer Martin Dawson lived on the property. Since there has been no archaeology at Snowdon, there are no specifics about how the members of this household augmented their diets and clothing beyond their ration. By 1770 Quash lived at Monticello, where he had a garden and grew potatoes. *MB,* 212, 261.

34. PJ Estate, 1757–1765; PJ Estate, 1759–1763. These six slaves represent about 19 percent of the adult workforce.

35. *VG,* Hunter, Nov. 7, 1751, no. 45. The whipping will be discussed below.

36. Again, which slaves went to RJ is based on negative evidence. TJ's Farm Book tells us which slaves did *not* go to the younger brother. The numbers here reflect only the slaves in the 1757 list and do not account for children born or people dying in the interim.

37. The sum total of what is known about this episode is the record in TJ's Case Book: "The defendant IB, overseer for RJ, had 'by a cruel whipping killed a negro woman Hanah,'" along with the dates of action in TJ's Memorandum Book. In June 1770 TJ produced alias capias, a second writ for the arrest of Bates. The suit was still being settled in December that year. Case Book, No. 433, cited in *MB*, 177, n. 177, 200.

38. The last mention of Dawson in Harvie's accounts was 1760, but the records are less than complete in the years following. Nicholas was clerk of court for Albemarle from 1749 to 1792. In 1768 he hired the young TJ as a lawyer for Bates, who was plaintiff in a case of undetermined nature against one John Cannon (both Bates and Cannon lived in Buckingham County, which formed in 1761 from Albemarle). Nicholas, as PJ's executor, may have hired Bates to oversee the Snowdon plantation. *MB*, 65.

Since we do not know exactly when Bates killed Hannah, we can only ask the question of whether slaves were moved from Shadwell's home quarter because of the fire at the Jefferson's house there. Such an abrupt move could have contributed to the overall unsettled conditions.

Rachael's age is based on the estimate that she was born after her mother reached the age of sixteen. Her mother, Little Sall, was born in 1752. PJ Estate, 1759–1763, 10. Rachael may have stayed at Shadwell with her family until she was older, however; Little Sall died in an accident at Shadwell in 1774. *MB*, 370, n. 13.

Most of what is known about RJ's plantation when he becomes master of it is because of letters and exchanges with his older brother; see *Brother*. Netti Schreiner-Yantis and Florene Love, *The Personal Property Tax Lists for the Year 1787 for Buckingham County, Virginia* (Springfield, Va: Genealogical Books in Print, 1987).

39. Orange County Deed Book 2, 181–83.

40. Of course, we are at the mercy of the estate appraisers and recorders, who may have meant Goliath in place of Goliah; Bella, not Bellow; and so on.

41. Although Samson, Nimrod, and Caesar are biblical names, they are heroic in nature and rarely used to name white Virginians.

The boy Orange may have been named for another slave that his parents knew, but the elder Orange may have been named for his skin color or for Orange County, where he lived.

James Arnold in *Slave Ships and Slavery*, ed. George Dow (Port Washington, N.Y., [1927] 1969) 172.

Just as many slaves were known by diminutives, members of the Jefferson family were known to their slaves by diminutives or nicknames. A diminutive form of a name was not necessarily demeaning to someone, even someone held in bondage. Eugene Genovese makes the point that what might seem like a diminutive form to us could in fact be the person's name, such as "Sukey." Eugene D. Genovese, *Roll, Jordan, Roll: The World the Slaves Made* (New York: Pantheon, 1974), 448. See also Jefferson, "Memoirs."

TJ's slave Madison Hemmings reported that Dolley Madison promised his mother a gift for naming her child Madison (his mother never received the gift). Madison Hemings, in *Pike County [Ohio] Republican,* Mar. 3, 1873, reprinted as "Memoirs of Madison Hemings," in Annette Gordon-Reed, *Thomas Jeffferson and Sally Hemings: An American Controversy* (Charlottesville: University of Virginia Press, 1997), 245, 247. Other observations on naming can be found in Genovese, *Roll, Jordan, Roll,* 447–49; and in Mechal Sobel, *The World They Made Together: Black and White Values in Eighteenth-Century Virginia* (Princeton, N.J.: Princeton University Press, 1987), 156–60.

Chapter 5. Plantation Business

1. TJ's granddaughter Septimia Anne Randolph Meikleham reported hearing that PJ requested burial at Shadwell, and wrote: "After Mr. Jeffersons death the grave was lost sight of and now it cannot be found." If the grave had a marker, it was gone by the nineteenth century. See Meikleham, "Everyday Life at Monticello," Mss 4726-a Randolph-Meikleham Family Papers, 1792–1882, ViU.

Devereux Jarratt tells us that 40s., or £2, was the legal fee set by the church for a funeral. Jarratt, *The Life of the Reverend Devereux Jarratt: An Autobiography,* foreword by David L. Holmes, The William Bradford Collection, series ed., Barbara Brown Zikmund (Cleveland: Pilgrim Press, 1995), 57. PJ Estate 1757–1765, 5, 28, 30. A number of recipes in *The Virginia House-Wife* use the ratio of a pound of sugar, brown or white, per gallon of liquid for brandies and cordials. The sum of £2 6s. would have purchased about a hundred pounds of brown sugar or about thirty-five of white sugar, suggesting that these same quantities in gallons of punch were on hand. Mary Randolph, *The Virginia House-Wife,* ed. Karen Hess (Columbia: University of South Carolina Press, 1984), esp. 213–16. Estimates on sugar quantities from York County Wills and Inventories 22, 1771–1783, 337–41, from file, "Williamsburg Inventories in the York County Records," Colonial Williamsburg Research Files, Williamsburg, Va. See also Kern, "Report on a Burial Ground."

2. T. H. Breen, *Tobacco Culture: The Mentality of the Great Tidewater Planters on the Eve of Revolution* (Princeton, N.J.: Princeton University Press, 1985); Bertram Wyatt-Brown, *Honor and Violence in the Old South* (New York: Oxford University Press, 1986), esp. chap. 3; Eugene D. Genovese, *Roll, Jordan, Roll: The World the Slaves Made* (New York: Vintage, 1976); Rhys Isaac, *The Transformation of Virginia, 1740–1790* (Chapel Hill: University of North Carolina Press, 1982), esp. 131–35; Charles S. Sydnor, *American Revolutionaries in the Making: Political Practices in Washington's Virginia* (1952; reprint ed., New York: Free Press, 1965).

3. On the runaway slave, see *VG,* Hunter, Nov. 7, 1751, no. 45. There is another story that challenges the myth of the eminently successful PJ. Biographer Henry Randall reports that Archibald Cary was "at mortal feud with Colonel Peter Jefferson—as dauntless and unbending an antagonist as himself—at the time of [PJ's] death." PJ and Cary were married to cousins; both wives were daughters of a son of William Randolph of

Turkey Island. Cary lived at Ampthill in Chesterfield County. He appears in PJ's account book for business of an unremarkable nature. Cary and TJ became friends in Williamsburg. I can find no other sources for this story and no explanation. Its sum total is in Randall, *Jefferson*, 1:21–22; TJ's other early biographers do not repeat it as they do many of the family stories.

4. The Marxist view that unequal power relationships are inherently negative is not what I am exploring here. The power wielded by Jefferson and his peers is undeniable. My focus is what the historical record shows about how they used and maintained their power.

5. Isaac, *Transformation of Virginia*, 132.

6. PJ Estate, 1728–1758, 12. For discussion of all the aspects of a courthouse town, see Carl R. Lounsbury, *The Courthouses of Early Virginia: An Architectural History* (Charlottesville: University of Virginia Press, 2005), esp. chap. 6.

7. Clothing for the Jefferson children is treated in chap. 2. Clothing for the slaves is treated in chaps. 3 and 4. PJ Estate, 1757–1765, 36. What Peter Shepherd did is unknown. Eleanor (also Nel or Nelly) Shepherd worked for the Jeffersons as late as 1778. There is no record of Peter Shepherd after 1763. PJ Estate, 1759–1763, 1, 3; *MB*, 206, 470.

8. Six mills were road landmarks in Albemarle County by 1748. Robert Rose mentions an additional eight mills before 1751. Jefferson's mill was in operation before 1755, but that is the first date it is mentioned in his account book. County magistrates owned six of the fifteen early mills in the county, and a seventh was the property of John Carter, secretary of the colony. Nathaniel Mason Pawlett, *Albemarle County Road Orders, 1744–1748* (Charlottesville: Virginia Transportation Research Council, 1975); Rose, *Diary*, index for mill. The payment to Cobbs's estate included the sum for PJ's coffin; PJ Estate, 1728–1758, 19, 21, 23, 30.

9. PJ Estate, 1728–1758, 26; AlCWB, 2:41–47.

10. PJ Estate, 1759–1763, 9; PJ Estate, 1728–1758, 24; PJ Estate, 1757–1765, 26–27.

11. Goochland County Order Book, 1741–1744, 246, in "Education and Research Database Material Record," CWF; PJ Estate, 1728–1758, 1, 4.

12. John Biswell's debts translate to roughly $775 current money. Biswell's debt to Jefferson was greater than the value of 25 percent of all Albemarle estates in the colonial period (n=165). AlCWB, vols. 1, 2. See John J. McCusker, *How Much Is That in Real Money? A Historical Commodity Price Index for Use as a Deflator of Money Values in the Economy of the United States*, 2nd ed. (Worcester, Mass.: American Antiquarian Society, 2001), tables A-1, B-1. PJ Estate, 1728–1758, 2–6, 19, 51.

13. AlCDB, 3, 52. After four or five years as a teacher, Devereux Jarratt recalled, "My annual income . . . had been very small, yet, by frugality, I had saved enough to procure me a small poney and a saddle. I began also to get some credit in a store, and having prospect of getting 13l. at the end of that year, entered to go in debt for a tolerable suit of cloathes." Jarratt, *Life*, 23. To Jarratt, credit was something he had worked hard to earn and could use to better himself.

14. West's debt to Jefferson is roughly the equivalent of $96 in current money, about an eighth of the debt owed Jefferson by John Biswell. Biswell's debt was greater than the value of four estates (2 percent, n=165) listed in the colonial probate records. AlCWB, vols. 1, 2. PJ Estate, 1728–1758, 3, 14. Liberty Hall is in what is now Nelson County, formed from the part of Albemarle that became Amherst County, then Nelson. Cabell Papers, box 1, 1727–1776, acc. no. 5084, ViU. It is possible that PJ could offer living quarters at Tuckahoe or Shadwell to someone like West for the duration of his work there. At Monticello, TJ made available a house on Mulberry Row for hired craftsmen during the 1790s work on that house. Previously, the same building housed slaves.

15. Lois Green Carr and Lorena S. Walsh, "Changing Lifestyles and Consumer Behaviors in the Colonial Chesapeake," in *Of Consuming Interests: The Style of Life in the Eighteenth Century*, ed. Cary Carson, Ronald Hoffman, and Peter J. Albert (Charlottesville: University of Virginia Press, 1994), 122–23.

16. For a discussion of tobacco ports, see Malcolm H. Harris, "The Port Towns of the Pamunkey," *WMQ*, 2nd ser., 23 (1943): 493–516; for Shadwell crop figures and transportation, see PJ Estate, 1759–1763, esp. 7; PJ Estate, 1728–1758, 11, 15, 18, 22.

17. This same scenario took place across social strata, but I am interested here in exploring how the Jeffersons' legal obligations reveal the connections among their peers.

18. AlCWB, 2:32–34.

19. I added the commas in the excerpt from PJ's will. AlCWB, 2:32–34; PJ Estate, 1728–1758, 14, 16.

20. AlCDB 2, 1758–1761 (reel 1), 20–22. Turpin leased his house in Richmond to TJ when the government moved from Williamsburg during the Revolution. *MB*, 495, n. 72.

21. *Papers*, 1:3. I propose that RJ's boarding with his uncle Charles Lewis was engineered to impart this same set of practical lessons to the younger.

22. In 1805 Walker claimed that Jefferson made improper advances toward Mrs. Walker about 1768 when they were all close friends. Walker's deposition was a contribution to James Callender's politically motivated essays against Jefferson beginning in 1802. LC, 155:27117–21, as reprinted in Malone, *Jefferson*, 1:449.

23. It is not clear whether the Beverley Randolph whom Isham invokes is the one at Tazewell Hall in Williamsburg or the one at Turkey Island. Either created the same effect. Goochland County Deed Book 4, 1741–1745, 110–11.

24. PJ Estate, 1728–1758, 18.

25. Goochland Wills and Deeds, 1728–1736, 142; Rose, *Diary*, 339.

26. RJ's accounts in PJ's book are PJ Estate, 1728–1758, 1–9, 59–61. PJ Estate, 1757–1765, PJ Estate, 1759–1763, and PJ Estate, 1760–1761, are the accounts John Harvie kept for Shadwell. There are references to other PJ account books among the receipts that Harvie recorded. The daily memoranda of expenditure that PJ's son maintained included a vast array of information that did not concern most planters; see *MB*.

27. AlCWB, 2:17 (will), 59 (inventory); William Byrd, *Histories of the Dividing Line betwixt Virginia and North Carolina, with Introduction and Notes by William K. Boyd,*

intro. by Percy G. Adams (New York: Dover, 1967); Rose, *Diary*, 321, n. 90, 335. For more on the intellectual affinity of surveyors, see Hughes, *Surveyors and Statesmen*, esp. 161–62.

28. On Fry, see George W. Frye, *Colonel Joshua Fry of Virginia and Some of His Descendants and Allied Families* (Cincinnati, Ohio: n.p., 1966), 40. On PJ's brother Thomas, see "Jefferson Family," *Tyler's Quarterly* 7 (1925–26): 122.

29. Stith was married to another of JJ's first cousins, Judith Randolph of Tuckahoe (sister of PJ's friend William). Stith's brother-in-law the Reverend William Dawson also served as college president. William Stith, *The History of the First Discovery and Settlement of Virginia: Being an Essay Towards a General History of This Colony* (1747). Stith's cousin once removed wrote that Stith "had no taste in style. He is inelegant . . . and his details often too minute to be tolerable, even to a native of the country." Jefferson, *Notes*, 177. Collinson describes a journey to "A Gentlemen's house where my good friend Isham recommended me." The distance and placement of the house suggest strongly this could be Jefferson. See Edmund Berkeley and Dorothy Smith Berkeley, eds., *The Correspondence of John Bartram, 1734–1777* (Gainesville: University Press of Florida, 1992), 102–3.

30. Twelve was the usual number of vestrymen, although fewer generally came to meeting, even for the first service of a newly hired minister. Jarratt, *Life,* 45. Mountain Chapel likely later became Walker's Church, near Thomas Walker's. On the location of Mountain Chapel, see Bishop William Meade, *Old Churches, Ministers, and Families of Virginia,* 2 vols. (1857; reprint ed., Baltimore: Genealogical Publishing, 1995), 2:30; Rose, *Diary,* 33, 215, n. 376; Benjamin B. Weisiger III, abstractor and comp., *Goochland County Virginia Wills and Deeds 1736–1742* . . . (n.p., 1984). [Deed Book 3], 39.

31. Burgesses were James Holman, 1736–40, and John Smith, 1752–61. Vestryman Tarlton Fleming married Mary Randolph, daughter of William, and Charles Lewis married Mary Randolph, daughter of Isham, and became PJ's brother-in-law. *St. James Northam Parish Vestry Book, 1744–1850, Goochland County, Virginia,* abstracted by William Lindsay Hopkins (1987; reprint ed., Athens, Ga.: Iberian, 1993), 8. Jack Green's study of Virginia's political power finds that more than half of all burgesses served on their parish vestry. Green, "Foundations of Political Power in the Virginia House of Burgesses, 1720–1776," *WMQ,* 3rd ser., 16 (1959): 485–506. Douglas baptized sons and daughters of John Bolling and Mary Jefferson and of Dabney Carr and Martha Jefferson. *Douglas Register,* 8, 99, 101, 135, 159, 168; PJ Estate, 1728–1758, 12; *St. James Northam Parish Vestry Book,* 2, 8, 15, 16, 26, 30. TJ called Douglas's language skills rudimentary; see Autobiography, 4.

32. Archibald Henderson, "Dr. Thomas Walker and the Loyal Company of Virginia," *Proceedings of the American Antiquarian Society,* n.s., 41 (1931): 89; Malone, *Jefferson,* 1:40–45; Autobiography, 4.

33. When he died, Rose owned 103 slaves, more than anyone else who lived in colonial Albemarle County; however, Rose's slaves lived on plantations in Essex County and Orange County. Sixty-two of his people lived in Albemarle, on seven different quarters. PJ, with 60 slaves, was second. AlCWB, 2:pages inserted in back numbered 1–2. Rose, *Diary,* 98, see also 321, 335; "Jefferson Family, Bible."

34. Rose, *Diary*, 53, 250–52, nn. 545, 547.

35. Rose records many visits with Joshua Fry, and their friendship may have dated from when they both previously lived in Essex County. See Rose, *Diary*, 33, 60, 83, 92; and Marie Kimball, *Jefferson: The Road to Glory, 1743 to 1776* (New York: Coward-McCann, 1943), 23–24. On borrowed books, see Rose, *Diary*, 1, 112; also chap. 1.

36. Goochland County Wills, 1742–1749, 73.

37. Henry Fry's house was in Culpeper County. TJ served on the Committee on Religion and may have presented this petition and others like it to the meeting of Delegates and Senators, Nov. 1, 1776. "Petition of Dissenters in Albemarle and Amherst Counties," *Papers*, 1:586–89; Rev. Philip Slaughter, *Memoir of Col. Joshua Fry, Sometime Professor in William and Mary College, Virginia, and Washington's Senior in Command of Virginia Forces, 1754, Etc., Etc., with an Autobiography of His Son, Rev. Henry Fry, and a Census of Their Descendants* (n.p., 1880), 83–85; Edgar Woods, *Albemarle County in Virginia* (Charlottesville, Va.: Michie, 1901), 130–31.

38. TJ served the Saint Anne's vestry, 1772–85. Rosalie Edith Davis, *Fredericksville Parish Vestry Book, 1742–1787* (Manchester, Mo.: n.p., 1978); Meade, *Old Churches*, 50. Specifications for glebe houses suggest the minimum acceptable standards for men of professional standing. The 1748 act for support of the clergy required that every parish provide glebe lands of at least two hundred acres, with a "mansion and other convenient out-houses," including "kitchen, barn, stable, dairy, meat house, corn house, and garden, well-pailed, or inclosed with mudwalls, and with other conveniences as they shall think fit." William Waller Hening, ed., *The Statutes at Large; Being a Collection of All the Laws of Virginia . . .* , 18 vols. (Richmond, Va.: Samuel Pleasants Jr., 1809–23), 6:88–89. References to midcentury glebe houses reveal that the houses often had such amenities as plastered walls, brick chimneys, multiple glazed windows, and floor plans that acknowledged the growing need for separate social spaces. The vestry paid for houses that acknowledged the social rituals they shared. Susan A. Kern, "Virginia's Frontier Housing: Architectural, Documentary, and Archaeological Evidence for the Mid-Eighteenth Century," Paper presented at the Vernacular Architecture Forum Annual Meeting, Annapolis, Md., 1998.

Chapter 6. The Colony's Business

1. Sarah S. Hughes describes the social and political ranks of surveyors and the familial and intellectual connections between them. She observed that PJ was unlike many of his midcentury Piedmont surveyor colleagues, who were immigrants. Hughes, *Surveyors and Statesmen: Land Measuring in Colonial Virginia* (Richmond: Virginia Surveyors Foundation and Virginia Association of Surveyors, 1979), on family and political ranks, 90, on the Map of Virginia, 154–55. Dumas Malone, ed., *The Fry and Jefferson Map of Virginia and Maryland, Facsimiles of the 1754 and 1794 Printings with an Index*, with "Checklist of Eighteenth-Century Editions of the Fry & Jefferson Map," by Coolie

Verner (Charlottesville: University of Virginia Press, 1966). Margaret Beck Pritchard and Henry G. Taliaferro, *Degrees of Latitude: Mapping Colonial America* (Williamsburg, Va.: CWF, 2002), 154–159, also 160–63.

2. Fry was the first surveyor of Albemarle County in 1744. PJ inherited that position in 1754 (but had been county surveyor for Goochland in 1751). On the surveying "dynasties" and the position of commissioner (who could act for the colonial government and deputize surveyors), see Hughes, *Surveyors and Statesmen*, 21, chap. 8, esp. 90; and Mary M. Root, "Robert Brooke, Father and Son, Surveyors of Virginia," *Professional Surveyor* 24, no. 11 (2004), available at http://www.profsurv.com/magazine/archives.aspx. Fairfax Harrison, "The Northern Neck Maps of 1737–1747," *WMQ*, 2nd ser., 4 (1924): 1–15. Silvio A. Bedini, "William Mayo (1684–1744), Surveyor of the Virginia Piedmont; Part II," *Professional Surveyor* 24, no. 11 (2004), available at http://www.profsurv.com/magazine/archives.aspx. Thomas Lewis, *The Fairfax Line: Thomas Lewis's Journal of 1746*, ed. J. W. Wayland (New Market, Va.: Henkel, 1925). William Byrd, *Histories of the Dividing Line betwixt Virginia and North Carolina, with Introduction and Notes by William K. Boyd*, intro. by Percy G. Adams (New York: Dover, 1967). Although there is speculation that Fry and PJ met in Albemarle County in their professional roles, they may have known each other earlier through social connections. Fry worked closely at William and Mary under William Stith, who was JJ's first cousin and who was also married to another first cousin of hers, Judith Randolph of Tuckahoe, sister of PJ's friend William.

PJ's drawing of the dividing line survives; see "Plan of the Line between Virginia and North Carolina as Surveyed in 1728 and 1749," MS-38-628, ViU. Fry's expedition to the Ohio country as commander in chief of Virginia's forces also put him in contact with Christopher Gist, George Washington, and Conrad Weiser of Pennsylvania. See George W. Frye, *Colonel Joshua Fry of Virginia and Some of His Descendants and Allied Families* (Cincinnati: n.p., 1966), 36.

3. There is, however, almost no mention of slaves in the expedition journals, either traveling with the surveyors or at homes they visit. Lewis, *Fairfax Line*, 24; PJ Estate, 1728–1758, 9. See also Byrd, *Dividing Line*.

4. Randolph, *Domestic Life*, 19, 20; Lewis, *Fairfax Line*, esp. 60, 61, 66, 68, 69. Fittingly, TJ identified and helped the American Philosophical Society preserve Byrd's manuscript, which became known as "The Secret History of the Line." See Maude H. Woodfin, "Thomas Jefferson and William Byrd's Manuscript Histories of the Dividing Line," *WMQ*, 3rd ser., 1 (1944): 363–73.

5. Autobiography, 4; Malone, *Fry and Jefferson Map*, 7–8.

6. See, e.g., "Receipts, Pocket Plantation, 1750–1759," acc. no. 2027, box 1, ViU. See also chaps. 1 and 3.

7. AlCWB, 2:32–34.

8. The 1751 plan at ViU was drawn by PJ (and owned by TJ). PJ drew the 1756 plan now at DLC, cited by John W. Reps, *Tidewater Towns: City Planning in Colonial Virginia and Maryland* (Williamsburg, Va.: CWF, 1972). Sarah S. Hughes cites a plan of Beverley Town

drawn by William Cabell in 1751; Hughes, *Surveyors and Statesmen: Land Measuring in Colonial Virginia*, (Richmond, Va.: Virginia Surveyors Foundation and Virginia Association of Surveyors, 1979). Will of Beverley Randolph, Henrico Wills and Deeds, 1750–1767, 42. Lot description from PJ, Plat of the Town of Beverley, Henrico County, 1751 June 6 (Endorsed by TJ), Edgehill-Randolph Papers, ViU. See also Hughes, *Surveyors and Statesmen*, 135; Reps, *Tidewater Towns*, 226–28; Rose, *Diary*, 61, 79, 266 n. 613, 298, n. 769.

9. Lot owners from PJ, Plat of Beverley, ViU. For ferry lot, see *FB*, 32, 127. Rose, *Diary*, 61, 79, 266 n. 613, 298 n. 769. For Jefferson's ferry lot in Albemarle County, see PJ Estate, 1759–1763, 1:12, 43.

Nineteen men subscribed to more than one lot: eleven bought 2 lots, two bought 3 lots, three bought 4, two bought 5, and one bought 6; they include PJ (4 lots), Fry (3), Cabell (6), Rose (4), Carter Braxton (burgess from King William County, 5), Arthur Hopkins (burgess from Goochland County, 5), and John Nicholas (2). I have included in the count of burgesses men who served also before or after the dates of Beverley Town. Curiously, Richard Randolph and William Stith were the only Randolphs on the list.

Some of the sales were carried out, as TJ recorded his father's four lots in his land roles; *FB*, 32, 127. How much was actually developed is unclear.

10. The Loyal Land Company's holdings were effectively negated by the Proclamation of 1763, by which the British government promised Native Americans that Europeans would not settle west of the mountains. Loyal members were still settling their corporate business into the nineteenth century. Archibald Henderson, "Dr. Thomas Walker and the Loyal Company of Virginia," *Proceedings of the American Antiquarian Society*, n.s., 41 (1931): 87, 89. For comments about whose settlement should be on these vast lands, see Delf Norona, "Joshua Fry's Report on the Back Settlements of Virginia (May 8, 1751)," *VMHB* 56 (1948): esp. 31–41.

11. Henderson, "Dr. Thomas Walker," 87, 89; PJ, Plat of Beverley, ViU.

12. For summaries of the controversies over the Virginia–North Carolina line, see Byrd, *Dividing Line*, xxviii–xxxvi. See also Charles Royster, *The Fabulous History of the Dismal Swamp Company: A Story of George Washington's Times* (New York: Knopf, 1999), 258–62.

13. For the intellectual claims of this body of work, see John Calhoun Stephens, *The Guardian*, ed. John Calhoun Stephens (Lexington: University Press of Kentucky, 1982), Introduction. See also Jack P. Greene, "The Concept of Virtue in Late Colonial British America," in Greene, *Imperatives, Behaviors, and Identities: Essays in Early American Cultural History* (Charlottesville: University of Virginia Press, 1992), esp. 210.

14. A fireback is a metal plate that fits in the back of a fireplace to radiate heat from the fire out into the room. Iron firebacks were often cast with the makers' or owners' initials or crest or other decorative element, such as the royal arms on this one. I have assumed that the GR at Shadwell was for George II, though potters used the same cipher during the reign of George I; see Ivor Noël Hume, *A Guide to Artifacts of Colonial America* (New York: Knopf, 1970), 276–86.

15. AlCWB, 2:43. For the Governor's Palace, see Graham Hood, *The Governor's Palace in Williamsburg: A Cultural Study* (Williamsburg, Va.: CWF, 1991), 80–97.

16. AlCWB, 1:9, 2:59–62, 124, 135, 181–84, 188–90, 284–86, 328, 376–77, 20, 26–27. Hood, *Governor's Palace.*

17. TJ to John Adams, June 11, 1812, in *Papers: Retirement Series,* 5:124–25.

18. David I. Bushnell Jr., "'The Indian Grave': A Monacan Site in Albemarle County, Virginia," *WMQ,* 1st ser., 23 (1914): 106–12; Bushnell, *The Five Monacan Towns in Virginia, 1607* (n.p.: n.p., 1930); Peter W. Houch, *Indian Island in Amherst County* (Lynchburg, Va.: Lynchburg Historical Research, 1984). Jeffrey L. Hantman, "Between Powhatan and Quirank: Reconstructing Monacan Culture and History in the Context of Jamestown," *American Anthropologist* 92 (1990): 676–90; William Jack Hranicky and Floyd Painter, *A Guide to the Identification of Virginia Projectile Points* (Courtland, Va.: Archeological Society of Virginia, 1993).

19. On the Indian settlement patterns in the region, see Robert Steven Grumet, *Historic Contact: Indian People and Colonists in Today's Northeastern United States in the Sixteenth through Eighteenth Centuries* (Norman: University of Oklahoma Press, 1995), 292. See also Gary H. Dunham, Debra L. Gold, and Jeffrey L. Hantman, "Collective Burial in Late Prehistoric Virginia: Excavation and Analysis of the Rapidan Mound," *American Antiquity* 68 (2003): 109–28. The ridge that bears the name Shadwell was thoroughly plowed throughout the nineteenth century, providing a mixed, or plowzone, context for all artifacts from the top layer of soil, from the surface to a depth of seven to twelve inches. While intrasite distribution studies incorporate plowzone material to help determine areas of activity, only features extending below the plowzone can have solid historic or prehistoric proveniences. Deeper features include cellars, postholes, cooking pits, hearth pits, and middens. The possibility exists that prehistoric settlement was superficial and plowed away, but there is no regional evidence to support this thesis. Excavations between the Shadwell ridge and the Rivanna River, on sites of a historic-period burial ground and of eighteenth- and nineteenth-century mills, recovered no Indian material. See Benjamin P. Ford, "'A Profitable and Creditable Establishment': Industrial Textile Manufacturing and Capitalist Relations of Production in the Antebellum Central Virginia Piedmont" (Ph.D. diss., University of Virginia, 1998); Susan A. Kern, "Report on Shadwell"; and Kern, "Report on a Burial Ground."

20. Classification of lithic material by Martin Gallivan, University of Virginia, report on file, Dec. 20, 1994, Monticello Archaeology Department, TJMF, 1994.

21. Bushnell, "Indian Grave," 106–16; Bushnell, *Five Monacan Towns;* Hantman, "Between Powhatan and Quirank," 676–90; Jeffrey L. Hantman and Michael J. Klein, "Middle and Late Woodland Archeology in Piedmont Virginia," in *Middle and Late Woodland Research in Virginia: A Synthesis,* ed. Theodore R. Reinhart and Mary Ellen N. Hodges (Richmond: Archeological Society of Virginia, 1992), 137–64. C. G. Holland, Sandra D. Spieden, and David van Riojen, "The Rapidan Mound Revisited: A Test Excavation of a Prehistoric Burial Mound," *Quarterly Bulletin of the Archeological Society*

of Virginia 38, no. 1 (1983): 1–42; L. Daniel Mouer, "A Review of the Ethnohistory and Archaeology of the Monacans," *Piedmont Archaeology: Recent Research and Results,* ed. J. Mark Wittkofski and Lyle E. Browning (N.p., 1983), 21–39.

22. Hantman, "Between Powhatan and Quirank."

23. Jefferson, *Notes,* 100.

24. Henry Timberlake, *Memoirs of Lieutenant Henry Timberlake* (1765), 14–15.

25. Timberlake, *Memoirs,* 31, 35.

26. "The Treaty of Logg's Town, 1752," *VMHB* 13 (1905): 154–55.

27. Nathanial Turk McCleskey, "Across the Great Divide: Frontiers of Settlement and Culture in Augusta County, Virginia, 1738–1770" (Ph.D. diss., William and Mary, 1990), 249–52, 285–86.

28. Peter Fontaine Jr. to John Fontaine, June 11, 1757, in Ann Maury, *Memoirs of a Huguenot Family* (1852; reprint ed., New York: Knickerbocker, G. P. Putnam's Sons, 1907), 366–67.

29. L&B, 13:160; *VG,* Aug. 16, 1751.

30. *VG,* Dixon and Hunter, May 30, 1777.

31. William Marshman, "Dayly Account of Expenses [at the Governor's Palace]," Mar. 3, Nov. 9, 1769, extract from Botetourt Materials, files of Research Department, CWF. *Maryland Gazette,* Aug. 30, 1759, June 16, 1757, Apr. 4, 1757, in *Executive Journals, Council of Colonial Virginia,* ed. H. R. McIlwaine et al., 6 vols. (Richmond: Virginia State Library, 1925–66), 6:38.

32. At this dinner in 1762 James Horrocks was master of the Grammar School. He became president of William and Mary in late 1764. *Executive Journals,* ed. McIlwaine, 5:413–14; Timberlake, *Memoirs,* 112. See also "Treaty of Loggs Town," 154–155.

33. Timberlake, *Memoirs,* 50. *Executive Journals,* 5:225, 415. William P. Palmer, ed., *Calendar of Virginia State Papers and other Manuscripts Preserved in the Capitol at Richmond* (1875; reprint ed., New York: Kraus, 1968), 1:249.

34. *Maryland Gazette,* June 16, 1757.

35. Palmer, ed., *Calendar of Virginia State Papers,* 1:244.

36. Palmer, ed., *Calendar of Virginia State Papers,* 1:244. From around 1746 to 1752, the Jefferson family resided at Tuckahoe, where PJ was guardian of the Randolph children. Members of the Jefferson family occasionally returned to Shadwell, and slaves still worked the fields.

37. TJ to John Adams, June 11, 1812, in *Papers: Retirement Series,* 5:124–25.

38. *VG,* Nov. 10, 1752; *VG,* Dixon and Hunter, May 30, 1777.

39. Dinwiddie to Peter Randolph and William Byrd, in *The Official Records of Robert Dinwiddie, Lieutenant-Governor of the Colony of Virginia, 1751–1758,* ed. R. A. Brock, Collections of the Virginia Historical Society, n.s., 3–4, 2 vols. (Richmond, Va.: Virginia Historical Society, 1883–84), 1:303–4; Timberlake, *Memoirs,* 126.

40. TJ to John Adams, June 11, 1812, in *Papers: Retirement Series,* 5:124–25.

41. AlCWB, 2:43–44, 88, 111, 267–68, 320, 346, 351–52.

42. Timberlake, *Memoirs*, 51.

43. Lewis, *Fairfax Line;* Palmer, ed., *Calendar of Virginia State Papers,* 1:239–41; Dinwiddie, letters to PJ, 9 July 1755, 5 May 1756, in Brock, ed., *Records of Dinwiddie,* 1:95–96, 405; Rose, *Diary,* 105.

44. Randolph, *Domestic Life,* 23–24. Unfortunately, the family history leaves open to speculation which friend was the focus of this regular circuit.

45. Rose, *Diary,* 32.

Chapter 7. The Intangible Legacies

1. Daniel Blake Smith, *Inside the Great House: Planter Family Life in Eighteenth-Century Chesapeake Society* (Ithaca, NY: Cornell University Press, 1980), 226.

2. *MB,* 251. Jane Jr.'s slave Betty, daughter of Patt, wound up with TJ. Patt and her son Sancho may have gone to RJ. *FB,* 6. The remnants of Elizabeth's estate represent £200 and Elizabeth's portion of sister Jane's estate (£28 3s. 7 1/4d.) plus interest held by John Bolling, Charles Lewis, and Nicholas Lewis, a friend who helped administer TJ's Monticello accounts while TJ was in France. TJ to RJ, Feb. 28, 1790, in *Brother,* 15–16; *MB,* 23.

3. PJ Estate, 1757–1765, 1. TJ kept Fee Books for his siblings within what are now called collectively his Memorandum Books. *MB,* see index for each sibling. *FB,* 8–9; *MB,* 300, 346, 462.

4. AICWB, 2:32–34. TJ to Thomas Walker, Jan. 18, 1790, *Papers,* 112–14. TJ to John Nicholas Sr., Jan. 20, 1790, *Papers,* 115–16. TJ's handling of the debts of his parents and in-laws and his relationship with Thomas Walker is explored by Steven Harold Hochman, "Thomas Jefferson: A Personal Financial Biography" (Ph.D. diss., University of Virginia, 1987, esp. 166–70.

5. AICWB, 2:32–34.

6. Anna Scott and RJ did not receive the slaves from JJ's will, however. JJ wrote her will sometime between January 1, 1772, and September 29, 1773, the date she deeded those same slaves and others to TJ in payment of a debt. *FB,* 8–9; *MB,* 346. Elizabeth died before her mother and so did not receive her mother's legacy either. AICDB, 4:234. Fany had no immediate relation to Nan, who had gone with Mary in 1760, and I can find no special event in Mary's life that warranted an unusually large gift, unless it was the birth of Jane Bolling, a namesake for JJ, in 1766. JJ's namesake Jane Carr was four years old when the gift of Lucy was made. Rachel was born about 1768, making her two in 1770. The deed may have transferred ownership without actually changing Rachel's location, although Rachel's mother Little Sall died in 1774. *MB,* 177.

7. The average age at marriage for women during the second half of the eighteenth century was 22.2 years. The range for men was from about 25 to 28 years of age, so TJ was on the outside edge of that range. Allan Kulikoff, *Tobacco and Slaves: The Development of*

Southern Cultures in the Chesapeake, 1680–1800 (Chapel Hill: University of North Carolina Press, 1986), 50, 55, 60, esp. table 2.

8. AlCWB, 2:227, 233.

9. These distant ranges are estimates using modern map distances overlaid on the 1751 Fry and Jefferson Map, not accounting for actual distance by foot or road. Kulikoff found the two-mile radius determined the most likely marriage pool among freeholders in Prince George, Maryland, *Tobacco and Slaves,* 253.

In using such words as "successful" to talk about these marriages, I am evaluating the partnerships formed with other families to examine the strategies for preserving and maintaining the Jefferson's social standing. I am thus gauging the social "value" of the partnership, not whether the pairing meant a companionate mate for the individual, nor whether the mate was free of violent or drunken affliction (as we shall see below), nor any of the other criteria that might make a marriage good or bad from other standpoints. In looking at the failure of a strategy, I am certainly not implying that the marriages were not good ones in the sense that the people were not moral or worthy.

10. The Wayles and Skelton family connections are many-tiered. Martha Wayles (Skelton) Jefferson was the daughter of John Wayles and Martha Eppes. Wayles married twice more, the third time to Elizabeth Lomax Skelton (daughter of Lunsford Lomax, PJ's surveying colleague), whose first husband was Reuben Skelton. Martha Wayles married Bathurst Skelton, her second stepmother's brother-in-law. Wayles was an executor of Peter Randolph's estate and so was close friends with one of JJ's first cousins. PJ and Peter Randolph were friends, and PJ had a professional connection to Martha's second stepmother through the Lomax family and to her in-laws, so he likely knew John Wayles.

11. PJ Estate, 1728–1758, 9, 12, 17; PJ Estate, 1759–1763, 8. James Skelton and Isham Randolph served as magistrates together in Goochland County. "How a Murder Was Punished in Colonial Days," *Tylers Quarterly Historical and Genealogical Magazine* 8 (1927), reprint 1967, 61.

Bolling served Henrico County, 1742–49, and Chesterfield County, 1752–57. In fact, the Bolling-Jefferson association extends past the generation that includes Peter and John Sr. to TJ, John Bolling, and William Kennon, who all mustered with William Byrd in 1711. Wright and Tinling, *Secret Diary of William Byrd,* 410, 414, 486. Marks was a witness to Woodson's will (AlCWB, 2:374) and had occasional business with Monticello during 1774 and years following (*MB,* 376, 378ff).

12. Major John Bolling and his wife, Mary Kennon, lived at Cobbs in Goochland County, where he had been a burgess in 1727–28. Bolling Sr. died in 1757 and left his heirs 40,000 acres of land. Rose, *Diary,* 279. *St. James Northam Parish Vestry Book, 1744–1850, Goochland County, Virginia,* abstracted by William Lindsay Hopkins (1987; reprint ed., Athens, Ga.: Iberian, 1993), 9. PJ Estate, 1757–1765, 3. On botanical interests, see *GB,* 22, 27–28, 637; and *MB,* 415. On vestry duty, see *Douglas Register,* 8.

13. Almost every TJ biographer includes a brief biography of Dabney Carr, who was so important to the young Jefferson. See Malone, *Jefferson*, vol. 1; or Marie Kimball, *Jefferson: The Road to Glory, 1743 to 1776* (New York: Coward-McCann, 1943), esp. 45–47.

14. For other historians on TJ's courtship of Rebecca Burwell and Martha Wayles Skelton, see Malone, *Jefferson*, 1:80–86, 155–60; and Kimball, *Road to Glory*, 66–72, 174–77.

TJ inherited extensive land holdings, 135 slaves, and substantial debt from John Wayles; see Lucia Stanton, *Free Some Day: The African-American Families of Monticello* (Charlottesville, Va.: Thomas Jefferson Foundation, 2000). Malone, *Jefferson*, 1:161–65, 441–45. On the inherited debt, see Steven Harold Hochman, "Thomas Jefferson: A Personal Financial Biography" (Ph.D. diss., University of Virginia, 1987). TJ also paid the same fee to the rector of Westover Parish, the indebted William Davis, who was legally entitled to payment for a marriage in his jurisdiction. Recent scholarship suggests that Davis was not at The Forest and played no role in TJ's marriage. *MB*, 285, n. 285.

15. *MB*, 144, 438. Kulikoff reports that first-cousin marriage in Prince George County, Maryland, exceeded one half of all consanguineous marriages, which themselves counted for almost one third of all marriages in the period, 1760–90. *Tobacco and Slaves*, 252–55, esp. table 29.

16. On the Marks family, see Woods, *Albemarle*, 364, 365, 375, 379. Some of TJ's letters suggest that Hastings Marks's brothers were not viewed as upstanding citizens, or else they came to occupy a political camp opposite that of TJ's, but TJ cast no aspersions on Hastings. See, e.g., TJ to David Jameson, Apr. 16, 1781, in *Papers*, 5:468–69. TJ to Mrs. Anna Scott Marks, July 12, 1788, and TJ to Hastings Marks, July 12, 1788, both in Randolph, *Domestic Life*, 135–36.

17. Martha J. Carr to TJ, Dec. 3, 1787, in *Papers*, 15:639–40; also Boynton Merrill, *Jefferson's Nephews: A Frontier Tragedy* (Princeton, N.J.: Princeton University Press, 1976), 77.

18. TJ to Mary Jefferson Bolling, July 23, 1787, in *Papers*, 15:612–13. Mary Jefferson Eppes to TJ, Dec. 8, 1797, and TJ to Mary Jefferson Eppes, Jan. 7, 1798, in *Family Letters*, 149–50, 151–53. TJ to John Page, Feb. 21, 1770, in *Papers*, 1:36.

19. TJ to Mary Jefferson Bolling, July 23, 1787, in *Papers*, 11:612–13. This was some years before the letters noting John Bolling's drinking excesses and the problems that caused.

20. In tracing the stabilization of the Chesapeake family after the precarious mortality rates of the seventeenth century, Daniel Blake Smith notes that "an elaborate cousinry developed, which offered important marital, economic, and—at least among the elite—political opportunities." Smith, however, presents evidence that men rarely had strong ties to their in-laws. *Inside the Great House*, see chap. 5, quotation 177, also 188, 190, 196.

21. Ellen Wayles Coolidge Letterbook, 1856–1858, ViU 9090, 38–584. "Extracts from the Diary of John Hartwell Cocke, of Bremo, Fluvanna County, Virginia," as reprinted in *GB*, 637; *GB*, 41.

22. TJ to Mary Jefferson Bolling, July 23, 1787, in *Papers*, 11:612–13. TJ to RJ, Aug. 12, 1807, and RJ to TJ, May 26, June 21, 1813, Apr. 2, 1815, all in *Brother*, 21, 42–43, 46, 57. TJ landed in Norfolk on November 23 and arrived at Monticello on December 23. *MB*, n. 748.

23. TJ to RJ, Jan. 11, 1789, in *Brother*, 13–14. See Mary Jefferson Eppes to TJ, Mar. 20, May 27, 1798; and Ellen Wayles Randolph to TJ, Jan. 8, 1808, all in *Family Letters*, 157–58, 163–64, 320–21.

24. Mary Jefferson to TJ, c. May 22, 1786, and MJR to TJ, Jan. 1, 1796, both in *Family Letters*, 31, 135. Elizabeth Wayles Eppes to TJ, Jan. 6, 1788, in *Papers*, 12:497–98.

25. AICDB 4, 234. *MB*, 251. TJ to David Jameson, Apr. 16, 1781, in *Papers*, 5:468–69. Malone, *Jefferson*, 1:155.

26. TJ charged most purchases for his siblings to their father's estate. *MB*, 141, 352, 392, 480, 524.

TJ to John Page, Dec. 25, 1762, TJ to Anna Scott Jefferson, May 9, 1784, and TJ to Martha Jefferson Carr, Nov. 11, 1784, all in *Papers*, 1:3–6, 7:238, 500.

27. Some letters between TJ and his siblings are published in the *Papers of Thomas Jefferson* series. Others have not been found but were recorded in TJ's "Summary Journal of Letters." Letters between the brothers are included in *Brother*. Still others are in manuscript collections, such as the Papers of the Carr and Terrell Families, 1735–1894, at ViU. *MB*, 1020, 1272–73. Mary Jefferson Eppes to TJ, May 27, 1798, in *Family Letters*, 163–64.

28. Martha Jefferson Carr's letters are mostly in the Papers of the Carr and Terrell Families, ViU. Most historians who have looked at TJ's family focus on only his wife and daughters, and sometimes on his parents. Jan Lewis, "'The Blessings of Domestic Society': Thomas Jefferson's Family and the Transformation of American Politics," in *Jeffersonian Legacies,* ed. Peter S. Onuf (Charlottesville: University of Virginia Press, 1993), 109–46. Martha Jefferson Carr to TJ, Dec. 15, 1792, in *Papers*, 24:744. MJR to TJ, Feb. 27, 1793, and Anne Cary Randolph to TJ, Jan. 22, 1808, in *Family Letters*, 112–13, 323–24. Merrill, *Jefferson's Nephews*, 54.

29. TJ's own daughters did not seem to show any animosity toward their cousins who joined in their household. MJR's son Thomas Jefferson Randolph, however, created the thesis that the Carr brothers were among the candidates for having fathered Sally Heming's children. Lucia Stanton, "The Other End of the Telescope: Jefferson through the Eyes of His Slaves," *WMQ*, 3rd ser., 57 (2000): 140. Randall, *Jefferson*, 3:382, 384. TJ to RJ, May 25, 1813, in *Brother*, 35–37. TJ to Overton Carr, Mar. 16, 1782, and Peter Carr to TJ, Dec. 10, 1787, Mar. 18, 1788, all in *Papers*, 6:166–67, 12:414, 677. Malone, *Jefferson*, 1:161. MJR did not specify which Randolph trait or which Randolph line worried her; *Family Letters*, 360.

30. Anne Cary Randolph to TJ, Jan. 22, 1808, in *Family Letters*, 323–24. *GB*, 22, 637; *MB*, 415; also *Brother*.

31. For details of Carr's library, see William S. Simpson Jr., "A Comparison of the Libraries of Seven Colonial Virginias, 1754–1789," *Journal of Library History* 9, no. 1 (1974):

54–65; W. G. Stanard, "Library of Dabney Carr, 1773, with a Notice of the Carr Family," *Virginia Historical Magazine* 2, no. 2 (1894): 221–26; Douglas L. Wilson, *Jefferson's Books* (Lynchburg, Va.: TJMF, 1997), esp. 23.

TJ to Francis Eppes, Jan. 4, 1783, TJ to Alexander Donald, Sept. 17, 1787, and Peter Carr to TJ, Dec. 10, 1787, all in *Papers*, 6:219–20, 12:132–34, 414.

32. *Papers*, 1:144–49, 586–89, 664–68, 2:128–30. Nominee for clergy was Jefferson family friend and patriot the Reverend Charles Clay. "Subscription to Support a Clergyman in Charlottesville," and Bolling Stark to TJ, Apr. 30, 1781, both in *Papers*, 2:6–9, 5:579–80. (Bolling Stark was burgess from Dinwiddie County.)

33. TJ to RJ, Jan. 11, 1789, in *Brother*, 13–14. *Papers*, 6:219–20.

34. Boynton Merrill's study *Jefferson's Nephews* details the dramatic demise of the Charles Lewis family; see 74–75, 89, 183–84, quotation 184–85.

35. I give the number of slaves as about two dozen each because many of PJ's slaves died or bore children between the 1757 inventory date and when they became property of TJ (1764) or RJ (1776). There is no exact count of how many slaves each son received on reaching majority. Of course, some of TJ's slaves stayed at Shadwell, where they had been.

36. Lisa A. Francavilla and Ann M. Lucas, eds., *Thomas Jefferson's Granddaughter in Victorian England: The Travel Diary of Ellen Wayles Coolidge, 1838–1839* (forthcoming 2012), entry for July 9, 1838.

37. Sawney, the servant bequeathed from PJ, must have died before 1765, when TJ first recorded Jupiter as his attendant. Jefferson, "Memoirs."

38. See TJ visits, e.g., *MB*, 151, 257, 285, 479.

39. Nan's siblings were Lucinda, and possibly Caesar and Little Sall. Her brother Simon was born in 1765.

Peter left Shadwell as part of RJ's retinue. Nan's mother, Sall, was among the 11 slaves that JJ claimed. Myrtilla, Fany's mother, was among those kept "to not divide the children." AlCWB, 2:32–34; PJ Estate, 1757–1765, 3; PJ Estate, 1759–1763, 10.

40. The immediate family of the other Jefferson daughters' slaves is unclear, but they all left behind close friends and relatives, if not immediate family, when they left Shadwell. Quotation from TJ to RJ, Sept. 25, 1792, in *Brother*, 17. Squire's mother may have been PJ's slave Bellinda, in which case her other children Val, Lucy, Charlotte, Minerva, Sarah, Iris, and Jeremiah were among his family.

41. Netti Schreiner-Yantis and Florene Love, *The Personal Property Tax Lists for the Year 1788 for Chesterfield County, Virginia* (Springfield, Va.: Genealogical Books in Print, 1987). *FB*, 17; *MB*, 177, 957 n. 93, 1296, 1318, 1325, 1329.

42. AlCWB, 2:45; *FB*, 6, 29. Another slave named Robin also ran away from TJ's Shadwell, but he had not been PJ's slave. On other TJ slaves who joined the British, see Stanton, *Free Some Day*, 52–57; and Cassandra Pybus, "Jefferson's Faulty Math: The Question of Slave Defections in the American Revolution," *WMQ*, 3rd ser., 62 (2005): 243–64.

43. People dug into the ground to build, cook, and store things during the home quarter period (1737–76), but the slaves who lived at Shadwell during the quarter farm phase (1776–99) left almost no evidence of activity that penetrated below the ground's surface. Although the presence of only early artifacts in subsurface features does not rule out their use or deposition during the quarter farm period, only a single feature dates solely to a later period. Ceramics dating to the quarter farm and nineteenth-century tenant farm periods occur across the site in plowzone layers.

44. *FB*, 30, 51.

45. The book has inscriptions by four generations of Jeffersons and contains the family history of five generations, from Isham Randolph, born in 1687, to Septimia Randolph Meikleham, who died in 1887. TJ rebound four items from his parents' collection—his mother's Bible and the page his father wrote, a family Prayer Book, and a Concordance, into a single volume that he kept at Monticello. "Jefferson Family, Bible."

46. Jane Rogers Randolph died sometime between December 5, 1760, the date of her will, and July 21, 1761, the date her will was proved in Goochland County court. Goochland County Deed Book 8, 1759–1765, 168–169. "Jefferson Family, Bible."

47. The date of Elizabeth's death remains in question, but it certainly was not January 1773. RJ is perhaps the source of his brother's "error," noted by historians, of the discrepancy of Elizabeth Jefferson's date of death. In his memorandum books, TJ reported that his sister "was found" on February 24, 1774, but his Prayer Book has the January 1, 1773, date because he copied it from his brother's notation in their mother's Bible following his acquisition of the book after her death in 1776; *MB*, 370. (Malone noted the discrepancy, *Jefferson*, 6:430–31.) Perhaps the January 1 date is correct and RJ meant to write the year as "1774" but the turn of the year caused him to miswrite it. JJ wrote her will that included a bequest to Elizabeth sometime between January 1, 1772, and September 29, 1773, when she deeded slaves, including Little Sall, to her son TJ. So Little Sall and Elizabeth were still alive in the fall of 1773. The slaves that JJ deeded to TJ in September 1773 are all listed in the record he began January 14, 1774, as his Farm Book, except for Little Sall; *FB*, 7. This could be because Elizabeth and Little Sall disappeared in January and their bodies were not found until late February, or it could indicate that TJ respected his sister's need for Little Sall and thus did not include her in his Farm Book list. The fact that Elizabeth was not buried until March 7, 1774, twelve days after she was "found," may indicate unusual circumstances. Perhaps she and Little Sall had been missing for two months or perhaps the ground was too frozen or the weather bad enough to prevent a burial. TJ recorded a flood on March 6, "higher than the one which carried N.Lewis's bridge away"; *MB*, 370.

48. "Jefferson Family, Bible."

49. TJ recorded Martha's birth on or after September 27, 1772 (1:00 a.m.). TJ did not record the day of the month or the time of death of Jane, who may have died while he was in Philadelphia in 1775. For Lucy, who died in 1784 while he was in France, he recorded only the year. "Jefferson's Prayer Book," call number A1752.C87, ViU. This has also been

published in facsimile as John Cook Wyllie, *Thomas Jefferson's Prayer Book* (Charlottesville, Va.: Meriden Gravure, 1952).

50. "Jefferson's Prayer Book." TJ never recorded dates of his brother RJ's two marriages in 1780 or 1809, however.

51. "Jefferson Family, Bible." TJ had the Prayer Book and his mother's Bible rebound together. RJ turned fifteen the October following the Shadwell fire about the time for lessons in English grammar, according to Philip Fithian. Hunter Dickinson Farish, ed., *Journal and Letters of Philip Vickers Fithian: A Plantation Tutor of the Old Dominion, 1773–1774* (1957; reprint ed., Charlottesville: University of Virginia Press, 1968), 26. I thank Lou Powers for suggesting this as a source for determining the education levels of children at various ages.

52. Randall, *Jefferson,* 1:17. Malone noted that "Jefferson's statement . . . is approximately correct if applied to the Rivanna district; but the date which he give, about 1737, seems too early"; *Jefferson,* 1:18, n. 39. October 3 to June 27 is a statistically perfect gestation period of 267 days. See Fraser Neiman, "Coincidence or Causal Connection? The Relationship between Thomas Jefferson's Visits to Monticello and Sally Hemings's Conceptions," *WMQ,* 3rd ser., 57 (2000): 201. See also PJ Estate, 1728–1758.

53. "Jefferson Family, Bible."

54. See *MB,* 245–50; also cited in *GB,* 25–27. The Victorian sentiment of Sarah Randolph overshadows TJ's messages about his sister, but the heart of the stories passed on nonetheless. Randolph, *Domestic Life,* 34, 38–39.

55. *MB,* 246. Limited archaeological research on the burial ground at Shadwell revealed a number of unmarked nineteenth-century burials, others marked with fieldstones, and a single early twentieth-century burial with fieldstones marking the head and foot. There was evidence of earlier use, but those burials were not excavated. See Kern, "Report on a Burial Ground."

56. PJ's funeral embodied the traditions of public funerals in Virginia. The Reverend Peter Fontaine, who also died in 1757, requested the opposite. He wrote that his "will and desire is to have no public funeral, but that my corpse may be accompanied to the ground by a few of my nearest neighbors, that no liquors be given to make any of the company drunk," which he called "the great scandal of the Christian religion." He requested that "none of my family go in mourning for me." Peter Fontaine, "Extracts from His Last Will," in Fontaine, *Memoirs of a Huguenot Family,* 354–55, *VMHB* 14 (1907): 226.

On Jane Jr.'s epitaph, see *MB,* 245–50, quotation translation, 247 and note. Douglas Wilson notes the likeness of TJ's verse to one by Shenstone. Although TJ did not include Shenstone in his Literary Commonplace Book (LCB), this book was his source for other epitaphs. See LCB, 9, 12, 12n.

57. The story of TJ disinterring his friend's body in honor of their "boyhood pact" is repeated in the earliest TJ biographies. *GB,* 40–43; Randall, *Jefferson,* 1:83; Randolph, *Domestic Life,* 45. TJ's draft cites Mallet's *Excursion* as the source for Carr's inscription; as

reprinted in Randolph, *Domestic Life*, 47. For sources of the verses TJ chose for memorials, see LCB, 9, 132–33.

58. As reprinted in Randolph, *Domestic Life*, 47.

59. *MB*, 370–71; *Douglas Register*, 168. Wingfield was the brother-in-law of Martha's and Thomas's sister Lucy and brother Randolph, married to Elizabeth Lewis, sister of Charles Lilburne Lewis and Anne Jefferson Lewis. Wingfield also officiated at the burial of family friend William Mortimer Harrison, who drowned in the Rivanna River in 1812 and was buried at Monticello. *MB*, 1279. Malone, *Jefferson*, 1:498.

60. TJ to Wm. Randolph. C., June 1776, in *MB*, 415, 415, n. 76. In his Farm Book, TJ certainly distinguished between the various farms and specified Shadwell and other outlying fields as distinct from Monticello in his census of slaves and crop rolls. Perhaps this identity was not as clear in TJ's mind in 1773, when he used "Charlottesville" as the place of Dabney Carr's death. See Carr's epitaph, above.

There are no other details about JJ's funeral. Clay used a general funeral sermon during the years 1775 and 1776 at her funeral and at the services of least seven others. The text of the sermon and those for whom he used it he listed in his notebook, now in the possession of the Virginia Historical Society (VHS). The sermon offers no personal details about JJ (or any of the others), only Clay's take on scriptural references to Judgment Day, Clay Family, Papers, 1769–1951 (bulk 1769–1869), Section 2, VHS. The half-hour is roughly the time taken to read aloud the sermon, not accounting for whatever dramatic embellishments Clay may have added. On April 11, 1777, TJ recorded: "Pd. Mr. Clay for preaching my mother's funeral sermon 40/"; *MB*, 444. The mourning ring TJ purchased in Philadelphia later that year may have been to commemorate Jane; *MB*, 422 (I thank Bill Barker for this reference).

61. For the relationships of the Wayles and Eppes families, see Annette Gordon-Reed, *The Hemingses of Monticello: An American Family* (New York: Norton, 2008), chap. 1. Malone, *Jefferson*, 1:app. I.D., 432–33. Randolph, *Domestic Life*, 63. On Martha Jefferson's death, see Gordon-Reed, *Hemingses of Monticello*, esp. 141–46. Edmund Bacon, a Monticello overseer, reported hearing who was in the room. Other house servants may also have been there. Bacon himself was not yet employed by TJ when Martha Jefferson died; see Bear, ed., *Jefferson at Monticello*, 99–100.

62. TJ to RJ, Sept. 6, 1811, and RJ to TJ, Oct. 6, 1811, both in *Brother*, 26, 27. "Inscriptions on Gravestones in the Monticello Graveyard," in *Collected Papers to Commemorate Fifty Years of the Monticello Association of the Descendants of Thomas Jefferson*, ed. George Green Shackelford (Princeton, N.J.: Monticello Association, 1965), 253. In contrast, the inscriptions on his own daughters' gravestones included the names of their parents, Thomas Jefferson and Martha Wayles, and the dates they married their husbands. Martha's also included that she died at Edgehill, her home. "Inscriptions on Gravestones," 252.

63. TJ to RJ, Jan. 14, 1812, in *Brother*, 28. Randall, *Jefferson*, 1:666. "Jefferson Family, Bible."

64. Martha C. Lewis, Lucy B. Lewis, and Ann M. Lewis (written by Charles L. Lewis) to TJ, Sept. 17, 1810, in Merrill, *Jefferson's Nephews*, 218. Mayo and Bear speculate

that RJ was buried at Snowdon, although there is no marked burial there; *Brother*, Introduction, 5.

65. Randolph, *Domestic Life*, 431. "Inscriptions on Gravestones," 252.

66. *Family Letters*, 479–80. Quotation is Garrett to Mrs. Alexander Garrett, July 4, 1826, in *Family Letters*, 480. Malone, *Jefferson*, 6:498.

Chapter 8. Thomas Jefferson's Shadwell Stories

1. Peter Onuf, "The Scholars' Jefferson," *WMQ*, 3rd ser., 50 (1993): 686.

2. *Brother*.

3. Randall, *Jefferson*, 1:16, n. 1.

4. Autobiography, 3.

5. Jay Fliegelman, *Declaring Independence: Jefferson, Natural Language, and the Culture of Performance* (Stanford, Calif.: Stanford University Press, 1993), 99.

6. Randolph, *Domestic Life*, 23–24.

7. TJ to Thomas Jefferson Randolph, Nov. 24, 1808, in Merrill D. Peterson, ed., *The Portable Thomas Jefferson* (New York: Penguin, 1975) 511.

8. *MB*, 246; TJ to Mary Jefferson Eppes, Feb. 12, 1800, in *Family Letters*, 185; TJ to Thomas Jefferson Randolph, Feb. 4, 1800, DLC; *MB*, 376–77.

9. Joshua D. Rothman, *Notorious in the Neighborhood: Sex and Families across the Color Line in Virginia, 1787–1861* (Chapel Hill: University of North Carolina Press, 2003).

10. Jefferson, *Notes*, 162.

11. Jefferson, *Notes*, 162. Recent historians who offer unyielding critiques of the slaveholder Jefferson on an international stage include Paul Finkelman, "Jefferson and Slavery: 'Treason against the Hopes of the World,'" in *Jeffersonian Legacies*, ed. Peter S. Onuf (Charlottesville: University of Virginia Press, 1993), 181–221; Annette Gordon-Reed, *The Hemingses of Monticello: An American Family* (New York: Norton, 2008), see esp. chaps. 8, 11; and Garry Wills, *"Negro President:" Jefferson and the Slave Power* (Boston: Houghton Mifflin, 2005), xi–xv.

12. TJ to Robert Skipwith, Aug. 3, 1771, *Papers*, 1:78; Rhys Isaac, "The First Monticello," in *Jeffersonian Legacies*, ed. Onuf, 79.

13. Autobiography, 3; Malone, *Jefferson*, 6:24.

14. Annette Gordon-Reed, *Thomas Jefferson and Sally Hemings* (Charlottesville: University of Virginia Press, 1997), esp. xv–xvii, 210–23.

15. Ronald L. Hatzenbuehler explores how TJ's Garden Book entries about peas show his embrace of systematic observation and Enlightenment learning as evidence of his gentry education—the garden book is that. But the garden book also can only exist because the entire apparatus of the plantation economy and gentry social system already hold up the young Jefferson. Hatzenbuehler, *"I Tremble for My Country": Thomas Jefferson and the Virginia Gentry* (Gainesville: University Press of Florida, 2006), 13–17.

16. TJ to John Adams, June 11, 1812, in *Papers: Retirement Series*, 5:124–25.

17. Jefferson, *Notes*, 163; Edmund Morgan, *American Slavery, American Freedom: The Ordeal of Colonial Virginia* (New York: Norton, 1975), chap. 18; Herbert E. Sloan, *Principle and Interest: Thomas Jefferson and the Problem of Debt* (New York: Oxford University Press, 1995), esp. 91–101; Francis D. Cogliano, *Thomas Jefferson: Reputation and Legacy* (Charlottesville: University of Virginia Press, 2006), esp. chap. 7.

Index

Page numbers in italics refer to illustrations.

—horses (*continued*)

315n35; slave carried TJ on horseback, 26, 100–101; slave skills with, 99, 106–7, 179, 202, 223; stray, 152

—livestock: cattle, 21, 63, 64, 67, 139, 185; pig(s) or hog(s), 21, 63, 64, 139, 152, 185, 308n5; poultry, 61, 82, 84–86, 131, 137, 179; sheep, 21, 59, 64, 67; sheepdog, 220

—wild, 175, 192, 227, 251; bear, 190, 197; deer, 61; fish, 61, 80, 82, 86–87, *87*, 88; game, 61, 80, 82, 138; hunting, 17, 88, 137–38; oyster, 61, 138; wolf bounties, 176

—*See also* foodways; slave life

archaeology

—field quarters, method: change in site use, 340n43; excavations, 1950s, 4, 26, 309–10n10; feature, definition, 309–10n10; map of Jefferson land and quarter sites, *133*; plowzone, 229, 305n46, 307n5, 309n8, 333n19, 340n43

—home quarter, artifacts: agricultural implements, *128*; beads, *105*; buttons and scissors, *98*; colonoware, 92–94, *93*, 103, 188, 313n25; cooking pit, *87*; field quarter, 138; gaming pieces, *105*; grindstone, *135*; home quarter training, 81–82, 108, 113–14; hunting and fishing, *88*; iron pots, *81*; knife and fork, *81*; marble, *104*; Native American finds, *187*, 192; ointment pots, *91*; pencil, *104*; pipe blank, *102*; slaves and consumer goods: alternate use, *105*; surface distribution medicinal, tobacco, *104*; utilitarian wares, 87–88

—home quarter, buildings and landscape: kitchen and quarter site, 79; map of Jefferson land and quarter sites, *133*; Shadwell landscape, *20–21, 23*; Shadwell survey, *20–21*; site plan, *76*, 309–10nn9–10; surface distribution, 1737–1820s, *228*

—issues and methods: ceramic types as chronological evidence, 64–66, *65, 66, 228*; change in site use, 340n43; excavations, 1950s, 4, 26, 309–10n10;

fashion cycle of consumer goods, 89–90, 299–300n36; feature, definition, 309–10n10; lifecycle purchases, 312n20; plowzone, 229, 305n46, 307n5, 309n8, 333n19, 340n43

—house of JJ, 64–68; artifact distribution, 66; cellars, 65; new creamware, 67, 306n49; surface distribution, 1737–1820s, *228*

—Jefferson house, artifacts: coin scale, 153; dining room, 30–31; fireback, *182*; knife and fork, *81*; Native American finds, *187*, 192; parlor, 65–68; sets or services of wares, 296nn20–21; silver teaspoon, *31*; Spanish real, *153*; stoneware GR jug, *181*; surface distribution, 1737–1820s, *228*; surveying and drafting instruments, 25; tablewares as indicators of slave cook's skills, 81–82, 308n6

—Jefferson house, buildings and landscape: artifact distribution post-1770s house, 66; chambers, 38; dining room, 29–32; Jefferson house, 6, 28, *29*, 65, 290–91n2; office, 33–38; parlor, 32–33; Shadwell landscape, *20–21, 22–26, 23*, 229; Shadwell survey, *20–21*

—kitchen, artifacts: beads, *105*; buttons and scissors, *98*; chamber pot, 79; colonoware, 92–94, *93*, 103, 188, 313n25; gaming pieces, *105*; hunting and fishing, *88*; inventory, 269; iron pots, *81*; knife and fork, *81*; Native American finds, *187*, 192; ointment pots, *91*; pencil, *104*; surface distribution medicinal, tobacco, *104*; surface distribution, 1737–1820s, *228*

—kitchen, buildings and landscape: archaeological site plan, 76; kitchen and quarter site, 79; map of Jefferson land and quarter sites, *133*; Shadwell landscape, *20–21, 23*; Shadwell survey, *20–21*; surface distribution, 1737–1820s, *228*; TJ duplex, *137*

Augusta County, 191, 194

Austenaco. *See* Outassetè

Bacon, Edmund, 342n61
Ballow, Susanna, 56
Baptist Church, 167, 321n18, 330n37.
    See also "Petition of Dissenters"
Bartram, John, 19–20, 58, 62, 164, 305
"Batchelour's Dinner," 202
Bates, Isaac, 141, 325
Bath Parish, 164
beer, 34, 319n12; bottles for storing and
    brewing, 60; brewing, 21, 34, 60, 80,
    262, 297n22
Bell, John, 57–58, 152, 159
beverages. *See* beer; cider; coffee; food:
    sugar; persico; punch; rum; tea; wine
Beverley, Robert, 202
Beverley Town (also Westham), 159, 163,
    166, *173*, 176–79, *177*, 210, 331n8, 332n9.
    See also Westham
Bible, 230–33. *See also* books
Bickham, George, 201
Big Island (Holston), 190
Biswell, John, 99, 151, 153–55, 327, 328
Bolling, John Jr., 71, 210–11, 220–22, 241.
    See also Jefferson, Mary (TJ's sister)
Bolling, Major John Sr., 210, 336nn11–12
Bolling, Mary Kennon, 336n12
books: authors, 163, 167–68; furniture,
    27, 36, 38; JJ's, 54–55, 56, 60, 230–33,
    231, 232, 238, 297n22; Jane Jr.'s, 51;
    library, 33–38, 63–64, 180, 261,
    262–63, 297–99nn24–33; lost to fire,
    26, 294n11; owned by women, 33, 56;
    PJ to TJ, 43, 233, *234;* as repositories
    for history, 230–40, 340n43, 341n51;
    shared, 37, 211, 220; sizes, 35–36; TJ,
    52, 233–39, *234, 235, 237*, 245. *See also*
    Jefferson, Thomas: at Shadwell
Borchardt, Susan, 303
Bourke, John, 166
Braxton, Carter, 332
breast-feeding. *See* childbearing and
    health
Breen, Timothy H., 148, 169
Brooke, Robert Jr., 172
Brooke, Robert Sr., 172

Buckingham County, 142, 325n38
Buck Island. *See* Lewis, Charles Lilburne
burgess. *See* House of Burgesses
Burstein, Andrew, 4
Burwell, Rebecca, 337n14
Byrd, William, II, 17, 163, 172, *174, 175*,
    176, 293, 331, 336
Byrd's Warehouse, 139, 156. *See also*
    Westham

Cabell, Nicholas, 40, 155
Cabell, William, 163, 178, 332
Callender, James, 328
Caroline County, 178
carpenters, 99–100, 106–7, 129, 136–37.
    See also Biswell, John; Cobbs, Samuel;
    Dunkin, George; Dunkin, John;
    "Negro carpenter" (Charles Lewis's);
    slaves owned by Jeffersons at Shadwell:
    Jupiter, Samson, Sandy; West, Francis;
    Whilkill, Francis
Carr, Dabney, 52, 71, 165, 208, 210, 211,
    214, 215, 217, 220, 251; death and burial,
    240–46
Carr, Lois, 156, 296, 299, 300
Carter, John, 327
Carter, Mrs. Robert (Frances Anne
    Tasker), 48
Carter's Grove, 310
Cary, Archibald, 52, 161
Castle Hill (Thomas Walker's), 194, *195*
Charles City County, 17, 191, 208, 212, 293
Charlottesville, 242, 302, 312, 342
Cherokees, 40,183–86, 190–99, *195*,
    200–201, *201*, 251. *See also* Indians
Chesterfield County, 302n15, 315n11,
    327n4, 336n11
Chickahominy River, 194, *195*
childbearing and health, 47–49; elite
    women using wet nurses, 48–49;
    natural fertility population, 48,
    318–19n9; nurse, slave or wench, 48;
    patterns of conception: JJ, 265, 272,
    273; patterns of conception: slave
    women, 123–25, 272; Sall, 273

chocolate pot, 82

Chote, 190

Church of England. *See* Anglican Church

cider, 60, 140, 198

Clark, William, 189

Clarke, Charles, 101, 125, 319n12

clothing and dress, gentry, 223; druggett clothes, 19; hair curls, 111, 299; hair dressing, 223; Jane Jr., 51–52, 55–58, 208, 296n21; JJ, 56; PJ, 55, 281; Jeffersons, 8, 9, 33, 42, 223; TJ advice on, 59; wigs, 58, 101, 111, 299

clothing and dress, slave, 57, 95–98, *98*, 103, 126, 139, 314n28; adornment, 103, *105*, 106; "children's slaves," 110, 114, 206, 223, 314n33; seamstresses, 57, 159, 270, 280. *See also* archaeology: buttons; archaeology: buckles; tailors

Cobbs (Bolling House, Goochland County), 210, 336n12

Cobbs, Samuel, 130, 146, 151, 159, 327n8

coffee, 30–31, 39, 61, 67, 182, 305n48; wares, 31, 67, 82, 296nn20–21

College of William and Mary, 40, 43, 160, 163–64, 167, 192–93, 211–12, 329n29, 334n32; Grammar School at, 52, 167, 239, 334n32

college professors and presidents, 163, 329n29, 334n32. *See also* Dawson, William; Fry, Joshua; Horrock, James; Small, William; Stith, William

Collinson, Peter, 19, 58, 62, 164, 329

colonoware, 92–94, *93*, 103, 188, 313n25

commissioner of treaties, 190, 196, 200

Cook, David, 130, 152

Coolidge, Ellen Wayles (Ellen Wayles Randolph, granddaughter of TJ), 17, 70, 216, 223, 254

Culpeper County, 330n37

Cunningham, Nobel E. Jr., 4

Cumberland County, 46, 159

currency: coin, 153; corn, 151–54; credit, 151–55; grain, 154

dance, 7, 26, 39, 56, 62, 100, 155, 192, *195*. *See also* music

Dandridge, William, 174

Dawson, John, 324

Dawson, Joseph, 129, 136–38, 275, 321, 324

Dawson, Martin, 96, 129, 139–41, 275, 321, 324–25

Dawson, William (clergy), 167, 329

Dinwiddie, Gov. Robert, 190, 193, 196, 200

Dinwiddie County, 339n32

dissenters. *See* Anglican Church; "Petition of Dissenters"

Dos Passos, John, 69

Douglas, William, 52, 164–65, 243, 329n31

Dungeness, *18*, 18–19, 45–46, 52, 62, 215, 217

Dunkin, George, 130

Dunkin, John, 130

education

—boarding, 41, 62–63, 165, 208, 252–53

—dance instruction, 7, 39, 62, 100, 155

—Douglas's Latin School, 165

—Jeffersons: PJ, 19, 251; RJ boards, 52, 239; siblings' language skills, 305n43; TJ boards, 50, 52, 233, 251–53, 314–15n35

—music instruction, 39, 46, 62, 100, 155

—schooling, 45, 62–63, 160–61, 208, 219, 239

—tutors and teachers, 14, 19, 43, 47, 52, 62–63, 100, 208, 251–52; payment to, 62–63, 152, 305n44

—*See also* College of William and Mary (esp. Grammar School); Douglas, William; Fithian, Philip; Maury, James; slaves owned by Jeffersons at Shadwell: Benjamin, Sawney, Sneed; Wythe, George; *individual Jeffersons*

Ellis, Joseph J., 4

Eppes, Elizabeth, 216–17, 244; and Francis, 216–17, 220–21

Eppes, John Wayles, xiii, 246

117; port towns, 176–78; slave population shift on upper, 124. *See also* tobacco; transportation

Jamestown ferry, 194

Jarratt, Devereux, 17, 164, 326n1, 327n13, 329n30

Jefferson, Anna Scott (TJ's sister, Mrs. Hastings Marks, Anna Marks, Aunt Marks), xiii, 209, 231, 237, 265, 273; death, 233, 236, 245; death of spouse, 218; education, 43, 63–64; familiar name, 26; family stories, 303n22; during fire, 53; home after Shadwell, 208, 212; JJ's estate, 64, 207; letters and visits, 61, 216–18, 245, 335n6; living at Shadwell, 302n13; marriage and housekeeping, 207–13, 213–18, 225; moves to Monticello, 218, 236, 245; niece named for her, 71; PJ's estate, 97, 206; sibling's estate, 205; slaveowner: Eve, Nance, 64, 97, 222–25; spouse status, 210–13, 337n16; TJ shops for, 206, 217–18. *See also* slaves owned by Jeffersons at Shadwell: Eve; slaves owned by TJ at Monticello: Nance

Jefferson, Elizabeth (TJ's sister), xiii, 231, 237, 265, 273; death, 53, 64, 108, 233, 241, 243, 301n4; death date questioned, 340n47; deeded JJ's clothes and bed, 58, 207, 335n6; education, 43, 63–64; estate, 205, 335n2; letters, none, 305n43; living at Shadwell as adult, 53, 302n13; mental capacity questioned, 53, 208, 303n22; slaveowner: Cate, Sall (Little Sal), 53, 97, 108, 111, 206; unmarried, 208. *See also* slaves owned by the Jeffersons at Shadwell: Cate, Sall (Little Sal)

Jefferson, Isaac, 26, 49, 223. *See also* Jefferson, Thomas: slaveowner

Jefferson, Jane Randolph (JJ; TJ's mother, wife of PJ), xiii, 209, 231, 237, 265, 267, 273

—family and personal: childbirth, 47–50, 166, 265, 272, 273; children, 17, 41, 43–44, 203–4, 214–19, 230–33, *231*, 265, 267, 273; children's education, 5, 7, 8, 20, 28, 39, 41, 62, 204; clothing, 57–58, 206; clothing bequeathed to daughter, 58; dancing and music education, 39, 62; death, 50, 71, 226, 342n60; Dungeness, description, 19–20, 45, 62, 62; family, 5, 8, 11, 19–20, 44–45, 301n4; fertility, 124, 265, 272, 273, 302nn10–11; funeral and burial, 71, 243–44, 306n52, 342n60; health, 47–50; literacy, 50, 294n8; manners, 19–20, 30–31; marriage, 17, 165; nursing, by slaves, 48–49, 124, 272, 273, 302nn10–11; parents, 11, 45–46, 233, 301n4; siblings and cousins, 45–46, 146, 159, 161, 164, 167, 204, 208, 212, 233, 294n9, 296n45, 329n29, 331n2, 336n10; widow, 41, 266; will, 22, 50, 64, 205, 207, 340n47

—history: accounts, estate, 39, 64, 161, 206–7, 316n48; "aristocratic blue [blood]," 3; comparison with PJ and Jane Jr., 55–56, 297n22, 305n48; domestic or everyday, 42–43; gentry culture, 14, 40, 41, 248, 257; historiography, 68–72, 256, 301n2, 306n51; inventory, probate or estate, 53–54, 64, 66–67, 129, 294n11, 304n36, 304n39, 306n49, 316n52, 317n2; kin networks, women as guardians, 204; legacies, 11, 12, 46, 203; material culture, 72; mythology and family, 3, 5, 14, 47, 49–50, 68–72, 250, 256, 306n51, 294n8; name, 7, 71, 203, 267, 335n6; old style/ new style dates, 231, 233; relationship with TJ, 68–70, 306nn51–52; wealth, 56, 303n30, 312n20; and women's history, 42–43

—house and household: beer, 34, 60, 80; candles and candle molds, 60–61; coffee, 31, 61, 67, 305n48; cookery and food, 61–63, 67, 305n48; craft, 8, 34, 59–63, 304n36; dining, 30, 67, 114; homes, 1–2, 17, *18*, 19, *44*, 44–45, *45*, 53, *228*, 301n4; hospitality, 197; JJ's,

—house and household (*continued*)
post-fire, 53–54, 64–68, *65, 66,* 90,
228, 294n11; London, 17, *18,* 19, 43, 163,
301n4; manager, 8–9, 42–43, 50, 54,
257; medicine, 49–50, 92, 302nn11–12;
parlor, 32–33, 63–64; post-fire, 53, 64;
punch, 146; Shadwell Parish, London,
17, 43, *44, 45,* 301n4; social ritual, 40;
spices and seasonings, 61, 67, 83;
status, signaling through material
goods, 28, 40, 65–67, 89–90, 248; table
manners, 30–32, 114; tea and tea
wares, 31, 32, 61, 67, 89, 305n48; wine,
60–61, 80
—intellectual pursuits: books, 33, 34,
298n24; Bible, 46, 230–33, *231, 232,*
239–40; Bible inscriptions, compared
to TJ's, 236; cookery, 61–63; gardening, 61–62; historian, 8, 46, 203, 204,
230–33, 231, 239–40; horticulture, 62;
refinement, 28, 65; spinning, 59,
304n36
—plantation manager, 47–48, 64, 67,
320n14; hires workers, 58, 156; planter's
wife, 47–48; property, control or
ownership, 22, 33, 43, 54–56, 66–67,
77, 109, 161, 205–7, 266, 268n*a,* 282n*a,*
316n52, 335n6, 339n39
—slaveowner, 56–58, 77, 108, 109, 113,
316n52; clothing, 57, 97, 156, 314n33;
deeded or given to children, 22, 50,
68, 109, 119, 141, 224–25, 266, 268n*a,*
282n*a,* 316n45, 335n6; domestic (house)
slaves, 48–49, 50, 82, 83, 97, 146, 273,
314n33; families recognized, 77, 109,
113, 142, 224, 339n39; management,
8–9, 41, 80, 82, 113, 272, 273, 311n16,
314n33, 320n14; personal servants, 97,
101; as status, 114–15; wealth, 56
Jefferson, Jane Jr. (TJ's sister), xiii, 231,
237, 265, 273; adulthood 50–52; birth,
17, 19, 239; books, 33, 51, 298n25;
clothing, 55–56, 58; craft, 59, 304n36;
death, 51, 240–41, 341n56; health,
51–52; intellectual pursuits, 51–52;

inventory, probate or estate, 129, 217,
303n18, 303n28, 304n33, 306n51; keys,
51; letters, none, 305n43; marriage,
none, 51, 208; siblings divide estate,
205; singing, 240; slaveowner, 51,
335n2; tea, 51; wealth, 56, 208. *See
also* slaves owned by Jeffersons at
Shadwell: Betty, Cloe, Pat, Sancho
Jefferson, Lucy (TJ's sister, Mrs. Charles
Lilburne Lewis), xiii, 209, 231, 237,
265, 267, 273; birth, 233, 239; children,
xiii, 71, 219, 245; death, 236, 245;
education, 43, 62–63; home after
Shadwell, 53, 100; letters and visits,
60, 72, 219–21; marriage and housekeeping, 53, 207–8, 213–18, 342n59;
PJ's estate, 206; slaveowner: Cachina,
Phebe, 97, 100, 111, 206, 222; spouse
status, 210–11; TJ shops for, 218.
See also Kentucky; Lewis, Charles
Lilburne; Monteagle; slaves owned by
Jeffersons at Shadwell: Cachina,
Phebe
Jefferson, Martha (1746–1811, TJ's sister,
Mrs. Dabney Carr, Martha Carr),
xiii, 209, 231, 237, 265, 267, 273; birth,
239; children, xiii, 26, 71, 214–15, 267,
302n10, 329n31; death, 53, 71, 236,
243–46, 342n59; death of spouse, 215,
218, 240–44; education, 43, 62–63;
familiar name, 26, 71; home after
Shadwell, 52, 216; letters and visits,
52–53, 60, 62, 203–4, 213–20, 244,
254; marriage and housekeeping, 52,
207–8, 213–18, 222; Monticello, 53, 71,
216–18, 240, 303n21; portrait, *218;*
slaveowner: Rachel, 52, 97, 111–12,
222–25; spouse status, 210–11; TJ
advises nieces and nephews, 53,
219–20, 244–45. *See also* Carr, Dabney;
slaves owned by Jeffersons at
Shadwell: Rachel
Jefferson, Martha (1772–1826, TJ's
daughter, Martha Jefferson Randolph,
Mrs. Thomas Mann Randolph,

168, 254, 259, 303n25; slaves, 92, 112,
142, 224, 226, 252–53. *See also* Jefferson,
Thomas; slaves owned by TJ at
Monticello
—museum: Thomas Jefferson Foundation, 2
—quarter farm of PJ, 19, 20; archaeology, 132, 136–38; Shadwell as quarter
farm of, 225–29, *228, 229;* slaves on
Quarter III, 117–18, *133,* 134, 136–40
Moore, John, 129, 303n25, 321
Moore, Letitia (Letty), 129, 270, 321
Moore, Matthew, 128, 270, 321
Morgan, Philip D., 301–2n8, 318–19n9;
and Michael L. Nicholls, 317–18n1,
318n7, 319n11, 324n33
Mount Vernon, 172, 324n30
Mountain Chapel (also Walker's
Church), 164, 329n30
mulatto, 112, 316n50. *See also* slaves
owned by Jeffersons at Shadwell:
Rachel, Sandy, Sawney; slaves owned
by TJ at Monticello: Hemings family
music, 26, 46, 55–56, 62, 100, 155, 179, 255,
295n15, 303n29, 315n38; gentry women's
training, 47; Indian song, 192, 197;
Jane Jr., 51, 240; and language, as part
of material culture, 26; RJ, 26; slave
song, 26, 131, 295n15, 315n38; song, 179,
192, 197, 240, 295n15, 315n38; TJ, 26;
vocal, 26, 131, 179, 192, 240. *See also*
dance
musical instruments: fiddle, 26, 55, 303n29;
flute, 303n29; instruments not in probate inventories, 303n29; spinet, 55,
303n29; violin, 55, 183, 303n29; violon-
cello, 55, 303n29

Native Americans. *See* Indians
"Negro carpenter" (Charles Lewis's),
100, 130
Nelson County, 40, 328n14
New Kent Courthouse, 194, *195*
Nicholas, John, 141, 159–62, 167, 206,
325, 332

Nicholas, Robert Carter, 159
North Carolina, xvi, 172, 185, 220.
See also Virginia–North Carolina
dividing line
Northern Neck, 172, *173*
Notes on Virginia, 38, 175, 189, 220, 253,
258

Ohio, 193–94, 245, 331n2
old style/new style dates, 233, 236, 246.
See also Bible; Prayer Book
Orange County, 118, 142, 179, 292n3,
325n41, 329n33
Ostenaco, 190. *See also* Outassetè
Outassetè (Outacite, Austenaco,
Ostenaco), 183–84, *184,* 189, 192–93,
197–98, 200–201, 251. *See also* Indians
overseers, 16, 66, 84, 92, 99, 140, 156,
162; brutality, 140–41, 145, 207, 225,
325nn37–38; identification of quarters,
125, 128–29, 138–39, 270, 275, 323n28,
324n32; Jeffersons as overseer class,
4; number at Shadwell, 128–29, 275,
321n18; payment, 126; supplies, 96, *128,*
270; wives, 95, 126, 147, 156, 270; work
routine, 129, 138, 275, 321n19. *See also*
Bacon, Edmund; Bates, Isaac;
Dawson, John; Dawson, Joseph;
Dawson, Martin; Gillam, Fred;
Gillespy, George; Gooch, Lucy;
Gooch, William; Moore, John;
Moore, Letitia; Moore, Matthew

Page, John, 217, 294
Page's warehouse, 156, 194
Pamunky River, 156, *157,* 194, *195*
Parson's Cause, 168
Pasteur and Galt apothecary, 312n22
Patton, James, 191, 194, 195, 198, 200
persico, 293n6
Peterson, Merrill D., 3, 68
"Petition of Dissenters in Albemarle and
Amherst Counties," 167, 221, 330n37
Potomac River, 163, 172
Prayer Book, 233–39. *See also* books

blacks, 111, 112, 252–53; leisure, 102–6; mulattoes, 112; names, 142–43; privilege of house slaves, 106–12; teaching planters, 101–2, 108, 111, 222–24, 252. *See also* archaeology; clothing and dress, slave; foodways; slaves owned by Jeffersons at Shadwell; slaves owned by TJ at Monticello; tobacco; *individual Jeffersons*

slaves owned by Jeffersons at Shadwell, xv, *133*, 271

—Adam, 144, 268

—Agey, 132, 277

—Bella (at Monticello Quarter), 318, 325

—Bellinda (Belinda), 124, 266, 307n4, 339n40; family, 78, 134, 144, 266, 268, 272, 277

—Bellow (child), 139, 142, 277, 318, 325

—Bellow (mother), 139, 140, 142, 277, 325

—Betty (at Snowdon), 139–40, 277

—Betty (Patt's daughter, belonged to Jane Jr.), 51, 335

—Billey, 277

—Cachina, 53, 97, 111–12, 209, 212, 223, 268, 307; bequeathed by PJ to Lucy, 111

—Cate, 53, 97, 124, 206, 268, 272–73; bequeathed by PJ to Elizabeth, 111

—Cesar (Caesar), 142, 144, 268, 273, 325, 339

—Charlotte (Sharlott), 144, 339

—Cloe, 51, 96–97, 110, 142, 268; bequeathed by PJ to Jane Jr., 110

—Crummel, 139, 142, 277

—Cyrus (Sirus), 108, 316

—Dinah, 116–17, 134, 142, 143, 144, 244, 277

—Eady, 134, 277

—Ephey, 132, 277, 296

—Eve, 63, 97, 111, 144, 209, 223, 268; bequeathed by PJ to Anna Scott, 111

—Fan (daughter of Hannah), 141, 268

—Fany (Fanny) (Quarter I, daughter of Myrtilla, deeded to Mary), 50, 207, 209, 217, 224–25, 266, 268, 335n6, 339n39

—Fany (Quarter III, husband is Gill), 117–18, 137, 272, 277, 279

—Farding, 116, 118, 125, 142, 143, 319n12

—Flora, 132, 271, 277

—Gill, 117–18, 137, 272, 277, 279

—Goliah, 116–18, 134, 142, 143, 247, 279, 325n40

—Hannah, 144, 268, 307n4; killed by overseer, 141, 207, 316n45, 325n38

—Harry, 134, 277; ran away to join British, 225

—Hercullus (Hercules), 142, 268; married Island Betty, 78

—Jack (father of Bellinda's Charlotte?), 134, 277

—Jack (sold near Tuckahoe), 101, 125, 143

—Jammey, 144, 268

—Jenny, 134, 277

—Jesse, 144, 266, 268, 296n20

—Juno (also Juna), 117–18, 136, 142, 143, 224; excused from labor, 272nc; family, 277, 279; pregnancies, 272; purchased by PJ, 142

—Jupiter (1743–1800), 113, 142, *143*, 209, 223, 252, 266, 268, 273; carried TJ's "Summary View," 252; manservant to TJ, 73–74, 77, 111–12, 339n37; mourned by TJ, 74, 112, 252; mulatto question, 316n50; parents, 316n50

—Jupiter (d. before 1757), 125, 142; worked on mill, 78, 99, 151

—Leah, 144, 268

—Lucey, 117–18, 277, 279

—Lucinda, 266, 273, 316n52, 339n39

—Lydia, 97, 144, 223, 268

—Minerva, 144, 339n40

—Moll, 78, 132, 268, 272, 277

—Myrtilla, 78, 111–13, 142, 224, 266, 268, 307n4, 339n39

—Nan (daughter of Sall, inherited by Mary), 78, 222, 268, 273, 307n4, 335n6, 339n39; bequeathed by PJ to Mary, 110; to Fairfields, 50, 209, 211, 224–25

—Nanney (daughter of Toby and Juno), 117–18, 136, 142, 143, 277, 279

Smith, Daniel Blake, 204, 337n20
Smith, John (burgess 1752–61), 329n31
Smith, John (c. 1580–1631), 175
Smith, Russell, 229
Sneed, Benjamin, 52, 62–63, 152, 208
Snowdon, quarter farm in Shadwell
   system, 125–26, *133*, 139–41, *270*, *274*,
   275–76, *277*, *278*, *282*. *See also* Jefferson,
   Randolph
Soane, Henry, 292–93n6
South Anna River, 156, 194, *195*
Spiers, Mary, 270
spirituality. *See* medicine; religion
Spotswood, Alexander, 165, 172
Stark, Bolling, 339n32
Staunton, 60, 194, *195*
Stith, Mary, 301n4
Stith, William, 164, 166–67, 301n4,
   329n29, 331n2, 332n9
sugar. *See* food: sugar
surveying, 92, 162, 171–75, 178, 331n3;
   chain, 101, 172, 175, 178, 181; commissioner of survey, 172, 174, 200;
   (defined) 331n2; drawing, 11, 147–49,
   163, 166, 171, 179, 319n12; fraternity
   and dynasty, 162–63, 165–66, 171–75,
   331n2, 336n10; immigrants, 330n1;
   instruments, 163, 182; pole, 24, 295n13;
   slaves, 101, 331n3; social standing,
   330n1. *See also* Fairfax Line; Fry-
   Jefferson Map; Northern Neck; *Notes
   on Virginia;* Virginia–North Carolina Dividing Line; *individual surveyors:* Brooke, Robert Jr.; Brooke,
   Robert Sr.; Byrd, William II; Cabell,
   William; Fontaine, Peter; Fry, Joshua;
   Jefferson, Peter: public offices; Lewis,
   Thomas; Lomax, Lunsford; Mayo,
   William; Rose, Robert; Turpin,
   Thomas
surveyor(s), 163, 172, 331n2; county office,
   14, 17, 19, 46, 176, 294n10, 331n2;
   expeditions, 54, 92, 101, 162, 171–75,
   201, 215; instruments, 11, 24, *25*, 37, 63,
   163, 180; PJ as, 4–5, 54, 147, 154, 165–66,

171–78, *177*, 198; road, 294n12; at
   Shadwell, 5, 19, 20–21, 22, 24, 27; TJ
   as, 20–21, 24, 221, 241, 257; for
   Virginia, 40, 200, 331n2
Sydnor, Charles, 148

tailors, tailoring, 57–58, 100, 111, 147, 152,
   155, 206; for slaves, 95, 97, 100. *See also*
   Bell, John; Twynman, George
tea, 30–32, 51, 61, 67, 89, 305n48; basket,
   30, 61, 67; board, 67; bowl, 30, 97;
   chest; 30, 32, 51; cream pot, 82; cup, 7,
   30, 40, 67, 138, 296n20; kettle, 30, 32,
   51, 67; milk pot, 30; saucers, 30,
   296n20; strainer, 30; sugar dish, 30;
   table, 30–32, 297n22; tea service, 7,
   34, 63, 296n21; teapot, 30–31, 67, 82,
   89–90, 97; teaspoon, 30–31, *31;* tong,
   30; trivet, 67
tea wares: 89, 114, 296n20; fashion, 67,
   89–90, 296n21, 300n36; minimum
   vessel count, 296n20; secondhand,
   89; slaves, 82, 89–90, 138
Tennessee, 40, 103, 193–96, *195*
Thornton, William, 3
Three-Notch'd Road. *See* roads
Timberlake, Henry, 190, 193, 197–99,
   201
tobacco, 94, *102*, 102–3, *104*, 126–29, *157*,
   166, *275–76. See also* Beverley Town;
   Rose, Robert
transportation: carriage, 99; cart box,
   152; infrastructure, 151; riding chair,
   99; wharf, 118, 151, 156
Trist, Nicholas P. (TJ's grandson-in-
   law), 246
Tuckahoe: architecture and furnishings,
   40, 155; distance, 290n1; Jefferson
   family, 20–21, 54, 161–62, 164, 166–67;
   Jeffersons and Randolphs, 161–62,
   215–16, 294n9, 328n14, 334n36; JJ at,
   18, 45–46, 166, 233, 239, 265; slaves,
   100–101, 112, 315n38, 319n12; TJ at,
   14, 26
Tucker, George, 250

Turner, Frederick Jackson, 17, 257
Turpin, Thomas, 159, 328n20
Twynman, George, 57–58, 152

Upton, Dell, 29

Varina Parish, 293
Virginia Gazette, 38, 196
Virginia–North Carolina dividing line,
 17, 163, 172–75, 180, 332

Walker, Betsy (Mrs. Thomas Jr.), 328n22
Walker, John, 165
Walker, Thomas (doctor), 41, 92, 100,
 167, 194, 198, 200, 329n30; Loyal Land
 Co., 165, 178–79; PJ's executor, 159–61,
 164, 206
Walker, Thomas Jr., 161, 328n22
Walker's Church. *See* Mountain Chapel
Walsh, Lorena, 156, 296, 299, 300, 311
Washington(s), 172
Washington, George, 331n2
Wayles, John, 211, 244, 246, 253, 336n10,
 337n14
Weatherburn (Wetherburn), Henry, 17
Weiser, Conrad, 331n2
Welsh, Eleanor, 150
West, Francis, 30–31, 40, 155, 328
Westham, 156, *173,* 176–78. *See also*
 Beverley Town
Westover, 15, 17, 191, 248
Westover Parish, 337

wet nurse. *See* childbearing and health
Whilkill (Whitehill), Francis, 130, 151
Whitechapel Parish, London, 44
Williamsburg: businesses and trades, 17,
 36, 40, 58, 91, 302n13, 306n49, 312n22;
 colonial government, 40, 180–81;
 distance from Shadwell, 2, 39, 191,
 208, 290n1, 300n37; houses, 27, 180–81,
 192, 296n18, 301n4, 328n23; Indians,
 40, 147, 184–86, 192–94, *195,* 197;
 Jefferson kin, 44, 52, 161, 296n18,
 301n4, 327n3, 328n23; JJ, *18, 44;* Jupiter,
 252; metropolitan center, 2, 14, 40,
 300n37; PJ, 17, 111; Sawney, 14, 111;
 TJ, 14, 52, 58, 217, 242, 327n3
Williamsburg, The (ship), 163, 293n6
Wills, William, 92
Winchester, 154, 194
wine, 80; bottle, 60–61, 84, 88, 138, 249,
 304n38; cellar storage, 60–61, 308n6;
 decanting, 60–61; Lisbon, 60, 304n38;
 Madeira, 60; wine glasses, 31, 81
Wingfield, Charles, 243, 342n59
Winston's Ordinary, 194, *195*
Wood, Gordon S., 4
Wood's Gap (Jarman's Gap, also
 Jarham's Gap), 194, *195*
Wythe, George, 27, 52, 251

York County, 326n1
York River, 156, *157*
Yorktown, TJ I's land, 292–93n6